Globale Gesellschaft und internationale Beziehungen

Series Editor
Thomas Jäger, Köln, Germany

More information about this series at http://www.springer.com/series/12384

Ariel Macaspac Hernandez

Taming the Big Green Elephant

Setting in Motion the Transformation Towards Sustainability

Springer VS

Ariel Macaspac Hernandez
German Development Institute &
University of Duisburg-Essen
Bonn, Germany

This book is an open access publication. The book manuscript corresponds to the written requirement ("Habilitationsschrift") submitted by the author to achieve the "Lehrbefähigung" for Political Science. The completion of the Habilitationsschrift was supported by the German Federal Ministry on Education and Research (BMBF) through the Fellowship Grant at the Käte Hamburger Kolleg/Centre for Global Cooperation Research in 2016 and 2017 as well as by the German Development Institute.

ISSN 2626-2339 ISSN 2626-2347 (electronic)
Globale Gesellschaft und internationale Beziehungen
ISBN 978-3-658-31820-8 ISBN 978-3-658-31821-5 (eBook)
https://doi.org/10.1007/978-3-658-31821-5

Responsible Editor: Stefanie Eggert
This Springer VS imprint is published by the registered company Springer Fachmedien Wiesbaden GmbH part of Springer Nature.
The registered company address is: Abraham-Lincoln-Str. 46, 65189 Wiesbaden, Germany

For Sisa—my ever-loyal companion

Preface

"*The solution often turns out more beautiful than the puzzle.*" Richard Dawkins

Thinking about where I came from, I cannot help but be extremely grateful for how different puzzle pieces fell into places to pave the way for an academic path. Where I come from, the best thing that was possible was to only finish high school, find a job and spend a lifetime trying (and failing) to get to the other side of the wall. In this world, life is solely defined by extreme poverty, violence and resignation. And yet, I found solace in reading books, particularly books on historical events and politics. My passion for knowledge was awoken and I started to ask questions—sometimes too many and too critical. When my guardian forced me to leave high school at the age of 14 and pushed me into working as a waste picker in a neighboring dumpsite, this passion for knowledge served as the rock of my resistance. She falsely and maliciously denounced me as a drug addict to get me expelled, but with the help of my teachers, she was proved to be lying. She eventually agreed under the condition that I worked to pay for my school expenses, which I was already doing for years. I eventually moved out at 16 to pursue my B.A. studies in Philosophy with the help of the Marian Missionaries of the Holy Cross and a scholarship grant from the university treasurer, Father Roberto Pinto, O.P., of the University of Santo Thomas in Manila. With unimaginable luck, perseverance, and the good intentions of sponsors, scholarship committees, and mentors, many years later I wrote this manuscript as a requirement for a professorship qualification degree. I am now, finally, where I want to be.

In the last eleven years, I have explored different "training grounds" to collect the necessary academic and professional expertise as well as the methodological and technical skills to enable me to see different views and versions of the bigger picture. My employment (2008–2010) as a researcher and program coordinator of the Processes of International Negotiations (PIN) Program, which, during my time, was hosted by the International Institute for Applied Systems Analysis (IIASA) (now hosted by the German Institute of Global and Area Studies (GIGA) in Hamburg), was my first academic training ground. The PIN steering committee members at that time, Prof. Dr Gunnar Sjöstedt, Prof. Dr I. William Zartman, Prof. Dr Oliver Faure, Ambassador Franz Cede, Prof. Dr Rudolf Avenhaus, Prof. Dr Rudolf Schüssler, Prof. Dr Mark Anstey, Paul Meerts, Prof. Dr Fen Osler Hampson, Prof. Dr Valerie Rosoux, Mordechai Melamud, and Prof. Dr Victor Kremenyuk accepted me as one of their own. Working with these bright minds was very illuminating and is something I would recommend highly. The projects that I coordinated, such as the Caspian Dialogue, the research on climate change negotiations, and the large-scale simulation of the point-of-entry negotiations for the Comprehensive Nuclear Test Ban Treaty Organization were the first cases of negotiations that I became familiar with. Eventually, the negotiation perspective and systems analysis as a method of scientific inquiry became the main foundations of my academic profile. I also learned how to develop negotiation games to better explain the challenges of multilateral decision-making. I internalized the idea that conflicts and differences are not part of the problem, but are opportunities to advance human well-being. Here, my eyes were trained to look at **processes**.

It was also during these first years that I finished my doctoral studies at the University of Vienna in Austria and afterwards my second PhD at the University of Cologne in Germany. While the first thesis was on identity-building in the Philippines, the second was on facilitating decision-making processes. My supervisors Prof. Dr. Eva Kreisky and Prof. Dr. Thomas Jäger trained me to ask the appropriate questions and seek and find the probable answers to these questions, but to still doubt the answers that I found. I learned that when answers become self-evident, they cease to be useful.

Afterwards, I was employed as a (post-doc) researcher at the Institute for Infrastructure and Resources Management (IIRM) at the University of Leipzig (2011–2014). As part of the Faculty of Economics and Business Management Science, this training ground made me realize that there are different entry points to understanding problems. My main task at IIRM was to support Prof. Dr Thomas Bruckner in his function as the coordinating lead author of the chapter on energy systems of the Fifth Assessment Report (AR5) of the Third Working Group of the Intergovernmental Panel on Climate Change (IPCC). This position exposed me to management styles based upon knowledge cooperation. In addition, I assisted him in his lectures on the integrated assessment of the impacts of climate change by preparing obligatory readings, writing the script and the reader for the lecture, standing in for the professor when he was away and conducting his lectures, formulating questions for the examinations, evaluating students' outputs (exams, term papers) and supervising eight master's theses. As I undertook a course in pedagogy during my master's studies, I particularly enjoyed supporting the faculty's two master's degrees: The Joint International Master of Sustainable Development and the German-Russian Double Master of International Energy Economics and Business Administration. In my free time, I took additional courses and received training in scenario-building and scientific models such the TIMES-VEDA modeling course offered by the Energy Technology Systems Analysis Program (ETSAP), which is part of the International Energy Agency (IEA). Fortunately, my four-year position as Chapter Scientist (Assistant) of the IPCC AR5 chapter on energy systems required me to read thousands of articles, books, and reports on the role of energy systems in mitigating climate change and reading the work of these and other authors allowed me to synthesize everything that is known (and still unknown) about the related issues. In addition, I was tasked with reading, collecting, evaluating, classifying and even proposing responses to more than 6,000 pieces of feedback and reviews of hundreds of experts from all over the world for the different drafts of the chapter. This task in particular developed my understanding of the critical aspects behind technical issues, as well as the policy relevance of technological innovation. After two years, I was already confident enough to teach more than 500 students in more than 15 seminars and lectures on climate change, energy systems and energy & environmental politics not only at the University of Leipzig, but also at other universities in Spain, Estonia, Mexico, Jamaica and the Philippines, which was made possible by EU teaching mobility programs. Connecting my expertise in negotiations and decision-making to my newly found technical expertise in related environmental issues and appropriate methods of scientific inquiry, I developed innovative simulation games as an experimental approach to revisiting theoretical concepts, which were extremely useful in my courses. They were also a great deal of fun for the students and for myself. To sum up, this position enabled me to explain the relevant **issues** in the **context** of complexity and uncertainty.

My employment at the Fraunhofer Institute for International Management and Knowledge Economy (Fraunhofer IWM) in Leipzig (2014–2016) was a different training ground. It exposed me to a different research landscape, where applied research project acquisition was highlighted. I spent thousands of hours writing research grant proposals, building up networks for research consortiums and managing applied research projects. The highlight of this position was when I was tasked by GIZ and CARICOM to support the development of the curriculum for the master's degree in Sustainable Energy and Climate Change at the University of Technology in Kingston, Jamaica. For this project, I designed and implemented 7 of the 12 modules (sustainable energy systems, energy and environmental data management, environmental policies & politics, sustainable transport, smart grid management, ocean resource management, and energy management in buildings and industry). For each module, I wrote a module script for lecturers and a workbook for students. For me, it was important to highlight the Caribbean and Jamaican context in each of the modules. For this, aside from months of literature research, I conducted a series of face-to-face interviews with Jamaican policy-makers and local stakeholders. With the help of Prof. Dr Andrew Isaacs and Prof. Dr Ruth Potopsingh, I visited and discussed concrete issues with decision-makers in several ministries, Jamaican bus companies, the Jamaica chamber of commerce, the railway company, industry representatives, NGOs, and other local academes. I rented a car and drove through Jamaica visiting energy utilities, grid stations, communities dependent on mining companies, and housing projects with smart technologies to experience the context. In addition, I was able to personally teach the module on Environmental Policies & Politics to 16 Jamaican professionals from different sectors. This experience vindicated my approach towards highlighting stakeholders' perspectives when understanding technical issues. This training ground allowed me to learn how to understand the preferences and behavior of **actors** and use this understanding as an entry point to solutions.

My fellowship at the Käte Hamburger Kolleg/Centre for Global Cooperation Research (KHK/CGCR) at the University of Duisburg-Essen (2016–2017) gave me the **space and time** to connect all the dots. For a year, I immersed myself in academic discussions to better understand the role of cooperation as a framework of decision-making. During the various KHK/CGCR research colloquia, I listened and was inspired by the discussions on concrete areas of cooperation such as development assistance cooperation, peace-building and migration. I presented my initial ideas on this book. At first, I found myself struggling to find a cohesive storyline when considering the different aspects that I want to connect. I simply needed structure. With the guidance of my fellow colleagues Prof. Dr Sigrid Quack, Prof. Dr Jon Hovi, Prof. Dr Aridl Underdahl, Dr Katja Freistein, Prof. Dr Babacar Kante, Prof. Dr. Tobias Debiel, Prof. Dr Larry Crump, Dr Xavier Mathieu, Dr Charmaine Misalucha-Willoughby, Prof. Dr Detlef Sprinz, **and** Matthias Schuler, among others, the structure of my book slowly emerged. During this time, I also presented early drafts of selected parts of this book at different international conferences, such as the 2017 WISC Conference in Taiwan, the 2017 Risk and Asia Conference in Duisburg, and the 2017 Global Studies Conference in Singapore, where I received constructive and valuable input from peers. In addition, my presentation at the 2017 *Research Forum @ UBT Philosophy* in Bayreuth, Germany, through the invitation of Prof. Dr Rudolf Schüssler, was a welcome reality check, which made me re-evaluate the sense and purpose of this book.

The chapter on knowledge diplomacy, the prescriptive part and the conclusion of this book was completed during the first six months of my employment at the German Development Institute/Deutsches Institut für Entwicklungspolitik (DIE) and at the Institute for Advanced Sustainability Studies (IASS) (2018–2019). Through these two positions, I found the solution to my 'anti-climax' dilemma. How should I end the book in a way that it does not disappoint? These positions made me realize that the best way to end is to look at the beginning. My discussions with colleagues, particularly from Managing Global Governance Program (Dr Sven Grimm, Dr Wulf Reiners, Dr Tatjana Reiber, Dr Anna Schwachula, Dr Johanna Vogel) and SDSN Germany (Adolf Kloke-Lesch, Janina Sturm, Jacqueline Götze), helped me clarify the remaining issues relating to the sense and purpose in this book. So, what happens now with the knowledge I have developed? How can I make my research transformative? How can I encourage people to listen to what this book has to say? The results of these discussions are the last three chapters of this book.

My main *confidante* for this book was my main supervisor, Prof. Dr Dirk Messner. His passion for knowledge surpasses even that of my own. His professional and personal guidance was more than what a student can usually expect from a mentor, especially as this mentor is one of the busiest people of my acquaintance. Our discussions were phenomenal, and I one day hope to be able to structure my thoughts in the way he does.

Special thanks are to be given to Anni Hellwig, Nora Pierau, and Conny Hornschild who supported me in editing the language of this work. I appreciate the assistance given to me by the University of Duisburg-Essen, especially the efforts made by Prof. Dr. Michael Käding. Thank you also to the funding agencies, such as the DLR, GIZ, BMBF, DAAD, EU Mobility, and especially the *Bundesagentur für Arbeit* in Duisburg for the valuable financial grants and assistance that made this book possible.

Finally, my incredible journey would not have been possible without my friends and family. I found friends and *Wegbegleiter* such as Gunnar & Eva Licke, George Lemon, Astra, Grazie, Christoph, Tita Jojo (and the PGG community in Vienna, Austria), Yuni, Tanja, Steffi, Raquel, Tobias, Judith, Fatma, Ferhat,

Andreas, Jing, Adrian, Teagan, Reto, Philipp, Klaus and Gregor, who stood by me through the years. I cherish my former work colleagues such as Tanja Huber, Romeo Molina, Amalia Priyatna, Suchitra Subramanian, Maren Rath, Theresa Weinsziehr, Hendrik Kondziella, Mart Verhoog, Mario Götz, Angel de la Vega Navarro, Urban Kaiser, and Henrik Beerman who inspired me in various ways. My family (mother Lagrimas, stepfather Ian Henry, sisters MJ and Gigi and brother Aries) gives me purpose. And of course, the source of my joy (and oxytocin), Sisa.

Ariel Macaspac Hernandez

Contents

Abbreviations and Acronyms

UTECH	University of Technology, Kingston, Jamaica
CARICOM	Caribbean Community
GIZ	Gesellschaft für Internationale Zusammenarbeit
UNFCCC	United Nations Framework Convention on Climate Change
CFTP	Conceptual Framework of Transformative Pathways
RCP	Representative Concentration Pathways
OECD	Organisation of Economic Cooperation and Development
IPCC	Intergovernmental Panel on Climate Change
TBL	Triple Bottom Line
ICLEI	International Council for Local Environmental Initiatives
UNEP	United Nations Environmental Programme
NGO	Non-Government Organization
WBGU	German Advisory Council on Global Change
ICT	Information and Communication Technology
SA	Systems Approach
MLP	Multi-Level Perspective
AIM	Asian Institute of Management
IEA	International Energy Agency
PA	Process Approach
COP	Conference of Parties
IIASA	International Institute for Applied Systems Analysis
SPM	Summary for Policymakers
APEC	Asia-Pacific Economic Cooperation
SDSN	Sustainable Development Solutions Network
AOSIS	Alliance of Small Island States
ODA	Official Development Assistance

GATT	General Agreement on Tariffs and Trade
WTO	World Trade Organization
WMO	World Meteorological Organization
CLA	Coordinating Lead Authors
AR5	Fifth Assessment Report
DAC	Development Assistance Committee
SDG	Sustainable Development Goals
GDP	Gross Domestic Product
GHG	Greenhouse Gas
SME	Small and Medium-Sized Enterprise
TIS	Technology-Intensive Suppliers
NDC	Nationally Determined Commitment
ESMAP	Energy Sector Management Assistance Program
CCP	Central Communist Party
NEDA	National Economic and Development Authority
EO	Executive Order
PDP	Philippine Development Plan
DENR	Department of Environment and National Resources
CCC	Climate Change Commission
PEP	Philippine Energy Plan
LGU	Local Government Unit
CA	Commission on Appointments
CEO	Chief Executive Officer
LULUCF	Land Use, Land-Use Change and Forestry
LNG	Liquefied Natural Gas
CAFE	Corporate Average Fuel Economy
EPA	Environment Protection Agency
UTECH	University of Technology, Kingston (Jamaica)
BAU	Business-as-Usual
JLP	Jamaican Labour Party
IMF	International Monetary Fund
RPs	Risk Points
UPs	Unhappiness Points
EDPs	Ecological Damage Points
PNP	People's National Party (Jamaica)
CFTP	Conceptual Framework of Transformative Pathways
BMU	German Federal Ministry on Environment
BMF	German Federal Ministry on Finance

CDU	Christian Democratic Union
BMVI	German Federal Ministry on Transport and Digital Infrastructure
BMJV	German Federal Ministry on Justice and Consumer Protection
BMBF	German Federal Ministry on Education and Research
BMWi	German Federal Ministry on Economy and Energy
BMZ	German Federal Ministry on Economic Cooperation and Development
BMAS	German Federal Ministry on Employment and Social Affairs
BMG	German Federal Ministry on Health
EU	European Union

List of Figures

List of Tables

Introduction—That Big Green Elephant in the Room

1

Transformations, transitions and structural changes are not new to human civilization. Transitions can be *emergent*, that is, a subservient response to changes such as technological breakthroughs, or *purposive*, that is, a strategically instigated effort to achieve certain goals. Changes are constantly occurring and define identities, aspirations and how we see our human nature (*Menschenbild*), how we interact with each other, and how we make sense of the world (*Weltbild*). Changes can also be both fortuitous and expected. It is often during sudden changes that we feel disoriented, our identities dismantled, and that our way of life is threatened. Changes can cause ambivalence towards the stability of our political, economic or social systems. While some changes can be ground-breaking in improving the quality of human lives, they can also involve backlashes, which, if not properly understood and facilitated, can lead to system ruptures and the collapse of fundamental values and social contracts. Very often, transition periods are confronted by vacuums that may pave the way to "horrendous events" such as the violent seizure of power by armed groups or the suspension of *habeas corpus* fraudulently justified by the need to restore stability. Unstable systems promote the 'romanticizing' of nostalgic memories of the past when 'everything worked,' whereas other conditions such as a high mortality rate, non-existent welfare system or poor living conditions are neglected. Particularly when the imminent change or the public call for changes was met by violence by those 'status quo agents' in power, the *caveat* against using violence from all sides diminishes as "challenging times" can suddenly legitimate excessive use of coercion or the disregard for the rule of law. As Ian Bremmer (2018) contends in his book "Us vs. Them: The Failure of Globalism," insecurities behind paradigm-shifting changes such as globalization have paved the way to the current emergence of the "era of strongmen."

Transformations and transitions are often linked to subversion through which existing principles and norms are changed, leading to changes in power relations,

A. M. Hernández, *Taming the Big Green Elephant*, Globale Gesellschaft und internationale Beziehungen, https://doi.org/10.1007/978-3-658-31821-5_1

which mostly motivate those in power to delay or even reject transitions. Individual societies may react differently to a specific change depending on the '*Zeitgeist*' of change. These differences in 'absorption' and 'diffusion' of change can be attributed to existing lock-ins and path dependencies that are deeply rooted in socio-political systems. Change also depends on the availability of and trust (social capital) in formal and informal channels for change agents who can push for change within established provisions. For example, in societies with low social capital, changes in power relations can be fatal, especially when the narrative "the winner takes it all" defines contestation. Powerful actors can resist change, because of the perceived threat to the power. At the same time, weaker actors can resist change, because they perceive that changes will only deteriorate their positions. Because existing structural inequalities, for example, may limit the scope and functionality of representation and verification, they might fear being powerless when burdens are disproportionately distributed to them. Hence, it remains difficult for *academe* to grasp the real meaning of change for each actor, often because of the lack of precedents. It is also almost impossible to determine the 'retrospective' value of something that has allegedly prevented negative effects.

Because this book intends to address transformation towards sustainability, one must inevitably look for other "Great Transformations" to understand and explain the dynamics, issues and effects behind such metamorphoses. One example of such a Great Transformation is the industrial revolution, which is often seen as the event that foreshadowed modernity (see Hobsbawm 1965; Riello & O'Brien 2009). The industrial revolution was responsible for major shifts in human relations that resulted not only in positive effects linked with urbanization, the emergence of the middle class, economic growth and changes in the role of women in society, but also in negative effects such as air pollution, child labor, and inhumane labor conditions (see Scott & Baltzly 1958; Stearns 1993). In addition, industrialization was instrumental in justifying colonialism and imperialism as reflected by the narrative of civilizing others as a 'White Man's Burden' and a "noble enterprise of civilization" (see Chrisholm 1982; Murphy 2010). A rather speculative and yet compelling question is whether these negative effects were necessary for development or if they could have been relativized or even prevented if decision-making was inclusive. If the multiple trade-offs were already clear and properly understood, and if the weak had credible representation in the policy-making process, would economic growth still have been attained? Was child labor in factories a necessary evil of the Industrial Revolution?

Centuries later, human civilization is experiencing another kind of revolution—one that is driven by 'sustainable low carbon' developmental goals. Like the industrial revolution, this sustainable low carbon development is highly dependent upon technological advancement. However, in contrast to the Industrial Revolution, it was initially motivated by threats to human welfare such as climate change, environmental degradation, social inequality and diminishing resources, with solutions requiring fundamental changes in structures, paradigms, institutions, behavior, and identities. It is therefore purposive, which, unlike the Industrial Revolution, was more of an emergent occurrence. Nevertheless, this "great 'green' revolution" is inhibited by several complex problems, multiple trade-offs and dilemmas such as the public good dilemma, normative traps, the prisoner's dilemma, the not-in-my-backyard dilemma, and the indecisiveness dilemma. These dilemmas require proper, additional reconceptualization to adequately address the specificities of sustainable low carbon development. The absence of a proper understanding of numerous factors and causalities will not only lead to missed opportunities but will also empower those who wish to discredit the essence of changes. The failure to effectively address the negative aspects and fatal synergies linked to sustainable low carbon development has supported or even mobilized counter-movements such as anti-intellectualism, anti-factualism, anti-establishment, anti-globalization, anti-environmentalism, and anti-liberalism that threaten to reverse "hard fought" advancement in climate protection and sustainable development.

The parable of the blind men and an elephant can elucidate the complexity and uncertainty of sustainable low carbon transformation. The parable is about a group of blind men, who have never come across an elephant before and who learn and conceptualize what the elephant is like by touching it. Because each blind man feels a different and distinct part of the elephant, their individual description of the elephant is expected to contrast to those of the others. My entry point as one of the "blind men" is the linkage between multiple policy goals to achieve sustainable low carbon development. While these policy goals are inter-related, they are still addressed separately not only in the international system, but also by national governments and local communities. Each one of these often has its own socio-political and socio-linguistic context, set of (status quo or change) agents and (domestic/endogenous or global) audience.

This book employs a 'negotiative' and systems perspective as well as a process outlook on sustainable low carbon transformation. As such, I look not only at agents, context, audience, sectors and subsystems relevant to transitions towards sustainability, but also at processes including functional, institutional, and bargaining interactions that define collective, multi-level, and fragmented decision-making. The reason for this 'integrated' approach is that the success of transformations will most likely depend not solely on technical solutions but also on how consensus is negotiated and how decisions and actions promoting sustainability become self-enforcing. In addition, the stability of the transition process will depend on its agents, context, and audience, implying the relevance of sociotechnical narratives in ensuring legitimacy.

1.1 Research Objectives

1.1.1 Background

Studies of global transformation are often regarded as highly ambitious. The difficulty of studying (global) transformation starts with the term "transformation" and continues with the question of "what transforming actually is". Synonyms of transformation include shift, transition, structural change, conversion, revolution, transfiguration, transmogrification, switch and metamorphosis. Furthermore, related disciplines such as international relations, history, sociology, anthropology, and political science are still struggling to fully understand and grasp global transformation as a subject of scholarly work. One reason for this is that while transformation touches on concepts or categories that transcend disciplinary boundaries, fundamental research questions tend to be formulated using "boxes of disciplines." As such, academic debates on global transformation towards sustainability tend to be 'fragmented' and therefore limited within each scholarly discipline. In addition, the answers provided by these disciplines rather create more questions instead of providing useful answers.

Another challenge refers to the process of how notions behind concepts are established and reinforced. Current concepts of global transformation may include 'faulty assumptions' that further blur the understanding of the contemporary world. Because analyzing transformation will touch upon human cognition, such intentions, motivations, preferences, and decisions can also be made out of ignorance ("omission") or out of malicious motives and intentions ("commission") (see Spranca et al. 1991). For example, referring to global transformation as merely changes in the global economy may be too simplistic and therefore misleading, because it fails to provide understanding of non-monetary values such as social trust and cohesion which are necessary to define human well-being.

The difficulty of studying global transformation is further aggravated when transformation is linked to sustainability, which is itself a normative concept. This particular coupling of transformation and sustainability has increasingly gained attention from both *academe* and policy-makers, because of the distinct 'body' that emerges. Global transformation towards sustainability is a concert of multiple and multi-level linkages. Many universities across the globe are now incorporating the study of transformation/transitions towards sustainability in their curricula, with many others starting to branch out into more specialized areas of this emerging discipline including, for example, climate, environment, energy, water, governance, policy, regulations and business. In addition, several governments have created special agencies to address this linkage. For example, China's Third Plenary Session of the 18th Central Committee of the Communist Party of China initiated the creation of the task force "National Governance Capacity for Green Transformation" and mandated it to propose a comprehensive framework for enhancing governance capacity for a successful green transformation through 2030 (CCICED 2015).

1.1.2 Objectives

The primary objective of this book is to provide a comprehensive and integrated **analytical framework** that promotes **understanding** of multi-level (global, national, local and sectoral) transformation towards sustainability. This analytical framework seeks to contribute and enrich the current discourse on transformation towards sustainability by linking climate protection and sustainable development not only to each other, but also with transformation/transition studies, change management, negotiation and conflict management studies, and with decision analysis. This linkage will not only necessitate new methodologies and assessment approaches but also new concepts that specifically address issues and dynamics that only arise through this linkage. This analytical framework that is built upon *negotiative* and systems perspectives as well as process outlook aims to help define, design and facilitate functional, institutional, and bargaining interactions to align collective actions in order to execute the principles of sustainability.

Interestingly, due to the conceptual and methodological challenges of studying global transformation towards sustainability, the formulation of concrete objectives of this book has already entailed the justification of arguments as well as the clarification of the rationales and logic behind these objectives. These rationales and logic will be further elaborated in Chapters 3 and 4. These objectives are:

1. **The Sharp-edging of the inter-, multi- and trans-disciplinarity of studying global transformation towards sustainability:**
   a. Understanding and concretization of conceptual and receptive gaps that arise through the enforcement of closing or blurring boundaries between disciplines
   b. Identification and assessment of 'discriminative contrasts' that paradoxically promote learning about transformation towards sustainability

2. **Support more strategic and purposive approaches in planning, designing and implementing new branches of studies of transformation towards sustainability:**
    a. The effective design and implementation of new curricula or subdisciplines that highlight trade-offs by 'coupling' issues such as human rights and climate change, sustainable development and law, energy systems and governance.
    b. Identification of new channels or venues for academic discourse, particularly when considering 'peripheral scholars' from the Global South who do not have access to conventional scholarly channels such as peer-reviewed journals and conferences.
3. **Promote the adequate combination of incremental (step-by-step), regressive (going back to basics), decremental (backward-sorted) and saltatory (leapfrogging, by leaps and bounds) learning in a global transformation towards sustainability:**
    a. The critical assessment of varying paces of development among sectors and technologies (e.g., efficient procurement procedures in the energy sector) through incremental learning.
    b. A pragmatic and yet critical evaluation of 'best practices', for example among traditional modes of governance, which highlights the advantages of regressive and decremental learning (critiques of modernity).
    c. The efficient and critical design of innovative concepts that aim to circumvent traditional stages of development through saltatory learning.
4. **Advance academic and public discourse on transformation towards sustainability by highlighting linkages that uncover new conflict cleavages, co-benefits, synergies, fatal synergies, *caveats*, trade-offs, positive and negative externalities as well as self-enforcing dynamics resulting from such linkages:**
    a. The identification of novel approaches and methodologies to grasp and resolve collaboration and coordination problems, including the prisoner's dilemma, free-riding, and the indecisiveness dilemma.
    b. The delegitimization of "counterfactual" claims on global transformation towards sustainability.
    c. An assessment of the ontological and epistemological baggage of ideas, concepts and notions to allow out-of-the-box thinking and to prevent the reproduction of 'cognitive lock-ins' that frame the understanding of causalities.
    d. The evaluation of transition costs, for example, the costs of 'unlocking' carbon lock-ins.

5. **Empower decision-makers (policy-makers, policy entrepreneurs) by enhancing their capacity to empathize:**
   a. Resolve challenges in the monolithic architecture and polycentrism of multi-level (global, regional, national, local, sectoral) decision-making to abrogate existing blurred or competing jurisdictions, inefficient governance structures, structural imbalances and inequities, lock-ins in utility and value systems and volatile social contracts.
   b. Enhance evidence-based decision-making that profits from studies of various futures, each of which is defined by context, agents and audience.
   c. Strengthening of the value of (knowledge) diplomacy and a critical outlook on consensus-building and policy models (e.g., deliberative, democratic, authoritarian, post-democratic).

1.1.3 The definition of a Global Transformation Towards Sustainability—Clarification

This book defines transformation towards sustainability as:

the shifting from the initially chosen (or taken) pathway to another pathway as goals have been revised to enable the system to adapt to changes.

Pathways are sets of critical junctures and lock-ins that have framed decisions and collective actions. With this definition, sustainable low carbon transformation is then depicted by shifting from one pathway to another by shouldering transition costs, that is, the costs of detaching a system for example from existing carbon lock-ins. Each transformative pathway is always 'negotiative' in nature. The negotiative pathway pursues the convergence of objectives, principles, visions, goals and the necessary instruments through collaboration and coordination. However, emerging collaboration and coordination problems in various modular sub-systems need to be resolved among others by institutions in various modular sub-systems. For example, transformation cross-cuts various levels (global, regional, national, local, and sectoral). Nevertheless, while relevant vulnerabilities and risks, as well as opportunities and benefits, tend to have a global impact, responses are constituted and concretized following a local contextualization of vulnerabilities. In addition, transformation is dependent upon economies-of-scale. As one country achieves benefits and competitive advantages after choosing the sustainable low carbon pathway, other countries will follow and when a critical mass' is reached, this sustainable low carbon pathway will become the 'new normal.' However, we have a long way to go before we can achieve this new normalcy. Countries need additional information to identify benefits and assess their capacity to shoulder the costs of switching pathways, particularly when (carbon) lock-ins of the current non-sustainable high-carbon pathway seem insurmountable.

Figure 1.1 can be helpful in explaining the definition of sustainable low carbon transformation. While the figure illustrates the different radiative forces of the **representative concentration pathways** (RCPs), it also demonstrates the level of climate protection pursued—the lower the radiative forces, the higher the climate mitigation that needs to be done. If the line representing RCP8.5 is the pathway with the least emission reduction efforts and the line representing RCP2.6/RCP3PD is the pathway with the most mitigation efforts, shifting from the RCP8.5 line to the RCP2.6/RCP3PD refers to the **'transformation'** depicted in this book through the dashed arrow. The dashed arrow reflects an example of a change of pathway from the initial pathway to the 'purposive' pathway, which reflects newly implemented principles.

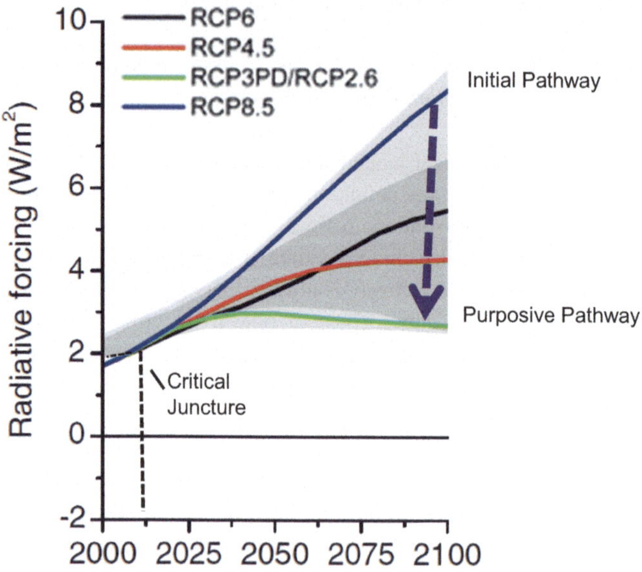

Figure 1.1 Radiative Forcing of the Representative Concentration Pathways. (van Vuuren et al. 2011) (modified)

The success of a facilitation of transformation towards sustainability depends on the 'shifting or transition costs' of moving from one pathway to another. The critical juncture points to the decisive point in defining the transition costs, because this represents the point with the lowest transition costs. As the transformative pathway unfolds, transition costs also increase. As new technologies are developed, or new sustainability-friendly policy and market instruments are introduced, a specific pathway, here for example the RCP3PD/RCP2.6 line, becomes more beneficial. However, some countries, while willing to shift pathways, may need additional capacities to be able to shift from their current pathway to the more efficient one. Shifting will therefore depend on flexibility measures that do not encourage free-riding, technology transfer that caters to innovation, capacity-building that does not reinforce inequalities and even transition cost relief that does not hamper autonomy.

In this book, transformation is understood as an 'umbrella-concept' that encompasses *shifts* (e.g., a behavioral shift favoring energy-efficient cars), *transition periods* (e.g., a 'grace period' given to companies to adapt to the new legislation), *structural changes* (e.g., a government changing its policies following the increased importance of the service and information sector), *conversion* (e.g., the monetary value of heritage sites included in the assessment of policies), *evolution* (e.g., changing the social mandate of universities following new demands from the private sector), *revolution* (e.g., new business models or new technologies as game changing factors), *transfiguration* (e.g., new technologies that rearrange the competitive positions of countries), *transmogrification* (e.g., changing the landscape by building a public park on the former elevated freight rail line tracks of the "High Line" in New York), *switch* (e.g., using of an alternative IT standard or energy source instead of the conventional standard or preference) and metamorphosis (e.g., a change in the utility of resources such as agricultural waste-to-energy). All these terms connote causalities and associations relevant to changes. This book will make distinctions if deemed necessary.

1.2 Research Design and Methodology

Achieving the objectives of this book requires a coherent research design. Figure 1.2 illustrates the research design strategy of this project and describes the various stages and processes involved.

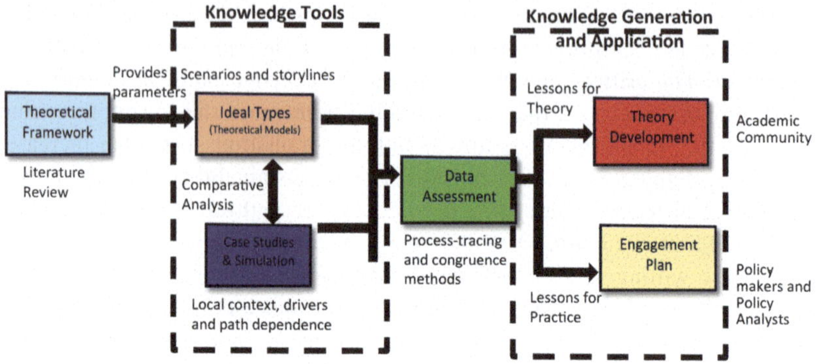

Figure 1.2 Research Design Strategy

Parts B and C of this book refer to the descriptive part that introduces the theoretical framework. Chapter 2 synthesizes the literature on transformation and introduces clusters of scholarly research on entry points in understanding the concept of sustainable development pathways (SDPs). Chapter 3 discusses the trade-offs as major drivers of transformation towards sustainability. Chapter 4 highlights the critical process outlook on decision systems by addressing the 'paradoxical' assumptions that influence how decisions are made. Chapter 5 conceptualizes knowledge diplomacy, how knowledge relevant to sustainable low-carbon transformation is generated, and how it reproduces and reinforces asymmetries in the international system. Chapter 6 illuminates a systems perspective on transformations to adequately address problem contexts and policy objectives particularly in countries with emerging economies.

Without the intention of relativizing the impact of historical emissions brought by now-developed countries, the perspective of developing countries is selected, not only because they currently represent the sources of the most growth on GHG emissions and are confronted with environmental degradation, but primarily because they tend to be confronted with multiple transitions such as political transitions (e.g., from a military junta to a democratically elected regime) and economic transitions (from a planned economy to a market economy), which make their transformation towards sustainability more complex and highly contextual. This high level of contextuality increases their resistance to the best experiences of developed countries.

Chapters 2 to 7 provide some necessary background and parameters for the development of ideal types as theoretical models (chapter 8). They also consolidate the theoretical pillars of the case studies and simulation game and introduce the benefits of using scenarios and theoretical models (ideal types) as tools for understanding the complexity of transformation under conditions set by policy models. Chapter 8 introduces the ideal types (theoretical models) of policy pathways—democratic, authoritarian, institutional, '*activistic*,' technocratic and post-democratic. These ideal types summarize the assumptions and storylines of policy models and identify linkages between policy models and policies on sustainable low-carbon transformation. These theoretical models are compared with country-specific case studies (to highlight the local context, drivers and path dependence of policy-making processes).

Chapters 9 to 12 are country-specific case studies that provide retrospective analyses, with the ideal types serving as theoretical models. This part of the project demonstrates how ideal type analysis can promote the further development of theories by highlighting the historicity of pathways taken by countries.

The theoretical chapters as well as the case studies coherently lead to the subsequent chapters: Chapter 13 introduces a conceptual framework of 'transformative pathways,' which is inherently derived from the contextualization of theoretical models. Through the case studies, this conceptual framework aims to provide additional theoretical inputs to better grasp the complexity of shifting from the pathway initially chosen (business-as-usual) to other pathways. Chapter 14 highlights the empirical value of this book by creating a check-list that comprises reflective questions for stakeholders to develop awareness of the complexities of the transformation process when engaging in various functional, institutional, and bargaining interactions.

1.2.1 Ideal Types: Theoretical Models and Scenarios from the Negotiation Perspective

Like most of the scientific studies on climate mitigation and low carbon transformation, this book orients itself on the use of scenario methods. Because the outcomes of present mitigation actions will only be realized after years, if not decades, decision-making is inevitably conducted in the context of complexity and uncertainty. Without the support of decision tools, decision-makers can be easily overwhelmed by issues, structures and processes, encouraging them to either delay or refuse necessary decisions. However, it needs to be highlighted that scenarios also have limitations. While scenarios aim to structure complexities and uncertainty in a way that helps decision-makers find orientation, they cannot be followed blindly.

Scenarios such as decision (analytical) tools can be useful in defining the view of the form, contents, and purpose of decisions. While scenarios cannot predict or forecast how, and which decisions will be made under specific conditions as the transformation process unfolds, they can provide answers to questions such as how decisions should be made (normative analysis) and how to ensure their compatibility with existing norms and principles. In such cases, theoretical models such as scenarios can be useful in determining the content and extent of norms and principles. However, the use of normative frameworks in evaluation policies has its own short-comings, particularly when reflecting upon how and from whom such normative frameworks are determined. Here, scenarios can highlight causalities between factors. Finally, and of equal importance, scenarios can demonstrate how decision-makers can facilitate multi-dimensional and multi-level negotiation processes (negotiation analysis) through a stakeholder perspective approach (see Zartman 1988; Young 1991; Sebenius 1992b; Raiffa 2002).

In this book, scenarios (policy models) have been developed that apply 'ideal types' of analysis to policy-making. Like scenarios, these ideal types express specific 'storylines' that have been defined from the perspective of negotiation studies. The so-called 'ideal type analysis' pertains to ideal types acting as analytical instruments by formulating hypotheses that are verifiable through the observation of empirical proceedings. The usefulness of ideal types is expressed through comparing the 'storylines' of each ideal type with empirical case studies. The purpose of ideal types is to enable researchers to ask appropriate underlying questions.

1.2.2 Case Studies and Simulations

This book employs a structured and systematic presentation of selected country-specific cases to verify theoretical models (ideal types). The interactions and relations between and the influences on implementing policies that support or inhibit transformation towards sustainability will be highlighted. A coherent framework for an analysis of cases has been developed for this book to implement a step-by-step evaluation using different sets of criteria. The implementation of these case studies using the framework will also address the significant shortcomings of using (historical) case studies to evaluate transformation processes. Through these shortcomings, new conceptual questions can be identified and retrofitted to the locality of the context.

Using case studies as methods of scientific inquiry has its own challenges. For example, Audley Genus and Anne-Marie Coles (2008 p. 1441) criticize the "flawed use of secondary data sources" as well as any study which "uncritically accepted accounts" and assumptions of the importance of certain events, intentions and actions (or non-actions). To address this, this book intends to re-visit and re-evaluate rationales and assumptions (see chapter 4). In addition, case studies that pertain to the transition or transformation processes of countries are often characterized as being rather descriptive or "illustrative" rather than analytical or systematic (Geels 2011 p. 36).

Moreover, by using case studies and simulations, this book aims to address the broader trade-off that is typical of mainstream social science. As Frank Geels (2011) and Peter Abell (2004) contend, this trade-off pertains to the tendency of social science to over-emphasize methods (e.g., the procedures for gathering data, data analysis, and replication) at the expense of ontology, i.e., a set of concepts and categories in a subject area that depicts properties and relations. Similarly, **process theories tend to have a more complex ontology, but less developed methodologies**. Studying transformation processes is not only constrained by this trade-off, it is also restricted by misleading or absent precedents that undermine the usefulness of existing concepts for explaining the various dynamics of transformation towards sustainability. A possible solution is introduced by this book by exploring comparative and nested case studies, event-sequence analysis, network analysis, negotiation analysis and decision analysis.

This book primarily depicts the sustainable low-carbon policies of selected countries representing selected groups of countries and how these policies are implemented in the context of various historical specificities:

OECD	United States (case study), Mexico (comparative case study)
High Income and Emerging Economies	China (comparative case study), the Philippines (case study)
Middle and Low Income	Jamaica (case study & simulation)

Mexico is a democratic country and an OECD member with clear visions on where the country should stand in the future. While these visions seek transformation towards sustainability, legitimacy deficiencies and coordination gaps are found to inhibit the achievement of these visions. The deficiencies pertaining for example to the formal and material participation of civil societal groups such as indigenous communities limit the legitimacy of policies. The lack of genuine deliberation processes undermines the realization of sustainable developmental goals.

China is often taken as the 'best example' that supports the argument that stable authoritarian regimes are in a better position to develop and implement more ambitious environmental policies. It is argued in this book that when climate protection is "securitized", it inevitably becomes an indicator of human well-being. It also modifies the context through new socio-political and socio-linguistic narratives, which alter relations between status and change agents, and re-define the relevance of audience. In China's case, the need for authoritarian regimes to ensure a high degree of output-legitimacy has promoted climate protection as a high-priority policy goal. The case study on China highlights how the securitization of climate protection and sustainable development has empowered "change agents" that push transformation towards sustainability.

The case study on the **Philippines** pertains to a transformative pathway defined by weak governance and the authoritarian tendencies of a democratic regime. The inability of the Philippine State to provide key services or its strategy to franchise the implementation of policies not only limits the sets of possible actions, but also undermines the effectiveness of policy implementation. The change of administration every six years tends to result in a disruptive return to "default" policies as the new administration seeks to first discredit its predecessor in order to consolidate political capital. While there are cases that illustrate strong governance systems, particularly in local levels and civil society participation, this strength ironically indicates weak national governance. National governance mechanisms are highly dependent on non-state actors or local political dynasties, which further strengthen the fragmentation of governance. In addition, one result of the state's low capacity and low autonomy is the diminished *caveat* against politicians abusing the state apparatus to implement policies, which is further reinforced by the current, stable culture of impunity.

The case study on the **United States of America** focuses on how change agents have been mobilized under the Trump administration. With the business and industry sectors as well as civil society pursuing more ambitious, sustainable low-carbon policy goals, it can be argued that under a federal government with ambitious sustainability policy goals, civil society and the private sector would not have been mobilized in the same way they have been now. The case study analyzes how the private sector and civil society can substitute the role of the federal government in pursuing sustainable developmental goals.

The case study on **Jamaica** commences with an assessment of the country's transformation process towards sustainability. The assessment identifies the carbon lock-ins and path dependencies of Jamaica's key sectors as well as potential entry points to mitigation. In addition, an experiment involving a simulation game was conducted to better understand some of the dynamics of decision-making, looking in particular at the carbon lock-ins that inhibit decision-making and support sustainability. Jamaica is a democratic island-state with an insular economy that is isolated and, at the same time, highly dependent on imports from other countries. It derives almost 100% of its electricity and other energy supplies from oil imports, which implies Jamaica's vulnerability.

1.3 The Analytical Framework—Negotiation Studies as an Entry Point to Transformation Towards Sustainability

When reflecting on global, sustainable, low-carbon transformation, understanding the concept of transformation will provide decision-makers from all levels and sectors (government agencies, business companies, and other societal groups) with the capacity to understand and capitalize on information and knowledge in order to come up with effective decisions and 'drive' the process in a way that is tolerable for all stakeholders. This book intends to come up with ideas to better understand and explain this process. As Wayne Booth and colleagues (1995) argue, "tell me something I don't know so I can understand better what I do know."

This book introduces negotiation studies as entry point to the analysis of sustainable low-carbon transformation. The focus on entry points helps to better think through the problem and to guide attention firstly to relevant questions and problems in order to come up with the appropriate normative foundation and an agenda for collective actions. While the implementation of transformation towards sustainability covers multi-level and multiple conflict cleavages, the value of negotiation studies tends to be underestimated and neglected. The reason for this is that negotiation is, as a process, assumed to be self-evident. **Negotiation studies address how conflicts can be resolved by focusing on the process of collective decision-making**.

The current debate on transformation or transition towards sustainability with regards to decision- and policy-making tends to evolve around deliberative democracy, regime/governance studies and organization studies. For example, Teresa Haukkala (2017) highlights the importance of a green-transition advocacy coalition for launching the transition take-off phase for renewable energy in Finland. This implies the significance of a robust deliberative democratic model which nurtures advocacy. Nevertheless, while a deliberative democratic model can promote transformation towards sustainability, **it cannot be fully argued that countries with alternative models will not be equally capable of achieving transformation towards sustainability**, especially those stable authoritarian states with technocratic elements that can also achieve audience's approval through output performance.

In addition, Franziska Ehnert *et al.* (2018) demonstrate how national and subnational institutions enable and/or constrain local agency for sustainability transition. However, while they identify the linkage between local and national agencies for sustainability transition, they do not address the fact that institutions are themselves evolving and adapting to changes. **This evolution is itself a concert of negotiation outcomes**. Furthermore, Brendan Haley (2017) identifies the high demand on the capabilities of the state in designing and implementing policies tailored to technological innovation systems and socio-technical niches and regimes. This implies that the state is expected to facilitate innovation through "game rules" that will further send useful signals about appropriate behavior. In his case study, he demonstrates that an organization's formal and informal rules can make the design principles mutually reinforcing, while a stronger political consensus is needed to manage tensions between accountability and stability. However, he does not consider that the state itself can be either an agent for change or for the status quo. Therefore, the state as an agency cannot be absolutely autonomous in designing formal and informal rules. Conflict of interests may arise when the state becomes not only a "rule-setter", but also a player that needs to abide by the rules. This can be problematic when states tend to bend the rules to their advantage at the cost of their role as facilitator.

Other authors who focus on the socio-technical dimension of transformation towards sustainability tend to highlight technologically optimal solutions as drivers of transformation. For example, Farzin Hossein (1996) suggests the possibility of the optimal pricing of environmental and natural resource use with stock externalities. In addition, Hans Werner Sinn (2007) argues for the relevance of *pareto* optimality in determining the appropriate extraction of fossil fuels to stabilize the greenhouse effect. However, as asserted by the IPCC (2007), while optimal solutions are often proposed as benchmarks for actual negotiations, these optimal solutions tend to be far from the negotiated solution, which causes frustration among technical experts. In addition, as Allard van Mossel *et al.* (2018) argue, the application of solutions will most likely be confronted by resistance. Some actors, even indifferent ones, will very likely seek to protect their autonomy to enable them to react to varying (local) context conditions. Ronan Bolton (2018), for example, identifies the problematic relationship between high-level grand visions of an integrated European system and more pragmatic bottom-up processes of electricity system development.

Negotiation studies highlight the process of reaching agreements through collaboration. Negotiation requires that there is a conflict that needs to be resolved (see Hopmann 1996) Moreover, the inability to resolve, a stalemate, is "mutually hurting" (Zartman 1978, 1988; Young 1991). Negotiated agreements are necessary, particularly in cases of common vulnerabilities where no single actor can effectively resolve the vulnerability (Krasner 1983). This confirms the relevance of negotiations when addressing global environmental concerns such as climate change. In addition, particularly when addressing complex (Druckman 1977; Crump & Zartman 2003) and uncertain issues such as sustainable development and climate change, negotiation serves as a tool for adaptive learning and for improving social relationships (Kramer & Messick 1995; Cross 1996).

However, the negotiation process is itself not self-enforcing. It requires purposive structure and adaptable organization (Malnes 1995; Lewicki et al. 1999; Kremenyuk 2002). Negotiation studies can provide 'anchors' or 'focal points' of transformation from which decisions that promote or inhibit the transformation process can depart. Some authors have already initiated the linking of negotiation studies with sustainability, particularly with environmental sustainability. As one of the leading figures in negotiation studies on environmental issues, Gunnar Sjöstedt (1993; 2013 with Penetrante) highlights the benefits of focusing on negotiation as a process when resolving global environmental issues. Others, such as William Moomaw *et al.* (2003), suggest focusing on innovations in negotiations in order to push forward environmental negotiations. This includes effectively addressing free-riding problems and the tragedy of the commons. Furthermore, studying negotiation is dependent on the analysis of perspectives. Mechanisms are needed to enable actors to analyze, reflect, evaluate and modify the perspective of their peers. Because conflicting parties cannot unilaterally achieve agreements, and the factors hindering particularly weaker parties from committing to agreements are regarded as equally the problems of the stronger parties, empathy is enhanced. Adil Najam *et al.* (2003) and Ariel Penetrante (2010) argue that the enhancement of the negotiation capacity of developing countries is inevitably linked with any global agreement on climate and environmental issues.

In addition, negotiation studies relativize the influence of power asymmetry (Habeeb 1988; William & Rubin 2002; Larson 2003). Because the stronger party requires the help of weaker parties, it is in the interest of stronger parties to prevent the use of coercive power. A probable explanation for this is that the outcome of coerced negotiation will very likely be challenged the moment power has shifted. For example, Joseph Nye (2010a) prefers the usage of "smart power" for global climate negotiations. For him, the conventional utility of power does not have the same meaning in climate negotiations.

Gregory Northcraft *et al.* (1995) contest the necessity of accommodating the non-linear preferences of actors when it comes to the reasons why actors engage or leave negotiations. This is particularly the case when there are multiple issues under consideration, the parties value the issues differently (Lax & Sebenius 1986) and there are initially no obvious benefits for participating actors. Because the transformation process consists of multiple 'negotiation' or 'bargaining games,' transformation towards sustainability is equally non-linear. As such, the relationship between the objective value obtained through the achievement of transformation goals and the subjective utility experienced by all relevant actors cannot be characterized by a straight line (see Northcraft et al. 1995). Because sustainability transitions are goal-oriented and purposive (see Smith & Tushman 2005), attention needs to be given to the preferences not only of the actors, but also of the approving or disapproving audience. In addition, because sustainability is an ambiguous and contested concept, the directionality of sustainability transitions is itself the subject of negotiations or what is referred to in this book as '**knowledge diplomacy**.'

From the negotiation perspective, against the backdrop of multiple possible transformative pathways of adapting to changes, 'status quo agents' and 'change agents' can employ various ways of interacting in order to elaborate which practices and rules need to be maintained to avoid system ruptures. In addition, the formalization of interactions (negotiations) between change and status quo agents will be guarded by a context that is expressed through narratives. Socio-technical and socio-linguistic narratives are the outcomes of multiple, multi-level negotiation or 'elaboration' processes. Pathways are the sum of policies, institutions, norms and narratives that aim to achieve predetermined goals, whereas path-dependent factors and critical junctures may promote or inhibit the course of the paths taken. Shifts from one pathway to another also mean resolving many types of conflicts that emerge as (power) relations between actors when hierarchies are realigned. Transformation produces new conflict cleavages, as tensions between the "old" and the "new" will most likely be projected into many issues, platforms and forums. As an implication of the conflicting nature of transformations, various types of functional, institutional, and bargaining games emerge. These games or interactions can be regarded as the 'fibers' of the transformation process, because these interactions compel collective actions.

Furthermore, the manner by which the monolithic architecture of global decision-making promotes or inhibits transformation towards sustainability in a specific country can be answered by looking at how this architecture determines how basic and policy games are pursued (i.e., connected or disconnected). The usefulness of the negotiation perspective is also demonstrated when addressing gaps between global, regional, national and local policy-making. The two arguments that 1) sustainable low carbon transformation requires global visions, a purpose and structural changes in the global sphere; and that 2) decision-making at the global level still uses a national lens are already widely accepted. It is necessary to account for many kinds of contextual influences that can stabilize or destabilize systems. Connecting these two arguments together will lead to additional questions that can be adequately formulated and answered by negotiation studies.

Negotiation studies calls for a deeper analysis of how decisions can be made, for example, to manage the balancing act between the global vision and the national reality. The literature on global transformation underestimates the proximity between the merely assumed analytical value of global transformation and its actual practical value in individual countries. So, if policy-makers are able to fully understand global transformation, will this help them make appropriate decisions domestically? In several cases, the disconnect between global visions and domestic priorities leads to a refusal to commit to decisions or the so-called "indecisiveness dilemma," that is, the lack of will to make decisions not because decision-makers reject the assumed solutions (Allison & Zelikow 1999; Raiffa 2002), but because they do not fully grasp or make sense of the potential effects of these solutions. When the complexity of sustainable low-carbon transformation is perceived to be manageable, decision-makers will eventually find resources to circumvent the 'indecisiveness dilemma' that has effectively inhibited the unfolding of the process.

1.4 Reflexivity and Stakeholder Engagement for Transformation Towards Sustainability

This book intends to present a practical approach to strategically facilitating sustainable low-carbon transformation. The recommendations that can be made are presented using the Weberian understanding (*Verstehen*) of various variables and dynamics that has been crystalized through this book's theoretical foundation (chapters 2 to 6), methodological tools (chapters 7 and 8), case studies (chapters 9 to 12), simulation game (part of chapter 12) and theoretical claims through the conceptual framework (chapter 13). The theoretical outputs of this research as synthesized in chapter 13 can be used by stakeholders as "political models" (*politische Leitbilder*) as well as guides for interpretations of various discourses

Chapter 14 provides the empirical value of this book with a reflexivity analysis and a stakeholder engagement plan. Reflexivity is itself a form of intervention that allows systems to adapt while preventing ruptures. The analysis of reflexivity can help better structure institutional, functional, and bargaining interactions from the negotiating perspective on context, agencies and the audience of transformation towards sustainability. **Reflexivity analysis is a matrix or collection**

of concrete questions that resonate with the (meta-level) theoretical/conceptual, methodological and practical challenges relevant for each analytical level (actors, issues, structures, processes and outcomes). In addition to the reflexivity analysis, a roadmap or "stakeholder engagement plan" is introduced. The roadmap provides a structure that can facilitate interactions by highlighting the roles of stakeholders, their power base as well as how they tend to behave at various bargaining games (negotiation analysis). The conflict analysis covers how stakeholders define conflicts and how they believe the conflict can be resolved. Moreover, potential measures of engagement are presented, as well as their possible entry points to transformation towards sustainability.

2 Global Transformation Towards Sustainability—Clusters of Current Scholarly Discourse

Studying global transformation towards sustainability is a colossal task. The difficulties in determining the scope, boundaries and levels of the analysis have ramifications for the conceptual value of attempts to understand global transformation towards sustainability. Because of the plurality of possible entry points as well as the complexity of various issues involved, providing an overview of the academic debate, if one can speak of a single debate on global transformation towards sustainability, is highly challenging. Hence, ensuring the 'epistemological acuity' of transformation towards sustainability is still in its elementary stage. Linking the debate of transformation or transition with the studies of sustainability has its own merits, but it also leads to further fragmentation of the debate. Moreover, without a clear definition of the normative concept "sustainability" as the goal of transformation/transition or the scope of conceptual analysis, designing and verifying methodologies becomes equally multifaceted. This blurriness implies that gaps will most likely arise during the calibration of theoretical and empirical models. Furthermore, the plurality of methodologies, for example, will most likely lead to many different types of mutually complementing and competing evidence.

A. M. Hernández, *Taming the Big Green Elephant*, Globale Gesellschaft und internationale Beziehungen, https://doi.org/10.1007/978-3-658-31821-5_2

When the term "sustainability" entered various policy circles, both on the global and national scale, the proliferation of interpretations and responses, especially with the absence of verification mechanisms, inevitably call for flexible approaches. In this regard, as the US Natural Science Foundation (2000) contends, the term 'sustainability' is laden with so many definitions that "*it risks plunging into meaningless(ness), at best, and becoming a catchphrase for demagogy, at worst. It is used to justify and legitimate a myriad of policies and practices ranging from communal agrarian utopianism to large-scale capital-intensive market development.*" Therefore, because of the existence of many possible definitions (Hopwood et al. 2005b) and divergent interpretations and variations applied in practice (Gibson 2005), sustainability has become an "overused misunderstood phrase" (Mawhinney 2002). With the intention of providing a useful overview of the academic literature, this chapter synthesizes the debates on transformation towards sustainability by developing a detailed characterization of drivers, actors and barriers to change as well as an overview of potential anchors for deliberations. Table 2.1 illustrates the different identified clusters and compares them in terms of context (offering a systems perspective by focusing on entry points and drivers), agency (addressing power and purpose by highlighting anchors for a deliberation process), and audience (in reference to legitimacy and social contract *vis- à-vis* a transformation process).

Table 2.1 Clusters of Current Scholarly Debates on Transformation towards Sustainability (own representation)

Cluster	**Context**		**Agency (anchor for deliberation)**	**Audience (meaning of transformation)**
	Entry Point	Drivers		
Cluster 1: Triple bottom line (TBL)—the sustainable development discourse	Brundtlandt Report 1987	Economy, society and environment as 3 pillars of sustainability (symmetrical relations)	Establishment of principles and rules such as the "Equitable Access to Sustainable Development"	Sustainable development also achievable without transformation
Cluster 2: Technological innovation and change management—the Industrial Revolution discourse	Industrial Revolution	Asymmetrical and/or vertical relationship between the triple bottom lines); purposive economy as champion and emergent society & environment	Technological innovation as background of deliberation (agenda-setter, rules for procedures like sectoral approaches and solution)	Industrial revolution as comparative model for the "Great Green Transformation" and innovation as enabler of transformation
Cluster 3: Systems Approach (SA)—Transformation management and socio-technical discourse	Transformation management discourse in the Netherlands	3 action levels: niches, sociotechnical regimes, exogenous sociotechnical landscapes	Human agency and multi-level structures of governance, meaning different levels of social mandates and fragmented deliberation	Inclusion of social relations in addressing technological configurations
Cluster 4: Systems Approach (SA)—Global shifts and globalization discourse	Globalization	Processes that support transition, interlocking and permeability	Power-based relations between actors	Transformation as means to address vulnerabilities as by-products of globalization

(continued)

Table 2.1 (continued)

Cluster	**Context**		**Agency (anchor for deliberation)**	**Audience (meaning of transformation)**
	Entry Point	Drivers		
Cluster 5: Process Approach (SA)—Center-Periphery and Global South discourse	Alternatives for participation	Cultures and societies, national identities and citizenship as determinants of human well-being and welfare	Availability and viability of alternative spheres for decision-making (including non-consensus-based processes)	Value-free perspectives on pathways
Cluster 6: Process Approach (PA)—Climate negotiations discourse	Norm and rule-based procedures for decision-making	Co-benefits and trade-offs resulting from the nexus of economy and environment as well as the nexus of society and environment	Justice and fairness over the attribution of responsibilities (and commitments) and distribution of burden	Agenda-setting and norm diffusion (convergence)

2.1 Cluster 1: Triple Bottom Line (TBL)—The Sustainable Development Discourse

The literature categorized in the cluster Triple Bottom Line (TBL) refers to the sustainability and developmental discourses that evolve around the Brundtland Report in 1987. The literature on sustainable development has achieved a consensus about the three pillars of sustainability—social, environmental and economic (see Byrne & Glover 2002; Hopwood et al. 2005b; Elliott 2013). They were inherited as these three categories—later labelled as the Triple Bottom Line—and have been standardized in most UN agencies addressing sustainability since the 1980s. The Triple Bottom Line, originally introduced by John Elkington (1994, 1997) is an accounting framework traditionally used in economics and business administration that refers to the society, the environment (ecology), and economy (see Willard 2002; Savitz 2006; Slaper, Timothy & Hall 2011).

The TBL has functioned as a catalyst for the sustainability debate, whereas social cohesion, environmental integrity and economic affluence are taken as goals toward which transformation processes are heading. The usage of TBL as a framework was institutionalized by the public sector when it was used as the cost accounting standard by the International Council for Local Environmental Initiatives (ICLEI), which was founded in September 1990 at the United Nations in New York. This international association has more than 1200 cities, towns, and regions from 84 countries as members (ICLEI 2018). The private sector has followed the TBL accounting standard and used the phrase "people, planet and profit" as the goal of sustainability, which later framed the elements of corporate social responsibility for companies wishing to embody these three Ps. Subsequently, as climate change negotiations have produced the principle of "Equitable Access to Sustainable Development" as a major anchor for any acceptable climate agreement, these TBLs have been incorporated into most discussions about transformative pathways.

Because of the functional importance of sustainable development in achieving climate mitigation, this cluster highlights the perspective of sustainable development through transformation. However, from this perspective, environmental integrity (i.e. climate mitigation) is only one of three equally important pillars. The distinct origin and constitution of the debate on sustainable development limits the capability of this discourse (cluster) to support the overall discussion on climate mitigation. The actors participating in the debate on sustainable development are diverse, probably too diverse for the climate regime. Furthermore, as will be highlighted in this cluster, sustainable development can also be achieved without transformation. This is in contrast to the discourse on climate mitigation, wherein transformation (labelled as 'transformative pathways') is inevitable and a precondition. Those from the public and business sectors in particular belong to the "weak sustainability" group (see Solow 1974; Hartwick 1977; Solow 1986). They argue that sustainable development can also be reached without major structural changes that require insurmountable sacrifices. In contrast, proponents of strong sustainability view the natural system as intrinsically valuable and not substitutable (see Brand 2009; Dedeurwaerdere 2014). Hence, there is a hierarchy of norms between the natural/environmental and human system.

Bill Hopwood *et al.* (2005b) classify debates on sustainability into three schools—*status quo, reform* and *transformation*, which strongly correspond to the categories of weak and strong sustainability. According to them, the "Status Quo School" is the dominant view of most governments and business groups. Those belonging to the Status Quo School tend to be proponents of weak sustainability who see economic growth as the solution to addressing climate change. For example, the Green New Deal Group, through its published report on July 21, 2008 (Green New Deal Group 2008) calls for a "return to pre-war Keynesianism" and an increase in public investment spending and international finance to address climate protection (Lynas 2008). Other notable proponents such as Thomas Friedman (2007), Mariana Mazzucato (2015), Van Jones (2008), the Heinrich Böll Foundation of Germany (French et al. 2009) advocate for fiscal policies that provide stimulus packages to address both financial crises and environmental issues such as climate change.

The combination of fiscal instruments such as investment in the deployment of renewable energies and the enhancement of resource efficiency is the solution (French et al. 2009). Edward Barbier (2009) published the report "Global Green New Deal" which was commissioned by the United Nations Environment Programme (UNEP). The report calls on governments to allocate a significant share of stimulus funding to green sectors order to achieve economic recovery, poverty eradication and climate protection through reduced carbon emissions.

Bill Hopwood *et al.* (2005b) continues with the "Reform School," which is the dominant view of academic communities and mainstream NGOs. The "Limits to Growth" report of Donella Meadows et al. (1972) is often considered to have initiated challenges to the idea that growth was the only way to improve environmental integrity. Subsequent authors and environmental groups such as Friends of the Earth, Greenpeace, WWF and Sierra Club have voiced their concerns about economic growth as the generic solution through political lobbying (Hopwood et al. 2005b). Other proponents of the Reform School attribute the root of the problem to imbalances and a lack of knowledge and information. For example, the Real World Coalition, a group that consists of 25 UK NGOs, sees the necessity of revitalizing democratic governance to empower the government and society to address mounting inequality and poverty, environmental degradation and world instability (Christie & Warburton 2001). This school also suggests there is a need for significant shifts in policies and behavior. In their book "Factor Five," Ernst Ulrich von Weizsäcker *et al.* (2009) suggest that sustainability can be achieved by improving resource productivity for some sectors of the economy, while maintaining quality of service and well-being. This argument for using technological solutions partly contradicts the Status Quo School by suggesting a significant degree of degrowth, particularly in consumption and production.

The Third School, as Bill Hopwood *et al.* (2005b) elaborate, sees transformation as fundamentally necessary to avoiding a mounting crisis and even a possible system rupture. Linking this cluster to the global transformation towards sustainability debate, it is implied that this cluster sees transformation as only one of the options and that sustainability can also be achieved without transformation. Authors that tend to represent the "Transformation School" call for "strong sustainability." This school is the dominant view of grass-root environmental justice groups and indigenous environmental movements. For most of these groups, there is a need for a new system and a new distribution of power (a shift from center to the periphery) (O'Riordan 1989). For the others, there is a need to re-visit the dogmatic realization of growth, whereas the logic of growth is considered the essence of *economicity* (Bonaiuti 2014). Because fundamental problems as well as imbalances are deeply rooted in society, more efforts and commitments are needed to address the conditions that produce and reinforce imbalances.

The Transformation School is also represented by views that are counterintuitive or even counterfactual to the goals of global transformation towards sustainability. In fact, extreme "transformationists" such as socialists, deep ecologists, and eco-fascists are not concerned with sustainable development. Other proponents belong to what some have called the "School of Post-development," from which the "partisans" of degrowth or "growth objectors" have originated (see Bonaiuti 2014). For example, David Foreman (1989), one of the founders of Earth First!, justifies the starvation of people in Ethiopia as nature's way of self-preservation (quoted in Bradford 1989; Hopwood et al. 2005b). In addition, Arne Naess (1989) observes that in the eight points of the deep ecology platform, human needs are sacrificed, and equity concerns ignored.

Nevertheless, this Transformation School also represents "transformation with sustainable development." One example is the Report of the German Advisory Council on Global Change (WBGU) (2011) that argues that transformation is a constant development brought about by changes. As new problems emerge, societies seek solutions. In most situations, these solutions require systemic or structural changes to alter the obsolete conditions that have caused the problems in the first place. For example, after analyzing the tendency of returns on capital to exceed the rate of economic growth, leading to extreme inequalities, Thomas Picketty (2014) argues that "economic trends are not acts of God." Hence, political actions are needed to design and implement social policies that reduce inequality and do not grow the GDP for its own sake. It is therefore implied that transformation is not only emergent, i.e. merely a response to changes, but also purposive, i.e. transformation goals are pre-determined. In addition, as the WBGU (2011) continues, advancing sustainable development will not only require modifications to social contracts as a means of adapting to changes, but new social contracts will most likely also challenge existing governance structures, for instance, because of the transboundary nature of vulnerabilities. More arguments from the Transformation School will be introduced in the Cluster on the Multi-Level Perspective.

2.2 Cluster 2: Technological Innovation and Change Management—The Industrial Revolution Discourse

While the discourse that belongs to this cluster uses the triple bottom lines as levels of analysis, its focus also lies in the linkages between them, particularly in the analysis of the effects of innovative and technological changes on small organizations such as industrial and commercial companies (Kristof 2017). Furthermore, there is an implied asymmetrical or vertical relationship between them, with the economy receiving the primary focus. The common denominator in the literature included in this cluster is the use of the Industrial Revolution as a comparative model or as precedent that frames the analysis of the scope and processes behind the "Great Green Transformation." For example, Tom Delay (2009) argues that the low carbon economy will transform the world much like the first industrial revolution did.

The Industrial Revolution from about 1760 to 1820/1840 was driven by technological innovations, which led to new manufacturing and production processes as well as commercial relations between countries (see Hobsbawm 1965; Landes 1969; Reisman 1998). The unprecedented, sustained economic growth throughout the Industrial Revolution is claimed to have marked a major turning point in history that changed almost every aspect of society (see Feinstein 1998; Lucas 2002).

In this cluster, the incorporation of the rationales of the Industrial Revolution is evident, hence the entry point to transformation in this cluster is rather **technologically driven**. Nikolai Kondratieff's (1926) theory of the "Long Waves of Economic Change," or the so-called "*kondratiev* waves or cycles," is often cited as pioneer research work on long cycles theory. Through his studies of industrial behavior using historical facts and economic data, he argued that economic growth is not linear, but rather has a sinusoidal form. Kondratieff further argued that it was possible to forecast and foster economic growth, because cycles are found to consist of growth and decay phases, whereas market economies tend to go into the development cycle, where new technological inventions have been employed.

Further developing Kondratieff's theory and putting Kondratieff on the radar of international debate is Joseph Schumpeter's Theory of Economic Development (1935, 1954), which argues that changes come in the form of significant technological innovations. For example, Schumpeter refers to railway construction as the cause of another wave, because it further enhanced modern the mining industry and promoted urban development. He continues that while all economic activities are essentially repetitive and follow a familiar, routine course, changes need to take place to make the static circular flow a dynamic and discontinuous process. According to him, for this to occur, innovation is required: "*spontaneous and discontinuous change in the channels of flow, disturbance of equilibrium which forever alters and displaces the equilibrium state previously existing*" (Schumpeter 1934 p. 64).

Gerhard Mensch (1975) further developed Peter Schumpeter's Theory of Economic Development through his Theory of Innovation. In his 1975 publication, "Stalemate in Technology", he attributed economic stagnation to the lack of basic innovations. He identified that "basic innovations" (*Basisinnovationen*), as an expression of knowledge development, are the drivers of economic booms (Mensch 1971, 1972). According to him, basic innovations create new economic sectors following the introduction of new products and production processes, leading to new jobs and new sources of income. He differentiated basic innovations from "improvement-innovations" (*Verbesserungsinnovation*), which further develop existing sectors by reducing production costs and increasing productivity levels. Finally, the so-called "pseudo innovations" (*Schein-Innovationen*) are those that do not possess economic value at all. This refers to those innovations that can increase consumer wealth even though these inventions neither move demand nor supply side curves. The effects of pseudo innovations such as changing the color or original form of products to long waves or cycles are too minor, because they do not, for example, significantly increase final consumer satisfaction levels.

As such, the economy, which serves as a "rallying point" for technological innovations, is implied as the driving bottom line with the environment and society becoming emergent or even subservient. Several authors coming from the Great Transformation discourse tend to connect the categories, here labelled as the 'triple bottom line', in a vertical or asymmetrical manner. Some directly or indirectly claim one bottom line "dominating" or "maneuvering" the others. For example, Karl Polanyi's book "The Great Transformation" (published in 1945) (2015) pertains to the economy as a driver of the Industrial Revolution and highlights the historical evolution of the current dominance of the market economy. This book provides an important understanding of global transformation, but it only focuses on the market drivers of transformation, such as market logic, as a framing factor of the evolution. While it is difficult to imagine a society without a market-based economy, Polanyi stressed that markets are not a natural feature of human society and that there are also non-market mechanisms to distribute goods and services. The dominance of the market has emerged and cemented by certain ideologies and principles, which relate to land, labor and the market, in particular profit, and which now define the basic fibers of societies.

Others highlight one bottom line as the main driver of global transformation, while the two other bottom lines are merely responding as subordinates (or even merely as circumstances). For example, Yoshikazu Sakamoto (1994) argues in his book "Global Transformation: Challenges to the State System" that while the global economy should not be analyzed as an isolated entity, but rather in conjunction with the political society, economic drivers are both causes and effects of global and national societal conditions. In his analysis of how uneven development and democratization has led to gaps between capital internationalization and political democratization, he focuses on the importance of economic drivers to the basic framework of the modern international order. While the book provides insightful causalities between global economy and the international order, it does not provide an understanding of how uneven development affects the prospect of cooperation between actors when forging decisions. Sakamoto focuses on global transformation as driven by capital internationalization and political democratization.

Other scholars have a micro-perspective and do not clearly identify technologies as the catalyst of global transformation towards sustainability, but rather as "enablers" of transformation (see Goldemberg 1998; Bibby 2012; Guo et al. 2015). For example, Manahem Anderman (2007) identifies battery technologies for hybrid electric vehicles as an example of such "enablers" of transformation towards sustainability. In addition, Richard Baldwin (2016) provides an analysis of how revolutionary changes in information communication technology (ICT) has fundamentally changed globalization. Through ICT, economic, political, cultural and military power has shifted in favor of countries with emerging markets, whereas the boundaries of competitiveness between countries are increasingly controlled by firms who run international production networks. In present times, global competitiveness means countries are required to look for new impulses of economic development. Low-carbon technologies and innovations can be the new "basic innovations" that can create new industrial sectors and jobs. On the other hand, Wiebe Bijker's (1995, 2010) constructivist outlook on technologies claims that technologies can be "treated" or "created" differently depending on various social factors such as changing gender relationships. He calls for the establishment of a basis for science, technology, and social change that addresses the social roots of technology (Bijker 1995).

Most of the literature classified to this cluster do not clearly address social, cultural and political processes of change as being of a technological nature or determined by technology. Some authors, such as Marko Hekkert *et al.* (2007), are critical of the fact that while technological innovation systems are multidimensional, they do not fully address structural change and how emerging innovations struggle against existing systems (and vice-versa). They propose a method for systematically mapping processes taking place in innovation systems and resulting in technological change. In addition, Clayton Christensen *et al.* (2006) argue that innovations and technologies can also be disruptive. Some innovations and technologies do not bring better products to existing markets, but rather disrupt and redefine trajectories, and that increased attention needs to be given to interactions between new entrants and incumbents. As Richard Baldwin (2016) argues, an outcome of a transformation process changes the role of distance and policies. New conflict fronts are established, particularly as declining sectors and skill groups fall into disfavor, are mobilized, and struggle for their relevance. Furthermore, some challenges that currently inhibit transformation towards sustainability transcend technologies, such as changing lifestyles and preferences (see Jackson 2008; Roy et al. 2012). For example, with the ability of transportation technologies to address traffic congestion, some governments prefer "basic technologies" such as bicycles rather than expensive and less environmentally-friendly technologies. The introduction of new technologies often means the increased consumption of exhaustible natural resources, which is counterintuitive to sustainability. New voices have emerged claiming that sustainability also means less technologies or less dependence on technologies, because as new innovations are introduced, consumption increases.

2.3 Cluster 3: Systems Approaches (SA)—Transformation Management and Socio-Technical Discourse

The next cluster pertains to *transformation management theories* (that trace their origin to the Netherlands) as well as the *socio-technical transition theories*. The transformation management theories highlight the goal of effectively managing transformation by taking into account complexities and the multi-tiered nature and non-concurrency of transformation processes (see Loorbach 2010; Schäpke & Rauschmayer 2011). In the words of Rainer Grießhammer *et al.* (2015), this goal is motivated by the assumption that transformation processes can only unfold when the focus is not limited to technical innovations, but also includes social and institutional innovations. In addition, René Kemp *et al.* (1998) assert that managing transition is not only a useful option for many policy instruments, but "it may be the only feasible way to transform environmentally unsustainable regimes" (1998 p. 191).

The backdrop of this discourse is that **transitions are multi-level in terms of governance**. They cut across the local, national, regional and international. A significant consequence of this cross-cutting element is the emergence of several conflict cleavages, particularly when asymmetries, for example those in power, are re-aligned and relations need to be revisited. It needs to be highlighted that asymmetries are reproduced across levels. As such, the boundaries between the global, the national and the local become diffuse because of the emergence of new interdependencies. For example, the "local" assumes a "global touch" when communities, villages, towns and municipalities become recipients of technology transfer to support local sustainability projects. Best practices from these local projects will most likely be collected, inductively assessed, re-conceptualized and applied in projects in communities from other countries. An example is the use of the *Talanoa* Dialogue, a concept that originates from Fiji, in global negotiations pertaining to climate change (see UNFCCC 2016). In addition, the introduced technologies are expected to assume economic, social, cultural and institutional connotations (Bijker et al. 1987; Bijker 1995, 2010). New business models are sought to adequately capture the opportunities of new global-local settings. These interdependencies between levels are therefore multifaceted, non-linear and even fragmented.

The **socio-technical theories** emphasize the relevance and complexity of technologies and the inclusion of social relations in the analyses of technological configurations (Rip & Kemp 1998; Geels 2005; Geels & Schot 2007b; Geels & Schot 2009). The inclusion of human agency as reflected by the interests, behavior, and preferences of humans and organizations in the analyses of technologies sets the stage for the multi-level analysis. John Grin *et al.* (2010) identify three initially independent action levels: *megatrends, sociotechnical regimes* and *niche level*, which allow the consideration of path dependencies along which lie processes with distinct self-contained dynamics and actors' preferences. Through these three action levels, the scope of action for change agents can be explored. Similarly, Arie Rip and René Kemp (1998) suggest three analytical levels that host non-linear processes that result from the interplay of multiple developments. The niches (1) serve as the locus for radical innovations. Sociotechnical regimes (2) pertain to the locus of established practices and associated rules that stabilize existing systems. Finally, the exogenous sociotechnical landscape (3) refers to background variables such as the material infrastructure, political culture and coalitions, social values and the natural environment.

Relevant to the linking of transition research to sustainable development is the work of John Grin *et al.* (2011), who argue that transformation does not only foresee new societal practices, but also changes in the structures in which these practices are embedded. They further contend that new practices need to co-evolve with earlier practices ("the regime"). Frank Geels (2011 p. 26) claims that the regime needs to be given the primary focus, because transitions are defined as shifts from one regime to another. He classifies the niche and landscape levels as "derived concepts," because "they are only defined in relation to the regime, namely as practices or technologies that deviate substantially from the existing regime" (Geels 2011 p. 26).

One major strand of socio-technical theories is the multi-level perspective (MPL), which conceptualizes overall dynamic patterns in socio-technical transitions (Geels 2011). The multi-level perspective uses a combination of evolutionary theory and the sociology of technology in explaining that transitions are shifts from one stable socio-technical regime to another. Transitions occur when regimes are destabilized through pressures (Rip & Kemp 1998; Markard & Truffer 2008a). Frank Geels (2005; 2011) summarizes that MPL is an analytical framework that combines concepts from evolutionary economies (trajectories, regimes, niches, speciation, path dependence and routines), science and technology studies (sense making, social networks and innovation), structuration theory and neo-institutional theory (rules and institutions as "deep structures" from which knowledgeable actors draw their actions).

The multi-level perspective can provide relevant insights into helping developing countries, especially those countries with emerging economies such as China, India, Mexico, Brazil and Indonesia, to manage their transformation towards sustainability. By assessing the historical phases of economic, technological, cultural, and political changes, this multi-level perspective can help distinguish other transition patterns which destabilize the system as the transformation process unfolds. In addition, the analysis of multiple processes of "changing practices" and structural change during the course of transformation can be better aligned parallel to each other to produce non-incremental changes in practices and structures (Grin et al. 2010). Because these countries are often confronted by multiple transition processes (e.g. political, economic, post-colonial), causalities and related challenges can be better understood and resolved. For example, through this understanding, corrective measures can accompany technology transfer mechanisms to effectively target "deficient" regimes in these countries.

Through the application of the MLP, it can be inferred that sustainable, low-carbon development, as sociotechnical transition, will most likely involve alterations of various sectors such as transport, energy, and agriculture, which would entail technology policy, markets, cultural meaning and scientific knowledge. However, as Fernand Braudel (1958) argues, each of these sectors or subsystems may vary in pace and follow different historical timescales. Therefore, it is detrimental to managing transformation that the stage of transition for each sector be assessed. In addition, there are existing path dependencies that may inhibit a specific sector to support sustainable, low-carbon development. Hence, more rapid and widespread reforms are necessary to pave over path dependencies and restructure asymmetries.

New revisions of the MPL are emerging. Some of the literature is now looking at transition or transformation as a process, with various possible pathways (plurality of pathways towards one outcome) depending on different configurations and multi-level interactions (Smith 2005; Patwardhan et al. 2012). This is particularly interesting when assessing the relevance of policy models (democratic, authoritarian, hybrid) to the achievement of sustainability goals. While the MPL as an evolutionary approach on transformation entails a pre-determined "future" for a system, it also argues that changes merely reorient existing development trajectories. The regime adopts certain niche innovations into the system which leads to a gradual reconfiguration of the basic architecture including guiding principles, beliefs and practices (Smith 2005; Geels & Schot 2007a).

Although the multi-level perspective is largely confined to emerging technologies, it can shed light on how the motivation to accept change is created. As transformation follows a specific evolutionary continuum, it is understood as an initial one-pathway, whereas challenges to the incumbent and dominant socio-technical practice (regime) will eventually emerge as the transition process unfolds. As time passes, the actors that are profiting from change will be more powerful than those resisting change. As more jobs are created, for example through the expansion of the renewable sector, the renewable sector will possess more resources and the confidence to pursue more effective advocacy. This is something that is being anticipated, leading to a more difficult transition process as resistance becomes a question of survival for some.

2.4 Cluster 4: Systems Approaches (SA)—Global Shifts and Globalization Discourse

Another cluster of how (global) transformation towards sustainability is addressed pertains to the focus on boundaries between the global and the national/local. This cluster revolves around questions about processes that support transitions and the interlocking and permeability of various domains such as state boundaries, cultures, societies, national identities and citizenship. Transformation towards sustainability is inherent to globalization, because sustainability as a concept has emerged in the context of intertwined vulnerabilities that transcend state boundaries. These intertwined vulnerabilities confront the monolithic architecture of the global system, leading to debates not only on how diplomacy can achieve solutions, but also on how the convergence of standards and identities can be facilitated to support transformation towards sustainability.

Peter Dicken (2015) points out that global shifts are mainly attributed to empirical changes in the configuration of the global economy and to changing interpretations of, and attitudes towards, 'globalization'. Barry Eichengreen (2011) attributes Great Britain's control of fully a quarter of the world's population and land mass by the end of the 19th century to the industrial revolution, which marked a global shift. He depicts another shift in economic power from Britain to other continental countries in Europe such as Germany and France as the pretext for World War I. In the same manner, Charles Kindleberger (1973) argues that the Great Depression of the 1930s was a ramification of the global shift of power from Europe to the United States.

This shows that global shifts are to be explained in the context of power, which is manifested by how structural as well as technological changes have altered relations between countries. Barry Buzan and George Lawson (2015) highlight the impact of global transformation on international relations. They argue that the uneven distribution of economic development brought by a complex configuration of industrialization, rational state-building and ideologies of progress defines the uneven distribution of power in the international system.

In addition, this inequity further determines the configuration of undergoing wide-ranging political, economic and cultural transformations. These global power shifts changed the basic modes of power, stimulating the emergence of global modernity.

While Joseph Nye (2010b) makes claim to the relative decline of the power of the United States, as Barry Eichengreen *et al.* (2008) also argue, he claims that the ongoing global shift of economic power from the United States to the East Asian region has a potentially far-reaching impact not only on markets and environmental policies, but also on reshaping relations in the current multilateral system. Several authors see a new era marked by accelerated globalization, where new decisive elements are available to maintain a leading global position (see Bardhan 2010; Kappel 2011; Shambaugh 2013; Kappel 2014). With China as the main proponent of this current global shift, the authors have pondered the emergence of new impulses for transformation towards sustainability (see Fücks 2011; Volz 2015; CCICED 2015). China's "change of tune" in climate policies is the result of the securitization of climate change (see chapter 8). This change reflects China's current, more cooperative posture in international climate policy-making as motivated by its new sociotechnical and sociolinguistic narratives.

2.5 Cluster 5: Process Approaches (SA)—The Center-Periphery and the Global South Discourse

Transition and transformation studies are no longer confined to European universities. Research institutions and universities in Asia and the Americas have recognized the need to establish or modify their mandates and visions and re-align their positions to be able to participate in shaping the discourse on sustainability. For example, initial contributions to leading practices in sustainability in higher education in the Asia-Pacific region have explored the trajectories of key initiatives across the region through the contextualization of sustainability innovation in higher education. Alexandra Ryan et al. (2010) attribute a wider understanding of the learning dimensions of sustainability in the region to several creative initiatives in the Asia-Pacific region that have helped harness national policy, develop further local and regional initiatives towards more profound change in curriculum development, and establish collaboration with external communities and stakeholders. As many Asian and North/South American universities and post-graduate institutes join their counterparts in Europe in establishing new, dynamic programs that integrate sustainability into most aspects of their curriculum including business and management, "change agents" of transformation towards sustainability are now equipped not only with concepts or ideas, but also with the technical expertise to address the emerging challenges of transformation.

The increased participation of non-European universities and research institutes in sustainability discourse will most likely lead to challenges to existing well-established Euro- or West-centric assumptions about sustainability. Old evidence paired with old approaches will most likely be revisited and new ways of linking will emerge, particularly because of the inter- and trans-disciplinarity of sustainability studies. For example, trajectories of sustainable development tend to "favor" democratic or deliberative (consensus-building) policy models (see Baber & Bartlett 2005; Arias-Maldonado 2007; Purdy 2010). Nevertheless, selected case studies in the book, particularly the case studies on Mexico, China and the Philippines offer new ways of re-linking 'modern' policy models with sustainability.

Some questions arise as to whether alternative perspectives such as the 'Indigenous' Modernity (see Pratt 2002; Ravindran 2015), the 'Asian Way' (Dupont 1996; see Chesterman & Mahbubani 2010) and *Bienestar* (see Collier & Collier 1991; Feinberg et al. 2006; Etcheverry 2011) could be equally useful for studies of transformation towards sustainability. For example, Simon Chesterman and Kishore Mahbubani (2010) argue that while there is no coherent or systematic Asian approach to meeting global challenges, Asian policy-making tends to respond pragmatically to challenges and is less ideology-driven. This includes how Asian countries such as Japan, with its "reluctant realism" towards China (Green & Self 1996), address changes in the region.

Another strand of this cluster refers to linking the study sustainability transformation to the development of the welfare state, which has been made prominent in Latin American literature through the concept, "*estado del bienestar*" (state-of-well-being) (see André 2008; Seligman 2014). This strand is a proponent of the ideas of Abraham Maslow (1943), who suggested the pyramid of basic needs. In addition, this strand calls for political actors to pursue the enhancement of four areas of health: physical, mental, emotional and social (see Smith et al. 2012; Abers & Tatagiba 2014). The "wellness" concept may open more channels for discourse on transformation towards sustainability, because most societies, particularly in developing countries, have had a long-standing debate on welfare policies such as *Zakat* (charity) in Islamic Law and *Dharma* (path) in India that could be used to further promote sustainability policies (see Shadi 2003; Crone 2005).

As the understanding of transformation or transition towards sustainability is widely contextualized, it has become apparent that differences in approaches and *Weltbilder* (world views) exist that require the re-visitation of existing concepts. As some developing countries that demonstrate advancement in their transformation towards sustainability deviate from the ideal type of democratic policy models as the "formula" for successful transformation (see Baber & Bartlett 2005; Arias-Maldonado 2007), there is a need to revisit, among others, the 'purposive rationality' (*Zweckrationalität*) of sustainability. As proposed by Max Weber (2005), expectations are developed as a means for a particular actor to attain rationally-pursued and calculated ends. In this sense, while transformation is driven by "social actions" serving a particular end, preferences around policy models can be diverse. Following the 'value-free' argument of global transformation in their book "Global Transformation and the Third World," Robert Slater, *et al.* (1993) suggest that while the major element of global transformation pertains to democratization (the wave of political liberalization), the 'Third World' perspective may highlight military rule as the major alternative to democracy in most 'Third World' countries where military regimes can be, equally, both 'credible' as well as effective and efficient administrators. Therefore, when reflecting on sustainable, low-carbon transformation, a 'value-free' perspective on assessing sustainability pathways seems to be viable. This suggests that processes that are not built on consensus-building can also be practically used to achieve sustainability priorities.

2.6 Cluster 6: Process Approach—The Climate Negotiations Discourse

Another cluster can be identified, one that evolves around the discourse framed by or for climate negotiations, where major conflict cleavages, as reflected by the numerous bilateral and multilateral climate negotiations, are related to the perceived economic burdens of climate mitigation and adaptation as major pillars of addressing climate change (see Cullet 1998; Heyward 2007; Penetrante 2010). The demand from developing countries for exemptions or delays in their mitigation commitments due to their right to develop (see Ott et al. 2004; Kanitkar et al. 2010; Najam 2010; Penetrante 2010) collides with the demands of developed countries that developing countries make comparable commitments to mitigation (see Winkler et al. 2009a; Penetrante 2010, 2013). As such, the academic debate has focused its attention on the nexus economy and the environment as well as on the nexus society and the environment when addressing climate mitigation and adaptation.

Some authors have observed that the global transformation towards sustainability is currently framed by global negotiations, particularly the climate change negotiations (see Sjöstedt 1993; Sjöstedt & Penetrante 2013) and the multilateral process towards sustainable development (see Kalhauge et al. 2005). As climate negotiations proceed, problems come to light, agendas are defined and procedures of generating solutions emerge as outcomes of these negotiations. The tendency within debate has now moved forward towards the 'decoupling' of the three bottom lines (see Steinberger & Roberts 2010), as doing so is perceived to create the political will to commit to climate protection. In this regard, a number of studies now support the notion that a climate-compatible global economy is technologically possible (see McKinsey 2009; GEA 2012). For example, the International Energy Agency (IEA) (2016b) reported that global CO_2 emissions from energy-related activities have not risen since 2013 in spite of global economic growth, suggesting that the decoupling of emissions and economic activity is possible. The stabilization of emissions was attributed to the registered 1.5 percent decline in emissions in the United States and China.

A major obstacle to climate protection, and therefore also for low-carbon development, is primarily the 'undoing' of narratives and the perception of additional constraints, for example to food security and living space, particularly for countries already struggling to meet their needs. Because the discourse on climate mitigation in most countries is dominated by narratives of climate protection, for example exacerbating food insecurity, policy-makers focus on trade-offs rather than co-benefits. Some scholars question these narratives and argue that, with efficient structural changes including the promotion of inclusive participation (see Winslow 2005), food insecurity does not need to be an issue. For example, Julia Steinberger and J. Timmons Roberts (2010) highlight the possibility of decoupling of energy and carbon from human needs such as food and shelter. If the academic discourse on the decoupling of the three bottom lines is able to find a consensus that there are co-benefits to pursuing climate protection policy goals for the two other bottom lines (economy and society), negative externalities can be reduced or even prevented. Nevertheless, decoupling requires a more integrated understanding of causalities and process-tracing. For this, new methods of assessment and verification are needed to be developed and to mature, which requires more time and testing.

For scholars working on path dependencies, decoupling means identifying carbon lock-ins, particularly in the economy, which hinder the sets of viable solutions that support sustainability, including climate protection. New approaches are needed to recalculate economies of scale, revisit coordination and collaboration problems and redefine the impacts of policies (or the lack of them). As Claus Leggewie and Dirk Messner (2012 p. 10) maintain, the successful implementation of transitions towards sustainability will be highly dependent on cognitive models, concepts and narratives that foresee how "change agents" acquire power to realign the economy and society. **There is still, however, the need to move one step 'sideways' and link this newly acquired power with a debate about justice and fairness**. Existing formal and informal rules as well as norms will need to be improved to adequately address this newly acquired power. Transformation needs to be legitimized by the society, but this legitimization needs to be preceded by a "tolerable window" (see Bruckner et al. 1998; Bruckner et al. 1998; Petschel-Held et al. 1999). In addition, the temporal dimension of decoupling, for example, climate protection from the economic burdens of mitigation, necessitates the careful planning of stages and complementary mechanisms to absorb and make sense of the incremental learning process.

2.7 Interim Conclusion

This chapter contributes to this book's theoretical framework by identifying parameters for the knowledge tools (ideal types and case studies/simulation). The rationale behind the introduction of the six different clusters is to rethink boundaries, even between relevant debates surrounding transformation towards sustainability, in order to effectively establish frameworks. The six different clusters allow a clear comparison in terms of **context** (a systems perspective, by focusing on entry points and drivers), **agency** (the power and purpose, by highlighting anchors for the deliberation process) and **audience** (in reference to legitimacy and the social contract *vis-à-vis* the transformation process).

Interestingly, the differences between these clusters of debates are themselves results of the contextuality of the process of academic debate. While looking at these differences, it can be argued that some difficulties in designing and implementing sustainability policies can be attributed to the continuous development of a specific debate. For example, while the debate surrounding climate change negotiations problematizes the coupling of climate protection goals with developmental goals (emission reduction can be achieved with increased economic development), the debate surrounding sustainable development calls for a much closer coupling of climate protection and developmental policies. For many developed countries, climate mitigation assistance to developing countries should be counted as official development assistance. For most developing countries, climate mitigation assistance from developed countries should be counted 'in addition' to official development assistance. Furthermore, because the audience of climate protection policies does not always correspond to the audience of sustainable development policies, some gaps between policy outcomes arise. There are different types of resistance within a specific debate that might later limit the usefulness of concepts to policy-making. This 'anti-climax' following intense debate can lead to frustration and resignation.

Trade-Offs and Turnstiles as the Main Drivers of the Transformation Process Towards Sustainability

3

This chapter is a major pillar of the theoretical framework and reiterates how this book understands the **intricacies of decision-making** in the context of transformation towards sustainability. It looks at how power, identities, path dependence, emotions, norms, institutions and paradigms can promote or inhibit effective decision-making. This understanding aims not only to achieve the 'deconstruction' of paradigmatically 'given' terms, which are widespread within and across disciplines, but, equally importantly, to also develop and/or refine decision tools to address complexity and uncertainty. This understanding also provides benchmarks and indicators to help ease the justification, verification and monitoring of decisions, paving the way for the effective 'management' of complexity. Because 'decision science' is still in its infancy (see Skorepa 2011), there is still a need to clarify the definitions, terminologies and concepts of decision-making processes that are relevant for this book. In addition, because of the complexity of relevant issues, a 'salad bowl' of perspectives, approaches and methodologies should be expected.

Moreover, as this chapter highlights, the *contextuality* of decisions and the conceptualization of the processes of achieving these decisions **require a different stance on normativity**. What is 'good' or 'bad' can no longer be easily determined, because of the lack of clear boundaries between perspectives. This complexity of issues, which implies the diversity of perspectives, prevents a 'black-and-white' distinction between 'good' and 'bad.' As context is reproduced and reinforced by narratives, there will be no single version of reality, or of the future. For example, while democratic principles, such as formal and material participation, are generally considered 'good,' such principles may also lead to

A. M. Hernández, *Taming the Big Green Elephant*, Globale Gesellschaft und internationale Beziehungen, https://doi.org/10.1007/978-3-658-31821-5_3

'bad' conditions, such as inefficient environmental protection measures, thinned out to accommodate the interests of the stakeholders. Trade-offs between poverty alleviation and emission reduction will very likely motivate policy-makers to prioritize poverty alleviation policy goals. In the same manner, purportedly 'bad' principles typical of authoritarian regimes that do not have 'respect' for human rights may actually be more effective in protecting the environment. In such cases, for example, a military junta leader that grabbed power from corrupt but democratically elected leaders through a violent coup may turn out to be an adamant 'protector' of the rule of law, including the protection of ethnic minorities, which may not have been practically respected by previously democratically elected administrations. Nevertheless, it is not being argued by this book that the value of human rights and democracy are to be diminished or disregarded. In this sense, **the analyses of decision-making processes need to be aware of 'normative biases' in order to maintain proximity to Eurocentric worldviews and to accommodate 'indigenous' ideas on modernity**. Analyses of decision-making processes need to be able to evaluate 'alternative paths' (e.g., the Chinese way, the Asian way, the Russian model, etc.), isolate 'best practices' and come up with 'adapted versions' of these practices.

Contextualizing decision-making to achieve sustainability is a situated and interactive activity. The contextualization of decision-making employs descriptive, analytical and prescriptive approaches. It also requires the re-visitation of dominant theories and assumptions that are often taken for granted or presupposed. In addition, **because the world system is in a transitional stage, collective decision-making is also in transition or transformation**, as the number of issues, actors, and complexities increase along with the scope (see Kremenyuk 2002). The monolithic architecture of the global system is complemented by fragmented decision-making that often leads to gaps that are still being conceptualized and understood.

The analysis of decisions and the processes needed to achieve them involves multiple disciplines and methodologies. Multiple disciplines are used by this book to come up with qualitative and quantitative as well as 'systemic' benchmarks and indicators: decision analysis, behavioral science, game theory, sociology, logic, negotiation analysis, etc. Furthermore, the systems approach identifies the different units of analysis to enable an understanding of the processes within such units, their interactions with other units, the dynamics defining their interconnectivity, and the resulting positive and 'fatal' synergies. These units of analysis are: *actors, issues, structures, processes* and *outcomes*.

In terms of context, as will be demonstrated through the case studies in this book, important main drivers of transformation towards sustainability are identified and evaluated. In this evaluation, the functional, institutional and bargaining interactions are highlighted. This structural analysis is key to understanding how transformation towards sustainability can be facilitated. For example, the case studies present potential entry points to transformation towards sustainability for the selected countries. These entry points may involve resolving current path-dependent impasses such as carbon lock-ins or identifying opportunities that have been so far overlooked. In addition, the case studies analyze how the context defines the agency and audience by, for example, pinpointing how bargaining interactions create more values that further promote sustainability. Nevertheless, there is a need to take one or two steps back and define the main drivers of transformation towards sustainability through trade-offs and turnstiles.

The main drivers are evident, and latent factors behind decisions can be external or internal. Their effects can be regarded as subjective, as the effects of these drivers can only be 'substantiated' when they relate to the actors' dispositions. As Andrea Trianni *et al.* (2016) suggest, these drivers can be *economic* (internal costs, opportunity costs, market barriers, demand, supply, etc.), *regulatory* (tariffs, taxes, public financing, fiscal subsidies, market instruments, etc.), *informative* (quantification methods leading to the consideration of additional or co-benefits), and *educative* (learning curves, technological maturity, etc.).

While these drivers ensure that similar decisions will be made as agents are eventually recalled and replaced, they are often highly contextualized, as these drivers may also occur only once or only as results of the uniquely constituted positive and 'fatal' synergies of various factors. For example, in a given developing country, the combination of a deficient element of governance, the unique effect of the global financial crisis due to the country's high dependence on foreign remittances and foreign direct investment, low social capital following decades of colonization, a recent natural disaster, and an on-going constitutional crisis, can only occur once. In addition, a triggering event may initiate a tipping point as this event may cross the boundary of what actors can accept, or this event may initiate a 'domino effect' which further blurs causalities between exogenous and endogenous factors. This event can either be a major game-changing occurrence, such as the natural death of the country's president, or a relatively unimportant event such as a successful, unexpected take-over bid of a company, which can push the last 'domino tile', leading to other events such as the mobilization of labor unions.

Analyzing these drivers, including the related dynamics, synergies, triggers, and tipping points through process-tracing, is a highly complex endeavor. It requires not only a comprehensive and integrated understanding of historical events, not to mention access to confidential decisions made during closed-door meetings, but also the identification and usage of adequate methodologies for content analysis, the definition of units of analysis (components, sequences, or complete models) and for data interpretation, both in terms of theories and in terms of its practical meaning and usability. Nevertheless, a shared understanding of the drivers behind one's own decisions and the decisions made by others is beneficial, especially when different actors can align their key goals, paving the way for a more mutually acceptable joint agreement.

The case study analyzed in chapters 8 to 12 of this book will highlight the main drivers of various transformation processes.

3.1 Trade-Offs

Trade-offs are paradoxes that inhibit, delay or prevent decision-making. They highlight the 'human factor' in decision-making, particularly in transformation processes, where 'losers' and 'winners' are expected to emerge. Without adequate decision tools to understand the complexity and uncertainty of the issues involved and of the potential ramifications of their decisions, decision-makers will mostly refuse to commit to any purportedly 'game changing' decisions, particularly when they will be eventually held accountable or responsible for these decisions.

Transformation processes towards sustainability will most likely touch upon various policy goals. In some cases, the achievement of one policy goal will diminish the possibility of reaching another goal or it may increase the monetary and non-monetary costs of achieving a later goal. Without proper coordination and facilitation when managing these trade-offs, new conflict cleavages will most likely emerge, which may be 'too much to handle' and lead to system ruptures. To address this, cluster 3 (transformation management and socio-technical discourse) in the previous chapter has provided impulses.

Table 3.1 enumerates the selected nexus that reflect trade-offs in transformation processes towards sustainability.

Table 3.1 List of trade-offs and *caveats* (*Source* Own Representation)

Trade-offs		
Global	vs.	Domestic/local
Unit	vs.	Collectivity
Cooperation	vs.	Sovereignty
Optimization/Efficiency	vs.	Consensus and Legitimacy
Choice	vs.	Control
Prototypes	vs.	Generics
Linearity	vs.	Non-linearity
Incremental	vs.	Leap-frogging
Adaptation	vs.	Latency
Causal Determinism	vs.	Self-efficacy/Free Will
Quantitative	vs.	Qualitative

3.1.1 Global vs. Domestic/Local

The global and the domestic/local can be regarded as two sides of a continuum. While they are, to a significant degree, interconnected with the national spheres and serve as sub-systems, the two can also be defined as two separate systems. Each system has its distinct processes and dynamics and although it will be difficult to 'think' of the global without the local (and vice versa), this is theoretically possible from an analytical point of view. Nevertheless, the uncooperative game theory characterization of a system where actors are rational, strategic, and opportunistic and that no outside actor will step in to enforce agreements can be generally applied to both domestic (national/local) and international politics (Martin & Simmons 2010 p. 43). Furthermore, as Lisa Martin and Beth Simmons (2010 p. 43) suggest, with a similar assumption about the nature of actors and their environment, the potential for learning offered by this level of analysis could be enormous.

At first glance, the trade-offs between the global and the domestic/local includes the need to give up a specific degree of sovereignty, that is, of control (see Biersteker & Weber 1996; Aspinall 2002). This means, on the one hand, 'outsourcing' some aspects of national decision-making processes to mechanisms outside of state governance and to non-state actors in a franchise-like system (see Hernandez 2014a). This is not only limited to government agencies seeking private providers of outsourced civil services to increase efficiency, but also to the substitution of tedious domestic constituency through mechanisms of various international institutions, where governments can play the "sovereignty" card to block decisions that are against their political agenda. This was, for example, the case when former US President Obama deliberately sidestepped the Congress and formally entered the United States into an international climate change agreement (Davenport & Prusak 2000; see DeMint 2016).

On the other hand, giving up a specific degree of sovereignty can also mean accepting a specific degree of dependence on international governance structures when forging national policies over lower-prioritized issues (see Cede 2012). National governments may, for example, accept the jurisdiction of international arbitration bodies in specific issues, particularly when disputes involve non-citizens (see Cede 2009). In addition, national governments allow themselves to be the subjects of external verification and sanction mechanisms which form a type of hierarchy, either because of rewards and sanctions (see Birnie & Boyle 1992; Boyle 1999), or because non-compliance will merely empower domestic pro-compliance constituencies to monitor and enforce national compliance (Dai 2007).

Another trade-off refers to identity-building and its meaning when accessing resources. When focusing on the above-mentioned distinct processes and dynamics related to transformation towards sustainability, opening the 'local' up to the 'global' may also promote disengagement among the locals. As the 'global' instils new and unfamiliar 'dominant' values and norms (often defined by historical experiences of the Global North) leading to the establishment of paradigms, the locals of countries belonging both to the Global North and the Global South are confronted by differences and conflicts between their homes (local) and the new romanticized 'society-at-large' (global). For example, in the Philippines, due to its colonial past and as enhanced by globalization, the use of the English language has been used as the defining factor for employment and status quo, whereas the ability to speak English with an American accent ('elitist English') promises more job prospects and social prestige. This ability is taken as an indicator of an individual's access to quality education or even of intellectual capability and therefore offers opportunities that are unreachable to others. Filipinos that speak English (or even Tagalog) with a clear 'provincial accent' are ridiculed as backward and uneducated (see Montalvan, III 2010; Hernandez 2014a). Many locals are then confronted with a clear disconnect between their 'primordial' identity and the social identity, as the language used at home (one of more than 100 local languages) and the English language they need to speak with an American accent to acquire better employment, for example, in the high-paying call center industry, imply two different incompatible identities. **This apparent disconnect implies that their relationships, activities and roles are restrained**.

3.1.2 The Unit vs. Collectivity

Trade-offs can also be observed when decisions are made by individuals or by a collectivity. Policies that need to be forged by individual actors in the name of the collectivity will need to address distinct challenges (see Olson 1965; Sandler 2004). In many cases, while unitary decision-making is considered to be efficient because decisions can be goal-oriented and made quickly, it is thought to circumvent proper representation and is therefore regarded as undemocratic and unwarranted. The connection between unitary decision-makers and the collectivity is contextually subjected to existing governance structures, which reflect the political mandate given to decision-makers (see Walker et al. 1988). This political mandate or legitimacy can be derived through electoral processes, for example in democratic countries, and in authoritarian countries through 'performance outputs' (see Easton 1975). In some cases, the effectiveness or integrity of decisions can be undermined by a failure to adequately consider the perspectives of all members of the collectivity. Nevertheless, the need to achieve consensus can also delay decisions and delays can incur additional costs or missed opportunities. In the same manner, when a unitary entity has made the necessary decisions alone without any form of consultation, it will most likely lead to the mobilization of opposition, disconnecting basic games from policy games.

Depending on the context, affected stakeholders that were not embedded in the process or did not agree to the decisions made by the majority may resort to legal or paralegal channels that could further increase the costs of decision-making (see Faysse 2006; Cheyns 2011). Furthermore, 'spoilers', or those actors that are not open to persuasion or bargaining are further empowered and vindicated and are provided with more arguments against the decisions made (see Mitchell et al. 1997; Pinkse & Kolk 2012). Nevertheless, while collective decisions resulting from consensus-building processes will most likely have fewer difficulties when being implemented, the integrity of these decisions can be doubted, as they can be significantly 'watered-down' as a result of compromises (see Ostrom 1990; Sandler 2004). A major trade-off refers to risks of *disidentification* and *disenchantment*, where decisions made by the few promote the removal of the signs of identities of the many such as roles, titles and statuses as well as creating new 'worlds' that are not 'real' for many locals (see Adger et al. 2011). For example, the signing of the Paris Climate Agreement by their national government may mean distress for coal-dependent communities that have already assumed distinct identities. This agreement may also mean that in the medium and long term, they will need to 'unlearn' their perspectives in order to survive, which horrifies many. This distress is, for example, considered to be responsible for the loss of the Democrats in Wisconsin and Michigan during the US Presidential Elections in 2016.

3.1.3 Cooperation vs. Sovereignty

While engaging in international cooperation has its distinct advantages, it also often means giving up some elements of sovereignty, whereas sovereignty and its indicators are regarded as matters of perception (see Biersteker & Weber 1996). In addition, trade-offs between international cooperation and sovereignty are often analyzed in the context of power asymmetry. For example, Johannes Urpelainen (2011) argues that under power asymmetry and in the context of cooperation, powerful states are willing to accept constraints on the use of power, as opposed to simply maximizing the supply of the collective enforcement power. Therefore, for weaker countries, engaging in cooperation with powerful states allows them to maintain their sovereignty, because cooperation also limits the motivation and capacity of powerful states to violate the sovereignty of weaker states.

International cooperation may also mean tolerating interference in domestic affairs, and this exclusion from the benefits of cooperation can be used as political leverage (see Axelrod 1984; Bunker & Rubin 1995). As international cooperation may also mean that sensitive information needs to be shared with the others, some countries may engage in 'tactical' cooperation to collect information. This means that cooperation could also limit one's competitive advantage (see Oye 2011; Urpelainen 2011).

In addition, international cooperation can be used by the government to define the paradigm of self-legitimization, particularly when there is a domestic legitimacy crisis. Nevertheless, because international cooperation is highly dependent on the kinds of issues involved, limitations to cooperation due to the demands of sovereignty are rather self-serving. When a government refuses to cooperate on issue A due to sovereignty concerns, and it cooperates on issues B and C, how can this government decide that cooperation on issues B and C do not undermine sovereignty? When such decisions are arbitrary, how can reciprocity, which is a major driver of cooperation, be built?

Limitations to cooperation often lead to questions about which issues should be dealt and to which degree sovereignty should be lost. For example, while it is evident that international cooperation on security will be confronted by different sets of political obstacles, and the national government will more likely prefer to limit the participation of social actors, what compels a government to reject environmental cooperation by claiming that it undermines national security? On the other hand, cooperation on trade and industry, such as free trade that requires involvement in the private sector, will more likely bear witness to a national government seeking the participation of business and industry actors. Why is sovereignty, then, defined by issues? Sovereignty is understood as independence from external influences and is a constitutive principle of 'legitimacy' *vis-à-vis* the audience, that is, one is sovereign not only in the eyes of the international community but also, and more importantly, in the eyes of the constituents.

3.1.4 Optimization/Efficiency vs. Consensus/Participation

Analyzing trade-offs between the efficiency of policy goals and promoting participation in forging and implementing these policies is tricky (see Walker et al. 1988; Cadman 2013). Although efficiency and participation can be regarded as the two sides of legitimacy, with participation serving as a category of 'input' and efficiency of 'output' legitimacy, they can be seen as competing in the eyes of policy-makers. Efficiency enhances the probability that the implementation of the measures and provisions of the decisions will lead to the achievement of the goals (see Barr 2012). Efficiency is often connoted in terms of the concept "Pareto Efficiency." Pareto efficiency, which has its origins in social welfare optimization, is the state of allocation of resources from which it is impossible to reallocate to improve one's own status without making at least one counterpart worse off (Krasner 1991; see Sinn 2007).

Meanwhile, participation means 'tailoring' and 'ownership' of the decision-making process. It also constitutes the 'acceptability' of these provisions in the eyes of the affected audience. In addition, it refers to the probability that the negative consequences of these decisions will be 'tolerated' and remain unchallenged by those affected, knowing that the 'pain' of indecision is worse than the expected consequences (see Luce & Raiffa 1957; Raiffa 1968). When the status quo ante or the 'alternative' to the 'business-as-usual' option is **better off** than the status under these (new) decisions, then legitimacy can be undermined, because of the high probability that the implementation will be rejected (see Tversky & Kahnemann 1986; Toth et al. 2001). Hence, efficiency can also be regarded as a category of legitimacy, as deficient decisions will also most likely lead to resistance.

The choice between efficiency and participation becomes challenging when there are trade-offs between them. In ideal cases, efficiency can be achieved without sacrificing a degree of participation. Nevertheless, particularly in climate protection, 'effective' measures and 'optimization formulas' will involve a degree of restriction on the part of the population or constraints to specific actors. Therefore, legitimizing channels need to be found to ensure the acceptability of such 'optimal solutions', particularly in front of a domestic audience. Because addressing trade-offs in (transformative) decision-making can be best understood, defined and conducted in the context of negotiations (see Winham 1977; Zartman 1994a; Watkins & Passow 1996), **efficiency calculations and indicators need to adequately address negotiation pay-offs.**

3.1.5 Choice vs. Control

Decisions are 'purposive,' because they are framed by goals. To enable decision-makers to evaluate the current status of decisions in terms of how the goals are expected to be achieved, there is a need to come up with indicators and benchmarks as the basis of verification or of performance control (see Freistein 2016; Boavida 2017). Nuno Boavida (2017) suggests that studies about the way indicators are used in technological innovation are significantly rare, despite the centrality of decisions. In addition, Greg Marsden and Carolyn Snell (2009) are critical of the fact that indicators can distort decision-making processes because of poor internal planning processes or unnecessary external constraints.

Indicators are needed to measure the progress of achieving predetermined goals. As discussed in the introduction, the transformation process towards sustainability is purposive due to the centrality of predetermined goals. For example, Greg Marsden and Carolyn Snell (2009) see indicators as crucial to transport planning processes as they can be used for decision-support in all aspects of policy development and assessment, from option generation, through to policy testing and appraisal, to monitoring and feedback. Moreover, indicators can provide insights into whether additional intervention or changes are needed to correct unwanted occurrences. Nevertheless, as indicators are often quantitative, focusing only on indicators may cause decision-makers to miss out on other signs of progress that cannot be measured numerically. For example, while climate protection goals can be measured through the amount of emission savings, specific co-benefits of these goals such as the prevention of destruction of historically important buildings and monuments or the improvement of health are often missed or inadequately included in assessing the benefits of such goals. Therefore, as Marsden and Snell (2009) suggest, an indicator framework needs to be an essential part of effective planning processes for internal management and decision support, as well as for external communication.

Trade-offs arise when decisions involving several actors are given more 'choices' as to how to fulfill their responsibilities and 'shopping' for indicators become a usual practice. In this situation, indicators are designed and developed to serve the vested interests of the actors. These self-serving indicators become useless in assessing various stages of transformation. Zachary Karabell (2014) argues that the twenty-first century is proving more challenging to measure. He continues that statistics cannot capture the multifaceted and complex national and global economic systems.

Another trade-off refers to choices available during collective decision-making. Choices, particularly long-term ones under certainty, are often linked to flexibility (see Fawcett et al. 2012). As a provision in an agreement, **flexibility means one unit less of possible control**. For example, the implementation of new policies is often combined with flexibility measures to enable affected actors to manage transition in an acceptable way. In addition to compensatory measures, flexibility may also include 'grace periods' or 'exemptions' until a given time. For example, Wigley et al (1996) found that the global time flexibility in GHG emission reduction given to developing countries can be justified to some extent. Particularly after the COP15 meeting in Copenhagen, developed countries have expressed their position that they will only commit if developing countries will agree to comparable commitments (Bodansky 2010; Penetrante 2010, 2011). Nevertheless, as Taishi Sugiyama and Liu Deshun (2004) argue, it does not necessarily serve as a rationale to delay the emission reduction commitments and efforts of developed countries.

In a similar way to flexibility, ambiguity in collective decisions increases the set of possible choices while limiting control. Trade-offs are evident in decision-making under uncertainty when policy-makers look for a 'way out' from the commitments before signing any agreement. From the negotiation perspective, while reaching an agreement is hard, honoring one may be even more difficulty. Martin Weber (1987) identified methods which are particularly suitable for handling decision situations with incomplete information. The decision-maker is unable to define a precisely defined and stable preference structure because probability distributions *vis-à-vis* the consequences are not known completely. Ambiguity in some provisions of the agreement would allow decision-makers flexibility, particularly in determining the "how"-provisions of agreements. However, difficulties arise when there are so many flexibility measures, or the goals are too ambiguous that verification (control) becomes useless. Ambiguity may also encourage 'bad faith negotiators' (see Churchman 1995) and 'spoilers' (see Stedman 1997), who have other vested interests when engaging in negotiations (e.g., to gather information about competitors) and who had no intention to commit from the start. Nevertheless, ambiguity is inevitable as agreements will not cover all possible aspects of interactions. In addition, ambiguity (and flexibility measures in general) encourages participation in bargaining processes. Ambiguity motivates actors to not leave the negotiation table, and should ambiguity and flexibility measures be inefficient, they can be re-negotiated. In these cases, there would be no need to start from square one of collective decision-making.

3.1.6 Prototypes vs. Generics

Decisions as solutions to new emerging problems may be either prototypes or generics. As new and previously unknown problems emerge, decision-makers can look for early samples or models as the basis for a decision. Prototypes intend to test various parameters relevant to the problem and to enhance future decision-making through replication and learning. As such, it follows the principle of '*trial-and-error*', which implies that unknown negative aspects or unwanted side-effects are expected and will be useful in reconfiguring decisions. Prototypes undergo 'learning-by-doing', defining their 'maturity process' as problems to be adequately addressed. Uncertainties about these negative side-effects will most likely be used by opposing actors to demand the recanting of previously-made decisions. Depending on how the opposition can mobilize popular support to form a counter-movement to reverse changes, the whole transformation process can be jeopardized. Therefore, decision-makers are highly dependent on verification measures to act as quickly as possible to address these side-effects.

Another approach that can be used by decision-makers when formulating decisions on emerging problems is to seek, or, if not available, to constitute 'generics'. There is often a 'general formula' to address such issues regardless of the unique specificities of these problems. Such 'standard operating procedures' (SOPs) are most likely general in scope and cannot address the specificities of these emerging problems. For example, Carlo Guipponi and Alessandra Sgobbi (2013) illustrate a generic decision/policy-making process with its main steps and the areas of influence of participatory planning, simulation planning and decision analysis: (0) political and normative triggering factors (e.g., water management plan); (1) problem exploration and framing (gaps, needs, potentials, constraints); (2) the actor's involvement and participatory process (stakeholder's dialogues, focus groups); (3) problem analysis (organization of information and knowledge, mental models); (4) data-processing, modeling and evaluation (simulation models, scenario analysis); (5) the analysis of response options (e.g., multi-criteria or cost-benefit analysis); (6) action-taking and monitoring (implementation plans, investment).

Decision-makers may, on one hand, see the need to look at each problem as it comes, that is, case-by-case. In these instances, decision-makers will start from a 'default' position, analyze the problems, investigate the factors responsible for cause-and-effect relationships and then come up with a solution for this specific case. On the other hand, decision-makers may prioritize a 'rapid response' to emerging problems and prefer to come up with 'generics,' where they have anticipated the problems and have already worked on protocols and SOPs. As a problem emerges, decision-makers will adhere to SOPs and will be less likely to tolerate deviations from presumed procedures.

Trade-offs are for example made between the effectiveness (in the context of usefulness) of the solutions and the speed of reaching decisions. Particularly when dealing with pressing issues while confronted by incomplete or soon-to-be obsolete information, decision-makers must absorb learning and establish adequate institutional memory or "stored knowledge within the organization" (Gibbons 2007). In addition, Jack Corbertt *et al.* (2018) contend that institutional memory is central to the pragmatic task of policy-making. They continue that memory can be "static," i.e. memory is singular and held in document form, or "dynamic," i.e. memory is dispersed across an array of actors that make up the differentiated polity. However, decision-makers in policy circles, particularly those at higher levels, often do not stay long in their positions. Therefore, because they do not especially have dynamic institutional memory, they may tend to prefer prototype decisions (based on static memory), while those at middle and lower levels tend to prefer generic decisions.

3.1.7 Linearity vs. Non-linearity

While the process outlook on decisions implies a 'holistic' or 'systems' approach, the negotiation perspective provides insights into the importance of different types of preference (utility) functions in collective decision-making, which can be linear or non-linear. An actor with a linear preference function will have strictly monotonous preferences through which larger quantities of a single good will be chosen (higher utility). Furthermore, the actor with a linear preference function will have 'weakly convex, but not strictly convex' preferences in which the mixture of two equivalent bundles is equivalent to the combined original bundles (see Gale 1976; Candeal-Haro & Induráin-Eraso 1995). In contrast, actors with non-linear preference functions will be confronted by differences between the 'objective' value of a negotiated outcome and the subjective utility attributed to the same outcome. In other words, **non-linear preference functions highlight the relevance of 'experience'**, which prevents a constant, subjective utility function. A non-linear preference can encompass both the decreasing and increasing marginally subjective utility of negotiation outcomes on a single issue (see Northcraft et al. 1995 p. 298).

The prevalence of non-linear preference functions is not only to be found in economics, but also in negotiation studies. Gregory Northcraft *et al.* (1998) have compared the effects of both linear and non-linear preferences on negotiated settlements. They claim that while non-linear preference functions dramatically alter the dynamics of negotiation exchanges by creating more value, called 'logrolling' (see Pruitt & Rubin 1986), they also promote 'concession cross-over' (see Northcraft et al. 1995). The paradox of concession cross-over occurs when an issue originally less valued by a negotiator becomes subjectively more valuable, merely because concessions were already made in the past. In addition, non-linearity implies that set-backs can also contribute to the achievement of the envisaged outcome, particularly when set-backs are understood as 'materials' or 'lessons' for future decisions. This 'non-linearity' of the decision-making process allows a more pragmatic stance on decision-making. Nevertheless, policy-makers often assume linearity of processes, as implied by their dependence on indicators and benchmarks to legitimize their decisions. The understanding of non-linearity allows a problem-solving outlook on process-related challenges that inhibit decision-making.

Nevertheless, non-linearity not only fails to consider more interconnected conflict cleavages that need to be addressed simultaneously, it also implies challenges on legitimizing policies, as policy-makers require indicators and benchmarks to assess the effectiveness of their decisions in terms of the value of concessions. While preference utilities can be non-linear, decisions cannot fully make use of these, especially when multiple issues are involved; therefore, they tend to use assessment tools that assume the linearity of preference utilities over issues and over the process in general. As Max Bazerman *et al.* (1985) as well as Margaret Neale & Gregory Northcraft (1986) claim, because actors can also have linear subjective utility (preference) functions, their preferences will most likely not change as their endowment, or holding, of other resources increases or decreases. For example, in negotiating monetary compensation for relocation due to the construction of dams for hydrogen power, a person might already have a specific minimum amount that he or she considers to be acceptable. The 'reservation value' or the 'walk away' (Raiffa 1982), or in this case, the minimum level of compensation that a person can accept, although subjective, is most likely linear. The person will most likely refuse relocation if not given any comparable values such as housing allowance, which can be 'converted' to monetary compensation.

Therefore, because concessions cannot always acknowledge or incorporate the diversity and complexity of possible subjective utility functions (see Northcraft et al. 1995), decision-makers will most likely be confronted by trade-offs between objective and subjective utilities. For example, to implement the low carbon transition of energy systems, the government plans to build two wind mills in the first year and another mill in each following year. Although the monetary value of this project increases every time a wind mill is installed, the utility function of the households living in the area may not increase to the same level or may even decrease after a specific threshold has been passed. Hence, trade-offs between linear and non-linear utilities or preferences need to be effectively addressed when facilitating transformation processes.

3.1.8 Incremental vs. Leap-Frogging

Transformation processes are dependent on technological innovation that supports the implementation of policy goals (see Carraro & Siniscalco 1994; Markard & Truffer 2008b). In some cases, innovation can initiate the transformation process, as societies find solutions to problems that have long existed. Step by step, as the transformation process unfolds, minor changes are made to achieve predetermined policy goals. Therefore, transformation processes are driven by incremental knowledge. Nevertheless, the maturity of technologies is often a result of constant exchanges with societal actors. During such exchanges, technology providers can adapt technologies according to the demand or to anticipated demand. While not all technological innovations are embraced by the population, those that have garnered attention will be further developed. Synergies are made as other products are developed that complement the initial technology (e.g., batteries and storage for new transportation modes).

In addition, synergies between technological and social innovation may improve transformation as shifted paradigms lead to new institutions and even new forms of governance. New information technologies will most likely lead to changes in modes of accountability and transparency. For example, a government prioritizing the elimination of corruption can further advance this policy goal by digitalizing various services provided by the government. Another example is that as it becomes evident that new green technologies can create new job opportunities, governments will have, ideally, started developing or adjusting existing political and market instruments. Nevertheless, because political actions depend on the incremental character of knowledge generation and technological innovation, the government and other state agencies might need to 'adjust' their mandate as well as some provisions in the 'social contract.' Digitalization might, for example, require new public debate and consensus related to data protection and freedom of speech.

Being incremental also means that a **learning process is inevitable**. However, in the national or global academic and political climate debate, there is a narrative that is gaining ground: that it is better for developing countries with emerging economies to omit this tedious, emission-rich and expensive learning process and accelerate transformation towards sustainability by bypassing certain stages of development. In current climate change negotiations, many governments and experts call for developing countries to 'leapfrog' (see Goldemberg 1998; Zerriffi & Wilson 2010; Correa d'Almeida & Poon 2015).

The concept of leap-frogging argues that it is possible for a country to change to a higher level of development without going through the intermediate stages. In other words, it means that developing countries should not follow the 'dirty' economic development path made by developed countries, and should accelerate development by skipping inferior, less efficient, more expensive or more polluting technologies and industries and move directly to more advanced ones (see Goldemberg 1998; Steckel et al. 2013; Jakob et al. 2014). When technologies as well as financing models are already available, why should developing countries not avoid the environmentally and socially harmful stages of development? In a highly globalized world, technology transfer can allow developing countries to 'assume' high technological development without the being country that has produced this technology.

Technological development needs to be complemented and guided by social change, which is highly context dependent. For example, as Victor Berrueta *et al.* (2015) conclude from their case study of Mexico's Patsari improved cook stove project, while a new low-carbon cooking technology can be easily distributed to poor households in developing countries, there is no guarantee that this technology will 'sink in' and be used, especially when cultural aspects have been disregarded. Moreover, new technologies may also lead to the reproduction or reinforcement of existing social fragmentation, as access to these technologies may further strengthen the hierarchy between urban (core) and rural (periphery) areas (see Jonas 1984; Meadowcroft 2005; Stirling 2008). Therefore, not only can too ambitious and rapid technology-driven social change disenfranchise a huge portion of the population and promote social division, it can also limit the potential benefits of technological innovation, as the society is not able to fully 'absorb' and 'replicate' innovation, which may lead to further frictions (e.g., legitimacy gaps).

3.1.9 Adaptation vs. Latency

Talcott Parsons (1951) highlighted in his AGIL-functions the systematic depiction of certain societal functions, which every social system needs to maintain stability. He argued that the stability of a social system depends on various functional prerequisites: adaptation, goal attainment, integration and latency. Adaptation refers to the capacity of the system to interact with its environment. Goal attainment pertains to the system's capacity to set goals for the future and formulate provisions and strategies to attain these goals. Integration points to the harmonization of the system through values and norms that are solid and sufficiently convergent. Latency, also referred to as latent pattern maintenance, refers to the capacity of the system to maintain integrative elements to 'mediate' or facilitate cohesion between different generations and actors within the system.

In the context of transformation processes towards sustainability, the trade-off or conflict cleavage that is often the subject of public discourse is between the 'old' and the 'new,' that is, between adaptation and latency. Some proponents of the 'old system' argue that there is no need to change something that has proven to have worked. One argument is that the system is constantly changing, and it needs to adapt to these changes if it wants to survive. Transformation can also be regarded as a self-preserving mechanism. With the ability to adapt to occurring changes, the system is able to avert perceived system ruptures. For Nietzsche, transformation is a matter of survival and well-being. In his work *"Also sprach Zarathustra"* (1883), he highlighted the necessity of allowing the three major episodes of the metamorphoses of the "human spirit" as a process of self-discovery. The camel, which is able to collect "burdens, conquests and scars," needs to transform into a lion over time to prevent the "risk of being poisoned by bitterness, despair and the spirit of despair." This "destructive" lion however needs to turn into a child, who represents a "new beginning" where the original "innocence" is revived.

Transformation is one of the most intuitive responses to a changing environment. Change management in organizations including business companies is an integral part of strategies in which their survival is highly dependent upon their capacity to adapt to changes and identify and utilize competitive advantages before their competitors do. For many major business companies, adaptation means seeing a different future for the company and being unafraid of making large scale changes (Simpson 2011). Now known as one of the world's largest chemical companies, DuPont (NYSE: DD) started as a gunpowder supplier. As new opportunities were identified, DuPont pioneered new plastics and synthetics, fertilizers and new healthcare and nutrition products.

Another argument is that the **system needs to maintain its basic fiber**. Latency does not resist changes in the system *per se* but focuses on maintaining basic structures or elements that mediate or facilitate between conflicting actors or elements within the system. Latency can be understood in terms of the governance theory introduced by Renate Mayntz (2009). Her definition of governance is functional and refers to how political facilitation (*politische Steuerung*) determines the agency or the capacity to act in vertically differentiated governance structures. For example, this definition can be referred to as channels of finding solutions to problems, realization of specific values such as climate protection and human rights, as well as the improvement of specific services such as energy supply security. For example, institutions such as the constitution can mediate belief systems and values between generations, ensuring social cohesion and therefore stability of the system. The literature has argued that transition or transformation is a process with various possible pathways that include low, moderate and extreme changes, depending on different configurations and multi-level interactions (Smith 2005; Patwardhan et al. 2012). As such, transition does not need to lead to ruptures, as it merely reorients existing development trajectories. Latency therefore means that the regime adopts certain niche innovations into the system which leads to a gradual reconfiguration of the basic architecture, including guiding principles, beliefs and practices (Smith 2005; Geels & Schot 2007a).

Trade-offs between latency and adaptation become relevant when decision-makers are compelled to maintain some elements of the system for it not to lose its identity, which binds differences between constituents while allowing some changes to adapt to the new environment, either globally or locally. María Eugenia Sánchez (2010) attributes a loss of identity to the process of creating a de-territorialized or multi-local world productive system, which is more informational than industrial and more speculative than productive. She argues further that the breakdown and disarticulation of institutional and symbolic mediations of the past have had a strong impact on identities. In addition, while some institutions can facilitate the identification of common ground, these institutions are themselves also subject to changes they need to adapt to. It remains a question of how much change these institutions can undergo before they lose their credibility as facilitators. For example, Patricia Gumport (2000) problematizes some changes in the academic landscape of public higher education in the United States over the past 25 years. She identifies a macro-trend whereby the mandate of public higher education has shifted from being a social institution to an industry. She explains that this pattern of academic restructuring that reflects multiple institutional pressures may lead to a loss of legitimacy, as universities move away from their historical character, functions, and accumulated heritage as educational institutions.

3.1.10 Causal Determinism vs. Self-Efficacy/Free Will

The assessment of possible decisions is often based on causal determinism, also referred to as cause-and-effect. Causal determinism is "the idea that every event is necessitated by antecedent events and conditions together with the laws of nature" (Hoefer 2008). In other words, all events have causes and identical causes will lead to same effects. While determinism can be less problematic in certain technical issues, attributing deterministic principles to collective decision-making can be challenging. **Determinism in decision-making implies predictability**. However, such determinants can also include human choices and actions that do not occur as a first cause but rather as responses. As events are perceived to be bound by causality, it makes sense to investigate how agents absorb information and constitute responses. Nevertheless, determinism is often considered to discard self-efficacy or 'free will', because determinism connotes predictability in human behavior (see Franklin 1968).

Furthermore, determinism seems to ignore self-driving and self-enforcing dynamics, where factor A leads to the occurrence of factor B, but only when factor C is near A, or where factor A leads to the occurrence of factor B, but the next occurrence of B is no longer dependent on factor A, because factor B is now able to reproduce itself. In these two examples, causality has ceased to be relevant, because of the lack of attribution. For example, the German government's "*Energiewende*" (energy transition) to the new German energy and climate policies (factor B) was primarily caused by the decision to phase out nuclear energy (factor A). It is often argued that the Fukushima incident (factor C) has influenced the decision to phase out nuclear energy (Hennicke & Welfens 2012; see Wille 2017). Regarding this matter, Dominik Smyrgala (2017) presents a statistical analysis of the impact of the 2011 Fukushima nuclear incident on the *Energiewende*. He argues that the decision of the German government to phase out Germany's nuclear plants triggered this "irrational" behavior. Nevertheless, for the proponents of determinism, irrationality is non-existent. There was a causality and this causality occurred. Furthermore, it can be argued that while the Fukushima incident motivated *Energiewende*, it merely provided the pretext for the decision and no direct causality between the Fukushima incident (factor C) and *Energiewende* (factor A) can be established, because if that was case, then other countries should have done the same as the German federal government

In evaluating transformation processes, it can be useful to analyze not only how a specific decision has come into being and how this decision will elicit further decisions and actions, but also why other (national) systems failed to reach similar decisions as well as how comparable decisions failed to elicit further decisions and actions. Nevertheless, the complexity and uncertainty of various issues will bring challenges, particularly when human accountability comes into the picture. For example, after low-carbon system transition costs are calculated, the next step is to find a formula to distribute these costs among actors, both perpetuators and recipients (victims) as well as both suppliers and consumers. The costs can, for example, be distributed according to the anticipated benefits, where actors expecting more benefits should pay more. In addition, costs can also be distributed according to their accountability.

The trade-off between determinism and free will can be particularly evident when mechanisms of rewards and sanctions are to be established as part of an international and national verification regime. Determinism foresees a clear attribution of negative externalities, while self-efficacy entails the responsibilities behind these decisions. Using the common understanding of fairness, equity and justice, those who have inflicted costs upon others (recipients) 'with intent' will need to be held accountable and responsible for the negative effects inflicted upon the others. Those perpetuators that did not, with free will, inflict the costs, are also held accountable according to their degree of guilt, but with lower sanctions after considering mitigating conditions. Therefore, the level of accountability (and the costs/sanctions linked with it) must also take into consideration causal determinism and free-will. However, this can be difficult, as there are no clear indicators that could objectively separate and measure factors that attest to causal determinism or free will.

3.1.11 Quantitative vs. Qualitative Valuation

Outcomes of a collective decision-making process are intended to reflect the goals and targets set by the actors prior to the process. This juxtaposition between the purported goals/targets and the negotiated outcomes is assessed through corresponding indicators. International organizations such as the World Bank and the IMF have developed 'measurement regimes' that have led to various paradigm shifts (see Freistein 2016), not only at the global but also at the domestic/local level. The development of these indicators is, however, also the subject of public debate, as 'control' over the development of these indicators can 'dictate' the paths of future policies (see Lyytimäki et al. 2013; Tokimatsu et al. 2013). Jari Lyytimäki *et al.* (2013) note that following the criteria for a good indicator does not guarantee that the indicator will be used, nor does it guarantee its use will produce the desired effects. For example, the scientists and experts drafting the Fifth Assessment Report of the IPCC have used the World Bank indicators to classify countries according to their level of income. This was a significant paradigm shift, because it was perceived to mean moving away from the UNFCCC's own categorization of countries through its Annex List. During the IPCC Approval Session of the Fifth Assessment Report of the Third Working Group in April 2014 in Berlin, developing countries, particularly the Gulf countries, protested against the use of the World Bank country labels (e.g., high, middle, low income countries), as this implied a different political understanding of historical responsibilities.

The functionality of indicators can also 'concretize' political mandates, because indicators are expected to enforce the unambiguity and applicability of provisions stipulated by the outcomes (see Underdahl 2002; Wilson & Wu 2016). Indicators can either lead to the success of implementation or can hinder implementation, particularly when the numbers reflected by indicators cannot be translated into realities. For example, Sarah Fredericks (2012) identifies definitions of justice used in sustainability discourse and evaluates how these concepts are aligned with different sustainability indicators and indexes, including the 2010 Environmental Performance Index and Eurostat's Sustainable Development Indicators. She concludes that while these indicators cover various aspects of justice, they are still confronted by limitations such as the availability of data and the inability of monitoring inequities between subpopulations. Finding appropriate indicators is a challenging task, as they not only need to fulfil several criteria such as the availability of data, their capacity of being monitored and their general suitability (see WRI 2009; World Databank 2011; Cobham 2014), but also because of the legitimacy impact of such indicators.

Particularly in the context of sustainable, low-carbon transformation, where quantitative and qualitative indicators are both used to monitor and verify compliance and progress, academic research on negotiations has been mostly qualitative and has depended on case studies to come up with insights useful for conducting negotiations (see Hopmann 2002). This is usually the case, because quantitative methods are not often seen as useful in negotiation studies. In addition, as Andy Scerri and Paul James (2010) explain, because achieving sustainability is often undertaken as a technical task, some methodological issues arise when setting out to develop and implement qualitative indicators of sustainability that incorporate quantitative metrics.

Additional challenges arise when quantitative indicators are bestowed with qualitative value to legitimize decisions and actions. A major concern refers to doubts about the universality of the results of quantitative measurements using merely a small fraction of the total population. In addition, it is not clear how quantitative indicators can make use of random and context-dependent occurrences. While quantitative indicators use average or median values, these can either 'water down' or exaggerate in a way that becomes useless for decision-making in a local context. Therefore, trade-offs between quantitative and qualitative valuation involves on one hand policy-makers who must be aware of the need of 'contextualizing' numbers, and on the other hand, the need to base their decisions on something 'objective' and 'representative'.

3.2 Interim Conclusion

Structural analysis is key to understanding functional, institutional and bargaining interactions in the context of the transformation towards sustainability. This chapter highlighted trade-offs and turnstiles as the main drivers of transformation, which define the contextualization of transformation. By clarifying which stumbling blocks (trade-offs) and opportunities (turnstiles) inhibit or promote transformation, the "ripeness" of decisions conducive to transformation can be strategically instigated.

These trade-offs and turnstiles are the "lever" that require proper management. They allow a degree of predictability in reproducing decisions. The trade-offs and turnstiles summarize the conceptual and methodological challenges of studying and managing multi-level transformation towards sustainability. Through the understanding of these challenges, policy goals can be more strategic and target-oriented. These trade-offs and turnstiles cut across scholarly disciplines and political jurisdictions. They uncover the dilemmas that might distort effective decision-making.

Referring back to the research design of this project, this chapter sets the stage for data assessment by providing parameters for process-tracing and congruence methods. By attributing distortions of decision-making to trade-offs, scholars and decision-makers can reflect more purposively and can strategize actions more effectively.

A Critical Outlook on Assumptions—Decision Systems in Transformation Towards Sustainability

4

Some assumptions about decision systems in the context of transformation towards sustainability will be presented in this chapter. These assumptions are backed by rationales, which highlight the utility preferences of agents and audience. In addition, trade-offs reflect the selection of the most important *caveats* that decision-makers are confronted with. These trade-offs were comprehensively discussed in the previous chapter. Moreover, turnstiles are enumerated that demonstrate possible 'silver-linings' and potential opportunities that may arise to strategically facilitate transformation processes. These turnstiles will be substantially re-examined in a later stage (prescriptive) of this book. The critical assessment of assumptions relevant to the studies of transformation processes towards sustainability needs to be part of any analytical framework. A critical outlook on transformation processes towards sustainability implies a systems analytical approach where the understanding of the parts of human thinking, or elements of reasoning, is given adequate attention. As Richard Paul and Linda Eder (2002) note, an understanding of elements such purpose, question, information, inference, assumption, point of view, concepts, and implications is a prerequisite of any critical thinking. Ignoring unquestioned and blindly accepted assumptions can lead to different types of bias that may have significant impacts, for example, on the relationships between the stakeholders of transformation towards sustainability.

As explained in Chapter 1, the negotiation perspective that defines the analytical framework of this book highlights the justifiability of decisions through the recognition of a diversity of viewpoints. Because most human thinking is inferential in nature (Paul & Eder 2002), there is a need to uncover, question, clarify and "reconcile" relevant assumptions that guide decisions and reasoning pertaining to dealing with complexity. 'Assumptions' refer to a collection of both justified and

A. M. Hernández, *Taming the Big Green Elephant*, Globale Gesellschaft und internationale Beziehungen, https://doi.org/10.1007/978-3-658-31821-5_4

unjustified beliefs or accurate and inaccurate inferences drawn from experiences, which are then used to interpret the world. Assumptions are those that are taken for granted or presupposed, because they are no longer questioned. Nevertheless, the diversity of inferences is inevitable, because individuals will tend to have different viewpoints or terms of reference on the same situations, which constitute experience and meaning. In other words, because different assumptions can be made about the same situation as reference object, and because assumptions are the basic foundation of decisions and reasoning, the importance of re-visiting assumptions in book needs to be highlighted.

4.1 Actors

Assumption 1: Power is to be understood through its 'relative' value.
Rationale: Excluding some actors to gain access to at least one source of power is impossible, as different types of structural changes unfold, but as different actors express different types of power, there is uncertainty as to which type of power is useful in a specific context or issue. It is important to accept that collective decision-making is a power game that motivates preparations as well as the formulation of short and long-term roadmaps, strategies and contingency plans to facilitate the achievement of goals (see Zartman & Rubin 2000; Hernandez 2014b). This preparation includes not only the 'calculations' of the 'relative' value of expected outcomes to the status quo to define the legitimacy behind such values, but also the relative value of one's preferred outcome to that of their competitors (Zartman 1994; Dupont & Faure 2002). In addition, these calculations will usually involve the examination of different types of leverages most likely to be available to oneself and to the others that will define subsequent interactions.

While changing sources of power as well as varying meanings and implications of power asymmetry can mean (old and new) opportunities, this can also be a source of anxieties and insecurities especially under high uncertainty (see Tversky & Kahneman 1974; Carraro & Sgobbi 2008). Therefore, it is highly important to assess how sources of power such as access to knowledge, military strength, moral power, and financial capacity can purportedly be converted into political actions by the others. An assessment of power needs must be performed to accommodate the complexity of specific issues. What are the advantages of a country's military strength in achieving climate protection goals?

In addition, the 'relative' value of power can be understood in terms of power asymmetry, whereas the unequal distribution of resources has led to more leverage for those with more (see Brooks 2006). It can be assumed that the different pools of actors within the global and national spheres will have different sources and uses of leverage. Nevertheless, having more power can also mean getting less, especially for the one actor with the most power. As power may also mean additional responsibilities and constraints, where the powerful actors are morally obliged to adhere to the rules that they themselves have established. The marginal benefit of one unit of power from the superpower is less than that of a weaker country, particularly because of legitimacy bias. For example, Gilbert Winham and Elizabeth DeBoer-Ashworth (2000) highlight that in the Canada-US Free Trade Agreement between 1985–1987, the more powerful United States was confronted by more urgent issues and so sent less experienced negotiators, while Canada sent its most experienced ones, leading to the best outcome Canada could achieve. Therefore, the concept of rational choice (see Simon 1955; Tversky & Kahnemann 1986) that assumes 'consistency' among goals and objectives relative to a particular action does not foresee that power asymmetry can mean both advantages and disadvantages. As such, power asymmetry is assumed to prevent many types of consistencies among goals relative to actions. Thomas Hobbes' notion of consistent, value-maximizing reckoning or adaptation within specific constraints (see Friedrich 1963; Gauthier 1969) need to be revisited as actors cannot be consistent with their decisions, as they are compelled to 'compare' values and strategize decisions.

Turnstiles:

- While the relative valuation of power is captured by its loss-aversion value function, the origins of loss aversion itself can be more effectively identified (and resolved) by framing power within the status quo.
- Power becomes a subject of analysis especially when linked with either maintenance or challenge of the status quo.
- Empathy towards the interests and perspectives of others can become more pronounced after the careful evaluation of relative values.
- Determining relative values can provide more appreciation, as useful insights emerge that can frame debate on values that cannot be measured, such as the value of world heritage sites for humanity.
- Focusing on the relative value of power will most likely allows changes in the distribution of power that may further promote 'decentralization' or 'poly-centralization' of the world order, with more regional powers assuming leadership.

- The emergence of 'new leaders' or new major players can promote finding 'fresh' ideas and develop innovative leadership styles.
- More deliberative negotiations can be more conducive to robust decisions compared with purely power-driven negotiations, whereas outcomes of deliberative negotiations are more resilient to changes as they are more capable of absorbing shifts in power.

Assumption 2: Power is not only an instrument for achieving goals, it is also a category of identities.
Rationale: As the analysis of power and power asymmetry motivates a more conscious articulation of the relative advantages and disadvantages (see Assumption 1), it can be assumed that behavior reflects purpose or intention. One's purpose or intention is in turn framed by one's expectation of the probability of actually realizing this purpose, which presupposes a calculation of one's power. Furthermore, as the connection between behavior and purpose becomes evident, it can be assumed that decisions (and actions) are framed by a 'value system' as rewards or sanctions are formalized. When an actor follows a value system in its decisions and actions, it is inevitably assuming an 'identity.'

Any form of representation, whether '*formalistic*' (see Warren & Castiglione 2004; Grant & Keohane 2005) (that is, institutional arrangements that precede and initiate representation), or '*descriptive*' (see Pitkin 1967; Young 1986) (that is, the close proximity of the interests between the representative and the represented, or 'symbolic' representation (see Pitkin 1967), presupposes the ability of the representative to project the interests of the represented to the others, as well as a degree of identity-building (see Hernandez 2014a).

In addition, as game theory would suggest, because actor A's choice depends on B's choice (and vice versa) it can also be assumed that the identity of A depends on the identity of B (and vice versa). This mutual causality implies that by making an adjustment to one's decision, an actor can already influence the decisions of the others. This understanding, which conceptualizes the connectivity of decisions, will more likely promote empathy among actors, particularly in the context of power asymmetry.

Turnstiles:

- As a state or a collectivity assumes an identity, its behavior can become 'predictable' and therefore manageable. Predictability of behavior decreases uncertainty in decision-making processes.

- Reciprocity can make it easier to forge collaboration and to execute coordination. As parties are able to 'estimate' and 'calculate' the behavior of other actors, they can look for similarities and assess differences. Motivations to agree on concessions increase, because reciprocity enables the creation of additional value.
- Identity-building can promote trust among negotiating actors, primarily because the counterparts are able to identify reference points which allow the others to come up with concrete strategies to respond to or develop a contingency plan to address power asymmetry.

Assumption 3: Rationality is to be decoupled from transitivity.
Rationale: Decisions are to a significant degree normative and will not always follow transitivity, as rational choice theory assumes. Actors can arbitrarily violate transitivity (A > B > C; but C > A) as they assess options (e.g., A, B or C) using their own context-based value systems. Actors may be willing to tolerate the negative aspects of C, although C's pay-offs are worse than those of A. Tolerance is a matter of perception, and emotions can amplify the importance of one or more elements behind an issue while underestimating the others. The consideration of emotions in decision analysis amplifies the human factor and needs to be included in any decision optimization effort (see Moore 1996).

Modern decision theory highlights rational choice in decision-making. Particularly because, in the selection among a set of given options (whose consequences are preferred in terms of the agent's utility function), each set of consequences is ranked according to the order of preference (see Raiffa 2002: 11). However, as suggested by game theory, rational choice can illuminate oversimplifications within the symmetrical normative orientation of actors. In addition, the compulsion to achieve equilibrium frames the set of actions, which highlight the importance of targets (see Raiffa 2002 p. 11). Transitivity is therefore the implication of such oversimplification leading to the failure to grasp complexity.

Turnstiles:

- By highlighting the 'human factor' (emotions), decision-makers can not only avail themselves of important qualitative impacts, they can also assume a more pragmatic outlook when seeking joint decisions.
- Decoupling transitivity from rationality can allow the development of more useful decision tools that are more effective in managing complexity.

Assumption 4: Decisions are changed following the adaptation of behaviors through the modification of expected outcomes.
Rationale: Decisions of actors in a joint decision-making process are made to achieve goals. As goals are converted to outcomes at a later stage, there is a need to conceptualize this 'conversion.' The first step of such a conceptualization is the examination of the 'trigger' that has caused the motivation to formulate goals (see Raiffa 2002 p. 16). The second step involves the format of realizing these goals. Is this format already evident or is there a need to constitute a new one? In cases of problems that can only be solved through cooperation with other actors, there is a need to evaluate how this format can scale up values from interpersonal to larger scales. Assuming the cooperative disposition of human-beings (Messner et al. 2013), it is inevitable that possible motivations for non-cooperation be highlighted. Is this format resulting from group identity formation or is this format an antecedent of such an identity formation? If the latter is the case, there is a need to have a closer look at their existing value system and how their value system dictates specific actions. The next step pertains to the analysis of the meso-level, where persons who represent groups in negotiations affect the course of negotiations, either by promoting or inhibiting the achievement of the goals.

As differences between actors are expected and will be reflected in their behavior when negotiating, the more urgent question is how behavior can be changed while acknowledging these differences. 'Manipulating' behavior refers to altering peoples' choices which will be most likely chosen under business-as-usual conditions. Michal Skorepa (2011) suggests that behavior can be manipulated by changing the outcomes of decisions or merely the perceptions about these outcomes. By modifying the volume or context of outcomes, new value is created, paving way for updates in perspectives and behavior. Such a manipulation can be conducted through educational campaigns, where pay-offs can be highlighted or differentiated. Other types of manipulation involve focusing on negative perspectives and on disadvantages (see Ganzach & Karsahi 1995).

Turnstiles:

- Modifying outcomes to accommodate changing goals can be done by changing the format of the decision-making process (e.g., from vertical to horizontal)
- Knowing the effectiveness of 'negative framing' in manipulating decisions, decision-makers can assess different types of manipulation, compare these to their own utility functions and 'convert' the negative frame.

Assumption 5: The compatibility and convertibility of perceptions of justice, fairness and equity define the resilience of decision systems.
Rationale: Sustainable low-carbon transformation encompasses different public goods that are indicated by different connotations and methodologies. As different public good problems (see Snidal 2010) are manifested through the plurality of connotations as well as the relevance of these public goods, several types of strategies emerge. When connotations compete for relevance, decision-making will need to touch on broader principles (environmental protection, civil liberties) and attempt to reconcile those principles in competition.

The existence of differences between actors intending to achieve collective decisions also encompasses differences in perceptions of justice, fairness and equity. The resilience of decision systems is contingent on mechanisms that facilitate the compatibility and convertibility of these differences. While existing orders will most likely reflect an asymmetrical distribution of privileges and (positive and negative) entitlements, the resilience of decision systems, that is, the capacity of these to survive internal and external shocks, will depend on how this asymmetry is reproduced or reinforced by the outcomes. Nevertheless, to understand how the asymmetrical distribution of privileges and entitlements is reproduced or reinforced in outcomes, it is first required to find the typologies of justice, fairness and equity.

Turnstiles:

- The typologies of justice, fairness and equity as well as the conceptualization of the facilitation of compatibility and convertibility of justice, fairness and equity can be helpful in re-framing conflict cleavages such as the North-South divide, the core-periphery dichotomy, and the urban-rural divide.

Assumption 6: The tolerance (and the acceptability) of biases which are inevitable in the decision-making processes that involve multiple perspectives is highly contingent on mechanisms of persuasion and the possibility of updating perspectives.

Rationale: Often regarded as an 'anomaly,' bias is inevitable for any person with a value system. As Johann Galtung (1990) claims, only 'dead people' are free of any form of bias. Human beings, either acting as a person or as a representative of a collectivity, cannot be free from every value system. Such a value system is a collection of life experiences, and although it can be updated, certain elements will remain and will define one's preconception or prejudice. Nevertheless, bias does not always need to inhibit decision-making. For example, neutrality or lack of bias is often regarded as a necessary requirement for mediators or chairs in negotiations. However, William Zartman (1988) claims that bias does not disqualify mediators *per se*, because this bias can be circumvented when mediators who are presumed to be biased are still able to deliver the 'message' from one actor to another. Assuming this logic, bias in collective decision-making processes should be defined as a stumbling block and assessed on how it can inhibit, delay or prevent the realization of presumed goals.

Decision biases are the tendencies to make decisions in certain ways that are systematic deviations from 'rational' or optimal judgment. Psychology and behavioral economics assess these deviations and look for explanations. Biases are often linked to 'heuristics' or 'mental short-cuts' that are cognitively produced to guide decisions. One prominent example of heuristics refers to 'self-fulfilling prophecies' where expectations dictate behavior and positive expectations call for appropriate behavior leading to the realization of goals. On the other hand, negative expectations lead to less motivation and less appropriate behavior, inhibiting the realization of goals. Another example of decision bias pertains to the valuation of 'sunk costs,' also referred to as 'loss aversion.' The pressure of sunk costs, which cause the overvaluing of past investments and the strong determinant of an irrational escalation of commitment (see Staw 1976; Bazerman & Shonk 2005), may eventually lead to decisions no longer honored, as escalated commitments are simply too expensive. When the disutility of giving up an object is greater than the utility associated with acquiring it (see Kahneman et al. 1991), costs can no longer be legitimized by their objective utility.

Other biases include *ambiguity effect* or the tendency to avoid options for which missing information makes the probability of an occurrence seem to be unknown (see Baron 1994); *anchoring* or *focalism,* that is, the tendency to rely too heavily on one piece of information, usually the first piece of information acquired, when making decisions (see Zhang et al. 2007); *availability heuristics* or the tendency to overestimate the likelihood of events with greater availability in memory (see Schwarz et al. 1991); *the backfire effect,* or the reaction to disconfirming evidence by strengthening one's previous beliefs (see Sanna et al. 2002); *the bandwagon effect,* or the tendency of one's action to occur when many other people are doing the same (see Colman 2003); *the bias blind spot,* or the tendency to see oneself as less biased than other people or to be able to identify more biases in others than in oneself (see Pronin & Kugler 2007); *the contrast effect,* or the enhancement or reduction of a certain perception's stimuli when compared with a recently observed, contrasting object (see Plous 1993); *hyperbolic discounting,* that is, the tendency for people to have a stronger preference for more immediate payoffs relative to later payoffs (see Laibson 1997); and *reactive devaluation,* or devaluing proposals only because they purportedly originated from an adversary.

Turnstiles:

- As decision biases are often inevitable, it can be useful to engage a more pragmatic outlook on evaluating biases. One possible step is to make such biases transparent to enable a case-by-case evaluation of their relevance to the realization of goals. As these biases will most likely lead to inconsistent decisions over time, decision-makers will require some mechanisms to document such inconsistent decisions. In addition, what needs to be analyzed is how perspectives can still be updated in spite of the occurrence of biases.
- Personal biases can provide insights into how issues and potential provisions of outcomes are prioritized, thus creating additional contingencies for possible agreements.
- Recognizing bias can allow the justification of compensatory measures, thus the internalization of bias.

Assumption 7: While emotions vindicate the importance of decisions, emotions define the unpredictability of decision-making processes.
Rationale: As the 'human factor' enters the picture, decision-makers are startled by the choices and decisions made by others. Interestingly, human emotions are often linked with irrationality, as emotions hinder humans from achieving the ideal type of *homo economicus*, which refers to a creature that takes into account all aspects of a situation to maximize its own utility (see Dubreuil 2010). In addition, there is the huge question of how poorly humans are able to relate to the negative emotions of the others, such as anger or fear. Without a sense of empathy, this perplexity leads to frustration. For example, when the lead negotiator of the Philippines delegation broke down in public and wept during the full plenary session of the COP18 climate talks and later staged a hunger strike to force a substantial outcome from the COP meeting, he was celebrated by the media and civil society groups. However, he was also later strongly reprimanded by the Philippine government and was reminded that the COP meeting is not a proper place for such emotional outbursts, as policy-makers need to "show a picture of strength to calm fears" (Cabacungan 2013).

Furthermore, as current developments prove, the rise of social media and other informational and communication technologies have led to the increased claim of 'opinions' as equal to facts and evidence. As such, the transitivity of decision-making becomes more difficult, as opinions often refer to an emotional basis. As everyone is deemed to have the right to his or her own opinion, and when policy-making needs to be justified by public opinion, it becomes a question of whether this justification through public opinion another source of unpredictability is, as opinions can quickly change or even be easily manipulated.

The failure to adequately address the gaps between (evidence-based) knowledge systems and self-perceived 'marginalized' individuals has often been addressed by 'correcting the facts.' Nevertheless, as these individuals have crystallized their own identity, stressing the factuality of decisions to 'correct' preconceived and emotion-based ideas and opinions is now counterproductive. In addition, such efforts are resisted as the knowledge system has also been placed into doubt and anti-intellectualism is now equated with 'anti-elitism' or 'anti-establishment' (see Tan 2017).

Turnstiles:

- New impulses can be found to stress a "we-identity," which can help solve other social cohesion problems.
- The social dimension of policies can gain more attention from policymakers and other stakeholders.
- As knowledge systems are re-visited as a reaction to anti-intellectualism, both methodologies and data assessment systems can be improved and matured.

4.2 Issues

Assumption 8: Understanding the domestic (local) in the context of the global and the global in the context of the domestic (local) will provide additional perspectives on the replication of best practices.

Rationale: While states and government agencies have the essential role of conflating global with domestic/local issues, non-government actors have been effective in both 'scaling up' and 'scaling down' good practices. Nevertheless, the replication of best practices, both upwards and downwards, will depend highly on the inclusiveness of decision-making. Increased participation and the enhanced role of particularly marginalized actors need to be dependent not only on the knowledge of what these actors will do, but also on what they could do. Inclusiveness promotes framing and controllability. While multiple perspectives allow issues to be framed differently, they also lead to trade-offs in goals, which highly depend on 'costing out' (see Raiffa 2002 p. 19), that is, converting different values to make them relevant, quantifiable, and comparable to other goals.

Inclusiveness also promotes the controllability of the decision-making process, making it more predictable and manageable. A common approach to ensuring inclusiveness is to support NGOs and other social movement organizations, which can serve as bridges between citizens and policy-makers (Princen & Finger 1994; see Andresen & Gulbrandsen 2003; Dong Wei 2010). For example, while social movements have developed 'champions' among target groups, they are lobbying for data-driven policies, monitoring and verifying the progress of government policies, seeking partnership or competing with other groups and local communities to advance their goals, and in some cases performing roles traditionally played by governments. Nevertheless, the relationship between governments and social movements is ambivalent and may reflect different developments depending on the local context. While in some countries NGOs have complemented governments in designing and implementing policies, others are viewed as being in 'opposition to the state' particularly when the activities of these NGOs focus on governance issues. In other cases, governments may 'tolerate' NGOs depending on the issues. While the diffusion of power is empowering states against their population, NGOs are also empowered against both their local state and transnationally, against other states, other NGOs and the international society. However, while NGO actions are informed by (liberal) normative concerns, NGOs also pay close attention to instrumental concerns that bear upon organizational survival and growth (Prakash & Gugerty 2010). Therefore, NGOs and other social movement organizations cannot be exempted from the analysis of power relations.

With the globalization of their means of communication as well as the globalization of their sources of funding, social movements have gained more leverage against government actors. In various cases, social movements have assumed deterrence and balancing strategies, have often been successful in containing state power. As NGOs seek to widen their range of goals and actions in order for them to stay relevant, governments have found ways to embed these groups into the political framework.

Turnstiles:

- The changing distribution of power between states and NGOs can expand the 'core,' lower barriers for peripheral states to enter the core, and make legitimacy more culturally pluralistic

Assumption 9: The negative synergies resulting from the interconnectivity of issues will most likely result in an assortment problem.
Rationale: As a 'portion' or a 'segment' of a (decision) policy is altered to address unacceptable trade-offs or negative externalities to other (decision) policy goals, the overall quality of this initial policy may significantly diminish and/or may no longer satisfy demand. Therefore, the 'removed' portion or segment needs to be substituted by an adequate component set to avoid 'adaptation loss,' 'linear substitution costs' and 'standardization gaps' (see Sadowski 1959; Pentico 2008). Assortment problems arise when it is difficult to decide which portions or segments of a policy can be altered or even taken out without undermining the overall effectiveness of the policy.

For example, the interconnectivity of promoting renewable energy, local community development, and innovation & entrepreneurship may result in negative synergies such as the loss of biodiversity which will motivate policy-makers to make changes to their overall sustainable, low-carbon policy to prevent or circumvent the loss of diversity. However, as policy-makers introduce new provisions, identify and implement substitute provisions, or alter existing ones, the effectiveness of the policy may lead to deficiencies.

Turnstiles:

- The effective management of negative synergies resulting from the interconnectivity of issues can be promoted by a clear understanding of relevant values and pay-offs (what does it bring to the table to address these issues, either only in terms of principles or only their practical meaning).

4.3 Structures

Assumption 10: The gaps between individual and collective rationality can be the results of varying levels of decision-making.
Rationale: While unitary decision entities are monolithic and ignore internal conflicts (see Raiffa 2002: 4), collective decisions emphasize the interactions and dynamics between multiple unitary decision entities. Expanding this idea and adopting the process outlook, these interactions and dynamics can be scaled up to various levels or structures. Each scale reflects specific principles, narratives and paradigms. Nevertheless, because these various levels are interconnected, contradiction of principles will only be evident at one point, which will require

integrated management. In addition, as a joint process is dependent on various factors, both fragmentation and convergence of these levels or structures will most likely be observed, which practically defines institutional complexity.

The implementation of the outcomes of decision-making processes is highly dependent on the connectivity between 'policy' and 'basic games.'

Turnstiles:

- As different levels of decision-making are highlighted, it can be easier for decision-makers to distribute 'ownership' among them and at the same time forge a shared identity.
- An integrated approach in assessing the various levels (as separate entities) can increase the proximity between policy goals and local conditions leading to enhanced legitimacy and effectiveness.
- The proper analysis of level-dependent rationalities can help develop new tools of evidence-based measurement, data interpretation, monitoring, and assessment.
- Hierarchies place 'anchors' at various stages of decision-making, thus defining expectations and limiting sets of possible outcomes of decision-making processes.

Assumption 11: Decisions cannot be 'freed' from normativity, particularly in the context of transformation processes that involve paradigm shifts.
Rationale: While the normativity of decisions is well accepted among policy-makers, particularly in the context of climate change mitigation, there has been louder calls for policy-makers to come up with decisions that meet the expectations of the various scientific communities. While these scientific communities, including the IPCC, argue that what they contribute are merely 'policy relevant,' but not 'policy prescriptive,' and when scientific knowledge defines the so-called 'decision maxim,' it inevitably becomes normative, that is, it assumes a prescriptive role. The 'detesting' of the normativity of scientific knowledge follows the self-definition of most scientists of their roles. In order to maintain independence as well as objectivity, scientists need to refrain from any type of normative actions. When politicians, business actors, social groups, etc., are able to dictate the subjects, methods and results of scientific studies, then science loses its integrity.

Nevertheless, particularly when scientific studies define a 'decision maxim,' new discussions are needed on how to address the normative character of these studies. A decision maxim is a general maxim (composed of principles and rules), designed such that decision-making may adhere to or violate it (Skorepa 2011: 40). For example, the scientific results synthesized by the various IPCC reports constitute the principles (e.g., 2 °C threshold) and rules (e.g., life cycle assessment methods) of the decision maxim framing political decisions. Nevertheless, as the next chapter of this book claims, the generation of this knowledge is subject to various norms. Furthermore, should there be consensus about the 'absolute' non-normativity of this scientific knowledge, the 'aesthetic argument,' that according to Michal Skorepa (2011 p. 42) proves the normativity of a decision maxim, shows that the principles and rules also encompass 'aesthetic' elements such as consistency, coherence, stability, symmetry, analogy, balance and simplicity. Scientific knowledge that employs one or more or all of these 'aesthetic' elements is normative *per se*.

Turnstiles:

- The acceptance of the normativity of scientific knowledge will most likely require new concepts and methods of accountability and transparency that reveal conflicts of interest.
- The normative outlook on scientific knowledge can be helpful in identifying and 'controlling' various types of decision biases.

4.4 Processes

Assumption 12: Global convergence has amplified the 'competition among concepts of modernity' leading to more embedded consolidation of national identities.

Rationale: The increased competition among states implies changes and shifts in the World Order. Nevertheless, the emerging 'Post-Western' World Order will most likely not see the immediate removal of these mechanisms of privilege and vulnerability, but rather maintain them, as these mechanisms are often 'coupled' with rewards and incentives. While some privileges have lost their meaning in terms of '*Realpolitik*,' some types of vulnerabilities are either too difficult to eliminate or provide additional political leverage. When this new 'meaning' of vulnerabilities has defined the prospects of alliances, they require a new assessment in terms of international politics. As Barry Buzan and George Lawson (2015) observe, the current World Order is shifting. They claim that the great, old, advanced industrial powers are "exhausted and weakened both materially and in terms of ideational legitimacy", debarring them from credibly fulfilling their roles as leaders and giving the impression that the World Order is now defined by the so-called 'G-zero,' which is a World Order where no country can step in to replace the United States. With these powerful countries voluntarily or involuntarily relinquishing their 'exclusive' dominance, more opportunities are given to developing countries with emerging economies to replace these developed countries and set the pace of global decision-making. Nevertheless, these new 'major players' are not always interested to the 'new privileges' linked with global leadership. While some of them have already started establishing and maintaining their 'spheres of influence' (e.g., China in Africa or Southeast Asia), they are resorting to strategies that fall short of global leadership and still demand more responsibilities from the 'old powers', against whom they bring their grievances. The changes and shifts in the World Order have produced a new consciousness and 'naturalness' (*Selbstverständlichkeit*) that still await conceptualization.

In addition, while the occurring global convergence, as further induced by information technologies, has moved countries closer to each other in terms of economic development, pop culture, Western science (e.g., medicine), democratization, industrialization, and secularization, new waves of 'indigenous modernity' emerge, where various societies recognize that as global convergence unfolds, their national or local identities should be 'empowered.' Various societies that are unable to adapt to new realities without losing their identities are confronted with 'counter-processes' that aim to 'bring back the old glory.' What follows is the 'paradox of modernity', where the struggle between 'competing modernities' (see Mauch & Patel 2010) has led to more diversity in the definition of modernity. As it is clear that there can be no consensus as to how modernity should be defined, many countries, particularly developing countries, have come up with their own 'indigenous modernity,' which is often seen as challenging, freezing, stagnating or even eroding the world's multilateral system.

Turnstiles:

- The conflation of global and local cultures will most likely promote co-authorship between the 'old' powers and the 'new' powers in terms of realigning intermediary global and regional institutions, leading to 'global decisions' with more expanded scope and significance.
- A more embedded and consolidated national or local identity will more likely increase the legitimacy of global decisions as it closes the distance between individuals and global decision-makers.

Assumption 13: Global convergence does not foresee the creation of 'melting pots,' but rather of 'salad bowls'.

Rationale: The global convergence of standards, norms, governance structures, economic transactions, (popular) culture, consumption, political identities and communication is not contingent upon the creation of 'melting pots,' where differences among actors are 'melted together' to create a homogenous identity. Melting pots address conflict cleavages by eliminating them, whereas alienation among individuals becomes cumulative. Therefore, global convergence needs to be understood as 'salad bowls' where differences mix but still remain in some cases, without causing system ruptures. For example, a melting pot definition of global convergence would see norms spill over to countries which are not always tailored to the local conditions. Melting pots will most likely ignore the relevance of addressing local conditions. In contrast, a salad bowl understanding will see new forms of '*glocalized*' decision-making that enjoys more support from local stakeholders (Princen & Finger 1994; see Roudometof 2015).

Nevertheless, melting pots will exist, but will maintain a rather regional scope, where countries of a specific region benefit from already existing regional cooperation regimes. Regional melting pots will define the thresholds of conflict cleavages, as global transformation will take place not in the global system, but rather in regions. Regional demarcations of knowledge production and representation of the world have defined transfers and synergies within regions. As Barry Buzan and George Lawson (2015) argue, global transformation will be a conglomerate of various (interlinked) transformation processes in various regions, issues and areas.

Turnstiles:

- New forms of *glocalized* decision-making will most likely increase the legitimacy of decisions
- Understanding that while problems can be global, their solutions can only be local, will most likely increase ownership of the processes and the solutions, leading to better and more sustainable implementation of goals.

Assumption 14: As decisions relevant to transformation are collective decisions, the achievement of global and domestic/local decisions will depend on how collective and individual 'pay-offs' can be bridged.

Rationale: Negotiations as joint decision-making procedures presuppose that parties voluntarily come together, as the expected 'pay-offs' of individual or unilateral decision-making is 'worse' than those of non-negotiation. Expanding upon this, parties will need to 'convert' collective pay-offs in terms of how much these will increase or decrease ones' competitive advantage. This creates the 'negotiation dilemma', where parties are reluctant to commit to negotiated agreements when there is uncertainty about the implications of these agreements in terms of their future negotiation leverage. Therefore, bridging collective and individual pay-offs will also require 'coupling' the costs of non-agreement or non-participation to 'individual loss.' For this to occur, the focus should be shifted from separate interactive actions to group actions, effectively dissolving game theory's 'prisoner's dilemma' (see Raiffa 2002). While parties make separate decisions, these decisions will need to make sense only when they interact with the decisions of others, leading to the production of joint pay-offs.

Nevertheless, joint pay-offs can only be useful when there is full information about individual pay-offs. This will require a specific level of mutual trust, which itself is a subject of learning processes. Joint pay-offs will also depend on reciprocity. On occasions where pay-offs cannot be divided equally, joint pay-offs will be distributed. What follows are exchanges of other resources to 'level up' distribution. Reciprocity plays a role in defining the level of possible trust.

Turnstiles:

- New methods on analyzing and understanding processes may lead to insights into methods and possibilities of 'coupling' as well as 'decoupling', leading to new values useful for joint pay-offs.
- Bridging collective and individual pay-offs may dissolve free-riding and social traps.

4.5 Outcomes

Assumption 15: The efficacy of outcomes of joint decision-making is contingent upon ambiguity that allows constituting exit-strategies from path dependence.

Rationale: While ambiguity may reduce the practical value of outcomes through multiple interpretations of outcomes, it expands the quantity and quality of participation in the decision-making process. Uncertainty around the implementation of outcomes can be relativized when decision pathways, defined as critical junctures, and locked-in sets of decisions, are accompanied by contingencies that allow revisions of path trajectories without forcing a system default or rupture. Decision-making processes that involve more than one actor are particularly dependent on provisions that allow flexibility, as there is most likely an asymmetry of departing points. In addition, uncertainty can be managed when decision-making guarantees the repetition of interactions between actors in order to collect experiences and information about the viability of reciprocities. Moreover, because participation in negotiations mutually 'reveals' the identities of participating parties, useful mechanisms of communication can be developed that could, among others, adequately address existing asymmetries.

In the context of negotiations on emission reduction to mitigate climate change, while one actor can easily commit to this mechanism, others will need more time or more capacities, and if not, these actors will not agree on any agreement in the first place. In this situation, flexibility measures entice them to be part of the 'system,' take advantage of the various learning processes and have access to incremental knowledge not only in terms of the technical content of the issues, but also the strength of reciprocities among actors. As such, ambiguity can be regarded as a principle that can initiate (but not guarantee) trust among actors.

From the path dependence perspective (see Arthur 1988; David 1988; Arthur 1994; Sydow et al. 2009), flexibility measures can decrease the 'magnetic' influence of critical junctures and lock-ins. Nevertheless, flexibility measures can be easily 'abused' in order to free-ride. Therefore, the provisions of ambiguity need to be transparent, context-dependent and focused on allowing exit strategies from path dependence. In addition, ambiguity provisions should be limited by complementing them with both quantitative and qualitative indicators of defined targets to promote the predictability of the resulting consequences of 'ambiguous' provisions. Furthermore, the definition of risk profiles (see Raiffa 2002 p. 20) should be clearly communicated. Moreover, the ambiguity of provisions does not always mean uncertainty, as uncertainty pertains to the likelihood of the implementation of the outcome, and ambiguity refers to scalable values such as ordinal ranking, monetary value, desirability value and utility value (see Raiffa 2002: 22).

Turnstiles:

- Ambiguity provisions for outcomes of joint decision-making can expand participation and deter or even 'convert' spoilers.
- Ambiguity can provide incremental knowledge both in terms of trust and the technical content of relevant issues.

Assumption 16: Because joint decision-making cannot expect complete information, the implementation of the outcomes of decision-making need to be open to permanent change through learning.

Rationale: In a 'perfect' world, decision-makers will be given a set of alternatives, a set of objectives (or attributes), and a known probability distribution of outcomes and the decision-maker will have a stable utility or preference function (Weber 1987 p. 44). Based on these, an optimal or satisfying solution can be found, whereas the decision-maker is required to provide all information. The decision-maker needs to provide his or her set of objectives to predict his or her behavior. In addition, methods such as conjoint analysis are needed to 'translate' holistic statements into preferences (see Weber 1987). Nevertheless, the 'real world' will be completely different. Not only can all relevant information be known but providing all information that one has can also be practical, particularly in a joint decision-making process involving negotiations. As a bargaining game, negotiators need to calculate how the information he or she gives can lessen his or her leverage. In addition, any prediction about the behavior of an actor based on a set of information can only ever be a model, because humans have both stable and unstable preference structures. Moreover, an incomplete preference structure itself can be the reason for incomplete information, as humans often do not always know what they want (Weber 1987 p. 51). Preferences can also change with or without new information. Therefore, joint decision-making should lower its requirement or expectation about the completeness of information.

Turnstiles:

- Acknowledging the limitations of information can motivate actors to think probabilistically and focus on what they could do and not on what they want to do. In doing so, expectations can be more consistent with the objectives of the decision-making process.
- Although decision-making under incomplete information can promote risk-aversion and increase intractability when achieving outcomes, provisions of permanent change (e.g., conflict management, review and monitoring, etc.) can further induce the learning process.

4.6 Interim Conclusion

This chapter is another important pillar of the theoretical framework. It identified theoretical and conceptual issues in **decision systems** that tend to be taken as self-evident and therefore ignored, both in theory and in practice. As self-evident assumptions, these issues in decision processes and dynamics tend to be taken for granted. Because of this, the evaluation and the management of these issues are often skipped or circumvented in most functional, institutional and bargaining interactions. They are no longer questioned and therefore they represent missed opportunities. However, they do represent conceptual and practical lock-ins that prevent out-of-the-box or without-a-box thinking that is needed when addressing complex issues of transformation towards sustainability. They can cause further distortions in decision-making. But when they are adequate questions, they might provide additional impulses for strategies and solutions. These issues in decision systems can be understood by exposing them and inviting scholarly discourse on how they can relate to the transformation process towards sustainability.

In this chapter, the exposure of these issues was conducted by explicating them as assumptions and by explaining where these assumptions come from and how these can inhibit or promote transformation towards sustainability. The rationales behind these assumptions intend to shed some light on the utility preferences of agents and audiences. Finally, turnstiles were identified that represent addition opportunities for facilitating the transformation process.

Knowledge Diplomacy as Facilitator of Transformation Towards Sustainability—The "New Diplomacy" and Consensual Knowledge

5

Negotiations over the best way to address climate change and sustainable development are heavily dependent on input from scientific and expert communities. While policy-makers seek to rationalize and thereby legitimate their decisions through evidence-based decisions frameworks, this unprecedented reliance on scientific knowledge has inadvertently led to a perceived erosion of state authority and a weakening of democracy. It has been strongly suggested that the use of scientific knowledge in policy-making is reducing the demand or need for concordant consensus-building, or distorting deliberation processes through the emergence of new forms of dependency (see Barett & Chambers 1998; Bijker et al. 2009). In addition, Wiebe Bijker et al. (2009) dispute that the more urgently scientific advice is solicited, the more vigorously scientific authority is questioned by policy-makers, stakeholders and citizens, who themselves have become reliant on scientific inputs.

Knowledge is becoming a powerful means of effectively asserting interests. This gives rise to new demands, related to accountability, for a critical assessment of how knowledge is generated, applied and monitored. Does the knowledge produced by scientific communities really facilitate or even justify interventions by policy-makers? Concerns have been expressed that the use of knowledge in policy-making is replicating existing structural imbalances and therefore reinforcing or even reproducing inequities (see Crouch 2008). With power established through knowledge, **equitable access to knowledge** resources requires additional discourse to prevent knowledge from reinforcing structural inequities. Furthermore, it is increasingly proposed that scientists and research institutions have assumed a "corporate identity" following the increased market logic being applied to the awarding of research grants and the emphasis on attracting paying students. Through this corporate identity, scientists and research institutions may

A. M. Hernández, *Taming the Big Green Elephant*, Globale Gesellschaft und internationale Beziehungen, https://doi.org/10.1007/978-3-658-31821-5_5

have ceased to reflect the image of "disinterested, rationalized" powerbrokers (see Crouch 2008; Rohde 2017). They have simply become another interest group seeking funding for growth and survival. Scientific knowledge, as Tora Skodvin (2000) suggests, no longer exists as an agency of transformation towards sustainability, but as a calculating policy entrepreneur.

This chapter introduces the concept of **knowledge diplomacy** as an instrument or "agency" of collective decision-making. After a brief synthesis of how knowledge diplomacy is understood by the academic literature, this chapter introduces typologies of knowledge diplomacy to structure the analysis of how knowledge can strategically facilitate the transformation process. The typologies reflect the two, complementary, negotiation perspectives on knowledge: *power-base* and *systems perspective*. To put knowledge diplomacy into context, it will be examined by analyzing the IPCC process of knowledge generation for policy-making. In addition, this chapter re-visits the concept of "new diplomacy", which was previously introduced by Bo Kjéllen (2007). This "new diplomacy" can be useful for analytical purposes, whereby the centrality of knowledge/information in framing functional, institutional and bargaining interactions can be highlighted. The concept can also help to distinguish the current collective (negotiative) decision-making on transformation towards sustainability from the traditional terms of diplomacy. Finally, the critical assessment of knowledge diplomacy offers an understanding of the perils and challenges brought by this "new diplomacy" as well as recommendations to address them.

Scientific knowledge and decision tools (as provided by scientific communities) that support climate protection are often the subject of political scrutiny. The complexity and uncertainty of climate change issues, the limitations of methodologies and the frequent ambiguity of scientific findings have led to allegations of manipulation, and the assertion that scientific results are divorced from the real world. It is necessary to analyze where these anti-intellectualist sentiments are coming from. This chapter discusses, through the analysis of the IPCC process, how current knowledge management practices are reinforcing structural imbalances. For example, the "sensation-seeking" media and the uncontrolled social media have provided platforms for condemning the so-called "climate conspiracy", a view that has gained significant public support, in particular after a few factual errors and inaccuracies were discovered in the WGII Contribution to the Fourth Assessment Report (AR4) of the Intergovernmental Panel on Climate Change (IPCC) and were used to cast doubt on climate science in its entirety (see Cogley et al. 2010). In addition, several political actors have managed to incriminate science by "shopping" for scientific studies, in which they choose only those that support their political agenda, while at the same time defaming studies that are opposed to it. Instigated by the political narratives of populist groups, for example on climate conspiracy, a significant portion of society now sees climate science as based on false and manipulated data that merely aims to suppress dissent (BBC News 2016; see Robertson 2016).

A current trend indicates that although governments have become knowledgeable about the importance of addressing climate change and sustainable development, these issues are still not the top priorities of national governments. A discussion is therefore needed as to whether the power of knowledge in setting the policy agenda is misleading, if not overstated. For example, the 2017 Report Card on International Cooperation of the Council of Councils (2018), a survey of global think tank leaders on which global issues were prioritized by world leaders in 2017, climate change and development are ranked merely 5th and 8th respectively. Preventing nuclear proliferation and preventing and responding to violent conflict between states have taken the top two positions in the ranking. In addition, the survey included an assessment of global issues in terms of how they are effectively addressed through international cooperation. Mitigation and adaptation to climate change was given a grade of C+in 2017 compared to B in 2016 (with A+as highest grade). This low grade (and deterioration) is attributed to the United States' climate policies, the end of US funding for the Green Climate Fund, and its withdrawal from the Paris Agreement. Moreover, development as a global issue also witnessed a decline, from B– in 2016 to C+in 2017. This decline is attributed to the failure of 22 members of the OECD to meet their development assistance target of 0.7% of gross national income. In addition, aid to least-developed countries fell by 3.9% in real terms from 2015.

Knowledge diplomacy in the post-factual era needs to revisit the social mandate of knowledge. Emerging narratives that couple knowledge with elitism are supported by arguments that target legitimacy deficits on how knowledge is generated, distributed and used to justify political decisions. Knowledge diplomacy is a multi-level (e.g., global and national) process of joint decision-making, using the art and science of negotiations, whereas knowledge serves as a facilitating agency to structure complexity and uncertainty. In addition, scientific communities need to take an active role in defining these narratives and to break the increasing monopoly of "anti-intellectualist" groups that abuse knowledge to serve their own political agenda. But for this to happen, an extensive multidisciplinary academic discourse is inevitable. The following sections aim to identify issues that can be the subject of such a discourse.

5.1 Knowledge Diplomacy and Consensual Knowledge

Knowledge diplomacy on climate change is evident in various forms and stages. The most intuitive type of knowledge diplomacy refers to negotiators (or decision-makers in a collective setting) consulting scientific knowledge experts as the basis for agenda-setting and the resolution of issues through agreements. The context pertains to sociotechnical narrative that the objectivity of knowledge can be trusted to ensure efficiency and legitimacy of decisions. **Knowledge serves as agency or facilitator by providing a framework for complexity and uncertainty**. For example, the RAINS model introduced by the International Institute for Applied Systems Analysis (IIASA) was used in the complex negotiations on long-range air pollution in Europe to address acid rain problems (Anstey et al. 2009). The approval of the audience is deemed evident, because decisions based on objective indicators are perceived to be less arbitrary. At the national level, most governments appoint technical experts in Scientific Advisory Committees to help government departments and agencies as well as other executive public bodies to access, interpret and understand the full range of relevant scientific information, and to make judgements about the relevance, potential and application of policy instruments (UK GOS 2011).

Looking at the process level, knowledge diplomacy can also refer to the efforts to collect appropriate **consensual knowledge** to prepare for upcoming negotiations. This type of knowledge diplomacy also focuses on the utility of consensual knowledge, including standards and norms. With clear consensual knowledge (e.g., the 2 °C threshold), future joint decision-making can save resources on procedures and concentrate on concrete solutions. One example is the IPCC process involving numerous assessment reports and special reports (see Schulte-Uebbing et al. 2015). The IPCC's Summary for Policymakers undergoes an approval session at the IPCC, with country negotiators directly verifying each word and sentence of the text of the Summary for Policymakers (SPM) in close collaboration with IPCC scientists. The SPM, as will be discussed later, becomes the departing point of upcoming UNFCCC negotiations.

One example of knowledge diplomacy refers to consultations through regional forums, which may not be directly connected to the UNFCCC. Prior to UNFCCC COP meetings, regional forums such as the Asia-Pacific Economic Cooperation (APEC), Association of Southeast Asian Nations (ASEAN) and the EU are used as preparatory spaces for upcoming COP meetings, where initial direction of consensual knowledge on several topics is harmonized and determined. For example, prior to the COP15 negotiations in Copenhagen, members of APEC used its November 2009 Summit to come up with a common agenda for COP15. Serving as a "political barometer", the APEC Summit did not produce any substantial agreement and this failure motivated the UNFCCC and the COP15 chair to lower their expectation, which may have motivated them to take a more pragmatic approach to reduce potential frustration (Penetrante 2010). Regional forums also include formal and informal coalitions such as the Alliance of Small Island States (AOSIS).

Another type of knowledge diplomacy refers to epistemic communities, including think tanks, NGOs, universities, research institutions and even the private sector, which actively seek to influence policy-makers (e.g., selection of policy objectives). In contrast to the IPCC, where scientists merely present policy-relevant knowledge without seeking to direct policy-making, there are certain epistemic communities that actively participate in forging policies through various formal channels available. For example, the Sustainable Development Solutions Network (SDSN) Germany, which is the local response to the global initiative for the United Nations, was formally launched in 2014 to promote the sustainable development of Germany as well as German efforts for sustainable development worldwide (SDSN 2018). This network aims to serve as a catalyst or accelerator of cooperation between research institutions working on sustainable development. The group involves leading think tanks, research institutions, foundations and networks, and maintains close partnership with government agencies and private sector stakeholders.

SDSN Germany can also be taken as an example of another type of knowledge diplomacy, in which scientists and experts cooperate with each other to produce evidence-based consensual knowledge. In this type of knowledge diplomacy, a process of consensus building occurs between different subgroups coming from different fields and disciplines. For example, social scientists have but a shallow knowledge of the natural scientific issues that are addressed by policy-makers. Therefore, the assistance of natural scientists is recommended to improve their capacity as issue experts. Similarly, natural scientists need to reach out for social-scientific knowledge in order to increase the actual operational usability of scientific knowledge (Anstey et al. 2009). Natural scientists strive to structure uncertainty by means of probability estimates, whereas policymakers tend to prefer unstructured certainty. In their capacity as process experts, negotiation analysts are, for example, in a position to help natural scientists to develop methods to cope with obstacles impeding their communication with the critical actors in an international organization (Anstey et al. 2009).

Other types of knowledge diplomacy are latent. For example, in the global level, achieving consensual knowledge for sustainable development is a process that involves convergence of norms, standards and practices that can also be achieved through knowledge or technological spill-overs through cooperation mechanisms such as the International Development Assistance (ODA) (see Carraro et al. 2006; Easterly 2007). A type of knowledge diplomacy can be observed in technological cooperation projects as well as technology-transfer activities. On the one hand, countries providing technologies can learn from recipient countries, allowing the further development and maturation of technologies involved. On the other hand, recipient countries can acquire the necessary human capital and technical expertise to initiate further technological development that is more tailored to local parameters. This is, however, highly dependent on how the transfer of ownership is envisaged.

5.2 Negotiation Perspectives on Consensual Knowledge

"Knowledge diplomats" or "knowledge entrepreneurs" are scientists and professional experts, often referred to as members of "epistemic communities", who have become central pillars of both international and national policy-making (see Adler & Haas 1992; Haas 1992; Sebenius 1992a; Haas 2010). Knowledge diplomacy is not a fully new concept in international diplomacy, but its increased importance in achieving global agreements related to climate change and sustainable development is leading to changes in how bargaining between countries is strategized or how individual bargaining games relate to specific policy games. For example, the profile of diplomats participating in climate negotiations has shifted from traditional diplomats sent by Foreign Ministries to delegation members recruited from a wide range of ministries who do not necessarily have the diplomatic training but do have the technical expertise on the core issues that are important to them. Interestingly, smaller countries tend to concentrate on selected specific issues, as reflected by the expertise of the members of their delegations. For example, during the COP23 meeting in Bonn, Germany, among the nine members of the Azerbaijan delegation, three represented the oil sector of the country. In the same meeting, as distinct from most countries, which have delegations led by their Environmental Ministry, Sri Lanka's delegation was led by representatives from the Ministry of Science, Technology and Research, reflecting the country's different outlook on addressing climate change. In addition, some countries have found a hybrid type of diplomats. For example, during the COP23 meeting, among Australia's delegation was H.E. Mr. Patrick Suckling, the country's "Ambassador for the Environment" (UNFCCC 2017).

Consensual knowledge establishes the parameters within which decisions can be made. Hence, it assumes a facilitating function in the multi-level transformation towards sustainability, because many issues addressed in various multilateral talks related to climate change and sustainable development need to be assessed in scientific terms to structure complexity and contingencies. This structuring is a requirement before these issues can be objects of functional, institutional and bargaining interactions that lead to collective decisions (see Zartman 1994b; Sjöstedt 2009). Consensual knowledge's acquisition of a facilitator role enables a negotiation outlook on consensual knowledge as an agency of transformation towards sustainability. To provide a comprehensive overview of knowledge diplomacy, Gunnar Sjöstedt (2009) initially suggested that two negotiation perspectives on knowledge diplomacy can be identified: *power-base* and *systems perspective*. The next sub-section synthesizes and further expands the previous collaboration between Gunnar Sjöstedt and the author of this book by elaborating these two perspectives and by defining how (consensual) knowledge facilitates the achievement of collective decisions through bargaining.

5.2.1 Power-Based Perspective on Consensual Knowledge

Knowledge can be seen as a critical component of the power base of individual actors involved in a game of diplomacy. After calculating the utility of engaging in negotiations, the next step is the estimation of one's power relative to that of one's counterparts. Although power is a merely a perception (see Dahl 1957), it still influences the behavior of actors. Even though the outcome of negotiations tends to benefit those actors with more power (see Habeeb 1988), as argued by I. William Zartman and Jeffrey Z. Rubin (2000), the clarification of power asymmetry motivates negotiating parties to know their roles and correspondingly prepare strategies to achieve their intended appropriate benefits. Furthermore, Zartman and Rubin contend that conflicts can be resolved more efficiently with clarified power asymmetry, because parties will avoid wasting time sending signals about their power.

In addition, the definition of power as an act designed to cause the other party to move in a desired direction allows a more detailed analysis to be made of preferences. Through a definition of power that separates power as a concept from its source and its effects, strategies can be forged to "equalize" power in a way that ensures that negotiation pay-offs justify the efforts made. For example, connecting different issues together allows one actor to have a bigger pool of possible concessions for bargaining. By focusing on co-benefits and synergies, negotiators can be more willing to accept concessions on one issue, when they anticipate pay-offs in other issues. However, this can only work if reciprocity has already been established and formalized. Another example of possible strategies to address more powerful actors is to build coalitions and alliances to balance the more powerful actor (see Dupont 1994). Such coalitions and alliances can share individual capabilities and the expertise of members, allowing them to improve their overall leverage.

Gunnar Sjöstedt (2009) identifies the international negotiations leading to the Convention on Long-range Transboundary Air Pollution in the 1970s as well as to the achievement of its eight protocols that concretize commitments as an example of where the power-equalizing characteristic of knowledge was demonstrated. The Convention, which was composed of a series of multi-lateral treaties, is witness to how 49 Parties were able to cooperate in developing scientific understanding of the problems related to long-range transboundary air pollution (Sliggers & Kakebeeke 2004). The negotiations involved many scientists representing different issues, whose contributions were used as a foundation on which policy-makers have based their negotiations on emission-reduction commitments. For example, the elaboration of the effects-based or critical loads approach, as well as the extensive use of integrated assessment models as the basis for policy-making, provided negotiators with objective indicators that addressed existing caveats due to uncertainty.

Negotiations on the Convention were known to be "arduous" (Sliggers & Kakebeeke 2004 p. 20). "Hard negotiations" were expected against the backdrop of the Cold War, where the lack of antecedent negotiation frameworks and experiences on a similar scale was aggravated by mistrust, particularly when procedures were being established. In addition, politicians and environmental experts were far from unanimous, which can be attributed to the lack of experience of cooperation and gaps in professional cultures (see Sjöstedt 2003; Penetrante 2014). Nevertheless, the negotiations also demonstrated different dynamics in the power game among the countries that participated (Sjöstedt 2009), which, although smaller in scale, can be compared to the climate change negotiations. In the acid rain negotiations, access to scientific and expert knowledge was linked to power, with smaller and weaker countries able to circumvent traditional power logics and assume leadership or to adopt an assertive negotiating style due to their technical expertise on certain issues. Another possible enabling factor was that the leadership of neither Norway nor Sweden was perceived as a threat by the United States and the USSR. The Convention was eventually signed by 34 governments of European countries, Canada and the United States, as well as by the European Economic Community (EEC).

The knowledge-based "convening power" of Norway and Sweden was supported by antecedents. Because Scandinavian countries were the first ones to experience the negative effects of acidification due to air pollution, these countries had large stakes in the negotiations. Therefore, Norway and Sweden were not only keen to participate, but they have indeed actively sought and demonstrated clear leadership. This tactical leadership was not only skillful in terms of diplomacy, but it also effectively addressed the critical power-base component of negotiations through access to expert knowledge on relevant issues related to the acidification problem and its international causes. This expert knowledge of Norway and Sweden was the outcome of interested and concerned individuals, organizations, and agencies in Norway and Sweden that analyzed and assessed the issue of acid rain earlier than other countries (Sjöstedt 2009). With expert knowledge, these two countries were successful in linking policy games with simple bargaining games, which further facilitated the negotiation process. In addition, with expert knowledge, Norway and Sweden were able to compete with more powerful countries and take the initiative in determining the negotiation agenda and the solution formula as reflected by their proposals for the agreements.

Similar dynamics can be observed with both the climate negotiations and the international talks on sustainable development. During the COP15 meeting in Copenhagen, in particular, Scandinavian countries demonstrated leadership not only because of Denmark's chairmanship but also through the technical expertise they had built through their experiences of previous environmental negotiations. However, it became evident that this expertise was not yet enough to achieve a comprehensive emission reduction agreement. Nevertheless, the COP15 meeting produced important consensual knowledge, such as the 2 °C threshold that set the stage and empowered "change agents" in achieving the Paris Climate Agreement.

5.2.2 Systems Perspective on Consensual Knowledge

The negotiation outlook also evinces the systems perspective on collective decision-making. The establishment, for example, of the climate regime is not only reliant on consensual knowledge but also runs parallel to the establishment of consensual knowledge on individual issues, which, in concert, "fuel" the phases of negotiation. For example, the Paris Agreement was preceded by numerous formal and informal agreements on roadmaps and procedures that specifically required procedural knowledge. In addition, when relevant issues are particularly complex, such as is the case with climate change, consensual knowledge scientific knowledge assumes a relatively high degree of authority and acceptance. Consensual knowledge not only legitimizes the outcomes of decision-making, but also the process that unfolds to achieve such outcomes. Gunnar Sjöstedt (2009) identifies the GATT/WTO regime as an example of how the neo-classical trade theory has provided direction to multilateral trade negotiations in the last 50 years. This theory, which argues, for instance, that all obstacles to the free exchange of goods and services on the world markets are to be eliminated, is acknowledged by brief references inserted into the treaty texts.

Another example is Provision 20 of the Johannes Declaration on Sustainable Development. The provision declares the commitment to ensure that women's empowerment, emancipation and gender equality are integrated in all the activities encompassed within Agenda 21, the Millennium Development Goals and the Plan of Implementation of the Summit. It can be argued that this provision has benefitted from the public discourse that was initiated by the suffrage movement at the end of the 19th century and beginning of the 20th century. Serving as an antecedent, the consensual knowledge on women's empowerment as a necessity for sustainable development has successfully debarred counter-arguments against Provision 20.

In this regard, several negotiation frameworks are dependent on their capability to "borrow" or "absorb" theoretical concepts and empirical models to build consensual knowledge that will accordingly give direction to the negotiation process. Consensual knowledge represents the common but specific understanding that parties have of the issues, and it subsequently defines the "tolerable window" for present and future decisions as well as the agenda and formula for functional, institutional, and bargaining interactions. Therefore, it can be argued that **negotiation frameworks are built on a system of multiple consensual knowledge**, which further highlight the strategic importance of the ability to influence the generation and systemic distribution of consensual knowledge. Serving as anchors, "negotiation lock-ins" can be established, which may increase the power of those who installed these anchors and at the same time impede the power of the others (e.g., market barriers established by "first movers").

5.3 Case Study: The IPCC and the Generation of Consensual Knowledge for Climate Negotiations

Negotiators and decision-makers on climate change issues are aware of their heavy reliance on science and research. This reliance opens new demands for accountability, as the lack of adequate knowledge management can distort existing social contracts. This section analyzes the IPCC process of generating consensual knowledge for climate negotiations. It highlights the power-based and systems perspective on consensual knowledge. Some of the analyses made in this section is based on the author's anecdotal experience as a chapter scientist, contributing author and informal reviewer of the Fifth and Sixth Assessment Reports. The IPCC was awarded the Nobel Prize in 2007 (shared with Albert Arnold "Al" Gore) "*for their efforts to build up and disseminate greater knowledge about man-made climate change, and to lay the foundations for the measures that are needed to counteract such change*" (Nobel Media AB 2014). The Nobel Prize Committee based its assessment on the scientific reports published by the IPCC over the preceding years, which had created an "ever-broader informed consensus about the connection between human activities and global warming" (Nobel Media AB 2014). While the prize confirmed the mandate not only of the IPCC, but also of scientific bodies providing policy relevant knowledge, it also placed them under more intense public scrutiny.

In the late 1970s and early 1980s, several scientific communities expressed concern about the potential severity of the increased CO_2 emission. The issue garnered political attention when the 1978 Carter administration sought to use domestic coal to solve the energy crisis, prompting the early forms of "knowledge diplomacy", in which evidence-based decisions are preferred, leading to various consultations with scientific communities. Increased public awareness following prominent environmental problems, such as the smog problem in London, the *Minamata*-sickness in Japan and the *Waldsterben* (death of forests) in Germany have further motivated national governments to listen to the scientific communities, as restrictive actions require a new basis of legitimacy.

The establishment of the IPCC by the United Nations Environment Programme (UNEP) and the World Meteorological Organization (WMO) in 1988 was a direct response to the increasing number of climate-change-related studies as well as to the increasing demand for the knowledge needed for policy-making. The IPCC is designed to provide necessary assessments of findings within fields and disciplines relevant to climate change, and to elucidate multiple linkages between possible policy actions and desired outcomes (Haas 2010 p. 186). As Evan Schofer (1997) as well as Gili Drori *et al.* (2006) referred to in relation to international organizations, the IPCC's aim includes the broad development of societies that promote the rationalization of decision-making.

The IPCC produces assessment and special reports by engaging thousands of scientists and experts worldwide, with recognized expertise and competence, who have been nominated by their national governments, appointed by the IPCC secretariat after it considers geographical balance, and have committed themselves to participate in the assessment-writing process without any form of financial remuneration. This voluntary participation of scientists reflects the shared set of normative and principled beliefs, which provide a value-based rationale for the social action of community members (Haas 2010 p. 186). The IPCC does not conduct its own studies, and its reports are constituted to reflect the international standard of scientific knowledge within a given time period.

While a mandate was given to the IPCC to provide reliable and policy-relevant scientific inputs through its various reports, national governments are able to influence the types and scope of scientific knowledge codified in the "Summary for Policy-makers" (SPM) during the IPCC approval session. Because this SPM is formally used as the basis of subsequent climate negotiations, most countries are keen to block certain technical information in the SPM that opposes their political interests or that can limit their future leverage. For example, Brazil, as a major bioenergy producer, is usually highly "vigilant" when wordings on bioenergy in the SPM are at stake, as are the United States, France and Austria regarding wording on nuclear energy. In the approval session of the Third Working Group of the IPCC in April 2014, several countries, for example China, India, Saudi Arabia, Iraq, South Africa, Ecuador and Bolivia, were "unhappy" with some chapters that used country classification based on income in the context of climate mitigation. These countries argued that the presumed political consequences of this reference include the "thinning out" of the "historical responsibility" of developed countries, because mitigation actions will no longer be defined by past emissions, but by the current country income.

Most importantly, due to the reliance on science and research when understanding the consequences of climate decisions, most climate negotiators are required to be experts on climate science. In various cases, IPCC lead authors are often later (or were earlier) invited to be members of country delegation in UNFCCC negotiations. Negotiators need to understand the scientific evidence as well as the methodologies used to come up with certain policy scenarios. The disparity among regions is further reinforced by the fact that most developing countries from Asia and Africa, without an extensive pool of scientific experts in their countries, are unable to send "experts" as negotiators. While some developing countries often hire Europeans or Americans as consultants or expert-members of their delegation, others are dependent on their diaspora, which is usually based in developed countries, while some have opted to tap "patronage countries" from the "North" to gain access to scientific knowledge.

When providing a synthesis of available literature, the IPCC assessment reports concentrate on peer-reviewed materials. Peer-review is one of the mechanisms to guarantee the reliability of the scientific literature (see Brembs et al. 2013). However, non-peer-reviewed materials, such as reports and data from international organizations, national governments and their agencies, and international non-state organizations—also called "grey literature"—are included in IPCC reports if these materials are deemed to meet the high standards of quality demanded by the lead authors of the reports. Nevertheless, the existing inequalities among regions are also reflected in the scientific literature, with scientists and experts from Africa, Latin America and Asia heavily relying on non-peer-reviewed materials, due to their lack of access to journals, which mostly require subscription fees. In addition, scientists and experts from developing countries have less opportunity to publish their works in peer-reviewed journals due to language barriers and the tendency of journal editors to reject papers that mostly cite grey literature.

At first glance, the analysis of the IPCC working process suggests that while there is political motivation to engage scientific experts from, for instance, Africa and Asia, most climate knowledge is generated in North America, Europe and Oceania. Among the 830 coordinating lead authors, lead authors and review editors of the Fifth Assessment Report (AR5), 301 (36%) are from developing countries (including countries labelled as economy-in-transition, such as Russia, Poland and other EU members from Eastern Europe). The regional distribution of all AR5 author teams further support this claim: Africa (8%), Asia (16%), South America (6%), North America, Central America and Caribbean (28%), South West Pacific (7%), and Europe (34%) (see IPCC 2017).

On a practical level, more than 69% of the authors and expert reviewers of the AR5 are from the "Global North". This implies that members of epistemic communities from the "North" have more opportunities to influence international and domestic climate policies. As they are able to "*illuminate the salient dimension of issues from which the decision-makers may then deduce their interests*" (Haas 2010 p. 187), they increase the likelihood of convergent behavior of states that "listen" to experts who are mostly from the Global North. This condition is structurally driven and path dependent, and the question is whether "better" alternatives are available. The scientific works assessed in the Fifth Assessment Reports of the three Working Groups were, with few exceptions, peer-reviewed as a requirement for them to fulfil the necessary scientific quality standard.

In addition, because the three IPCC Working Groups mainly consider peer-reviewed journal articles published in English, there is a rather high proportion of cited articles published in Anglo-Saxon countries. While some lead authors are willing to cite non-English sources, it is difficult for reviewers to assess the quality of the content cited, because only abstracts of non-English studies are provided in English. Therefore, the content will most likely not garner support from other lead authors and expert reviewers in the multiple draft-writing (e.g., zero, first, second order drafts) and review stages, and will be unlikely to be included in later versions of the report. As radical constructivists contend, the use of English language in IPCC outputs implies a socially constructed "material reality" that corresponds to the social circumstances under which descriptions, terminologies and concepts of English-speaking nations were inherited, which further alienates the applicability of concepts and models to peripheral countries (see Knorr-Cetina & Mulkay 1983; Woolgar 1988).

Moreover, the bias against journals not published in English is among others already institutionalized as defined by the current journal ranking system. The quality of academic journals is claimed to be determined by its impact factor, which serves as proxy to reflect the place of a specific journal within its field. The impact factor suggests the level of prestige of being able to publish one's article in that specific journal. It reflects the average number of citations to articles published in science and social science journals. Because of this, some journals adopt editorial policies to maximize their impact factors, including the "by invitation only" policy under which senior scientists, who tend to come from, or work in, developed countries, are invited to publish "citable" papers to increase the journal impact factor (see Moustafa 2015).

Because publication in peer-reviewed journals has become the major criterion of research evaluation in Anglo-Saxon countries and most of Europe (which determines one's competitiveness in attracting funding or employment), additional grants and resources such as language editing are provided by universities and research institutions to boost their publication performance, not to mention the professional grant application writers and consultants usually hired to improve the success rate of grant applications (e. g., the Euro 80 billion worth EU Research and Innovation Program called *Horizon 2020*). Journal articles often become both outputs of successful grants and inputs, simultaneously indicating a scholar's or research institution's ability to attract grants. In comparison, most researchers from developing countries, who are usually employed in universities, tend to spend most of their time teaching and fulfilling administrative tasks. For example, according to numerous interviews, Filipino scholars in Philippine universities are confronted by their heavy teaching load (an estimated 80% of their time, not including administrative tasks) as well as the lack of research grants (and experience in preparing for grant applications) which prevent them from doing substantial and internationally competitive research. Furthermore, most of the research done by local scholars is limited to local topics, which further limits the attractiveness of their research for international journals. In addition, there are usually fewer financial and structural resources available to support scholars in most developing countries to write peer-reviewed journal articles published in a language other than their own native language, not to mention their lack of access to expensive journals, which should be cited for their paper submissions to be accepted.

Moreover, journals published outside Europe and the Anglo-Saxon region and which are published in English are most likely to publish articles written by English native speakers or Europeans with excellent language skills or who can afford language-editing services. Furthermore, many of these journals have editors originating from Europe or the United States to save the cost of the necessary English-language editing (see Belcher 2009). In many cases, peer-reviewed journals do not offer language-editing services and the acceptance of submitted journal articles is therefore significantly dependent on the quality of English language. In cases where language-editing services are offered, researchers will need to bear these costs, adding further barriers to publication for non-English speaking researchers from Asia, Latin America and Africa. In addition, most journals often cater for certain methodologies and theoretical approaches when accepting submitted articles. Expertise on specific methodologies, such as modelling, or specific "theoretical schools" (e.g., Chicago school, Copenhagen school) is often established over a long period of time and is usually concentrated in a few research institutions and universities in Europe and the United States, promoting the tendency that articles written by scholars affiliated with these few institutions are preferred.

In the various AR5 meetings of the different IPCC working groups, this issue has often been raised not only by scientists from developing countries, but also by the IPCC secretariat. Efforts were made, for example, to ensure North–South balance by nominating and appointing Coordinating Lead Authors (CLA) of the different chapters, with one CLA coming from a developing country. Nevertheless, this CLA from a developing country needs to be equally qualified and there were often some shortcomings in this regard. In addition, the appointment of the CLAs, lead authors and chapter reviewers also took into consideration geographical balance. However, some CLAs and lead authors during the AR5 writing process expressed the view that some appointed authors from developing countries who provided no input in the writing process, nor participated in sessions for various reasons, were nevertheless included in the list of authors. The geographical representation reflected on paper is not always effectively translated into the process of building consensual knowledge.

The experiences from the IPCC AR5 writing process conceptualize a type of knowledge diplomacy demonstrated when synthesizing knowledge on climate change. It allows the convergence of shared notions of validity: intersubjective, internally defined criteria for weighing and validating knowledge in the domain of expertise (Haas 2010 p. 186). In addressing various shortcomings, the IPCC requested the InterAcademy Council (IAC) to perform an independent review of its processes and procedures, after which the IPCC adopted various changes to its processes and procedures. However, this resulted in even higher workloads for those involved in preparing the assessments and further becoming dependent on developed countries, which provided "chapter assistants" to CLAs from their countries (Schulte-Uebbing et al. 2015). As such, it becomes apparent that generating knowledge on climate change can also be a question of analyzing power relations and power asymmetries.

Because the IPCC experiences suggest that acceptable scientific quality standards for IPCC reports are dependent on what is currently "best" available, the IPCC process unintentionally reproduces or even reinforces structural imbalances and unequal inputs from regions in the generation of knowledge. While the transboundary character of climate change demands a global response, as codified through a global agreement, for example, solutions are dependent on regional and local actions, and decisions need to be coordinated and best practices exchanged between actors coming from various regions. Therefore, a transregional perspective towards knowledge generation and deployment and towards power relations in climate change negotiations can be helpful in understanding how knowledge becomes a subject of climate diplomacy.

5.4 Interim Conclusion: Convergence of Knowledge Frameworks as Opportunities and Risks—The Preceding Step Towards Global Convergence

While effective knowledge diplomacy is generally contingent on balance of power in terms of generating and applying knowledge, the critical assessment of the IPCC process as a type of knowledge diplomacy to address climate change has demonstrated that additional mechanisms are still needed to address certain legitimacy gaps of knowledge diplomacy. Such legitimacy gaps include the unintended reproduction of structural inequities due to structural imbalances that are systemic in nature and are therefore difficult to correct. While there are intentions to resolve these gaps, additional efforts are inevitable to "compensate" disadvantages. However, the ontological baggage of the concept of "compensation" aggravates these legitimacy gaps, because compensation connotes the admittance of guilt, which complicates any reform process.

Solutions need to be found and there are already conceptual impulses that can be further explored. For example, while the generation of knowledge relevant for climate negotiations is still concentrated in the "Global North," peripheral regions can still circumvent knowledge gaps by focusing on sub-frameworks of climate negotiations that address specific topics relevant to climate change. Furthermore, with regards to the norms, rules and practices institutionalized by the SDGs, developing countries are increasingly discovering regional bodies and forums through which to gain access to needed technical knowledge. Therefore, a further examination of regional knowledge generation and the way it promotes transformation towards sustainability in the global level would be beneficial.

6 The Systems Perspective on the Transformation Towards Sustainability

From the systems perspective, the ultimate '*Angst*' of societies is the occurrence of 'dystopian' system rupture, which can be the outcome not only of unexpected events leading to the elimination of principles that bind actors together (e.g., identity), but also by purported solutions that create further 'horrendous' events. System ruptures are not only linked with natural hazards such as earthquakes, hurricanes, floods, and pandemics (such as the Ebola outbreak), but also with collapsing national governments and regimes, for example following the outbreak of a popular revolt after a state-sanctioned escalation of violence (e.g., Mubarak's Egypt and Ghadafi's Libya) or an outside intervention (e.g., Saddam Hussein's regime in Iraq following the US intervention).

Assuming that transformation can be either a response to a collapsed system or a preventive effort to avert collapse, this chapter starts by looking at the cognitive aspects of transformation in terms of experiences. In addition, this chapter discusses how energy security reifies transformation, which highlights a major context of the transformation process towards sustainability. Moreover, a special focus on countries with emerging economies will be presented. This selection is set against the backdrop of these countries experiencing multiple parallel transitions that are, to a significant extent, mutually competing. The contextual predicaments (problem contexts) of these countries will be used to understand how impulses for change are both a threat and an opportunity, whereas the difference between a threat and an opportunity is inherently defined by how the states choose to respond and manage changes. Finally, this chapter will suggest policy objectives when addressing, for example, contextual predicaments related to energy security.

A. M. Hernández, *Taming the Big Green Elephant*, Globale Gesellschaft und internationale Beziehungen, https://doi.org/10.1007/978-3-658-31821-5_6

Much of the debate about system ruptures and disruptions is about the importance of an actor (e.g., a country) or an entity (e.g., a bank) to a constructed social system. More illuminating questions emerge as new issues tend to modify existing contexts, agencies, and audiences both in positive and negative terms. What will most likely happen to the system if an actor or entity fails to fulfil its function? Is the cost of helping this actor or entity to get back on track smaller or more tolerable than the expected cost of system ruptures? How do decision-makers assess both the monetary and non-monetary costs of actions and non-action? How will the system 'reboot'?

Moreover, other questions pertain to how changing power configurations allow individual actors and entities to gain preference when reshaping the existing order. Is the stability of the global system and order threatened by China as an emerging superpower? Or is China the necessary agent of change by assuming global leadership that can bring motion (and growth) to a global system that has stagnated and has become fragmented? How will China's ambitious development campaign, the *Belt and Road Initiative,* which is backed by 40 billion US dollars from the New Silk Road Fund, 900 billion US dollars from China's Development Bank, and 100 billion US dollars from the Asian Infrastructure Investment Bank (see Menon 2017; Philipps 2017) define international relations, particularly after the withdrawal of the United States from the TPP and the Paris Climate Agreement? How will sustainable low carbon transformation be embedded in China's long-term policy objectives? Or is sustainable development the long-sought-after principle that can bring China to the next level?

In addition, linking the discourse on system ruptures to transformation processes remains a huge challenge. While it is widely accepted that changes are imminent if not necessary for growth or even survival, it is a huge conceptual and methodological challenge to decide whether an impulse (or a trigger) is part of this imminent system change that ensures the relevance and functionality of the system, or if it is already the first step in a system rupture. Furthermore, there is a diversity of meanings and ramifications of such an impulse. For example, the massive decrease in coal prices could be an impulse to enhance the expansion of renewable energy. But for some coal-dependent countries such as Poland and the Czech Republic or other regions within a country such as Kentucky, West Virginia and Ohio in the United States, this impulse is not only a significant threat, but it mobilizes radical agents who have now found new channels to reverse other advancements such as in welfare and human rights.

6.1 System Transformation and Human Cognition—Power and Identities

The conceptualization of system transformation needs to begin by looking at the cognitive and behavioral aspects of changes (see Brewer & Stern 2005; Messner et al. 2013). Collectivities that represent people respond to changes by transforming themselves. While some experts, such as Anthony Robbins (2006), equate change with growth, others highlight 'distress' when addressing transformations (see France 2013; Benson et al. 2014). For example, Karl Polanyi (2015) reiterates that a "great transformation" is the result of a collapse of the system. Furthermore, as this chapter argues, **a transformation process is likely initiated when (at least) one of the three streams (policies, polities and politics) experiences at least one of the following symptoms of cognitive vulnerability:** ***disengagement, dismantling, disidentification, disenchantment and disorientation***.

Disengagement pertains to the loss of connection to the specific environment, whereas 'connection' means a sense of purpose and personal growth. For example, when the decline of profitability of coal technology had led to a significant loss of employment, private households may have experienced disengagement as they were forced to seek employment in other places or in other sectors, leading to the loss of their routines and comfort zones. Arguments that the renewable energy sector means new jobs do not mean anything concrete for those previously employed in coal mining industries, not only because of differences in qualifications, but also because of how they have built their identities.

Dismantling refers to vulnerability during transitions, where temporary structures are not able or are no longer able to provide the perception of stability and security. Vulnerability connotes the loss of control and autonomy. For example, the transition period that foresees a shift in the dominant use of fossil fuels to renewables may produce 'disturbing' vacuums due to a lack of experience around how challenges caused by transition can be effectively addressed. For example, the *Energiewende* in Germany led to a significant increase in electricity bill prices for private households leading to a perception of inequity, as most industrial and business entities were exempted from newly introduced levies to support the renewable energy sector.

Disidentification occurs when roles and status are no longer able to provide the same purpose (such as stability and security) that they have provided in the past, leading to a loss in the meaning of identities. The sense of belonging defines identity and its loss brings distress. Addressing a loss of identity requires an understanding of the 'stories' and narratives behind such representations. Through this, a more adequate understanding of how identities can be open or resistant to changes can be achieved. For example, when owning gasoline-intensive SUVs is no longer seen as a status symbol, individuals will have the chance to see the impractical aspects of owning such vehicles. This requires, however, the decoupling of status from emission rich cars by producing luxurious cars with less emissions.

Disorientation is the absence of perspectives or direction. A sense of purpose is translated into actions, leading to the achievement of goals. Actions, however, require a plan or a (road)map that serves as personal leverage for beliefs and behavior. Without a map, a sense of less certainty of actions will more likely arise. Disorientation reinforces insecurity, because caveats such as norms and values that have served as orientation for social relations often lose their meanings. For example, local communities affected by massive job loss may witness increased level of antipathy towards policy-makers, who are unable to effectively address the causes of job loss. Discredited policy-makers can become the targets of various forms of violence.

Depending on how inclusive (collaborative or positive-sum) or divisive (competitive or negative-sum) the decision-making processes are, some actors may, for example, use 'dogmatic' arguments to assert their interests, appealing to issues of higher political priority. For example, in 2010, vindicating the dominance of the market logic in German policy-making, five German car companies, supported by the then German Federal Minister of Economy Michael Glos, argued that lowering the threshold value for CO_2 emissions from cars to 120 grams per kilometer by 2012 will lead to elimination of jobs in Germany (Schulte von Drach & Schätzl 2010). In this case, 'change agents', such as environmental NGOs and social groups, are deprived of effective arguments, because as non-economic entities, they are unable to provide compelling arguments using market logic. **Resistance to changes that are compelling is not constructive, especially when the 'success' of this resistance is merely defined by the perception of power.** Depending on how effective groups protecting the interests of conventional energy are, implementing energy policies conducive to climate protection goals requires **a broader consensus-building framework where consensus will not be merely dependent on the inability of dissenting actors to organize resistance**, but rather on the notion that cooperation provides more gains (compared to non-cooperation).

Nevertheless, when considering the power resources available to societal groups, the successful transformation of systems needs to find ways to integrate the interests of societal groups irrespective of their power resources. In addition, identities may exist that do not correspond to that of the system. Often, it is assumed that a given system reflects one identity and that changing systems imply equally changing identities, which is misleading. For example, coal mining is deeply embedded in the social identity of many local communities. While the majority of the communities are enthusiastic in welcoming new job opportunities that are created through renewable energies, climate policies that aim to reduce emissions by closing coal mining pits are then perceived as targeting their communities, hence, their identities.

Therefore, energy policies promoting non-conventional energy also need to address the narratives behind these identities, which will require more time and different types of interventions or incentives. There is co-evolution within and between levels, processes at multiple dimensions and levels unfolding simultaneously (Hughes 2009), and these levels often have different paces of transformation (Braudel 1958). These processes may compete or reinforce each other, making decision-making more complicated and requiring a well-orchestrated integrated approach. As Frank Geels and Johan Schot (2009: 22) argue, transitions come about when processes link up and reinforce each other. This focus on the linkages of processes deviates from technology-push approaches, which can be found in punctuated equilibrium frameworks.

6.2 System Transformation—'Grasping' the Context of Sustainable, Low-Carbon Transformation

The historicity of the transformation process needs to put the focus of analysis on the meaning of collected decisions or actions for the system. From the system perspective, historicity can define and provide an understanding of self-driving dynamics as well as '*fatal synergies*.' Various subsystems such as governance, institutions, and civil society may have deficiencies which, when analyzed separately and individually, can be tolerated by the system in specific contexts (and not in others). However, when these deficiencies are combined over the course of the transformation process towards sustainability, they produce additional obstacles that pose additional conceptual and methodological challenges. For example, the lack of channels to formally and materially integrate political opposition into government, combined with structural inequalities in society and the high upfront costs of renewable energies, may increase the need for the security of sophisticated facilities and high-tech equipment (further increasing the costs of maintenance), as the lack of political integration into a specific context may have created and reinforced the use of paralegal means, wherein attacking expensive facilities becomes an effective means of leverage.

System transformation, as a non-linear process, is not self-evident and not self-enforcing. When changes remain unmanaged, shocks may lead to partial or total collapse of the system, thus, producing vacuums and uncertainty. Its management requires quantifiable indicators that could serve as 'benchmarks' to eventually decide on adjustments in priority areas. Quantification, in turn, necessitates appropriate procedures of data collection and content analysis as well as a clear definition of the units of analysis (components, sequences or complete models), encoding categories and the interpretation of data to determine patterns. Nevertheless, quantitative methods, which aim to eliminate coincidences, are confronted by the historicity of the transformation process leading to conflicts.

The difficulties in analyzing sustainable low carbon transformation processes are similar to the difficulties in analyzing historical events, with the distinct purpose of deriving lessons for other cases. Often, the comparison of different country cases with the intention of learning from the 'successful' (often developed country) in order to 'help' the less successful (often developing country) is trapped in the 'center-periphery' dichotomy, limiting the acceptance and even applicability of these lessons. Mainly following '*the center is capable, the periphery is not*' evolutionary narrative is frequently misleading, at least in its methodological function. As natural sciences may suggest, the individuality of historical events often undermines the scientific validity of historical analyses due to limitations in the generalizability and applicability of results. In addition, comparing the low carbon transformation of countries is often rejected due to claims of Eurocentric perspectives (see Fisher & Green 2004; Najam 2010).

Furthermore, when 'green technology' becomes the dominant agenda of a country's foreign policy, green technology is inevitably geo-politicized as it indirectly changes existing power relations between relevant countries, making it predominantly a mere subject of power games. For example, applying lessons from the "successful" German *Energiewende* (energy system transition) to developing countries is often regarded by critics as "a new form of imperialism." The German *Energiewende* was officially introduced after the Fukushima reactor incident in 2011 and was vindicated by challenges brought about by the Russian-Ukrainian conflict. It defines changes in Germany's policies and initiated the transformation of the country's energy system to a system with the increased use of renewable energies and energy efficiency technologies (see Ciuta & Klinke 2010; Die Bundesregierung 2016). Because the *Energiewende* is regarded as a result of the geopolitical and energy security discourse in the country, its application to other (mainly developing) countries which did not undergo the same discursive process implies latent coercion. As such, as claimed by Felix Ciuta and Ian Klinke (2010), the *Energiewende* has increasingly dominated and framed the debate on the domestic and external policies of Germany and has eventually defined the German geopolitical narratives. Germany has become a major proponent of renewable energies and energy efficiency technologies in various international forums, whereas, countries with a high dependence on conventional energies are pushed to the 'periphery' through these forums. In addition, Germany's international aid support, both from government agencies as well as from German NGOs, has increasingly become related to the promotion of renewable energies in developing countries, while the narrative "climate protection is sustainable development policy" has increasingly defined foreign and developmental policies (BMZ 2015).

6.3 Transition, Transformation and Leapfrogging—Sustainable Low Carbon Policy Priorities in Countries with Emerging Economies

Academic and political discourses about the transitions, changes and transformations of energy systems have been revived in the assessment of measures to mitigate climate change. The Fifth Assessment Report of the Third Working Group, in summarizing their results, claim that stabilizing greenhouse gas (GHG) concentrations will require large-scale transformations in human societies, from the way energy is produced and consumed to how the land surface is used (Clarke et al. 2014). Furthermore, Thomas Bruckner *et al.* (2014) raise the issue that the energy infrastructure in most developing countries is still undeveloped and not diversified. Therefore, energy system transformation will involve incremental costs. Nevertheless, while this may be the case, especially in the Least Developed Countries (LDCs), other developing countries such as Brazil, China, Turkey, India, Mexico, Indonesia and the Philippines do have the technical and financial capacity to deploy renewable energy technologies (La Viña 1997; van Asselt & Gupta 2009; Rong 2010). In fact, not only is China currently the biggest investor in renewable energy, the deployment of renewable energy technologies is also a top policy priority of the government (Feng Wang & Haitao Yin 2010; Mathews & Hao 2013).

There is a consensus that the any mitigation regime will need to address the requirements of energy systems, particularly of developing countries with emerging economies. As the UNFCCC (1992) identifies, preventing dangerous anthropogenic climate change will only be feasible with substantial emission reductions below the business-as-usual case in developing countries (Jakob & Steckel 2013; Jakob et al. 2014). While this consensus also recognizes that the sustainable low carbon transformation of energy systems of developing countries should not hamper economic development, the international community is fragmented when it comes to how economic development should define the emission reduction goals of developing countries (Najam et al. 2003; Winkler et al. 2009b). Some governments argue that developing countries have the right to emit all necessary emissions for the sake of economic development (Zhang & Cheng 2009; Lotfalipour et al. 2010; Ozturk & Acaravci 2010). Others argue that although developing countries should be given the right to emit emissions, the level of emissions should not surpass the average level that was reached by developed countries. Michael Jakob *et al.* (2014) suggest that reducing emissions in developing countries will require a fundamental break in the historical correlation between economic growth and GHG emissions.

The prospect of decoupling economic development from GHG emissions has become a popular notion. As Fred Pearce (2016) points out in an article in The Guardian, the International Energy Agency of the OECD has reported that global CO_2 emissions from energy-related activities have not risen since 2013, staying at 32.1 billion tons even as the global economy grew. As Pearce suggests, this implies the possibility of decoupling emissions from economic activity. This decline was led by China and the United States, which are the two largest emitters and which both registered declines in emissions of about 1.5 percent. Moreover, the decoupling is mainly attributed to the higher pace of increased deployment of renewable energies. The Frankfurt School of Finance and Management confirms that in 2015, more than twice as much money was invested into new capacities for renewables than into new power stations using fossil fuels. In addition, for the first time, the majority of this investment was in developing countries, with China responsible for 36 percent of the total global investment (Pearce 2016). Decoupling is therefore already on its way and has reached a stage in which renewable energy deployment has become self-enforcing.

6.3.1 Leapfrogging of the Developing Countries—A Way Forward?

An argument was presented by several governments in developed countries and by epistemic communities that developing countries should not follow the "dirty" economic development path made by developed countries. Instead, these developing countries should take advantage of 'leapfrogging', which is both more economical and lower in carbon. Technologies and financing models are already available to enable leapfrogging. However, while this is the case in theory, such a transformation of the global energy system would impose considerable additional costs on developing countries (Jakob et al. 2014). If developed countries decided to shoulder the costs of energy system transformation, a further question would be raised about the channels used to transfer the money. The first notion that usually comes into the picture is that this transfer is a development aid. There is a separate debate about developmental aids and how providing aid to developing countries is often defined by self-serving interests rather than the wish to support development (see Tandon 2008), not to mention the so-called "climate rent curse" through which financial inflows negatively affect the recipient's long-term economic performance (Jakob et al. 2014). Yash Tandon (2008) further argues that the conceptual understanding of developmental aid is dominated by the notion that the donors own the process. This notion would lead to additional conflict cleavages in any energy system transformation process where, unlike in the donor-recipient dichotomy, developing countries expect to own the process.

The concept of leapfrogging was originally developed in the field of industrial organization and economic growth. The main idea behind the concept is that small and incremental innovations are the responsibility of a business company wanting to dominate the market. As of more recently, the concept of leapfrogging is used in the context of sustainable development and energy system transformation, particularly for developing countries, as a theory of development which may accelerate progress by skipping inferior, less efficient, more expensive or more polluting technologies and industries and move directly to more advance ones. As José Goldemberg (1998) argues, by avoiding the mistakes made by developed countries, developing countries can circumvent environmental and socially harmful stages of development and do not need to follow the polluting development trajectory taken by industrialized countries.

Major challenges for the leapfrogging of developing countries to attain a sustainable and low-carbon energy system include the issues of knowledge/technology transfer and capacity-building, that is, how to help developing countries to build up new infrastructure, acquire knowledge and technological expertise, and formulate relevant policies in line with sustainable development and climate protection. Furthermore, the leapfrogging country needs to build an 'enabling environment' that includes good governance and the availability of local technical expertise that fosters innovation from within (see Zerriffi & Wilson 2010). Innovation should also be supported by an innovative culture, whereas innovation is the ultimate mantra of local entrepreneurship (Carraro & Siniscalco 1994; Lundvall et al. 2011). Innovation should also serve as the major driver of production and consumption that cuts across various sectors of the economy.

Another major challenge for leapfrogging to attain sustainable and low-carbon energy is how social inequalities can be reduced. Susan Cozzens and Raphael Kaplinsky (2009) note that innovation and inequality co-evolve, with innovation sometimes reflecting and reinforcing inequalities and sometimes undermining them. Innovation is only seldom seen as a potential driver of social and economic justice. Mitigation measures, including deploying renewable energies, could contribute to further deficits in public acceptance because of adverse distributional impacts. However, leapfrogging to attain sustainable and low-carbon energy, when managed properly, can also pose opportunities for reducing inequality. For example, individuals with lower incomes tend to be more dependent on public transportation than individuals with higher incomes. While leapfrogging is possible and feasible, both technologically and financially, why is it that some countries still opt to follow the "dirty" path? This book argues that **the technological and financial feasibility of leapfrogging is not enough to entice the shifting of energy systems**. There is a need to address transformation as a process of decision-making. Which requirements should be fulfilled, from the decision-making perspective, to enable the switch?

6.4 Problem Context: Energy System Transformation in Developing Countries with Emerging Economies

What makes the energy system transformation of countries with emerging economies different to those of developed countries and other groups of developing countries? Why is it worth analyzing? What is the value of learning the specificities of energy system transformation in developing countries? If no substantial emission reduction schemes will be relevant, developing countries are expected to follow China's carbon-intensive economic growth pattern and this will make any drastic emission reduction in developed countries unable to achieve the 2 °C target agreed by the international community (IEA 2011). As Michael Jakob *et al.* (2013) observe, households from selected developing countries with an income of the average European household exhibit a carbon footprint similar to that of the average European. In addition, richer households, for example from India, Indonesia and the Philippines, have considerably higher carbon footprints than poorer ones (Jakob & Steckel 2013; Seriño 2014) which suggests that income is the most important driver of variations of emissions over time and between households (Jakob et al. 2014). As such, the demand of developed countries that developing countries substantially limit their emissions, implies limiting the increase of income.

Moreover, putting pressure or even blaming the developing countries to the failure to reach the 2 °C target is not only unfair (La Viña 1997; Beyerlin 2006; Penetrante 2010), it is also counterproductive. For once, developing countries will not accept any emission reduction scheme which limits income growth. As carbon-intensive energies have traditionally met energy demand, there is a close correlation between human development and GHG emissions (Costa et al. 2011). No developed country has managed to achieve high levels of economic development without having crossed a threshold in final energy consumption of approximately 40 GJ per capita (Steinberger & Roberts 2010; Steckel et al. 2013). Expecting or even forcing developing countries to refrain from following the same path under business as usual conditions is not only inequitable, it is also not feasible (Najam et al. 2003; Winkler et al. 2009b).

Nevertheless, as already highlighted in this book, it is possible to decouple emissions from economic development. Leapfrogging can be viable in developing countries, particularly for those with emerging economies, if they are not left alone with the issues related to the transition processes. As Michael Jakob *et al.* (2014) argue, in a similar way to developed countries, per capita emissions in developing and emerging countries will only stabilize or decline at comparatively high income levels. Therefore, the question that needs to be asked is how developing and emerging countries can transform their energy systems before reaching high income levels. Leapfrogging will require substantial financial support to cover the incremental costs.

Developing countries with emerging economies will need to simultaneously manage various transitions in a shorter time frame than the developmental trajectory taken by developed countries. As increased income will call for social, cultural, and other types of changes that are beyond the economic sphere and developing countries with emerging economies will need to employ a holistic approach in policy-making. For example, these countries tend to experience more intense changes in demography, such as massive urbanization as job opportunities become more concentrated in bigger cities, internal migration and displacement as new infrastructures will require the relocation of communities, and some qualifications becoming obsolete as new types of expertise are demanded, among others.

In addition, developing countries with emerging economies tend to act as experimental grounds for new technologies that require maturation. As new technologies are deployed in non-OECD countries, new conflict cleavages arise as these technologies clash with existing cultural and societal conditions. Technological development is often driven by a specific societal need and deploying this technology to a different society will require significant adaptation. With no prior practical experience available, the current state of progress of deploying new technologies in these countries remains bleak, a "black-box" dilemma. Public acceptance of technologies is a process that can take time and forcing the deployment of these technologies without substantial public acceptance will not only make the deployment costlier, the deployment will remain uncertain as minor problems can easily be transformed into reasons to cancel deployment.

6.5 A Systems Perspective on Energy Transitions—Energy Policy Objectives for Countries with Emerging Economies

For any given energy policy objective, decision analysis is useful when analyzing the multiplicity of policy options and of policy evaluative criteria and can help policy-makers assess the trade-offs and synergies associated with one or a combination of policies. Countries with emerging economies will need an integrated outlook on policy objectives. This section analyzes the challenges of energy policy-making in countries with emerging economies. It also provides recommendations for how these challenges can be resolved.

6.5.1 Policy Objective 1: Increase Energy Access and Energy Efficiency by Reducing Income Gaps Between Urban and Rural Areas

One major barrier for many developing countries in ensuring universality of energy access is the gap between urban and rural incomes. A common trend in these countries is rapid urbanization, where opportunities are concentrated in cities (Kusno 2000; Grubler et al. 2012). Providing energy, such as electricity and the required infrastructures in rural areas, is often not cost-effective due to the lack of possibility of economies of scale. Under current conditions, private investment in energy projects in rural areas will be in most cases limited, because these projects are not expected to yield profits. Therefore, providing energy in rural areas will most likely involve certain amounts of subsidies. With many low-income households living in rural areas, government subsidies will be needed to avoid high energy costs being forwarded on to low income households. While subsidies are often seen as not sustainable and inhibiting innovation, rural communities will continue to require government assistance to ensure that rural areas will have access to a similar quality of living as in urban areas.

From the estimated 1.2 billion people (17% of the global population) who did not have access to electricity in 2013, more than 95% of this 1.7 billion lived in countries in sub-Saharan Africa and developing Asia. In China, 1 million people are without electricity. In India, 237 million people (19% of the total population, 26% of the rural population) do not have access to electricity (IEA 2015). The Philippines (21 million), Indonesia (49 million), Bangladesh (60 million), Vietnam (3 million), and Pakistan (50 million) are the other countries identified as EAGLE or N-11 countries with emerging economies (IEA 2015) with a huge portion of their population still without access to electricity. Providing access to these people will most likely lead to an increase in the national level of emissions but will at the same time promote the achievement of certain sustainable development goals (e.g. gender equality, affordable and clean energy).

In addition, the massive inflow of new residents into megacities will often require upgrades in energy infrastructures in urban areas to catch up with the increasing energy demand. The trend towards urbanization, now standing at 3.7 billion people, is expected to accelerate and double by 2050. Furthermore, 96% of all urbanization by 2030 will occur in developing countries (Runde 2015). This shift will create additional challenges to providing food, water and energy. Policies that aim to ensure a reliable energy supply will cut across other priorities. Paradoxically, in many developing countries, there is often the sentiment that cities tend to be major recipients of government spending, successfully competing for funds that could have been spent in the peripheries. In many developing countries, this sentiment fuels separatist movements, right and left-wing extremism, and further exacerbates social distrust.

Moreover, as cities become more congested, the more difficult and cost-intensive it will be to expand existing infrastructures. It becomes more difficult for governments to prioritize other policies than those that support, for example, energy efficiency. For example, in a highly populous city with a very high housing demand, governments will most likely prioritize providing affordable housing rather than low-carbon housing. Energy efficiency programs offered by governments such as tax cuts for solar panels on roofs will most likely experience resistance from the society as such programs are seen to favor high-income households and real estate property owners. In addition, with a very high demand for rental housing, property owners will have low or no motivation to refurbish in order to meet energy efficiency goals, as they will not personally benefit from such investments. Low-efficiency rental houses and apartments will easily find tenants in highly populated urban areas.

Governments in emerging countries need to identify a scenario that addresses the dilemma of policies that aim to increase energy efficiency and policies that aim to expand energy access. Incentives and other types of market instruments are available to avoid policies promoting energy efficiency from obstructing the state's ability to effectively provide other welfare services. Furthermore, policies should focus on co-benefits and synergies as promoting energy efficiency can lead to additional benefits such as job creation, health improvement, pollution control, entrepreneurship and local community development.

6.5.2 Policy Objective 2: Capacity Building for Energy Transitions

It is widely accepted that there is no one-size-fits-all strategy for capacity development. Efforts need to be tailored to the specific attributes of a given continent, region, country, and even sub-national region (Armitage 2005; Mytelka et al. 2012). The energy system transition of developing countries in the context of climate mitigation usually implies the need to build local capacity through technological, knowledge-based and financial transfer. Such a transfer intends to help developing countries in building local expertise and financial capacity to deploy necessary technologies for low-carbon development (see WBGU 2009). Michael Jakob *et al.* (2012) estimate these financial transfers will reach almost 400 billion US dollars by 2020. They further claim that this amount is comparable with many developing countries, raw material exports. In this regard, many experts argue that the rationales behind raw material export might be assumed in financial transfers leading to similar negative effects related to the so-called 'resource curse' or 'Dutch disease' (van der Ploeg 2011; Kornek et al. 2013). In addition, Ulrike Kornek *et al.* (2013) observe that countries that receive the highest transfers are generally confronted with low institutional quality as indicated by deficits in the rule of law and the control of corruption. Therefore, policies related to capacity building in the context of energy transition should adequately address their negative effects on local state-building processes.

Furthermore, to ensure the contextual relevance of their strategies, the ownership of capacity building as a process needs to be taken up by the recipients.

Capacity building often involves technology or knowledge transfer which implies the existence of the dichotomy of "donor" and "recipient", where the donor tends to be developed countries and the recipient developing ones. There is a need to find a concept for the capacity building of developing countries which is not based on the current OECD-Development Assistance Committee (DAC) vocabulary and their definitions of aid, which have also been adopted by the United Nations (see Tandon 2008). Furthermore, the new concept of technological, knowledge-based and financial transfer in climate mitigation should not be an extension of the 0.7 percent Official Development Assistance (ODA) model, which was adopted by the United Nations in October 1970. Public discourse about the responsibilities of developed countries towards developing countries has used this ODA model as a yardstick for measuring developed countries' commitment to the advancement of developing countries (Tandon 2008). The new concept of capacity building in the context of climate mitigation and low-carbon energy system development needs to be based on equal partnerships and cooperation.

Thus, technology transfer to build the capacities of developing countries to achieve successful energy transformation needs to have the perspective of an asymmetrical cooperation, where interdependence between the donor and the recipient defines the "mutual" relationship of the donor and recipient. The differing and often non-comparable commitments of developed and developing countries do not need to hinder cooperation. **Only when the donor is dependent on the success of realizing the objective of the transfer can the recipient occupy an equal rank and therefore co-own the process.** In addition, when the receiving country can reciprocate the transfer, the transfer ceases to involve the recipient as an object of generosity or charity. The benefits of energy transformation in developing and emerging countries should be clearly documented in order for developed countries to recognize that their efforts benefit them as well, and not, as many experts see it, that the capacity building of developing countries with financial commitments to developed countries is unfair to future generations of developed countries (Schelling 1995).

Reciprocity is therefore a key element that policies need to adequately address. This means that any international program that aims to support energy transformation in developing and emerging economies should also encompass provisions for reciprocating technology or knowledge transfer from the developing country to the developed country. For example, technology transfer projects tend to involve experts from developed countries coming to developing countries to build capacities. Reciprocity should promote experts from developing countries coming to developed countries not only for training purposes, but also to allow them to build capacities, for example, in developed countries with aging infrastructures. This would allow experts from developing countries to gain experience as well as international recognition. When the direction of technology transfer is two-way, additional benefits can be gained. Energy policies should therefore build on partnership and cooperation that aims to achieve mutual gains rather than mere developmental aid, which is often driven by vested interests and donor ownership of the process. Developing countries should also seek cooperation with other developing countries through South-South partnerships.

6.5.3 Policy Objective 3: Reduce the Environmental and Human Health Impacts of Energy System Transformation

A critical outlook on energy system transformation in countries with emerging economies includes a critical analysis of measures that are considered solutions. Renewable energies, such as biomass, may undermine food security and/or biodiversity. Wind mills may, for example, negatively affect ecosystems including bird migration routes (see GWEC 2010; Wiser et al. 2011). The necessity of expanding smart grid systems enormously may pose health problems to the population living near the high-voltage grids (see IRENA 2013). In addition to mitigation costs and potentials, the deployment of energy-related mitigation measures will depend on a variety of other factors that relate to broader economic, social and environmental objectives, driving policy choices and decisions in the relevant sectors. The implementation of energy-related mitigation measures can have positive or negative effects on these other objectives. To the extent that these side-effects are positive, they can be deemed as co-benefits. But if these side-effects are adverse and uncertain, they imply risks. Co-benefits and the adverse side-effects of mitigation measures, the associated technical risks and uncertainties, as well as their public perception and technological spill-overs can significantly affect investment decisions, individual behavior, and policy-maker priorities.

Developing and emerging countries' energy policies need to look at the technical, social, economic, and environmental risks of relevant measures, such as the deployment of renewable energies, the expansion of smart grid networks, etc. Particularly in liberalized energy markets, governments have to ensure that standards are met and that companies will take responsibilities when risks materialize.

6.5.4 Policy Objective 4: Accelerate the Rate of Energy-Related Technological Change

Innovative policy plays a central role in accelerating the rate of energy transformation (see Markard & Truffer 2008b; Mission Innovation 2015). It is fundamental in stimulating and managing the processes of knowledge generation, application, dissemination, and feedback that are involved as the transformation process unfolds. Policies supporting the supply of innovations or the development of technologies include investments in R&D, intellectual property protection, laboratory and testing infrastructure, training and skills, university-industry collaborations, formal and informal mechanisms of knowledge exchange, technology roadmaps to guide the direction of innovation, and financial incentives such as tax credits for private investment.

A major challenge to coming up with effective innovation policy is that it cuts across various jurisdictions. Policy instruments promoting investments in R&D are often addressed by the ministries responsible for research, technology, education or trade & industry. Intellectual property protection is addressed by the ministry responsible for justice, peace and order; training and skills by the ministry for education. Financial incentives are most likely provided by the ministry for finance or the ministry for economy and trade. In addition, in most developing countries, universities and other centers of higher learning tend to be run by private institutions and enjoy a significant degree of autonomy, as such establishing collaborations between universities is difficult if not unwanted, because of the highly competitive environment. Cooperation frameworks between universities and industries are also often not yet evident in developing countries, especially when local industries tend to cater to foreign markets.

Energy system transformation must be complemented by integrated policies that seek to promote innovation to effectively absorb the contingencies of technological change. Energy system transformation also needs to be complemented by expanding the domestic market, as innovation is a direct result of solving local problems. When a country's industrial sector is raw material export-oriented, which is typical of most developing countries, the required impulses that trigger innovation tend to be far-fetched.

Furthermore, policies should address cultural elements of technological change. Innovation is often the result of technological development responding to concrete societal needs. When innovation is exogenous, it might clash with local culture. For example, Ilse Ruiz-Mercado *et al.* (2011) note that the adoption of improved biomass cook stoves, which will not only improve the health conditions of households but also reduce emissions from developing countries, will depend on public acceptance. For many indigenous communities in Mexico, fire is an important symbol, and cooking practices that limit seeing the fire will tend not to be used. Therefore, policies that aim to promote technological change need to assess the level of public acceptance of the deployment of various technologies. Technological change requires an 'innovative culture' where the society is receptive to innovation.

6.5.5 Policy Objective 5: Coordinate and Implement International and National Energy-Related Policies

Globalization poses both risks and opportunities to a country's energy system transformation. A major instrument to promote energy transformation is direct, foreign investment in the energy sectors in developing countries. However, because imminent issues in many developing countries revolve around providing access to electricity in rural areas, foreign direct investment remains unattractive for foreign investors as these fields do not promise significant returns. Furthermore, foreign direct investment may also pose risks to the country's energy security goals.

Furthermore, as a vast array of agencies and structures are responsible for various aspects of energy sector governance, the national government requires a high level of institutional capacity to coordinate and facilitate interactions between the government agencies responsible for various elements of the energy sector. Many developing countries are confronted with political fragmentation in which government positions have been allocated based on the political interests of political parties and groups and not on technical expertise. This leads to crucial government agencies having other interests beyond their formal mandate. In addition, government agencies often compete for limited public resources.

Moreover, due to their wide-ranging and often cross-sectoral responsibilities, many government officials lack detailed knowledge of sustainable energy technologies, their economics and financial requirements, and alternative mechanisms for their effective support (see Ochs et al. 2015). There is also often the lack of a significant capacity dedicated exclusively to energy issues, often making it difficult to coordinate with other government officials and to provide the updated information necessary for renewable energy planning. Finally, the transformation of energy systems requires clarity in final decisions in the energy sector and that this final decision will be continued by subsequent governments or administrations. Thus, a broad general political consensus is inevitable.

6.6 Interim Conclusion—So What? Where Do We Go from Here?

This chapter highlighted the historicity of transformation processes, it focused on the cognitive aspects of transformation towards sustainability and explained how these aspects frame the set of possible actions. In addition, this chapter explained the systemic contextuality of policy-making by focusing on countries with emerging economies as well as on energy security as a major policy goal. The contextual predicaments (problem contexts) of these countries were used to understand how impulses for change are both a threat and an opportunity, whereas the difference between a threat and an opportunity is inherently defined by how the states choose to respond and manage changes. The chapter ended by recommending policy objectives when addressing, for example, contextual predicaments related to energy security.

From a systems analytical perspective, there are many reasons why developing countries, particularly those with emerging economies, find it difficult to commit to a low-carbon and sustainable energy system. As highlighted in this chapter, these reasons include the lack of a holistic and integrated perspective due to a failure of re-visiting existing assumptions, which was highlighted in chapter 4. In addition, after chapter 3 provided the understanding of how structural imbalances are unintentionally reproduced due to existing critical junctures, this chapter further explored the specificities of these imbalances by analyzing how human cognition reinforces such imbalances.

Finally, this chapter problematized the failure to consider co-benefits in calculating the costs and benefits of low carbon energy policies. As argued in this chapter, the possibility of decoupling emissions from economic development and some of the trade-offs between energy security and climate protection could be resolved, both of which are integral aspects of sustainable development. The policy objectives presented in this chapter use the premise of such decoupling to advance transformation towards sustainability.

7 Theoretical Models, Case Studies and Simulation Games as Knowledge and Decision Tools

The methodological challenges identified by this book reflect the limitations of or the constraints on the ontological conceptualization of transformation towards sustainability due to complexity and uncertainty. This complexity is exacerbated by the inevitable contextualization of sustainable, low-carbon transformation, where there is the need to find ways to assess and understand the political, economic, cultural, technological and environmental context from many analytical and governance levels, degrees and scales of causalities as well as making use of insights from these contexts to draw up lessons for others. The context, as reflected by socio-technical and socio-linguistic narratives, not only defines power relations between agents (e.g., between change agents and *status quo* agents), but also constitutes the audience as codified by social contracts.

The **historicity challenge** of sustainable low carbon development is driven by the inherent connection of the past to the present and future. Because historical events are usually analyzed in retrospect and as 'finished products,' the empirical value of historical analyses is defined by what has already happened. For example, the *life-course* analysis focuses on the overlaps between individual experiences and those coincident in history within specific structural, social and social contexts (e.g., changes in government policy) (see Elder et al. 2003; White & Klein 2007; Mayer 2009). As such, questions that are formulated in historical analyses tend to depict closed processes.

As the theory of path dependence implies, decisions made in the past limit the set of possible present and future decisions (see David 1988; Arthur 1994). Therefore, analyzing the historical components of current and future policies, governance structures and human behavior can only be useful for the analysis of transformation processes when the relevance of these historical components to the present and the future can be established and understood. However, as it will

A. M. Hernández, *Taming the Big Green Elephant*, Globale Gesellschaft und internationale Beziehungen, https://doi.org/10.1007/978-3-658-31821-5_7

be evident in the case study chapters in this book, arguments of historical inevitability based on formulating examples of historical contingency of how different choices could have led to different consequences may be misleading, because of the inability to test the occurrence of 'alternative paths'. The comparison of a 'real' development with its version in an 'alternate universe' has limited empirical value due to its highly speculative character. Therefore, due to the historicity of case studies, interpretations of cause-and-effect relations can only be tentative, and they need to be regularly revisited and corrected.

While 'learning from history' is intuitively accepted, there are limitations to the significance of history for studying the present and the 'futures,' primarily because the 'formalization' of historical analyses constantly needs further development. Charles Tilly (1987) identifies deficits in *formalization* in historical analysis as important factors in understanding the limitations of the value of historical analyses. Formalization requires the *conceptualization*, *measurement*, *modelling*, and *estimation* of historical events. However, as Charles Tilly (1987 p. 20) further claims, formalizing historians have devoted little of their ingenuity to the statement of an historical question as a problem susceptible to a formal statement (conceptualization), to the organization of evidence in a standard, comparable form (measurement), to the formal statement of an argument concerning the expected pattern of a phenomenon (modelling), and to matching models to evidence in order to see how the model fits (*estimation*).

Scholars working on sustainable, low-carbon transformation will need to ensure such formalization, which will very likely require multi- and interdisciplinary approaches and expertise. For example, conceptualization is likely to be conducted by social scientists with comprehensive and integrated knowledge that would allow the establishment and validation of concepts, labels, terminologies, and notions. Conceptualization needs to identify and justify the boundaries and scopes of the subjects of the analyses. It will also need to accommodate competing historical narratives. In addition, measurement and modelling will require scholars with expertise to identify and filter relevant data and information. These scholars should be able to simplify a complex system without losing empirical relevance. Additional scholars are needed to calibrate models and connect them to empirical reality to make them useful for decision-making. The assessment of the value of these models is often defined by how they can help provide policy-makers with the capacity to justify decisions.

Also relevant to the methodological challenge brought by path dependent historicity is the plurality of historical explanations due to limitations on accessing all relevant information. As many of the decisions were made in closed-door meetings, the assessment (process-tracing) of these historical events is confronted by a plurality of possible **explanations**. These explanations can be regarded as **storylines** that are composed of arguments supporting cause-and-effect relationships. This plurality is likely to be reproduced when establishing narratives and enduring issues.

In addition, analyzing the '*Gestaltungsmacht*' (shaping power) of historical events *vis-à-vis* the future is a contentious endeavor, particularly because of the need to clearly identify and trace the cause-and-effect relationships between factors and monitor the long-term developments that transcend spatial and temporal boundaries. Moreover, not only are there many ways of 'packing' a concert of historical events, there are also latent self-driving processes that can only be identified in retrospect, thus limiting the ability to predict the future. Another concern is that, particularly in sustainable, low-carbon transformations, there is not only one future caused by various possible concerts of historical events, but many futures that can be possibly caused by one or more concerts of historical events. Inserting the value of perspectives in the analysis brings the challenge that one future, say the sustainable, low-carbon transformation, cannot, under current conditions, be optimal for several actors, because they are confronted with other points of departure. As there can be more than one optimal future scenario, collaboration and coordination problems need to be resolved as forethoughts.

7.1 Scenarios as Methods of Analysis of Futures

The scientific literature on climate mitigation and low-carbon transformation relies heavily on the use of scenario methods. The complexity as well the temporal dimension of relevant processes and outcomes require decision-makers to use decision tools to structure decision-making. For example, the reduction of emissions will require years if not decades before substantial effects will be significant. As such, present decision-makers and their constituents will most likely not personally experience the outcomes of their decisions. Similarly, some positive effects might take place in other areas leading to these effects becoming intangible for those who would need to accept present burdens of actions. Nevertheless, as it is assumed that delaying decisions or even avoiding making decisions will lead to more 'painful' and, therefore, unacceptable costs, decisions are still to be made. Because decision outcomes can be theoretical at best, while actions are practical, tools are needed to bridge the gaps between these two analytical levels. Inevitably, decision-makers are required to formulate visions or goals that would frame decisions, or even set or change paradigms. Goals have a temporal dimension as they imply achieving a specific status in the future. Therefore, formulating policy goals will require tools that address the need to 'prepare' for the future.

Scenarios are constructed to investigate alternative future developments under a set of assumed or controlled conditions. Scenarios are instruments to help decision-makers cope with problem cases that are complex and uncertain. As Nick Hughes (2009) observes, recent years have seen a proliferation in the use of scenario methods to define low-carbon futures. '*Energy in a Finite World*' of the International Institute of Applied Systems Analysis is one of the first global studies that have used scenarios as a tool to assess future CO_2 emissions in the late 1970s (Häfele et al. 1981). The IPCC has used emissions and climate scenarios as a central component of its work as an institution that assesses climate change research. Working with authors and modelers, it has developed emission scenarios to be used for driving global circulation models to develop climate scenarios. The **SA90 scenarios** were introduced by Working Group 1 of the IPCC in 1990 (IPCC 1990).

Some questions that a scenario developer needs to address include how scenarios can provide insights not only into the integrated scope or description of the system being studied, but also how the system may have evolved into its current state and more importantly, how the system might continue to evolve, taking into consideration changing motivations and functionalities. What are the possible systemic effects of changes in the motivation and behavior of actors? This will most likely invoke the re-evaluation of various elements of the scenario, asking whether and how the actors could have decided to resolve these changes in a different manner. Asking these questions implies that scenarios have a normative undertone.

There are limitations on decisions based on scenarios. Scenarios often do not envisage changes in an actor's preferences, as well as in relations between *actors*. Therefore, scenarios are often limited to providing insights on behavioral change and paradigm shifts that are highly valuable in any analysis of transformation processes. Because choices will depend on temporal and spatial circumstances, humans can change their decisions when circumstances change. As Michel Godet (2000) argues, humans can be both rational and driven by the emotional faculties. While scenarios are often not able to capture these changes, they are also often designed assuming the rationality of decisions and actions. In addition, as circumstances change, human interactions also change. **Iterative actor interactions** imply changing coalitions, behavior and identities. Scenarios, therefore, need to be complemented by tools that support the anticipation of changes in an actor's preferences and relationships.

Furthermore, scenarios are often not able to properly address the **dynamics of social, technological, and economic change**. As social, technological, and economic changes unfold, new *issues* may arise, or old issues may gain a different meaning and significance, prompting the need to revise previous decisions. For example, the dynamics of change may imply a new importance on certain conflict cleavages that will touch on differences between actors in terms of their values and even ideologies. Because of this, the agreements and other outcomes of previously conducted bargaining games will require renegotiation and re-elaboration. In some cases, renegotiations will need to start by default. In other cases, particularly when the procedures of renegotiations were included in previous agreements, bargaining over new issues will be met by amendments or additional protocols to existing agreements.

One scenario is a collection of conditions and factors that jointly express a specific **storyline**. The storyline is heuristic in the sense that it employs an approach to problem-solving that does not guarantee or pursue 'optimality.' A scenario is an analytical instrument through which assumptions or 'stories' are made about the system under the conditions of limited knowledge and information. Therefore, a scenario inevitably pertains to a deviation from the 'optimal solution', as optimality presumes complete information. Nevertheless, it is not the objective of scenarios to present the optimal solution or the 'perfect story', but rather to look for a simple set of conditions sufficient to achieve immediate goals. This storyline serves as the *structure* in decision-making, limiting the number of possible decisions, thus, reducing indecisiveness. For example, the storyline of a scenario may highlight the necessity to adhere to human rights in present and future actions. It encourages decisions and actions by providing the scope of necessary actions and eliminating possible decisions and actions that do not correspond with the storyline. Nevertheless, the storyline, which is often a result of consensus-building processes, needs, as a normative approach, to be inclusive and should support the orchestration of various negotiation processes.

7.2 Theoretical Models and the 'Ideal Type'—A New-Old Method of Analysis

An ideal type can be regarded as a distinct type of model or scenario. One major difference between an ideal type and a model or scenario lies in its methodological implication. When a model or scenario depicts a historical or trajectory-based process, as is the case with the low-carbon transformation of energy systems, an understanding of purposes and the related causal interdependencies becomes necessary. Can properly identified indicators be adequately measured and interpreted? Are the benchmarks being fulfilled in order to achieve the predetermined purposes as the process unfolds? Is there room for tolerance and the adjustment of targets? Are there relevant self-driving dynamics that need to be addressed? The usage of ideal types allows researchers to focus on the individuality of actors, structures, issues, processes, and outcomes, without undermining the scientific validity of the results of analyses. It allows the 'systematic' management of indicators and benchmarks.

The 'ideal type' is a typological term most closely associated with the sociologist Max Weber (1864–1920), in which Weber claimed a better understanding (*Verstehen*) of historical development through ideal types (Weber 1976, 1985). Georg Simmel (1858 to 1918), a contemporary of Weber's, has adapted Weber's line of thought and developed a similar term called "categories," which are ideal types that not only serve as principles for constructing terms and concepts but as sources of theoretical knowledge (see Simmel 1908).

Similar to scenarios, ideal types can be identified as analytical instruments designed to strategically facilitate decision-making. Ideal types formulate hypotheses that are verifiable through the observation of empirical proceedings, providing resources for understanding patterns of actions, world views (*Weltbilder*), structural order and lines of development or trajectories. Ideal types are composed of basic concepts that define a "constructed world of ideas" or "idea constructs" (*Gedankenbilder*), with a distinct analytical functionality—to compare. Later, ideal types compel researchers to conduct a comparison between the constructed ideal type and the 'historical case.'

The ideal type is a normative and heuristic model or scenario that does not need to emerge from the experiences of a successful case (e.g., developed countries). It does not need to include optimally technical solutions, because it can also refer to a case where conditions are merely tolerated for pragmatic reasons. As George Jellinek (1900) suggests, ideal types can only be manifested as incomplete as they disregard one or more parts of reality, limiting the complex characteristics of the case. The divergence between the ideal type and the historical case serves as leverage point for formulating questions and constituting explanations.

The primary value of ideal types is to enable the formulation of relevant research questions that do not claim the ability to reproduce reality or to predict the future. An ideal type is not the 'perfect situation' or the utopia. While some critics argue that the ideal type tends to focus on extreme phenomena and overlook the connections between them, the ideal type developer can be flexible in designing the ideal type. In this book, the ideal type of the transformation process has been aligned to the stages of the negotiation process and assumes the perspectives of collective decision-making. Nevertheless, ideal types should also allow the construction of simple concepts and fictional conceptual extremes

(*Grenzbegriff*), which, however, can still occur in reality. Therefore, ideal types can contribute substantially when conceptualizing complex phenomena.

Ideal types are frequently also regarded as merely applying lessons from successful cases to less successful ones. European forms of democracy, governance, welfare systems and even climate protection schemes are frequently regarded as the end of the evolutionary process (Najam 2005; see Beyerlin 2006; Najam 2010), and this optimal stage is nothing else but the ideal type. This is, however, not how Max Weber and Georg Simmel define ideal types or categories. It is merely a methodological instrument of constructing ideas, a *Gedankenexperiment*. Moreover, as Alexis de Tocqueville (1856) stressed, although institutions or systems may be similar in some details, they cannot be reproduced as each system is unique. Therefore, borrowing lessons from one case to another, for example from a developed country to a developing country, will most likely involve incomplete information. Although there is still merit in looking at the evolutionary dimension of the development of developed countries, this is not the primary value of ideal types as depicted in this book.

7.3 Case Studies as Historical Analyses—The Value of Context

As a method of scientific inquiry and research, case studies have long assumed a well-established and prominent status in many academic disciplines (see McKeown 1999; Maiden 2004; George & Bennett 2007). While it is often thought that Frederic Le Play first introduced the case-study method into social science in 1829 (see Healy 1947), similar forms of case-study methods can be traced to earlier historical times, even to as early as Ancient Greece (see Lloyd 1992). Case study analysis involves a method that uses the up-close, in-depth, and detailed examination of an object of study (the case) in a specific spatial, temporal, cultural, social, political, and economic context. The usage of case studies in social science has often been chosen, particularly because of its descriptive value in explaining the outcomes or effects of variables. Nevertheless, the systematic further development of case study methods for the cumulative building of theories from various disciplines of social science is often neglected (see George & Bennett 2007).

A major point of debate on the viability or scientific validity of case study analyses as methods of scientific inquiry is the capability of formulating generalizations from single cases and applying these generalizations to other cases. Karl Popper (1959) has suggested the use of falsification or *falsifiability*, which forms part of critical reflexivity, as a test to determine the generalizability of the outcomes of case studies. He claimed that falsifiability defines the boundary between the scientific and unscientific, whereas that which is unfalsifiable is classified as unscientific. Based on this definition, the possibility that the outcomes of a case study are not applicable to other cases makes case study methods scientific.

7.3.1 Grasping Historicity and Plurality Through Case Studies—The Value of Perspectives in Knowledge Generation

What makes case studies interesting for this book is that it highlights the value of perspectives in generating, testing, re-testing, validating, rejecting and accepting knowledge. The use of perspectives in scientific inquiry ensures the acceptance of the pluralism of ideas, actions, normative systems and even of the concepts or understandings of fairness and justice. Such perspectives automatically provide a foundation for revisiting and the eventual modification of ontological concepts. While case study methods reiterate the uniqueness of each case, they are still able to identify and conceptualize patterns, as overlaps, cross-cuts and deviations contribute additional resources for further theory development.

Case studies of transformation processes highlight the relevance of historicity and plurality in understanding the process. Because each transformation process is unique, historicity can only be understood through the perspectives of actors, issues, and structures. Some scholars may even argue that when looking at the perspective of power (power-centric), interactions between actors can be explained and predicted. Perspectives can even define the sources and value of power. The case study approach takes a snapshot of a historical episode, assesses the interactions of various variables and comes up with historical explanations that can be used to explain other events, which could have happened in the past or the future as well as in other geographical areas.

As discussed in the introduction of this book, time is a central pillar in any transformation process. Case studies attempt to provide an account of relevant turning points, lock-ins, set-backs and leapfrogging moments that have occurred. A case study can only grasp one set of these events. Therefore, case studies are based on the presumption that there is a plurality of turning points, lock-ins, set-backs and leapfrogging moments, which are particularly dependent on perspectives. In order words, case studies most likely come from a specific perspective, depending on the preferences and purposes of the chosen actors and frameworks.

7.3.2 Procedures and the Design of Case Studies—The Role of Theoretical Models in Case Studies

The value of comparing case studies among themselves and comparing these case studies with theoretical models, here presented as ideal types, is measured by how these case studies and theoretical models complement each other and how differences can be understood and explained. In addition, the value of comparing case studies and ideal types can be measured by how complex contingent generalizations can be formulated to support decision-making.

In this book, looking for the evident complementarity of case studies and the ideal types will require the following assumptions:

- Ideal types serving as formal models and scenarios have storylines and concepts that can be tested using the case studies.
- Case studies examine how and why these cases overlap and/or deviate, while identifying the new variables or new interdependencies that are responsible for the deviance. As Alexander George and Andrew Bennett (2007) suggest, deviant or outlier cases may be particularly useful for heuristic purposes, as by definition their outcomes are not what traditional theories would anticipate. In addition, the ability to explain this deviance enriches theories, as they suggest new terrains that need to be further understood and explained.
- Case studies evaluate the causal mechanisms behind the correlations or patterns between variables that have been assumed by current theories. Case studies provide a controlling mechanism to check whether correlations are spurious or potentially causal, adding insights into how causal mechanisms can be newly understood as well as how new variables or the refinement of concepts can be specified and operated.

To ensure coherence in the chapters on case studies, the following design and procedures will be implemented:

7.3.2.1 Problem and Objectives

Each case study of this book aims to introduce a selection of the most important subjects and objects of analysis that will be used to examine the specificities of the transformation process. While the subject of the case study refers to the promotion or obstruction of the low-carbon transformation process, the following will be taken as objects of the case study analysis:

- Recent developments, particularly how the country refers to the Paris agreement and the Sustainable Development Goals (SDGs).
- The multiple entry points to SD, particularly climate mitigation and energy security
- The multiple goal-setting of policies through different scales and levels
- Challenges, barriers, trade-offs, *caveats*, gaps and risks
- Opportunities, synergies, and co-benefits
- System transition and/or transformation (multiple transitions) including socio-economic, cultural, technological, political, and demographic drivers and trends of change (e.g., GDP, population, migration, R&D)
- Path dependence and lock-ins: infrastructure, governance, behavioral aspects
- Enabling or hindering frameworks for behavioral and lifestyle change: policy instruments, non-mitigation policies, non-SD policies, state partnerships with private sector and civil society
- International cooperation and institutions
- Legitimacy: transparency, accountability and social inclusion in decision-making
- Innovation and technology development, diffusion and transfer

The analysis of these subjects will allow the inductive identification of new variables, hypotheses, causal mechanisms and causal paths that are needed to be understood in order to correct the paths or benchmarks of low-carbon transformation. In addition, the discovery of potential causal relationships may initiate new methods of quantitative and qualitative measurement.

7.3.2.2 The Execution of the Case Studies

The execution of the case studies as methods of scientific inquiry will be conducted through the following steps:

1. The formulation of the chronological 'narrative' that defines each chapter
2. The identification and assessment of causal mechanisms through congruence methods and process-tracing
3. A deviation analysis between the empirical case studies and the ideal types
4. A Comparative analysis of two selected (country) case studies (where applicable)

For each chapter, accessible primary literature, secondary literature and interview data will be used to construct a chronological 'narrative' that will structure historical inquiry. Such an inquiry aims to establish the values of independent and dependent variables.

In addition, the case studies aim to highlight the causal mechanisms that are substantial in promoting or obstructing low-carbon transformation. Looking at particular cases, it is argued that such causal mechanisms can operate only under certain conditions and that their effects are highly contingent upon interactions between factors. As Alexander George and Andrew Bennett (2007) claim, a causal mechanism may be necessary, but is not sufficient, in an explanation. In other words, effects or occurrences are brought about by a set or bundle of factors and configurations of mechanisms, through which the behavior of actors is defined. Nevertheless, the same bundle may constitute other effects or even counteract the effects when transferred to another country or even region within the same country. Therefore, one causal mechanism will be compared with another case study in the chapter as well as compared with the theoretical model (ideal type) to analyze how a causal mechanism offsets other causalities in some contexts and complements them in others (see George & Bennett 2007).

7.3.2.3 Congruence Methods—The Role of Process Tracing

The relevant theories are summarized through the ideal types. Linking these theoretical models to the case studies is an attempt to assess the ability of these theories to explain or predict the occurrence of events or factors. As Alexander George and George Bennett (2007) suggest, if the outcome of the case studies is consistent with the predictions of the theories, then there is the possibility that a causal relationship exists. Overlaps and cross-cuts can explain the applicability of theories to realities. In cases of deviations, explanations will be sought for these deviations, and hypotheses will be formulated about how these deviations will need to expand the existing theories. In cases of both congruence and deviation, factors and theoretical reasons will be taken into consideration to address how the hypothesized causes may be amplified, diminished, delayed or sped up (e.g., the self-fulfilling prophecy).

The next step pertains to the assessment of the possible causal significance of congruity (see George & Bennett 2007), where two questions will be asked:

- Is the consistency spurious or of possible causal significance?
- Is the independent variable a necessary condition for the outcome of the dependent variable and how much explanatory or predictive power does it have?

As suggested by Alexander George and Andrew Bennett (2007), spuriousness occurs when the observed congruence of the cause C and effect E is artificial because both C and E are caused by some third factor Z.

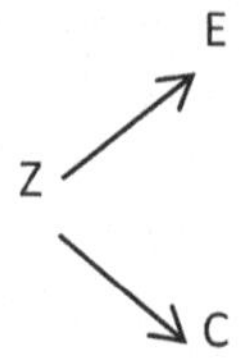

Alternatively, the putative cause C lacks causal priority if C is necessary for E, but C is itself only an intervening variable wholly or largely caused by a necessary prior variable Z. In this instance, both Z and C are necessary for E, but C has no independent explanatory value. The comparability of these country cases will be supported by the general questions formulated that link these *subjects of analysis* (see above) to the low carbon transformation process. The outcomes of the case studies will be explained by referring to the theoretical models (ideal types). Deviations will then be highlighted while providing theoretical and empirical explanations for these deviations. In many cases, the theoretical framework provided by the ideal types will need to be broadened to capture the major aspects of the historical elements. This broadening defines the analytical value of these case studies by allowing typological theorization.

To summarize, process tracing is a method that motivates one to take equifinality into account. This refers to an openness to the possible feasibility of alternative paths through which the outcome could have occurred. In addition, process tracing supports the possibility of mapping out one or more potential causal paths that are consistent with the outcome. As other cases are identified and tested, new typologies can be developed, leading to the further development of existing theories.

7.3.3 Theory Testing and the Implications of Case Findings for Theory and Practice

An analysis through case studies pertains to the testing of deductive theories. Theory-testing aims to strengthen or reduce support for a theory, narrow or extend the scope conditions or parameters of a theory, or determine which of two or more theories can best explain a case, type or general phenomenon (George & Bennett 2007 p. 112). As theories are tested using the data and information from the case studies, this testing may lead to an assessment that existing theories are not able to provide the necessary framework of understanding. Therefore, case studies can also initiate an inductive process of theory generation.

An analysis of deviations from theoretical models (ideal types) can link the gaps between deductive and inductive processes. As case studies uncover new or omitted variables, self-driving dynamics, hypotheses, causal paths, causal mechanisms, types of interaction, and network effects, the historical explanation that has been supported by existing theories can be improved upon (see George & Bennett 2007). This improvement highlights previously overlooked variables. In some cases, some of these new factors can be a highly significant factor that delays or obstructs the transformation process.

Developing or expanding upon existing theories through the analysis of case studies is an inductive process. Single case studies can produce observations that can initiate further questions, detect patterns (which can be supported by additional case studies as well as by other forms of scientific inquiry such as experiments), and hypothesize on tentative explanations of these observations. Hypothesizing can include distinguishing the subclasses or subtypes of existing typologies. In addition, 'concatenated' theories can be developed by dividing complex causal processes into specific component theories, or sequential stages, phases or episodes, as well by as focusing on the perspectives of identified actors (see George & Bennett 2007). For example, by focusing on actors' behavior and how it changes as the process unfolds will provide important insights into sequential stages and typical interactions and dynamics within a specific stage or episode.

As the deviance between the theoretical model and the case studies becomes clear and eventually leads to the specification of a new theory, generalizations can be achieved as to how the newly identified mechanism may play out in different contexts and how this new mechanism can be relevant in managing processes (George & Bennett 2007 p. 112).

7.4 Role-Play Simulation

Simulation as a method of scientific inquiry gained popularity in the 1990s as computer simulations were used to simplify and mimic complex systems. Considered the third pillar of empirical research, along with experiment and theory (see Drösser 1994), simulations are recognized as allowing the manipulation of complex systems that would be impossible, too costly or unethical to do so in natural systems (Peck 2004). Simulation can add to theory development and testing, can assist in formulating hypotheses and can limit the scope of which data are most important to gather (see Peck 2004; Gilbert & Troitzsch 2005).

This book does not intend to do computer simulations, but rather a so-called 'role-play' simulation. Particularly because this book highlights the aspects pertaining to functional, institutional, and bargaining interactions, a simulation was conducted using the role-pay format, where the participants were brought together to mimic interactions under conditions and parameters set by the game designer. For simplicity, when referring to simulations in this book, role-play simulations will be meant. In this book, more than 15 postgraduate students from the University of Technology in Kingston, Jamaica, participated in a role-play simulation. While the main goal of the simulation was educational, the role-play simulation was also designed to provide useful empirical insights into the analysis of sustainable, low-carbon transformation.

7.4.1 The Scientific Value of Role-Play Simulations

While the pedagogical value of role-play simulations in the classroom is less contentious, the value of the results from these games to scholarly research may require further discussion, if not further convincing of their scientific value. The engagement students as subject groups or 'human guinea pigs' may be perceived as self-serving and drawing empirical evidence from these games may be limited. Furthermore, most of the simulation games used in classes of international relations and political sciences depict complex cases such as climate change negotiations, where negotiators are required to have extensive institutional memory and technical expertise. While role-play simulations will mostly run for mere hours, these real-life negotiations occur for a longer period of time, with several preparatory meetings and consultations.

Nevertheless, the limitations of the empirical value of role-play simulations are not limitations *per se*, because there are distinct expectations and none of these expectations is to reproduce reality. Like computer simulations and models, role-play simulations aim to look at specific aspects of negotiations. Variables and parameters are adjusted to look at how processes are affected by such changes. In addition, particularly for this book, role-play simulations are used to identify interesting impulses that will then become subjects of further scientific inquiries. Moreover, some events in the role-play simulations are compared to the real-world and some theories and empirical statistics are drawn to explain differences. These explanations will inevitably test the relevance of existing theories and suggest improvement or even encourage the development of new hypotheses for further research. Therefore, in any case, role-play simulations can in actuality promote further theory development.

The purpose of conducting simulations as a method of scientific inquiry is to introduce the possibility of a new way of thinking about social processes that is difficult to understand through text books (Penetrante 2012). Based on ideas about the emergence of the complex mechanisms of interactions between actors, a holistic and meta-level analysis is made possible. Because simulation is akin to an experimental methodology, simulation can be executed many times to draw conclusions through analogies (Müller 1998). The variation of conditions through the researcher allows the exploration of the several effects of different parameters (Gilbert & Troitzsch 2005 p. 14).

7.4.2 The Procedures and Design of the Role-Play Simulation

This book puts forward the procedures and design of role-play simulations that highlight the process and negotiation outlooks on a complex system. As mentioned earlier, in role-play simulations, such as those conducted in this book, the dynamics of functional, institutional, persuasive and bargaining interactions initially depend on the parameters preconditioned by the researcher, who will define the initial point of behavior, based on assumptions made prior to the game. These assumptions are to be clearly communicated to allow the participants to understand the scope of the issues that are relevant to the game.

These assumptions can be formulated through the following steps:

First, **the role-play designer chooses an aspect of a complex system**. For example, in chapter 12, a cabinet meeting of the Jamaican national government on budget-planning under the conditions set by the International Monetary Fund.

Second, **the role-play designer identifies the problems and challenges he or she wants to be understood through the game**. The problems and challenges will define the agenda of the role-play game and will limit the scope of parameters. A game can be limited to a single problem. In chapter 12, the difficulty of consensus-building in achieving the budget plan will be presented as the over-arching problem. In this game, the agenda becomes clear, which helps structure the discussions of the participants. In addition, a game can also highlight several problems and challenges. Here, more than one problem was introduced, and these need to be resolved in parallel, in conjunction or in a specific order by the participants. In addition, each interacting participant has a different set of problems and challenges, where resolving them requires cooperation with other participants who may not have the same set of problems.

Third, **questions need to be formulated that will identify the parameters that will be manipulated**. For example, in chapter 12, one question refers to the effects of gender. In one group, all the members were females, in another all male, and in the other mixed. In addition, the parameters can be addressed by introducing control and experimental groups to allow direct comparisons.

Fourth, **the profiles of participants need to be prepared and distributed among the participants before the games**. These profiles need to include brief background information about the positions and interests of the country. These positions and interests are to be concretized in specific numbers (e.g., 20 million US dollars as compensation; or maximum 10 percent in GHG emissions by 2030). Each profile also needs to clarify the limitations of the negotiators. For example, a 'toxic' issue can be identified, where negotiators would need to walk away if this issue is involved. The profiles also include some instructions or recommendations as to how they should behave at the bargaining table: competitive, collaborative, avoidant, cooperative, emotional, arrogant, etc. to highlight the human factor at negotiations.

Fifth, **the role-play designer needs to plan the departure point of the game**. It may include requiring all participants to give a brief (ministerial) statement in a plenary session or to instruct each participant which bilateral or mini-lateral meeting he or she needs to prioritize first. These brief ministerial statements allow the participants to have an overview of potential partners and adversaries. This 'departure point' also serves as an 'ice-breaker', as participants will eventually 'warm up' during the game.

Sixth, **some flexibility and creativity should be encouraged in the game to allow the participants to come up with innovative and out-of-the-box solutions**. Furthermore, some provisions should be made leading to changes, for example, in the power or interests of one or more participants. In addition, while the simulation is running, the participants may choose to follow instructions and adapt to these parameters and frameworks, basing their decisions on certain rationalities and criteria. With the researcher intentionally changing the parameters and frameworks as the game unfolds, the effects of such changes should be observed, documented and discussed during debriefings. These observations would generate (simulated) data, which can be later compared to the data produced by other methodologies outside of the simulation (Penetrante 2012).

Seventh, **the results of the role-play should be clear and concrete**, such as forging an agreement with one or more counterparts, or 'sabotaging' and 'stalling' the negotiations. This allows closure in the game. Furthermore, the role-play designer needs to carefully plan the evaluation discussion and debriefing to encourage the participants to reflect on what they have experienced. The participants should also be asked about their feelings during the game, whether their expectations are met, whether they would like to change something about how they negotiated were they given the chance, or what struck them most during the game. Also, technical and logistical questions about the game should be encouraged. Are there some shortcomings in the game and whether there are things they would like to change about how the game was designed and conducted?

Eighth (and finally), **participants should be given a questionnaire or a written task that they need to do in few days after the experience has sunk in**. It should be submitted no longer than a week after the game. This questionnaire with both open and closed questions could include questions that can be useful for the researcher when assessing the empirical value of the results.

7.5 Interim Conclusion: Bridging Gaps Between Theory and Practice Through Knowledge and Decision Tools

The knowledge and decisions tools introduced in this chapter can be particularly helpful in identifying and assessing obvious and latent stumbling blocks to effective collective decision-making. These tools can also provide impulses for how these stumbling blocks can be addressed to allow actors to cope with them. Major challenges and barriers to low-carbon system transformation are diverse. The first step of bridging the gaps between theory and practice is to ensure the fluidity of the relationship between the two. Theory generation should be dynamic, as reality becomes more complex with the emergence of new issues that require multi- and interdisciplinary as well as an integrated outlook to grasp their essence and meaning. As challenges and barriers are identified by policy-makers (covered here by the case studies) and academes (covered by the theoretical models), their perspectives combine, and new insights can be found that can allow more effective measures to facilitate the transformation process.

It is the aim of this book that the theoretical models (ideal types), case studies and the role-play simulations will contribute to an understanding of how gaps between theory and practice can be bridged. The case studies and role-play simulations will be conducted to understand how low-carbon transformation processes can be facilitated. What kind of theoretical and practical knowledge is needed by decision-makers for dealing with challenges, risks, *caveats* and barriers related to sustainable, low-carbon transformation? How can these case studies and role-play simulations contribute to the establishment of general, conceptual models that can be helpful in designing and implementing policy instruments?

Ideal Types—Theoretical Models as Agent of Transformation Towards Sustainability

8

This chapter introduces the ideal types of a transformative policy pathway as the agencies of transformation: *democratic, authoritarian, institutional, activistic, technocratic or bureaucratic, and post-democratic*. Functioning as 'corridors' where transformation is facilitated, each of these ideal types of policy models may have distinct preferences regarding procedures of collective decision-making. These procedures are, for example, highly dependent upon existing path dependencies defined by how each ideal type tends to draw legitimacy in front of its audience.

A major purpose of this chapter is to 'unmask' the normative judgment of policy models, whereas the academic literature on transformation for example tends to link environmentalism with democratic governance (see Humphrey 2007). While democratic and authoritarian ideal types of policy pathways reflect the types of regime, institutional, activistic, technocratic and post-democratic ideal types of policy pathways can be considered as deviations, because they can be found in both democratic and authoritarian regimes. The separate analysis of these 'sub-types', or deviations, are significant as they suggest different dynamics in the transformation process, which will be illustrated through the integrated streams of transformation.

A. M. Hernández, *Taming the Big Green Elephant*, Globale Gesellschaft und internationale Beziehungen, https://doi.org/10.1007/978-3-658-31821-5_8

8.1 An Ideal Type of Transformation—The Democratic Policy Pathway

The ideal type of a democratic policy pathway pertains to a 'corridor' or a 'transformation roadmap' that identifies the multiple underlying stages, paces, episodes or parts of orchestrated transformation and the various conflict cleavages within a specific stage or episode. As figure 8.1 suggests, this integrated stream illustration identifies the relevant stakeholders for each stage and episode, whose interactions produce a collection of outcomes (both agreements and non-agreements). These interactions lead to the concretization and elaboration of the relevant issues and interests involved, allowing the integrated understanding of barriers into the transformation and eventually establishing possible procedures of resolution (Fig. 8.1).

Each box of the diagram represents a sub-system where various types of negotiations occur. Each of these subsystems have distinct actors, issues/agendas, processes, structures, and outcomes. Furthermore, the relationship between these inter-related subsystems may be complementary or competing. The different phases of negotiation—the opening of the process, agenda setting, the clarification of interests, generating solutions and ending the process—are reflected in the diagram (see Zartman 1978; Young 1991; Sebenius 1992b), suggesting the incremental nature of the transformation process.

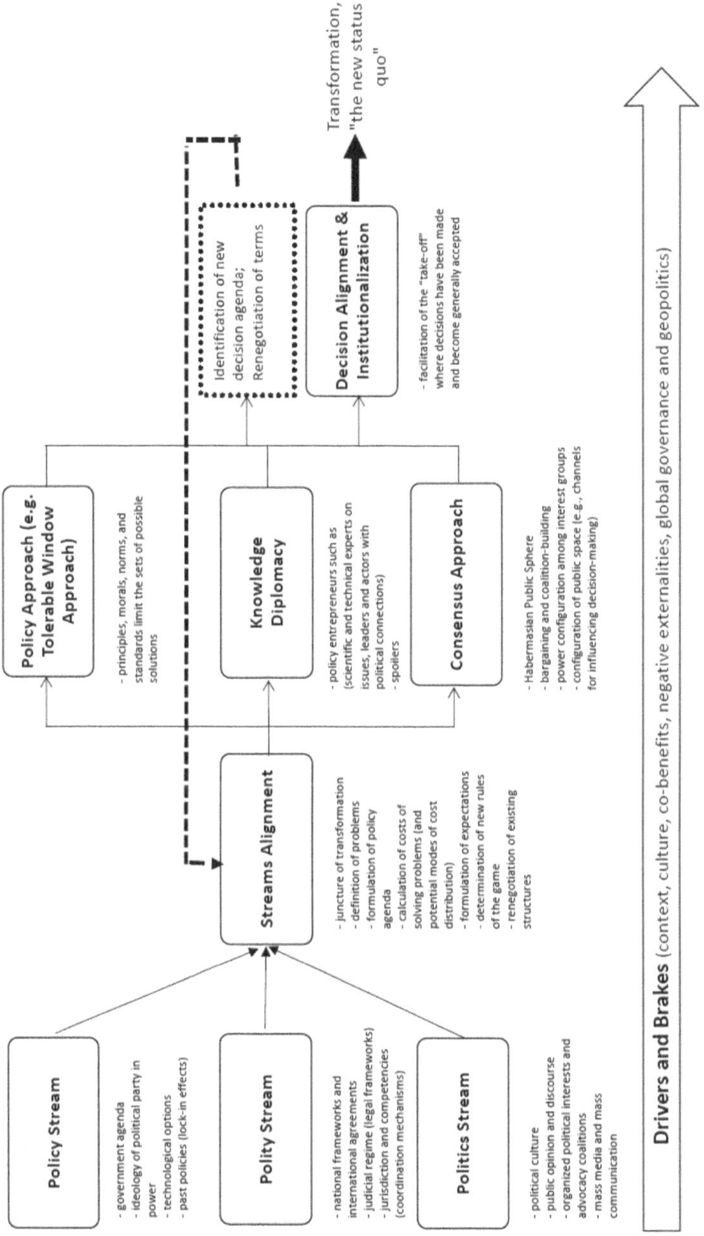

Figure 8.1 Integrated Streams of Transformation—An Ideal Type of Democratic Policy Pathway (own representation)

8.1.1 Context: Actors and Issues

Because the competitive advantage of political actors in democratic countries is defined by how they manage to align their political interests with public opinion or how they shape public opinion, bargaining interactions are important subjects of analysis in democratic pathways. In many cases, public opinion is not defined by a 'collective logic,' but by how arguments are made, communicated and exchanged. Moreover, public opinion is often heterogeneous and, in some cases, fragmented, as many societal groups with complementing and competing interests seek to claim representation of what 'society wants.' In some countries, universities and other academic institutions play a significant role in providing a 'public space' where various societal groups can meet and exchange perspectives.

The diagram highlights the role of drivers and brakes in either promoting or delaying the various negotiation processes. These drivers and brakes are frequently path-dependent, which can be properly addressed when transition costs are comprehensively identified and accommodated. Context, for example, is an important factor that needs to be discussed. It explains the occurrence of a decision in one setting while being unimaginable in a different setting. The Fukushima incident has, for example, led to policy shifts in Germany, yet not in other countries.

This illustration summarizes the different channels where a transformation process can be initiated: *policy, polity* and *politics streams*. Like in the first phase of negotiation, the left side of the diagram pertains to how transformation is initiated by the emergence of a specific challenge, which can only be addressed when changes occur. The policy stream refers to government agenda as significantly defined by the ideological preferences of the political party in power, the technological options available to implement policies, viable alternatives and the related costs of pursuing these alternative opportunities, and the locked-in policies that were made in the past. For example, a government may initiate new policies to implement electoral promises. However, the fulfilment of electoral promises may be dependent on how much change the constitution allows (e.g., *Rückwirkungsverbot,* or the principle of non-retroactivity in Germany).

In addition, a government may revise existing policies, for example, to adhere to international or regional agreements pertaining to climate mitigation measures. Although international agreements may contrast with a government's formal position, for example, in terms of climate mitigation, because expected gains will serve other, highly-prioritized political goals, the country opts for cooperation. For example, Poland and the Czech Republic, countries that are highly dependent upon coal energy and are staunch opponents of ambitious mitigation measures that relate to coal energy, have agreed to commit to more stringent climate protection policies to fulfil the agreements they have agreed to upon their ascension to the European Union (Darby 2014). Moreover, a reversal of past policies may be a product of crises and even of natural disasters.

The polity stream pertains to the national institutions in place. It includes the institutions responsible for monitoring, evaluating and verifying government actions. The politics stream is dynamic and is defined by the power relations between actors, as well as how existing polities serve as formal and material frameworks that allows weaker parties to cope with asymmetrical relations. The polities will then review if new policies are in accordance with the existing rules of the game while evaluating the resilience of the system. In most countries, new government policies most likely result in legal challenges from various sectors of the society. This possibility of check-and-balance promotes social trust; as weaker actors are assured that they have access to formal channels of decision-making.

Politics is the stream that refers to how public discourse will unfold and the various complementing and competing perspectives regarding concrete matters are mobilized and communicated. This stream also involves the expression of power games, as the societal actor that has most of the relevant effective resources will tend to dominate the discourse. Power resources do not only refer to money, but also to information, including how information is disseminated. For example, an environmental group with fewer financial resources could find more public support if it could present a more compelling argument based on scientific facts or at least the impression of serious evidence.

8.1.2 Agencies: Structures and Processes

The alignment of the three streams is a significant part of the transformation process, because it represents the critical juncture that determines subsequent steps. For example, as the policy stream identifies energy security as a political priority and agenda, the politics stream may agree on the importance of resolving threats to energy security especially when these threats to energy supply are causing higher energy prices. At this point, the polity stream may not have major reservations except when huge interventions are to be made by the state in the energy market that could reach the tipping point. In the streams-alignment stage, all the issues behind energy security will be collected and translated into the respective language of the different streams.

After the agreement on the agenda, the streams-alignment is followed by the identification of a mixture of approaches through which various interests are processed and evaluated. The process unfolds, leading to the combination of three possible approaches, where one approach can be more dominant than the others, depending on the importance of the issues involved. The policy approach involves the normative setting provided by past and present policies. While the government may set the limits of what is politically acceptable, for example, the same national government needs to adhere to these limits. It may define that changes in the country's energy system should not undermine the global competitiveness of the country. This normative setting may subsequently limit the financial burdens of transitions and legitimize financial incentives or tax exemptions to business and industrial companies affected by transition.

From the policy-approach perspective, the resolution of an issue needs to be within the boundaries set by pre-defined guard-rails that exclude the intolerable impacts of an emerging problem as well as any unacceptable measures used to address and resolve these problems. These guard-rails will eventually define and frame institutional interactions, in which certain policy principles need to be considered, no matter what policy area is involved. Such guard-rails can be directly defined by polities (e.g., the constitution) or be directly negotiated *ad hoc* by relevant actors determining principles that frame subsequent actions. For example, the "tolerable window" may include provisions for the protection of human rights, especially for indigenous communities.

8.1.3 Audience: Outcomes

The three approaches—the policy approach, knowledge diplomacy and the public consensus approach—interact in various forms by complementing, substituting or competing. The three approaches will eventually define the new social contract. In cases of stalemate, new agendas may be introduced, paving the way for new rounds of negotiations. Subsequently, decisions are achieved by following the conclusions of 'follow-up' negotiations. When decisions are then implemented, they call for the institutionalization of practices. Eventually, institutionalization will lead to new status quo and transformation that has followed a democratic policy pathway will have been completed.

8.2 An Ideal Type of Transformation—The Authoritarian Policy Pathway

Academic debate around environmentalism, particularly when addressing climate change, is increasingly focusing on the significance of the types of governance or regimes as agents of transformation towards sustainability (see Newig

& Fritsch 2009; Young 2009; Zelli 2011). For example, Derk Loorbach (2010) introduces transition management as a new governance approach for sustainable development. He highlights the impact of the long-term outlook on network and decision-making processes. While the definition of authoritarianism has become less contested in the last few decades (see Avritzer 1995; Altemeyer 2006), there is an emerging debate as to how authoritarianism relates to environmental policies. Mark Beeson (2010) argues that the intensification of a range of environmental problems reinforces authoritarian regimes, particularly in East Asia and Southeast Asia. To understand this presumed linkage between environmentalism and authoritarianism, the value of this policy model as an agent for sustainable, low-carbon development needs to be determined. Following Juan Linz's (2007; 2009) three major indicators of authoritarianism (the de-politicization of society, limited pluralism and a connection to a traditional mentality), this section focuses on how (environmental) policy-making in authoritarian regimes facilitates transformation towards sustainability.

In light of the various challenges that hinder effective and efficient climate policy formulation and implementation, arguments have been raised about the incapacity of democratic regimes to effectively respond to climate problems. A growing literature on 'authoritarian environmentalism' or 'ecological authoritarianism' has emerged, proposing a non-participatory approach to public policy-making and implementation to address environmental challenges such as climate change (see Doyle & Simpson 2006; Beeson 2010; Gilley 2012). On the one hand, how democratic countries can isolate environmental policies from other policy areas and purposely 'suspend' or 'limit' civil rights and liberties for climate protection is discussed (see Heilbroner 1974; Beeson 2010). On the other hand, several experts have focused on how stable authoritarian regimes can effectively respond to environmental challenges (Sowers 2007; Schreurs 2011). For example, the Chinese case study of Bruce Gilley (2012) provides a comprehensive analysis of how authoritarian environmentalism is practiced in China.

8.2.1 Challenges to Developing an Ideal Type of an Authoritarian Policy Pathway

In conceptualizing an ideal type of an authoritarian policy pathway, there are several challenges that need to be clarified. One significant challenge refers to the current diversity of existing authoritarian regimes. This diversity complicates the potential representativeness of this ideal type. There are different types of authoritarian regimes and these types can become even more complex and intangible when local cultural aspects enter the spectrum of analysis. For example, after differentiating authoritarianism from democracy as well as from totalitarianism, Juan Linz (2007; 2009) differentiates seven subtypes of authoritarian regimes: (1) bureaucratic-military; (2) corporatist; (3) mobilizing regimes in post-democratic states; (4) post-colonial; (5) racial and ethnic 'democracies'; (6) incomplete totalitarian and pre-totalitarian; and (7) post-totalitarian. Other authors have also introduced different subtypes of authoritarian regimes. While Wolfgang Merkel (1999) bases his subtypes on the holder of power (*Herrschaftsträger*), Armin Pfahl-Traughber (2004) defines the subtypes according to the legitimacy of authority. This book introduces **an ideal type of an authoritarian (environmental) policy pathway that focuses on interactions between actors and institutions as results of the interplay between agents, agencies and audience.**

Another challenge refers to the lack of a clear separation between authoritarian and democratic regimes. While there is common knowledge about how authoritarian regimes are to be distinguished from democratic regimes, certain democratic elements can still be observed in authoritarian regimes in the same manner as authoritarian tendencies can be identified even in the purportedly most democratic regimes. Because of this, it is difficult to clearly attribute environmentalism either to the democratic elements of an authoritarian regime or to the authoritarian elements of a democratic regime. Furthermore, democratic regimes may prefer authoritarian procedures when addressing specific issues, especially issues that can stir social division. In addition, constitutions of most democratic countries have provisions allowing limitations to political pluralism such as the implementation of martial law and the suspension of *habeas corpus* under specific conditions that can be easily 'abused' for other political reasons. Facing increased political opposition and the loss of political power, political leaders can "stage" different types of crises. Minor crises can be projected out of proportion for political gains. Moreover, as Bob Altemeyer (2006), a leading scholar on authoritarianism argues, a simple but significant majority can be mobilized to democratically elect a charismatic leader. He suggests that as time passes, the drive for authoritarianism may become stronger as this leader may see the need to suppress opposition to fulfil electoral promises. With the majority's support or with the passiveness (or ignorance) of the *silent majority*, democratic regimes can feel authoritarian, given their mandate to limit political liberties, for example those of minorities, and to suppress political opponents who can be easily cast as risks and threats to the stability of the system.

8.2.2 Advocacy, Social Movements and Authoritarian Environmentalism

A growing number of researchers are analyzing the role of social movements including NGOs in authoritarian states and many of them see environmental advocacy as a type often tolerated by these states (Sowers 2007; Mertha 2009). Especially because environmental groups tend to pursue interests that coincide with state policies of restricting rights and liberties of other actors such as business and industry, authoritarian regimes see their benefits when seeking inhibitions to the rule of law that will exclude corporate and business actors as well as other groups from participation in policy processes on the basis that they are mostly opposed to environmental action or that their existence is leading to environmental degradation (see Shearman & Smith 2007; Wells 2007; Gilley 2012). For example, while public policy processes in China are non-participatory, public policies involving environmental issues including air pollution or climate change have indeed engaged in an advanced level of societal participation (Gilley 2012). Nevertheless, broader public participation in environment-related public policies in China is limited to cooperation with state authorities (see Teng & Gu 2007; Lei 2009).

In response to the existing difficulties in forging agreements to effectively address the environmental challenges brought about by climate change, there is a growing literature calling for alternative public policy models. This growing literature often refers to the effectiveness of authoritarian policy models in confronting environmental problems. As the case study on the Philippines demonstrates, because the successful implementation of measures that would ensure environmental integrity implies restrictions, and because of civil society activism around environmental issues, there is an increasing preference towards authoritarian structures within democratic states (see Sowers 2007; Beeson 2010; Geronimo 2016; Pora 2017).

Most of the academic studies on authoritarian environmentalism address this policy model in comparison with democratic environmentalism. Many scholars argue that authoritarian environmentalism is more effective than democratic environmentalism in addressing the specific characteristics of environmental issues, including public ignorance, public irrationality, free-riding, the need for immediate action, the lack of resources to motivate social action and multi-stakeholder veto players (see Diehl & Gltsch 2001; Barrett 2003; Posner 2004; Arias-Maldonado 2007; Stone 2009; Beeson 2010; Gilley 2012). Authoritarian environmentalism refers to the concentration of state authority in executive institutions, which facilitates a rapid formulation and implementation of environmental policies through limitations on individual freedoms and the partial or total exclusion of social actors or their representatives (see Shearman & Smith 2007; Sowers 2007; Beeson 2010).

In comparison, democratic environmentalism pertains to a public policy model that spreads authority across several levels and agencies of government and where direct public participation from various groups of society is encouraged, if not guaranteed (see Holden 2002; Humphrey 2007; Gilley 2012). Participation takes place from the **upstream stage** (research and knowledge formation, problem identification, measurement and assessment, policy options identification and assessment) to the **midstream stage** (policy selection and formulation) to the **downstream stage** (policy implementation, leadership, monitoring, reporting, assessment and revision) (Birkeland 2005). In addition, participation occurs at different levels: low level (being targets of state propaganda, reporting public violations and attending informational meetings) and high level (legally-binding and deliberative forums, outright citizen autonomy, legislative sovereignty) (see Arnstein 1969; Plummer & Taylor 2004; Gilley 2012).

While authoritarian environmentalism is able to produce a rapid and centralized response to environmental threats and mobilize much needed public support, the society will most likely not always benefit from the outcomes of such policies, because of other emerging problems caused by the exclusion of key stakeholders in policy-making. Especially in many developing countries with weak governance and a highly fragmented society, the benefits of authoritarian environmentalism will more likely not contribute to sustainable development due to the authoritarian system's proneness to favoritism towards technocratic elites (see Shearman & Smith 2007). Looking at China, which is regarded as a positive example of the effectiveness of authoritarian environmentalism, opponents argue that the authoritarian model is causing poor policy formulation and poor policy implementation (Gilley 2012). Before summarizing the parameters of this ideal type, there is a need to clarify that this ideal type presupposes an authoritarian regime with continual stability and robustness, that is, an authoritarian regime that is deeply embedded in the society and in the culture of that specific country. The cultural integration of authoritarian rule is expressed through narratives and a psychological disposition of the constituents which are enforced by social institutions (see Adorno et al. 1950). Furthermore, there is a significant amount of the (formal) rule of law in such a regime that allows a degree of predictability of policies and political actions.

Figure 8.2 is the illustration of an authoritarian policy pathway that summarizes the steps typically taken as the process of policy formulation and implementation unfolds.

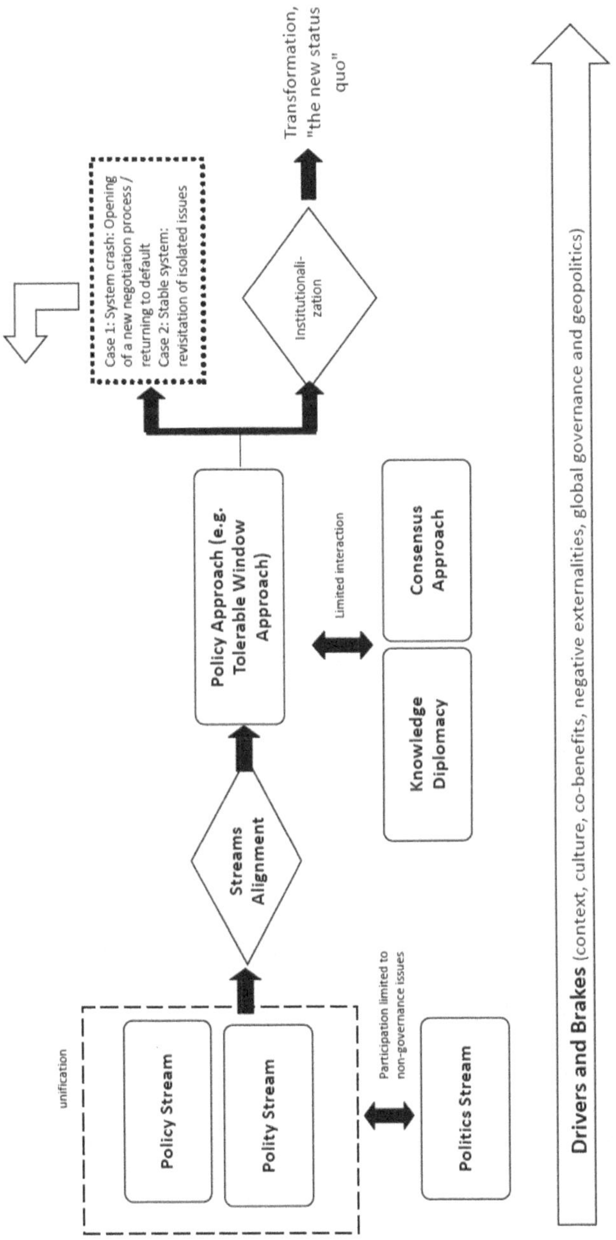

Figure 8.2 Integrated Streams of Transformation—An *Authoritarian* Ideal Type of Policy Pathway

8.2.3 Context: Actors and Issues

In an authoritarian policy pathway, (political) elites such as agents from the policy and polity streams historically dominate policy-making. This dominance is guided by socio-technical and socio-linguistic narratives that legitimate the control of state institutions. The recruitment of new members of the elite is structured and to a certain degree eidetic. Depending on the subtype of the authoritarian regimes, who will be in the next generation of leaders is most likely predictable. While from a normative perspective, the recruitment process is unjust and inequitable, this predictability of recruitment can ensure long-term stability as power is passed from one generation to another. For example, because a military regime will most likely involve military personnel in higher political positions, citizens who aim to hold political offices will need to enter the military and pursue a military career. In racial and ethnic 'democracies' (e.g., Apartheid South Africa), belonging to the ruling racial or ethnic group ensures access to political offices.

Nevertheless, the participation of the politics stream (civic society groups and those groups excluded from the political elite) is still possible or in some cases even encouraged. Compared to democracies, the consensus approach involves a different process in authoritarian regimes. Social movements are not dormant in this ideal type of authoritarian policy pathway, but rather stratified. Participation in social movements is limited to certain domains or issues and is 'tolerated' as long as it does not pose an opposition to certain state policies and to the political system in general. A social group can achieve 'non-threat' status when it has, for example, existing, informal connections with members of the political elites or when social networks are seen as beneficial to the legitimacy of the regime. Such informal connections often imply the personal guarantees of members of the ruling elite. In various cases, authoritarian regimes are keen to work with social movements as these can serve as pools of new recruits. Furthermore, the interaction between policy-makers and scientific communities often involves scientific and technocratic elites with long-standing relationships with the state. Knowledge diplomacy takes place in a rather controlled manner. In 'stable' authoritarian states, state universities and other research institutions are directly or indirectly managed or funded by government agencies. Therefore, scientific knowledge can easily be 'institutionalized' and interpreted in a way that supports government policies.

In stable authoritarian regimes like China and the United Arab Emirates, climate protection measures are most likely decoupled from political opposition. This is done by framing climate protection as an integral part of social policies that are concerned with human well-being. Embedded in existing social policies, climate protection becomes an indicator of output legitimacy through performance. Therefore, the regime will most likely allow more ambitious targets.

Authoritarian regimes that are able to achieve higher indicators of welfare are more likely to receive adulation from the audience as compared with democratic states. In addition, because a failure to achieve ambitious targets will not face drastic criticism domestically as communication channels are controlled by the regime, authoritarian regimes are most likely willing to set ambitious targets. Furthermore, modernization is framed as an indicator of performance that legitimizes the authoritarian system of governance. Aware of the risks of modernization to the system, stable authoritarian regimes have found ways to expand the benefits of modernization to a larger part of the population, thus, promoting social cohesion. This 'guided' modernization proves to be more effective than the use of violence.

8.2.4 Agency: Structures and Processes

Because the stable authoritarian regime derives its (output) legitimacy primarily from its performance in achieving indicators of modernization, bureaucracies of authoritarian regimes will most likely play a very significant role in planning. Stream alignment is rather simple, because state authority is concentrated in executive institutions. Decisions are expected to be swifter and policies tend to be predictable, as historically dominant policies will significantly influence the approach that policy-makers will take when addressing new areas. The characteristics of historical policies will be most likely reproduced in new policies. For example, in a country where an authoritarian regime has historically used generous welfare policies (e.g., United Arab Emirates) to uplift the well-being of its citizens to ensure its legitimacy, the regime will most likely apply similar principles to addressing other policy areas such as climate protection.

Although modernization is often argued as a threat to authoritarian rule, as modernization tends to 'balance' power among societal actors, it can also be used to legitimize authoritarian rule, particularly in highly paternalistic societies (see Kreisky 1979; 2008). Because of the authoritarian regimes' control of communication systems (e.g., censorship, state media), 'authoritarian culture' is enforced. When the authoritarian regime can effectively 'frame' the minds of citizens in terms of the meaning of ('guided') modernization, legitimacy is ensured.

Processes refer to various means of interactions that allow the achievement of decisions that advance the transformation process. As discussed above, although authoritarian countries are governed center-to-periphery and top-down, there is this predictability of institutional interactions (implying stability), as the character of historically dominant policies will define the policies adopted in new areas. Jurisdictions and hierarchies are well defined, implying a certain degree of accountability.

In addition, authoritarian structures define functional interaction, where actual or potential interaction between policies can be emphasized. Policy approach will most likely be highly functional, as fewer stakeholders will be involved. The tolerable window approach is defined by historical policies and will most likely not be subjected and open to intense bargaining with non-state actors. Moreover, bargaining interactions in authoritarian countries are framed and managed by the authoritarian regime. While the regime will allow the significant information participation of social elites and mid-level social movements and activists, the boundaries are well clarified, and violations are heavily sanctioned. In addition, bargaining interactions between elites and other social actors in authoritarian policy pathways tend to occur through informal and non-public channels.

8.2.5 Audience: Outcomes

It is assumed in this ideal type that while policy outputs are more easily achieved, these outputs are highly contingent on system stability. Because all governance structures of authoritarian states are construed to ensure system stability with low or no tolerance to challenges to the system, not to mention state control of communication channels, it is most likely difficult to anticipate when a rupture will occur. Therefore, system ruptures in authoritarian states will most likely 'catch everyone in surprise.' However, in case there is a rupture and the authoritarian system collapses, system default will most likely occur, and the transformation process will most likely need to start from zero, which implies a high degree of uncertainty. Nevertheless, a system rupture occurring in a democratic state may also lead to previous policies being disregarded, but it is assumed that dispersed decision-making as a result of factional politics following the separation and distribution of powers among various levels will mostly likely allow these 'dispersed' policies to be maintained.

The learning process is very important for authoritarian regimes. It is assumed that stable authoritarian regimes can adapt quickly to new challenges as decision-making does not need to undergo a rigid political debate among various political groups. The government can adapt faster to new conditions. In addition, because authoritarian regimes will most likely influence all aspects of the transformation process, outcomes will then require cooperation with state authorities from various levels. In addition, outcomes will be more embedded in existing historical policies. Persuasion interactions in authoritarian regimes will most likely be framed already by historical policies as these policies will identify the logic of the authoritarian regime.

8.3 An Ideal Type of Transformation—Policy Pathways Driven by Institutional Activism

In reality, democratic policy systems are often confronted with deviations. On the one hand, these deviations can be significant, but they cannot constitute another ideal type because of integral differences. On the other hand, these deviations still need to be 'isolated' to identify what is different in this scenario compared to an 'ideal' democratic system, and to analyze how deviations lead to changes in the structures and outcomes of decision-making processes. This section addresses a scenario that constitutes a subtype of the democratic policy ideal type—*the institutional activist-driven policy model.*

8.3.1 Literature on Institutional Activism—When Activists Hold Power

As Rebecca Abers and Luciana Tatagiba (2014) assert, most of the North American and European literature on social movements ignore the possibility that activists might work from inside government bureaucracy. The literature on new social movements highlights the need for civil society groups to maintain distance from the state, not only to ensure their credibility, but also their independence. Civil society groups, often formalized as non-government organizations, are expected to exert a significant degree of "self-limitation" (Cohen & Arato 1992), especially because proximity between bureaucracy and civil society would limit the latter's democratizing and transformative potential (Abers & Tatagiba 2014).

This theory is far from reality. While the majority of the academic literature looks at civil society groups as the consultants, contractors or partners of government agencies when implementing policies, it is not rare that governments hire activists due to their technical expertise and on-the-ground knowledge. However, as Federico Rossi and Marisa von Bülow (2015) suggest, the tasks of these activists are often limited to small-scale projects and they usually have to content themselves with making incremental changes while trying to maximize the effects of small actions such as a well-placed word in a decree or a training manual. Nevertheless, there are several cases of mobilized social movements which have successfully influenced or even dictated policy-making. For example, a whole generation in Germany were mobilized in the 1960s and 70s following a contentious public debate on nuclear energy leading to the establishment of the Green party.

8.3.1.1 Environmental Activism and Democracy

Environmental activism is considered to be a significant force behind decision-making concerning environment-related issues (see Wapner 1996; Sutton 2000; Chasek 2006). In general, the academic literature on democracy sees activism as a major pillar of deliberative or discursive democracy, in which deliberation and consensus is central to decision-making (see Bessette 1980; Gutmann & Thompson 2002; Dryzek 2010). In contrast to traditional democracy, deliberative democracy sees authentic deliberation and not merely voting as the primary source of the legitimacy of the system. The function of activism is to expand the base of public support as it goes beyond partisan politics (Goldberg 2013). Amy Gutmann and Dennis Thompson (2002) highlight the importance of the process, which not only guarantees fair terms of cooperation for all parties, but also the possibility of defection should the outcome of participation be proven to be non-reasonable.

The relation between state and civil society is traditionally adversary (see Tilly 1978, 1985), particularly when civil society groups emerge because of deficiencies in and failures of state instruments. Civil society groups are usually engaged in "collective challenges" to the political system (see Tarrow 1994). When the existing governance proves not to be receptive to the demands of civil society groups, these groups tend to resort to coercive means. In deliberative democracies, civil society groups act as participants in the consensus-building process, often identifying agendas and providing the technical expertise needed for the identification and implementation of solutions.

Environmental activism is regarded as the main driver of the inclusion of environmental issues in the political agenda (see Princen & Finger 1994; Wapner 1996; Andresen & Gulbrandsen 2003; Epstein 2005; Dong 2010). For example, Thomas Princen and Matthias Finger (1994) suggest that environmental NGOs challenge the traditional structure of politics, especially when states are reactive to various environmental crises, behaving both as independent negotiators and as agents of social learning. They continue that environmental activism identifies the political agenda by linking biophysical conditions to the political realm. However, environmental activism is to be differentiated from activism that pushes for other issues such as political liberties or gender equality. Civil society groups pushing for environmental integrity often enjoy more leeway, especially when their demands are in accordance with government policies and when these demands do not question governance structures (see Doyle & Simpson A. 2006; Sowers 2007; Beeson 2010; Schreurs 2011; Gilley 2012).

8.3.1.2 Relations Between Activism and Climate Protection—The Scientific Community as Norm Entrepreneurs?

Environmental activism is key to politicizing environmental issues and to bringing them to the political sphere not only at a national but also at a global level. Paul Wapner (1996) acknowledges that transnational groups such as Greenpeace, the World Wildlife Fund and Friends of the Earth use transnational social, economic and cultural networks to politicize environmental issues and mobilize the global civic society, aiming not only to alter norms and practices leading to the shifting of standards coinciding with the ideals of these groups, but also to define political agendas and determine the design of decision-making processes. Pamela Chasek (2001) documents how civic society groups have shaped the course of various negotiations directly or indirectly when dealing with environmental issues.

Environmental activists have regularly used science to convince policy-makers of the need for policies to address the increasing problems posed by environmental threats (see Eyerman & Jameson 1989; Fogel 2002; Epstein 2005). Environmental activists have identified the increase of public awareness as their main strategy to attract the attention of policy-makers (see Chasek 2006; Dong 2010). For example, activists have used the results of scientific studies, leading to their success in achieving the collective 1982 declaration of an international ban on commercial whaling (Aron 2001), ozone depletion (Litfin 1994), transboundary movements of hazardous wastes (Kempel 1993), and climate change (Andresen & Gulbrandsen 2003). Currently, it seems unimaginable to exclude NGOs and other environmental groups from climate change negotiations, given the high degree of public interest in and concern for the issues involved (Depledge 2005).

Expanding environmental activism to other issues such as sustainable development and energy security is regarded as inevitable, due to the interlinkages of these three policy priorities (Mawhinney 2002; Hopwood et al. 2005a; Kalhauge et al. 2005; Jabareen 2006). Nevertheless, environmental activism needs to expand its existing networks to include those groups whose interests complement their own. New alliances may be formalized with "sustainable activism" (see Goldin & Winters 1995; Fisher & Green 2004; Berrueta et al. 2015) and "green energy activism" (see Fitzpatrick 2014; Mission Innovation 2015), which will require prior evaluation of new conflict cleavages among these groups.

When activists are able to hold positions in one of these cooperating agencies, they will be confronted with the need to learn to consider procedures to be equally as important as results. The hierarchies, management and bureaucracy of different agencies are often diverse as they are defined by institutional memories, where the "due process" as coordination requirements may take longer and will eventually increase the frustration of activists, paving the way for more motivation to circumvent these procedures. Fig. 8.3 depicts the transformation process with activists predominantly in the driver seat.

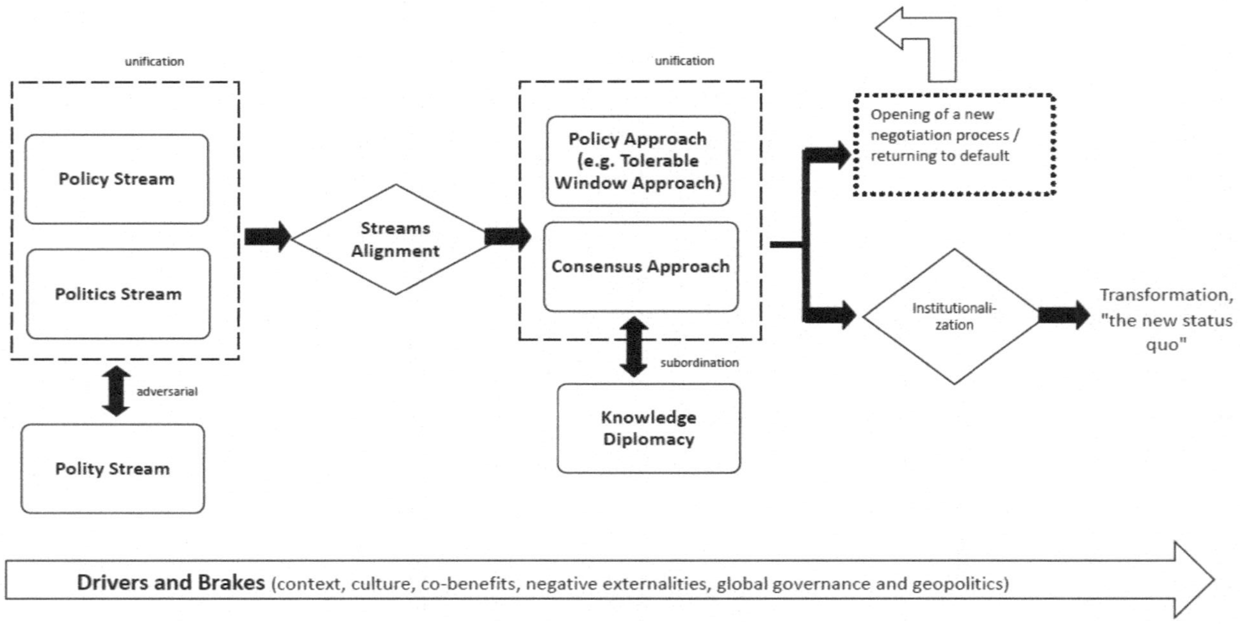

Figure 8.3 The Integrated Streams of Transformation—Institutional Activism as an Ideal Type (own representation)

The ideal type of institutional activism in decision-making is summarized as follows:

8.3.2 Context: Actors and Issues

The ideal type of institutional activism involves activists who are either elected or appointed to government posts, and who are mandated to define and implement policy goals. Activists hired in management positions can also be considered to be "institutional activists" if they are able to "shift" government policies in the direction coinciding with the activists' advocacies by introducing game-changing measures or strategies.

The previous figure (Fig. 8.3) illustrates the union between the "policy" and the "politics stream." In the two first phases of *negotiative* transformation, the opening of the process and agenda-setting for the negotiation process are dominated by institutional activists. In this ideal type, polities such as legal frameworks and other bureaucracies can be perceived as adversarial to the policy and politics stream. Stream alignment is often implemented with less participation from other institutions.

The union of the policy and politics streams dominates the identification of relevant issues. Because specific issues are non-negotiable for institutional activists, these issues are less receptive to compromise and are often based on ideologies or normative belief systems. The union between the policy and consensus approaches, as a direct consequence of the union between the policies and politics stream, leads to definition of the role of knowledge as a *subordinate* position. Science ceases to become a partner and becomes arbitrary and merely an instrument for legitimacy purposes. While issues are often backed with scientific studies, when scientific studies are unable to support arguments or when these are adversarial to the activists' arguments, other sources of legitimacy or methods of discrediting policy-makers are sought, such as mass demonstrations or public naming, blaming and shaming.

8.3.3 Agency: Structures and Processes

Institutional activists, prior to their government position, often complained about the biased structures of decision-making, where powerful actors such as corporations and business groups are able to dominate the process because of the resources at their disposal. Policy spheres (e.g., mining policy) are often established by dominant actors. Because of the lack of formal channels to effectively express opposition within this "policy sphere", activists tend to rely on social networks to mobilize popular support as leverage. However, now that they are in power, institutional activists are ironically taking advantage of the lack of effective formal channels to express opposition to their own advantage. As such, formerly powerful actors now look for other frameworks outside the distinct policy sphere to oppose decisions, such as courts or even social networks.

The transformation process in this deviating policy regime tends to circumvent existing bureaucracies and procedures for the sake of efficiency and effectiveness. The transformation process is less likely to be consensus-based. Therefore, the system will witness the emergence of new conflicting and highly competitive processes. The rhetoric will most likely be aggressive in blaming opposing counterparts, and the possible outcomes will also most likely be perceived as negative-sum. Instead of looking at potential synergies between the interests of actors, strategies will revolve around how the other actors can be disenfranchised, discredited and excluded. Furthermore, the transformation process is understood as "linear", as short-term "set-backs" for the sake of long-term strategies are most likely unacceptable.

8.3.4 Audience: Outcomes

Results tend to be the only things that matter for institutional activism. The outcomes are most likely short-term, as there will most likely be challenges after the activists leave office. New elections tend to be perceived as disruptive, as they will most likely bring uncertainties and instability. When opposing parties win elections, emerging vacuums will most likely define the relations between actors. In addition, because the results achieved through institutional activism are often reached by ignoring existing procedures, they will be confronted by legal and other types of challenges. A high proportion of the resources of institutional activists will be needed to address opposition, which may effectively "wear out" activists, prompting them to seek more drastic measures. Therefore, the implementation of these results will be the major hurdles for the institutional activist. The lack of broader support for policies produced by institutional activists increases the costs of transformation. In addition, the outcomes concentrate more on issues, rather than changes in the "social contract" or the mechanisms and procedures of decision-making. Therefore, the outcomes will most likely fail to address existing, biased structures and will therefore produce or reinforce existing power asymmetries and inequalities, because the activists need these biased structures to produce the results they want.

In this regard, while it is still possible for institutional activism to achieve transformation, it is a question of at which cost and at the expense of which actor. In addition, renegotiations of isolated terms or provisions are less likely, because of the highly competitive nature of the negotiation strategies used to achieve the results. New negotiation rounds, if they occur, will most likely encompass a default. Because of the high cost of renegotiations of terms, stalemates are most likely to occur, which may further delay important decisions to resolve problems.

8.4 An Ideal Type of Transformation—The Technocratic/Bureaucratic Policy Pathway

In policy-making in areas related to climate protection, sustainable development and energy security in particular, technocratic elements have become integral parts of decision-making structures and processes. While there is no concrete claim of being a purely 'technocratic' regime, current governments of both developed and developing countries as well as both democratic and authoritarian regimes have recognized the effectiveness of technocrats within their ranks (see McDonnell & Valbruzzi 2014; Shelton & Clark 2016; Rohde 2017). This section introduces an ideal type of a technocratic policy pathway. In addition, this section assumes that technocracy is reflected in the increasing importance of bureaucracies, where on the one hand, political decision-making is 'franchised' to technical experts and on the other hand, working groups such as scientific advisory councils have been tapped to assess problematic issues and to come up with solutions, and where politicians will most likely follow the 'recommendations' made by these 'expert committees.'

8.4.1 Technocracy and Governance

The academic debate about technocratic types of governance is becoming increasingly loud, particularly in policy discussions revolving around climate protection, sustainable development and energy security. The debate has evolved from its beginning and is now no longer concerned with technocracy in a classical or utopian sense where experts directly assume political power for the 'greater good.' The Platonic idea of philosopher-kings is often regarded as an early version of technocracy, in which the state is governed by those with expert knowledge of the 'good.' The 'technocratic narrative' has elevated the rule of the technocrats as one that has some problem-solving capacity and one that is linked with modernity (Shelton & Clark 2016).

Some academic scholars have coupled 'technocratic' qualification with profession or occupation. For example, the qualified minister of health is often regarded as someone who should have a medical background. There is then the question of how the evolution of a technocrat to a politician and vice-versa can be analyzed. When a medical doctor assumes the office of health minister, he or she needs to learn the challenges of bargaining interactions.

Technocracy can be found both in democratic and authoritarian regimes. As The Economist (2011) suggests, autocracy and technocracy are 'bedfellows', as authoritarian regimes prefer technocrats to run political offices. The Soviet Union is often classified as the first technocratic government. For instance, presidents of the Soviet Union often had a technical background in education. In addition, in 1986, 89 percent of *Politburo* members were engineers (Graham 1993 p. 74). As industrialization was promoted in the 1930s, engineers were rapidly promoted within the Communist Party. A similar development can also be observed in China. Similarly, military regimes often appoint civilian technocrats in government positions. Singapore and, to a lesser extent, Hong Kong, are often labelled as the 'best advertisement' for technocracy, where political and expert components of governance have merged completely, particularly through information technology (see The Economist 2011).

Several European democratic countries have seen the rise of technocrats as leaders, particularly in times of economic crisis. During political crises, technocrats are often the preferred 'compromise' candidate between competing political parties. Technocrats have, for example, assumed leadership during the financial crisis in Greece and Italy (see Grundle & Parker 2012), as they were seen as able to rise "above the paralyzing political rancor" (Blair 2011). Two bureaucrats—Mario Monti, an economist, and Lucas Papademos, the former vice-president of the European Central Bank—were seen as the 'saviors' of these two countries. Technocrats are often preferred by markets and international partners over 'indecisive' *Berufspolitiker* (career politicians) as they are able to provide concerted answers that political figures are unable to give (see Blair 2011).

While technocratic principles have their own merits, unelected technocrats holding political positions are required to 'evolve' into politicians as time passes by. Jürgen Habermas (2013) in his book '*Im Sog der Technokratie*' sees democracies with increased technocratic tendencies as weak democracies, as the elite is able to identify the quickest means to achieve their interests under the banner of efficiency. He continues to argue that technocratic governance structures are less receptive to persuasion and bargaining interactions. The European financial crisis has enforced technocratic principles and institutions in solving the crisis that many scholars argue was caused or at least promoted by technocrats, who failed to supervise financial institutions. In addition, Jürgen Habermas links the current 'political crises' of the European Union, including Brexit and the emergence of alt-right movements, to its technocratic tendencies.

Nevertheless, other academic scholars have argued that technocrats are primarily driven by their cognitive 'problem-solution mind-sets' (see Njalsson 2005), where relevant ideas and decisions are forged not or less by political ideologies, but by how information is assessed and interpreted. As such, technocrats are often regarded as being independent of lobbying. However, the absence of lobbying can also be 'undemocratic', as lobbying does not always need to refer to powerful business and industry groups influencing policy-making but can also refer to social movements and grass-root organizations aiming to persuade policy-makers.

Furthermore, as mentioned above, there is a need to clarify the idea that technocratic features can be observed in both democratic and authoritarian governments. While technocratic principles can be seen as undermining accountability in democratic countries, as these experts may not be elected through a popular vote, technical expertise can be a significant legitimizing factor in democracies, especially those experiencing a crisis. For example, the constitutional protection bestowed upon Central Banks and the judiciary to guarantee independence from political interference is an example of the technocratic characteristics of democratic political systems. Furthermore, in authoritarian states, technocratic principles can also be prevalent. With the practical absence of a popular election, technical expertise becomes a major criterion for recruitment to political offices (see The Economist 2011).

8.4.2 An Ideal Type of Transformation—The Technocratic/Bureaucratic Policy Pathway

The following illustration (Fig. 8.4) summarizes the various processes of a technocratic policy pathway in the context of transformation. Decision-making is initiated solely or predominantly by expert committees, forming the union of the policy and polity streams. Other societal actors belonging to the politics stream have limited channels to influence decision-making, and in many cases their involvement is tolerated only in agenda-setting. Stream alignment is, as expected, rather simple and the agendas are not subject to external contestation. Solutions are reached through closed-door expert committee meetings and there is the connotation that whatever solutions are produced, these are for the sake of the common good (Fig. 8.4).

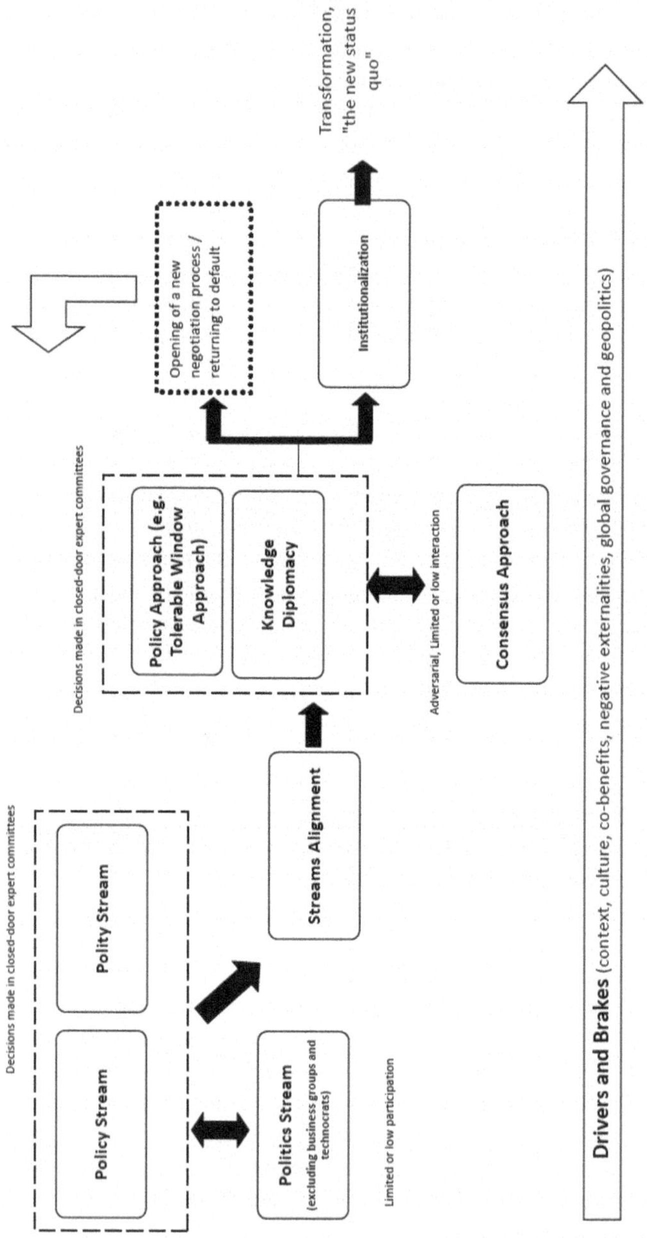

Figure 8.4 The Technocratic/Bureaucratic Policy Pathway—An Ideal Type (own representation)

8.4.3 Context: Actors and Issues

An elected or appointed politician (e.g., president, prime minister, minister) is defined as a technocrat if he or she has, prior to his/her (first) appointment or election, never held public office under the banner of a political party or is not a formal member of any political party. A technocrat can also be someone who is elected through an electoral campaign that emphasized non-political, technical expertise (e.g., a businessperson, scientist, teacher or athlete). He or she can also be appointed upon recognition of non-political expertise that is directly relevant to the role occupied in government (e.g., a military general as minister for defense, a doctor as minister of health, or a lawyer as minister for justice) (see McDonnell & Valbruzzi 2014).

A significant portion of the population is 'apolitical' if not defined by politically apathy. On the one hand, a technocracy can be the result of this increasing political apathy in the population. On the other hand, political apathy is reinforced by technocratic practices, with the public losing channels to influence policy-making. In addition, social movements that seek to influence the policy-making process will most likely employ 'technocrats' to represent them. Speaking the same language, NGOs that are able to manifest the same technical expertise will mostly likely be embedded in the decision-making process.

Relevant issues will most likely be identified, chosen for the agenda, and addressed by technocrats both from the policy and polity streams. The politics stream assumes a merely 'responding' or 'recipient' role. The assessment of the issues will very likely be conducted using presumed technical methodologies that are systematic and perceived to be representative. Conflicts evolving from these issues are seen as a matter of differences in methodologies and in the calibration of models and projections. Furthermore, issues tend to be de-politicized and are often not subjected to political debate, at least not the methodologies. There is an understanding that isolating these issues from the political sphere serves the interest of the public, particularly in times of crises.

8.4.4 Agency: Structures and Processes

Technocratic characteristics of decision-making are reflected in the structural design of governance. At first glance, the technocratic policy pathway will be highly dependent on institutions. The 'proliferation' of institutions will most likely imply a huge bureaucratic system. Institutions are most likely independent from each other, implying dispersed decision-making. Nevertheless, because of the highly formalized nature of governance, institutions will most likely be skeptical of engagement in new policy areas. Because interactions between institutions are also highly formalized, bargaining interactions are shifted towards back-channel communications. In addition, bargaining interactions with non-expert social groups are limited. In addition, the intersections or cross-cutting features of policy areas will require additional institutional mechanisms. Paradoxically, while technocrats can find quick answers to problems in the short term, in the long-term technocrats will most likely accumulate the control over procedures and structures to promote the efficiency of the system leading to a 'fat' bureaucracy.

A technocratic policy pathway will most likely imply a high level of social capital in the short term, as the public will tend to tolerate a lack of inclusiveness and transparency for the sake of technical effectiveness. Nevertheless, additional legitimizing actions will be needed as this tolerance tends to be short-term and challenges will be voiced in the long-run as the ramifications of policies move from the collective to the personal level. Without such additional legitimacy, the public will 'feel' the distance between decisions and society. The technocratic 'establishment' will then be highly criticized as 'undemocratic.' Institutional interactions are highly formally defined, with clear jurisdictions and mandates of government agencies. Unlike the situation in many democratic regimes, there is no or very low competition between government agencies.

Communication channels tend to be one-way with the technocratic regime merely informing the public about the benefits of decisions that it has made. Persuasion and bargaining interactions tend to be highly formalized. Technocratic policy pathways are also characterized by 'dispersed decision-making' as a result of the dynamics of factional politics (see Gilley 2012), as decisions are most likely 'bundled' according to the 'expert committees' formed. For example, as health issues will be addressed by health experts, there is a tendency that experts on energy will not be invited to the health committee. As such, additional processes are needed to structure functional interactions between 'policy issue groups.'

There is limited or low interaction with other societal actors in terms of assessing the ramifications of the solutions proposed. Knowledge diplomacy occurs solely within expert committees. At one point, these solutions will be implemented and institutionalized, leading to the new status quo and thus completing the transformation process. Due to the exclusion of some stakeholders who will be affected by such decisions, the regime will need additional resources to ensure that these solutions will not be challenged. For some regimes, additional legitimacy will be derived through output legitimacy (performance) or through international recognition of their 'efficient' structures. For others, the legitimacy of unelected technocrats is achieved through plebiscites or active information campaigns to gain popular support. Other governments resort to 'quiet' approaches, where solutions are not 'loudly' announced through the media.

8.4.5 Audience: Outcomes

The results of expert committee decisions are 'dispersed' and highly 'factional.' Therefore, outcomes of committee deliberations in a technocratic policy pathway will tend not to be integrative. As there is most likely no competition among government institutions and agencies with clear jurisdictions and mandates, additional measures are most likely needed to make sure that the 'technical' decisions made are cohesive. The proximity of decisions made by technocrats to the 'sentiments' of certain members of the society will most likely lead to the rise of anti-intellectualism.

8.5 An Ideal Type of Transformation—The Post-Democratic Policy Pathway

As an ideal type, a post-democratic policy pathway is not a 'continuation' or a later version of a democratic pathway. Rather, it is a policy pathway that is democratic in nature but has some features that are typical of pre-democratic political systems (see Crouch 2008). In this ideal type, the role of the finance, business and industry sectors refers not only to the involvement of the representatives from these sectors in the policy-making processes either as direct appointees or elected officials, but also to the installment of market-based principles and a logic in the narratives that legitimizes political actions. The emphasis on money and economic values in the political goals of policy-makers is a significant deviation from a democratic policy pathway, where social, political, cultural, economic and environmental interests are of the same rank. As a deviation, there is a need to conceptualize how post-democratic characteristics shift institutional, functional, and bargaining interactions in the context of a transformation towards sustainability.

Although there are similarities, post-democratic policy a pathway is differentiated from a technocratic pathway. While a technocratic policy pathway pertains to an emphasis on knowledge-based decision-making through technical experts, which may also include financial experts, a post-democratic policy pathway solely or dominantly employs experts from the financial, business and industry sectors. These 'money' experts are directly or indirectly mandated to make decisions relevant to non-economic issues.

8.5.1 Post-Democracy and Institutional Interactions

Post-democracy is a concept that has emerged from protest movements. As the European financial and economic crisis of 2008/2009 unfolded, there was criticism of how current democratic systems have shifted away from the 'ideals' of democracy. Post-democracy is labelled as 'unhealthy' democracy, where indicators of pre-democratic eras can be recognized without moving back to these times. Colin Crouch (2008 p. 13) argues that while democratic institutions are still formally unimpaired, political procedures and governments increasingly manifest structures typical of pre-democratic times. **One of these developments refers to the retraction of democratic participatory requirements and the replacement of these requirements with outputs and performance**. The discrepancy between the formal democratic legitimacy models of governance and the political actions increasingly legitimized through efficiency distorts democratic procedures.

The 2008–2010, the economic and financial crisis in Europe led to new discussions about institutional deficits in the European economic and financial system (see Sell, Friedrich, L. & Sauer 2011; Ullbrich & Lipponer 2011). Most authors see the economic and financial crisis in 'small boxes', and often ignore the 'spill-overs' between different policy domains. The analysis of institutional interactions occurring between political actors (such as ministers, members of the parliament and bureaucrats) and banks as well as the financial service sector has led to insights into how democratic principles have been changed or re-defined. Particularly because the state is regarded as the guarantor of economic stability, deriving its output legitimacy through the level of its economic welfare, the question arises as to whether the same state can act as 'referee' in the society, where social welfare or even climate protection can be undermined by the primacy of economic welfare.

Post-democracy is a political science concept that aims to explain how certain societal actors are extruded through the dominance of economic actors that leads to the establishment of state structures that favor money interests and focus on economic values. For example, the erosion of state monitoring and verification mechanisms in a post-democratic state is a consequence of the typical devolution of state functions to private actors, particularly because 'privatization' tends to be equated with rationalization and efficiency. This development is regarded as being a feature of post-democracy, which often leads to a legitimacy crisis. Armin Schäfer (2008) argues that trust in the capability of the state decreases, particularly because the privileges given to these economic actors are often translated into a decrease of social welfare.

The following illustration summarizes the interactions of the different streams as well as the processes leading to the achievement of the transformation (Fig. 8.5).

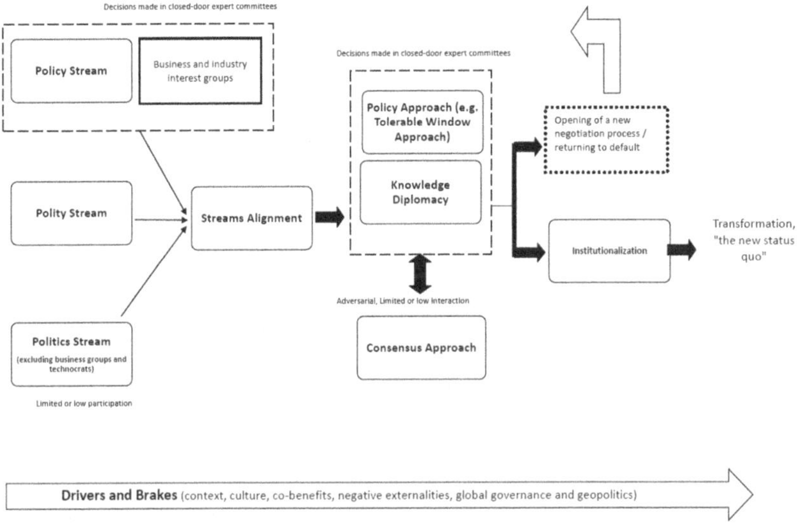

Figure 8.5 The post-democratic policy pathway—an Ideal Type (own representation)

8.5.2 Context: Actors and Issues

In this ideal type of policy pathway, representatives or proponents of the finance, business and industry sectors have been able to establish themselves in the policy stream. As various financial actors such as the 'rating agency' Moody's are able to use the threats of lowering the solvency ratings of countries to compel political actions, governments are most likely to assume the socio-technical and socio-linguistic narratives of these agencies when legitimizing unpopular austerity measures and other market instruments such as cuts to subsidies to the coal energy sector. Particularly in a post-democratic state, governments have become highly dependent on loans and investment from the private sector. With a negative rating, governments will find it difficult to access loans with acceptable terms. Moreover, particularly in times of economic hardships involving deficit-tainted governments forced to bail out financial institutions and business or industry companies that are too big to fail, austerity measures are expected to be implemented to prevent further negative ratings. These austerity measures tend to limit expenses relating to social welfare, further vindicating the dominance of economic actors.

A further characteristic of a post-democratic ideal type refers the state ceasing to be the sole holder of monopoly of authority and welfare services, as it has privatized most of its functions. The state will most likely be concentrating on the bureaucracy (polity stream). As the state has privatized most of its functions, policies are now in the hands of the 'private sector.' As 'bidding' for the state functions were conducted in an 'auction' like process, economic actors would have eventually won the biddings. Through the dominance of 'money actors' in policy-making, the state will most likely assume 'money logic' in constituting the 'rules of the game' in the bargaining space. As a consequence of privatization, the state will be *de facto* substituted by the private sector, similar to how the Medicis controlled politics in Florence in the 15th century. As dominated by the private sector, the state ceases to be the genuine regulator, becoming a player itself and leading to further legitimacy crises due to the bias favoring the interests of 'money actors.'

A major characteristic of a post-democratic policy pathway is the reduction of the functionality of the State to being merely a 'security instrument' through diverse waves of privatization. Indeed, in some countries, even security services have been outsourced to private security companies. As such, a further reduction of the quality of democracy is implied, as diminished transparency and unclear accountability are to be expected (see Crouch 2008). Nevertheless, not all sectors of social life can be privatized. The state will need to take over sectors that cannot yield profits and which no business company is willing to take. This will most likely lead to a further erosion of the quality of government services as the 'poor', without a political voice, will be the only remaining direct 'dependents' of the state (see Hirschmann 1974; Crouch 2008). Following 'market logic,' government expenses for the poor—who are considered the 'others'—will be eventually reduced over time as these will most likely not yield profits.

Due to the perceived bias of the state, other societal actors (politics stream) will most likely be motivated to seek alternative channels outside state mechanisms. While a significant portion of the population will resort to resignation and political apathy, others will mostly likely be motivated to use paralegal instruments. As such, societal actors will most likely be perceived and will understand themselves as part of 'protest movements', stirring further political apathy in the population. Issues and agendas for policy-making will be primarily determined through economic lobbyism. Because of the access of economic elites to political power, political authority lies *de facto* on the table of the CEOs and directors of financial and economic institutions and actors. The lobbyism of economic actors in post-democratic policy pathways is highly effective, because economic elites can threaten governments with the idea that policies limiting the activities of economic actors will lead to a reduction of employment. In addition, most economic actors see lobbyism as an investment, which promises revenues in the future. This is part of the logic that investment should only be done in areas where profits can be expected, and no longer in areas that serve common good.

Issues will most likely entail 'horror scenarios' should governments fail to effectively address emerging issues. The importance of actors that are specialized in developing such horror scenarios, such as rating agencies and, to a lesser degree, industry associations, will most likely be reinforced in post-democratic policy pathways. Non-economic issues such as animal protection and human rights protection will often be secondary in government decisions. Economic sanctions on countries that regularly and systematically violate human rights will be harder to legitimize and implement. As such, proponents of these non-economic issues will need to find ways to couple these issues with existing economic interests. They will need to speak the language of 'money actors,' and employ the same methodologies, further reinforcing the dominance of market logic in the society.

8.5.3 Agency: Structures and Processes

Decision-making in post-democratic pathways are highly dependent on structures such as institutions and bureaucracies. The polity stream complements the policy stream in framing the agenda for further interactions. Nevertheless, in contrast to technocratic pathways, jurisdictions and mandates of individual institutions are not fully clear and there is a market logic preventing the clear separation of powers. As the market logic implies the necessity of 'healthy' competition among state institutions, institutional interactions will be limited. Due to the privatization of most of the public services of the state, the state will most likely have low autonomy and low capacity. As it is merely functioning as a regulatory body, should the government initiate and pursue more ambitious targets it would need more assistance and collaboration from other actors such as the finance, business, and industry sectors. The success of government-led programs will be highly dependent on how the economic actors will think they will profit from these programs.

Streams alignment will be more likely structured using practices typically used in the finance, business and industry sector. For example, issues that promise the most economic value will be prioritized over the others that are merely of 'symbolic' importance. In addition, the methodologies that will be used to assess the feasibility of political actions will most likely use monetary, cost-benefit analyses. The tolerable window approach will be de-politicized and commercialized. What is acceptable is what brings economic value compared to costs. Maximizing benefits with the lowest possible costs will frame political actions. Structures that regulate the actions of all stakeholders will be stable, primarily because adhering to these rules and regulations will bring more value and not because of equity concerns. Cost-benefit calculations will define the effectiveness of structures in managing functional interactions. In addition, serving as a basis or criteria for rationality, cost-benefit analytical methods will further reinforce the privatization or commercialization of public services and welfare. At some point, cost-benefit thinking will define equity as it penetrates all sectors of social life. Bargaining interactions in a post-democratic policy pathway follow the market-driven and market-defined frameworks for assessing the feasibility of policies. Consensus-building is exclusive to only the economic value of decisions. Knowledge plays a significant role merely in providing inputs on costs and benefits as well as risks and opportunities.

Policy-makers in a post-democratic policy pathway will most likely follow the approach of 'system relevance' or 'too big to fail.' Government bail-out programs using tax-payers' money to the finance, business and industry actors will depend on how their failure to do so would have fatal consequences for the stability of the financial system and the economy. As such, post-democratic pathways will most likely require additional legitimizing mechanisms, particularly when profits are privatized while risks and losses are socialized. Furthermore, the 'system relevance' approach will most likely distort bargaining interactions, because actors such as labor unions and welfare associations, which do not enjoy the status of system relevance, will be confronted with an unfair bargaining sphere.

Of equally importance is how the concentration of power within the inner ellipsis in the context of a 'low intensity democracy' (Kreisky 2002 p. 60) will promote the further personalization of politics. Political communication will focus more on the people involved as the proximity between the electorates and governance structures increases. A further implication involves the increased importance of communication channels, such as conventional media and social media, in producing 'positive', image-building material relating to the policies and people behind policy-making. Problematic issues will most likely be solved not by looking at the root causes of the problems but through strategic PR activities. Because governments will be more inclined to keep a positive image, they will most likely want to control more of these communication channels, further reinforcing transparency deficits. For example, the highlights of closed-door meetings and conferences will no longer be the exchanges of ideas and bargaining interactions, but will tend to be the press conferences (Guehenno 1994).

8.5.4 Audience: Outcomes

Decisions and policies will be less likely the results of bargaining and persuasion involving all relevant stakeholders. Moreover, policies will not be developed through compromises and collaboration with societal groups but will rather be predominantly achieved through direct and indirect interactions between government officials and representatives of the finance, business and industry sectors.

Moreover, the privatization of major state services will on the one hand lead to dispersed decision-making. On the other hand, outsourcing state services also means that governments will simultaneously rely heavily on consultants and experts (see Crouch 2008). Dispersed decision-making and factional politics will be complemented by a centralized concentration of power to the inner ellipsis of decision-makers, further reinforcing transparency deficits.

As the development and implementation of policies in the transformation process are exclusive, the outcomes of various bargaining, institutional and functional interactions will be mostly fragile in terms of input legitimacy. Nevertheless, as an implication of the assumption of market logic as an indicator of the efficiency of performance, the relevance of output legitimacy will surpass that of input legitimacy.

Outcomes will be confronted with social distrust. The tendency of governments to rely heavily on positive image-building ('branding') is counterproductive to promoting social trust. In addition, the political apathy of a significant part of the population will be reinforced by governments' increased control of the media, with critical voices easily labelled as enemies of the state.

8.6 Interim Conclusion

The usage of the ideal types as theoretical models of policy-making can be useful in analyzing current irritations resulting from contradicting processes. While ideal types represent the "ideals" of selected policy regimes, the analysis of the reasons behind deviations in real-life regimes can provide important inputs to allow a more grass-roots understanding of decision-making. A comparison between the ideal types and the real-life policy models can identify the 'corridors' in which transformation can occur. The ideal types uncover the potentials of connecting policies with the assumptions made in the previous chapters. For example, it could be the case that policy-makers in democratic regimes are generally inclined to consult civil society groups. However, the same policy-makers may then prefer to exclude civil society groups, for example, from foreign policies or from climate mitigation policies. The attention of the analysis can be directed towards understanding how this change of preference arises. For example, these policy-makers may have learned from their own personal experience that civil society groups may be highly competitive when it comes to climate mitigation projects.

In addition, because some experts argue that authoritative or semi-authoritarian governments are also capable or even more capable of achieving success in climate protection projects (see Schreurs 2011), some policy-makers in democratic countries (referred to as "*eco-authoritarians*") are currently more willing to "sacrifice" inclusion (as a democratic principle) and other democratic principles for the sake of efficiency, especially when accountancy is increasingly measured by the formal success of economic development plans and external security (see Hardin 1968; Heilbroner 1974; Porritt 1984). Nevertheless, other experts argue that some authoritarian or semi-authoritarian states can only 'tolerate' environmental activism as long as its advocacy is not directed at governmental agencies.

9 Mexico and China—Sustainable, Low-Carbon Transformation Processes in Democratic and Authoritarian Regimes

Mexico and China are two dynamic countries that can 'challenge' existing normative views on regimes, governance, and institutions. On the one hand, Mexico is a vibrant democratic country that has managed to become a member of the OECD and its economy has benefitted from open borders, direct foreign investment inflows and integration into global value chains (OECD 2017b), but yet it still reflects governance deficiencies, particularly in the formal and material representation of relevant stakeholders, and especially in marginalized communities. On the other hand, although China is governed by an authoritarian regime, particularly when environmental issues are involved, societal groups' interests seem to find effective ways to influence policy-making. In addition, as the Chinese government has discovered the opportunities of integration into global value chains, moving into higher value-added production by improving the quality and relevance of innovation (OECD 2017a), it is able to achieve the approval of its domestic audience, which further consolidates the standing of the Communist regime.

Strategically, the Chinese regime was able to 'link' this 'upskilling' policy goal with climate protection and sustainable developmental goals, paving the way for the achievement of 'moral power', both domestically and internationally, and eventually assume global leadership. With certain European countries currently confronted with financial crisis, austerity measures, and legitimacy gaps, a vacuum has emerged, which may derail the climate negotiation process. Such a leadership in China will most likely require focusing on a partnership with urban clusters or networks of cities (*chengshiqun*), local societal groups, business and investment groups aiming to advance environmental integrity, sustainable development and energy security. As it becomes apparent that global leadership is becoming a key aspect of Chinese foreign policy, China has increasingly moved

A. Hernández, *Taming the Big Green Elephant*, Globale Gesellschaft und internationale Beziehungen, https://doi.org/10.1007/978-3-658-31821-5_9

into either creating new platforms for global and regional partnerships of development such as the Belt and Road as well as the Beijing-Hebei-Tianjin Corridor, or reconfiguring the rules of existing international institutions by assuming different types of leadership. Nevertheless, as Thomas Hale (2017) highlights, China still needs to find new avenues for climate leadership that cater to non-traditional channels of diplomatic influence.

Mexico and China are very seldom compared. In this chapter, the Mexico-China comparative case study suggests each are using the other as the 'alternative setting.' Particularly in the context of sustainable, low-carbon transformation, such a comparative approach can provide interesting insights, especially when 'normative traps' become evident. For example, the short-comings of democratic regimes and the advantages of authoritarian regimes in policy implementation are often downplayed, because the success of policy implementation tends to be merely defined by input legitimacy. However, an important requirement for such a comparison is to initially put aside, at least for analytical purposes, the normative lens of democratic and authoritarian regimes. Here, context beats the purported logic of policy models. This should not, however, be taken as an argument supporting authoritarian regimes. Understanding how authoritarian regimes are able to effectively address specific problem issues of low-carbon transformation can contribute useful knowledge to democratic regimes and vice-versa.

Hypotheses: Identifying New Variables and New Interdependencies

Any system transformation is highly contextual. Therefore, as argued in Chapter 7, each case study will most likely lead to the identification of new variables and interdependencies or re-discovering old variables that assume new meanings or significance, which can be later conceptualized. This approach aims to instigate further theory development.

The following hypotheses intend to highlight the overlaps and deviations between the ideal types (chapter 8) and the case studies on China and Mexico.

> **Hypothesis 1:** The successful implementation of sustainable, low-carbon policies is highly contingent on the capacity and autonomy of the state.

Relevant questions include: are democratic regimes more effective than authoritarian regimes in achieving sustainable, low-carbon developmental policy goals (policy formulation, coordination, implementation, verification and modification)? Are hybrid regimes the solution? If yes, which elements of both governance models should be selected when designing the regime?

> **Hypothesis 2:** Both democratic and authoritarian regimes can manage transformation processes.

Paradoxically, participative bargaining interactions do not exclusive occur, nor are they guaranteed in democratic countries. By understanding how institutional, functional and bargaining interactions can be planned and executed, both democratic or authoritarian regimes can establish effective transformation management.

> **Hypothesis 3:** The historicity of transformation processes implies that decisions or policies are to be designed and implemented case-by-case or point-by-point.

As such, analytical methods that allow the analysis of scales, episodes and subsystems are needed. Ideal type analysis suggests additional subjects and additional ways of analyzing historical, social processes for further research, allowing a more integrated approach to problems and solutions.

> **Hypothesis 4:** The effective management of transformation processes requires 'negotiative' mechanisms that allow continuous the revisiting of decisions made.

By focusing on various negotiation episodes, levels, or stages, the resilience of transformation processes can be ensured. Through this, distinct conditions of each episode, level or stage can be highlighted, allowing retrofitted solutions.

9.1 Context—Transformation Processes and Governance Models

The evaluation of the state of sustainable, low-carbon transformation in Mexico and China entails a participatory approach through which the different levels and scales of the 'involvement' of relevant stakeholders will be highlighted.

9.1.1 The Paris Agreement and Responses from Mexico and China

9.1.1.1 Mexico

Ahead of the UNFCCC COP meeting in Paris in December 2015, Mexico had already ratified the agreement in March 2015. Mexico was also the first developing country to submit a climate pledge to the 2015 COP meeting. By doing so, the Mexican government had officially committed to meet its climate goals by upscaling its 'Intended Nationally Determined Contribution' (INDC) from mere intentions to formal policy goals (see Secretaría de Relaciones Exteriores 2017). Mexico understands itself as a major climate champion while its government aims to achieve the following:

- Unconditionally reducing GHG emissions by 22 percent and black carbon by 51 percent of business-as-usual levels by 2030. With assistance, the government aims to increase these reductions by 36 percent (GHG) and 70 percent (black carbon).
- Conditionally reducing GHG and black carbon emissions (35 percent and 70 percent respectively), contingent on international support.
- Achieving peak net emissions from 2026 and reducing emissions per unit of GDP by around 40 percent from 2013 to 2030.
- Reducing emission intensity per unit of GDP by 40 percent between 2013 and 2030.
- Committing to various adaptation measures to lessen the vulnerability of local communities to climate change and to ameliorate climate impacts on ecosystems, infrastructure and productive systems. In addition, the Mexican government commits to achieving zero percent deforestation by 2030.

To achieve these goals, Mexico introduced a major new policy on clean energy through the 'Energy Transition Law'. With the energy sector responsible for 70.8 percent of Mexico's GHG emissions (Climate Links 2017), this new policy envisions generating at least 25 percent of its electricity through clean energy by 2018, 30 percent by 2021, and 35 percent by 2024. Nevertheless, even though many of new reforms in Mexico call for sustainable development and climate protection, many policies still favor the fossil fuels sector. In 2015, petroleum and natural gas accounted for most of Mexico's total fuel consumption for transportation and electricity generation, at 45 percent and 40 percent respectively (EIA 2016a). This is because the energy sector (electricity and hydrocarbons) is generally open to private investment, which tend to favor the exploration and exploitation of shale gas as a key goal. Therefore, as the Special Program of Climate Change of the Mexican government (PECC) recognizes, energy reform and the exploitation of shale gas in Mexico could actually lead to an increase in greenhouse gas emissions, which means that the reform would actually go against the national climate commitment (Energy Transition 2014).

In addition, the Energy Transition Law still needs to be complemented by additional knowledge of the impacts of targets that are yet to be quantified. Furthermore, because this law assumes a definition of clean energy that includes co-generation, which means natural gas—a CO2 emitting source of energy—will be playing a crucial role, doubts among the scientific community have emerged (Climate Action Tracker 2017b). The consumption of natural gas now accounts for 23.6% of fossil-fuel CO2 emissions (see Boden et al. 2017; CDIAC 2017). For example, this could mean that the emissions will be 6 percent higher in 2030 and that the share of renewables in 2024 will be merely 29 percent. Therefore, Mexico will need to commit to additional policies in order to reach its NDC target.

9.1.1.2 China

China ratified the Paris Agreement on September 3, 2016. The Chinese government has identified and centered its policies on reaching its NDC goals. Some important elements of its NDC include:

- Peak CO2 emissions by 2030, or earlier if possible;
- The reduction of the carbon intensity of its GDP by 60 to 65 percent below 2005 levels by 2030
- An increase of the share of non-fossil energy sources in the total primary energy supply to around 20 percent by 2030
- An Increase of the forest stock volume by around 4.5 billion cubic meters (40 million hectares of forest coverage) by 2020 compared to 2005 levels

Nevertheless, while the policies and intended actions of the Chinese government could be adequate to enable China to overachieve its NDC as well as its national targets, the Chinese NDC is seen as not ambitious enough to be consistent with holding warming to below 2 °C as required under the Paris Agreement, and is instead consistent with warming between 3 °C and 4 °C (Climate Action Tracker 2017a). However, while China is currently the biggest source of CO2 emissions with around 30 percent, followed by the United States with 15 percent (Boden et al. 2017), it cannot be blamed alone for this failure to achieve the global 2 °C target. China's emissions are merely half of U.S. emissions on a per capita basis.

In addition, most of China's emissions are attributed to manufactured goods exported to the United States and other European countries. Moreover, based on historical CO2 emissions, U.S. climate-damage responsibility is twice as much of that of China, even without normalizing for population. Most importantly, China's emissions have been stabilized and have now been constant over the last three years (Carbon Tax Center 2017).

When the 18th National Congress of the Communist Party of China initiated the concept of 'eco-civilization' as a new model of the modernization of harmonious human-nature development, it sets the new framework for present and future strategies on planning to conform to the world trend. China has already built the world's biggest installed capacity of wind and solar power, and its climate policies are embedded in its current five-year economic plan. With China's slowing economic growth, the Chinese government has identified the potentials of expanding its dominance in low-carbon technologies, which can serve as the engine of the next phase of its economic growth. In 2016, China invested USD 102.9 billion in renewable energy and installed half of the world's new wind power, as its coal consumption has peaked and has begun to decline.

9.1.2 Multiple Entry Points to Climate Mitigation in Mexico and China

Entry points can be understood as problem-issues related to other policy priorities such as sustainable development and energy security, **whose resolution can be coupled with climate mitigation**, that is, with emission reduction through renewables or through energy efficiency technologies. By focusing on synergies and co-benefits, policy-makers might find it easier to push for more ambitious climate protection policies. Sustainable development goals can be coupled with climate protection goals particularly after trade-offs between these policy goals and policy implementation measures can be identified and managed.

The entry points that will be discussed below do not comprise a complete list of all entry points to climate mitigation in Mexico and China. This selection intends to highlight the most relevant as underscored by the theoretical models (ideal types).

9.1.2.1 Mexico

There are various entry points to climate mitigation for Mexico. A potential entry point to climate mitigation for the Mexican government is its political priority of addressing **the social and economic impacts of migration to the country**. As extreme weather events cause economic damage, climate change increases the probability that Mexicans migrate to the United States and from rural to urban areas within Mexico (see Jessoe et al. 2016). The effects of climate change, such as water scarcity, diseases, food scarcity and rising sea levels, induce the increasing rates of internal and external migration, which are becoming more of an economic and political concern in terms of both the origins and the destinations (see Nawrotzki et al. 2015), climate mitigation needs to be a central element of any policy that aims to address migration. Nevertheless, as the effects of Mexico's climate mitigation efforts cannot be easily converted to concrete outcomes in the affected areas (e.g., observable resolution of water scarcity), **Mexico's climate mitigation efforts need to be accompanied by short-term successes in terms of containing migration.**

One example of such coupling of climate mitigation and addressing migration is **to ensure local community development**, particularly in areas where renewable energies such as wind, geothermal and solar are developed and expanded. Renewable energy projects in rural areas should be reliable sources of both high- and low-skilled jobs. **The promotion of intelligent growth in rural Mexico, for example through geothermal energy, needs to be driven by innovation and by the expansion of value chains in the context of community development, gender equality, empowerment of indigenous communities, social innovation, youth empowerment and innovative entrepreneurship**. Furthermore, renewable projects in rural areas need to be accompanied by the development of local infrastructure and expertise in order to build new capacities while reversing emigration. A huge challenge for various renewable projects (e.g., *Mareñas Renovables* in Oaxaca) is to address the situation that most workers in such areas are fishermen or farmers who will most likely be negatively affected by such projects (e.g., noise, water and air pollution leading to less catches or less agricultural yields). Therefore, **the creation of knowledge-intensive sectors and services needs to be equally beneficial for other sectors** (e.g., agriculture).

The sustainability of economic development processes based on the utilization of renewable energies in Mexico depends not only the Large and Multinational Companies (MNEs), but to a large extent on the incorporation of local traditional partners in this process—the Small and Medium-Sized Enterprises (SMEs). Climate mitigation projects need to initiate not only national and regional, but also local value creation by fostering the role of renewable energy and energy efficiency technologies in creating new market opportunities and the promotion of technology-based entrepreneurship with a focus on SMEs.

To avoid the traps of natural resource abundancy (the 'resource curse', or the 'paradox of plenty'), local economic development strategies need to utilize the energy project as an entry point to support new knowledge-intensive businesses, thereby upgrading the local economy in terms of capabilities and knowledge. Its focus is on the development of Technology-Intensive Suppliers (TIS), characterized by skilled activities such as manufacturing specialized machinery & production inputs and knowledge-intensive services. For instance, the utilization of geothermal energy in Mexico can open diverse new opportunities as well as challenges for SMEs, as specialized supplies and expertise in automation, precision, and scientific instruments, among others, are needed. Supporting the local supply of these goods and services avoids development in the form of enclaves, which export much of the production and import key inputs, capital goods and specialized services. In order to support this process, the project will actively promote, guide, and sustain the development of competitive new business models arising out of the energy project.

Another point of entry to climate mitigation in Mexico is **the promotion of social cohesion** by recognizing the importance of integrating societal groups into the value chain, preventing future conflicts that could delay mitigation projects. Social cohesion, or the lack thereof, has been a huge deficit in Mexico's democratic system, where the political elite has often pursued a top-down approach in policy-making, resulting in civil society groups concentrating more on governance issues rather than other important issues such as environmental protection and sustainable development. The participation of civil society groups can not only ensure a high level of public acceptance of renewable energies and the elimination of *caveats* against behavioral change, it can also promote evidence-based debates, which can further contribute to the maturity of technologies. Understanding the social ramifications of renewable energy technologies can help improve these technologies.

In addition, **promoting gender equality** can be a significant entry point to climate mitigation. The studies and investigations on gender elaborate upon the perspective of gender in analyzing how organizations and society produce inequalities through social positioning based on gender. Gender inequality is therefore an indicator of structures that produce various types of imbalances. Addressing and correcting gender inequality will most likely produce synergies and co-benefits that will resolve other types of imbalances. Masculinity and femininity are understood as cultural and social constructs through which society is organized and through which symbolical differences are defined. The category 'gender' fulfils the function of manifesting mechanisms and dispositions which create and reproduce spaces for the subordination, discrimination and marginalization of women in societies (see Kreisky 1979; 2008). The rationale for addressing the issue of gender equality and gender mainstreaming in research and innovation revolves around the principles of non-discrimination and equality, efficiency and competitiveness, preventing the waste the talent and potential contributions of highly educated women, increasing innovation potential and ensuring the conduct of socially responsible and accountable research and innovation through the integration of sex/gender analysis. Furthermore, integration of the gender dimension creates new ideas and opportunities for innovation. Thus, gender diversity and the consideration of the gender dimension in research content has a direct effect on improving scientific quality, social responsibility, and the robustness of research and innovation.

9.1.2.2 China

China has numerous entry points to climate mitigation. A major entry point to climate mitigation refers to China's efforts to **sustain and enhance its global economic competitiveness**, which legitimizes the current political regime. The Chinese government understood that from the examples of South Korea and Japan, its next phase of economic development involves a significant upgrade in its capacity to produce advanced and higher-value technologies, where China is able to own intellectual property rights. In addition, while there is still some resistance to its low-carbon energy transformation, traditional energy companies in China have fewer political resources to obstruct low-carbon policies. As such, these companies often pursue a pragmatic approach by cooperating with authorities and supporting policies that pose constraints to their own business interests. This is another entry point to climate mitigation in China, where the political system limits dissent and fosters a political culture where authorities are 'trusted.' Whether this trust is based on decades of propaganda through state controlled media, on collective narratives about the 'incorruptible' leaders (Hsu 2001), or on the persecution of dissenting voices is at this point a subject of a separate debate.

After a political crisis in the 1980s where intellectuals were able to draw upon the traditionalist collective narrative of corruption to blame the communist leadership for social problems, the Chinese government and the state-controlled media revised the narratives of corruption. In the 1990s, the role of the state was then no longer understood as a moral or ideological leader, but as that of an economic manager. As Hsu (2001) argues, Chinese leadership managed not only to control the corruption crisis, but it also found an effective channel for ensuring political legitimacy through the narrative "*economic prosperity*." With the slowing economic growth in China, the leadership has become more open to new policies that could sustain the very economic growth that legitimizes the current political order.

Another major entry point for climate mitigation is the **coupling of emission reduction with the recognition of the social, economic and health impacts of environmental degradation**, especially of air pollution (see Cao 2018; Trombetta 2019). Finally, shortly before and during the Beijing Olympic games, the Chinese leadership recognized the environmental effects of three decades of an economic growth that builds on high-carbon energy technologies. The social, economic and health impacts of air pollution in major cities, the loss of biodiversity, the water crisis, and soil contamination have created a sense of political urgency. These impacts of environmental degradation, as well as the impacts of climate change (extreme weather events and floods) are seen as threats to economic well-being. This urgency has opened another entry point for climate mitigation, paving way for the Xi Jinping administration (2013 to present) to adopt "ecological civilization" as a political vision. This vision was translated into actions including the restoration of decimated forests, efforts to stop the expansion of the Gobi Desert, the promotion of electric mobility, and eco-friendly urbanization. The most recent plan to realize this vision is the 4,500 km long 'Green Wall of China' or the 'Three-North-Shelterbelt Program' which is a huge ring of newly planted forests. This program, which was conceptualized as early as 2001, is planned to be completed by 2050 and aims to stabilize the soil, retain moisture and act as a buffer against further desertification (see BBC News 2001; Petri 2017).

9.2 Case Study: The Agency of Transformation Process in Mexico—Gaps in the Discursive Function of Governance

Some of the main challenges and barriers to Mexico's low-carbon transformation are defined by the dilemma of the self-fulfilling prophecy, whereas Mexico's current efforts, which are already perceived by Mexico as highly ambitious, are assessed as not enough to allow the country to achieve its NDC. This dilemma can be categorized as a structural barrier, as it limits the set of possible future actions. Particularly because Mexico's targets as concretized by its NDC are not consistent with limiting warming to below 2 °C, let alone with the Paris Agreement's stronger 1.5 °C limit, additional perspectives are needed. The Climate Action Tracker evaluates Mexico's current pledges. While Mexico has pledged to reduce its GHG emissions by 22 percent below baseline in 2030, equivalent to an increase of emissions by 56 percent above 1990 levels, the long-term pathway (red dashed lines) from 2030 to 2050 is simply, according to current knowledge, not attainable. Therefore, there is a need to conceptualize strategies that can be isolated from the anchors set by the knowledge that Mexico's efforts are not enough to attain the 2 °C goal.

Another challenge for Mexico's low-carbon transformation is to increase the clarity of strategies for reducing emissions in key sectors, particularly electricity and transportation. There is consensus in the policy, polity and politics sides that Mexico has the potential to move rapidly towards a low carbon future (ESMAP 2016). Although Mexico is a significant oil producer, it seeks to develop its vast potentials on renewable energies including geothermal, bioenergy, solar, and wind, because of steadily decreasing oil production since 2005. Nevertheless, Mexico still has a long way to go before it can depart from its dependence on fossil fuels, which constituted a total of 93 percent of the total energy consumption in 2015 (EIA 2016b).

With this background, low-carbon transformation in the country will require scenarios that provide fossil fuels with a bridging role to assure a bearable transition. New constitutional and policy reforms were already introduced by the government to promote transition, through diversification of the energy portfolio including tax reform, the liberalization of electricity supply, and ending the monopoly of the state-owned *Petroleós Mexicanos* (PEMEX). However, the volatility of world oil prices inhibits clear decisions, as the government might reverse some of its reforms when oil prices increase. Therefore, new arguments aside from low oil prices should be found as to why the development of renewable energies should be further expanded.

The current efforts of the government to achieve low-carbon economic development are defined by the country's national development policy as outlined in the "*Estrategia Nacional de Cambio Climático—Visión 10-20-40*" (National Climate Change Strategy) (SEMARNAT 2013). The national strategy is based on a study that encompasses various scenarios of emission reduction. The World Bank, in collaboration with the Energy Sector Management Assistance Program (ESMAP), conducted the study "*Mexico-Estudio Sobre la Disminución de Emisiones de Carbon*" for the Mexican government. The study assesses the potential for GHG reduction in Mexico in the next few decades. The main objective of the national strategy is to allow the country to significantly reduce it GHG emissions without hindering economic growth (ESMAP 2016). This principle mainly defines the tolerable window for Mexico's low-carbon economic development. Present and future decisions are required to follow this principle.

Based on this national strategy of the government, five principal sectors have been identified, indirectly identifying the different actors that need to be part of the negotiations—electric power (e.g., electricity utilities, transmission line providers), oil and gas (e.g., oil importers and suppliers, refineries, distributors), energy end-use (e.g. manufacturing and construction industries, residential, commercial and public sectors), transport (e.g., road transportation companies), and agriculture and forestry (e.g., crop and timer producers, forest land managers and biomass energy producers). Aside from the evident actors, societal groups, including indigenous communities, the urban poor, farmers and fishers, will want to participate in all decision-making processes, as their livelihood, culture, and self-determination will be affected by any changes made in these five sectors. The concrete roles of these actors are, however, not explicitly discussed in government policy papers. In addition, there is no clear reference to formal procedures that would allow stakeholders to be fully integrated into the formal decision-making process.

Low-carbon transformation in Mexico requires 'strong' and strategic policies. However, it is argued by this book that Mexico needs to complement these ambitious energy, climate protection, and sustainable policies with reforms of its governance system, particularly how state institutions should function as a nexus of social integration. As it will be discussed in this section, democratic structures in Mexico further conflate various conflicts, with challenges to climate protection merging with governance issues, further increasing the complexity of low-carbon transformation. As many conflict cases involving renewable energy projects in Mexico suggest (e.g., wind power in Oaxaca), it will most likely make no difference whether Mexico will be successful in designing policies that will make it achieve its NDC or not, as in both cases these policies will lack legitimacy, as they often do not carry social acceptance, particularly in local communities. **Without this social acceptance, the ambitious climate protection policies of the central government will be initially framed and defined as intrusion.**

9.2.1 Analysis between the Ideal Type and the Empirical Case Study of Mexico—Causal Mechanisms through Congruence Methods and Process-Tracing

Chapter 8 has introduced the democratic policy pathway as an ideal type of transformation. The following are the most relevant provisions of this ideal type in the context of transformation towards sustainability:

- The competitive advantage of political actors in democratic countries is defined by how it can manage to align their political interests with public opinion or how these political actors can shape public opinion.

- Universities and other academic institutions play a significant role in providing 'public space' where various societal groups can meet and exchange perspectives.
- Consensus-building mechanisms have the purpose of defining consensual knowledge.
- The government agenda on low-carbon transformation is significantly defined by the ideological preferences of the political party in power, which determine the feasibility of technology options and other viable alternatives in achieving the policy goals.
- Institutions are responsible for the monitoring, evaluation and verification of government actions.
- Politics is dynamic and is defined by power relations between actors
- Existing polities serve as formal and material frameworks that allows weaker parties to cope with asymmetrical relations
- Polities review how new policies are in accordance with the existing rules of the game while evaluating the resilience of the system.
- While the government may set the limits of what is politically acceptable through guard-rails that exclude intolerable impacts to both the issues involved and the instruments chosen to address these issues, the same government needs to adhere to these limits.
- The transition process and the transformed stage need to accommodate calls for re-negotiations through pre-defined measures.

The next step pertains to the enumeration and analysis of the deviations, where theoretical and empirical explanations to these deviations will be introduced. These explanations will focus on causal mechanisms.

▶ Democratic structures conflate various conflicts, delaying the sustainable, low-carbon transformation process.

One major deviation of the Mexican transformation process from the ideal type is that Mexico's **democratic structures actually conflate various conflicts**. For example, with climate protection policies reduced to mere questions of 'governance,' the effective implementation of climate protection policies will be contingent on how deficiencies of governance are effectively addressed. While the climate agenda can be defined by the ideological preferences of the political party or administration in power, with the conflation of various conflicts, the feasibility of technology options to achieve low-carbon transformation is no longer defined by the ideological preferences of the ruling political actor *vis-à-vis* low-carbon transformation, **but rather by its ideological preferences on governance.** This delays the sustainable, low-carbon transformation process.

This deviation can be explained by how **the state monopolizes the public sphere**. Compared to the provision of the ideal type, which suggests that the competitive advantage of political actors in democratic countries is defined by how they can manage to align their political interests with public opinion, or how these political actors can shape public opinion, the political elite in Mexico is able to profit from unequal, old practices and traditions based on dependence, such as clientelism, corporatism, and patrimonialism, which further reinforces legitimacy gaps, as political actors have a high degree of structural autonomy from the society (see Olvera 1997). Furthermore, the concomitant absence of operative legal institutions as well as the limited public space for normative political discussions further contribute to the state's monopoly of the public sphere, which motivates the **'over-politicization' of specific issues** (including climate protection and sustainable development) in order to maintain state control.

Mexico's capacity to host representative public discourse is yet to be developed in a way that is inclusive and that moves away from the center-periphery structure of decision-making (see Aguilera Portales & Gonzáles Cruz 2010). The current lack of opportunity to participate and express interests in forums is seen to increase and further justify violence towards politicians, which further motivates politicians to defer consultations. Mexican civil society faces various difficulties inhibiting their full participation in decision-making (Aguilera Portales 2010; Aguilera Portales & Sánchez Garcia 2010). Alberto Olvera (1997) argues that the unstable character of a civil society composed of social movements without, or with limited, operative civil, political, and social rights and capacities limit any type of transformation process. These difficulties are perceived to have roots in the colonial period, where a small but powerful elite was successful in politically, socially, and economically disenfranchising the majority of the population by completely insulating itself from societal influences. While local communities are usually able to influence local decisions, several decisions made in the capital city, especially those involving international partners including multinational companies, are often already finalized in closed-door meetings without prior consultation at the local level. These decisions often face resistance, further politicizing issues. This can be regarded as the result of Mexico's complex, segregated and decentralized policy processes, whereas the coordination and fusion of public and private resources are still controlled by the federal government, especially when these resources are provided by donors from abroad. Particularly when international projects follow a strict time schedule, the lengthy process of consultation at various levels will most likely motivate policy-makers to skip tedious consultations.

> Relevant stakeholders, particularly in the civil society, are unable to participate in the consensus-building process, because they are unable to influence the definition of consensual knowledge.

The ideal type of democratic policy model denotes a highly educated and informed civil society that is capable of understanding and defining problems and their technical aspects, identifying relevant agendas, and assessing the effectiveness of proposed solutions. As Mexico needs to come up with a clear plan to implement its transition from fossil fuels to renewable energies through robust policies and regulations, the government needs to mobilize local partners, which include social groups, to enable rapid deployment of policies. For the civil society to be able to identify and assess the social and environmental impacts of the implementation of policies, it requires the opportunity to contribute to consensual knowledge.

In Mexico, a significant vacuum in the technical expertise of its civil society representatives is seen as a major hindrance to including them in technical consultations (Aguilera Portales 2011). Without a proper understanding of the technical issues involved, their potential participation in any type of knowledge diplomacy (see chapter 5) is merely "rhetorical" and is therefore not expected to yield constructive discussions and solutions, which further motivates the political elite to exclude them. In addition, the ideal type entails that all decisions made by policy-makers are happen after consultation with societal groups in a self-evident manner. Deviation from the conditions of this ideal type can be explained in various ways. One possible explanation is that organizing consultation processes is dependent on existing networks. As a network, stakeholders have already been identified and cooperation is self-evident. Similar to many countries in Latin America, advocacy by non-governmental organizations in Mexico is usually connoted as opposition to state actions, which are often seen as lacking transparency and political accountability (Aguilera Portales & Gonzáles Cruz 2010). With this background, Mexican societal groups are distrustful of cooperation with perceived authoritarian state agencies (Franco et al. 2010; Natal et al. 2010; Martínez-Cárdenas et al. 2015). This manifests as the reality that social capital is yet to be strengthened in Mexico. High social capital means state agencies can be trusted to pursue the interests of society even when these interests contrast with their own personal interests.

Mexican civic society initially mobilized the broader society in the 1980s to form urban social movements, and continued in 1990s to demand transparent political processes and political accountability following the electoral fraud in 1988 (see Fox & Hernandez 1992; Aguayo Quezada & Parra Rosales 1997). This mobilization was highly repressed by the federal and state governments, as it was seen as a threat to the political stability of the country. From that point to the present, the attention and resources of Mexican civil society has been primarily directed towards good governance (see Feinberg et al. 2006). Environmental issues that affect various parts of society are more often addressed as merely a question of political governance, particularly regarding the political inclusion of marginalized sectors of society. Here arise various missed opportunities, both for Mexican civil society and policy-makers. For example, the resistance of indigenous communities to the wind farm project of *Mareña Renovables* in Oaxaca is merely seen as a political conflict, with the indigenous opposition not allowing any talks, taking the attention of the debate away from the concrete environmental and livelihood problems arising from the project (see McGovern 2014).

Another deviation of Mexico from the ideal type pertains to the lack of self-evident relationships between policy-makers and epistemic communities, between policy-makers and advocacy groups, and between epistemic communities and advocacy groups. The National Strategy refers to the potential role of civil society groups and of the research community. However, it is not clear whether all relevant civil society groups were involved in any form of the consultation process when drafting this national strategy or when writing the background paper through the World Bank. Low-carbon economy development in Mexico will affect all aspects of human life, from land use change to livelihood, from forms of housing to transportation. Therefore, the national strategy should also define consultation processes with both civil society groups and epistemic communities.

- The history of Mexico 'disqualifies' presumed hosts or facilitators of public discourse

As identified by the ideal type, universities and other academic institutions can play a significant role in providing a 'public space' where various societal groups can meet and exchange perspectives. Universities and other academic institutions are often chosen as venues of public debate as they symbolize objectivity and neutrality. In several European countries, public discourse is often hosted by such institutions. In other countries like the Philippines and Thailand, the church often provides 'venues' or actively facilitates dialogues between conflict groups. Historically, however, both universities and the church are not seen as suitable and credible facilitators in Mexico. The Revolution of 1910, where the Catholic Church in Mexico served as one of the hallmark supporters of the dictatorship of Porfirio Diaz, reminds social movements that the Catholic Church is a force of the right and that it only pursues its own interest (see Quirk 1973). In the same manner, universities have traditionally played the role of (left) opposition to the government (see Lorey 1993). With this background, looking back at the ideal type diagram, the public consensus approach still needs to be developed in Mexico.

This case study on Mexico is not a comprehensive analysis of the transformation process of Mexico. Using the ideal type, relevant questions can be formulated that could be subjects of further studies.

9.3 Case Study: The Agency of Transformation Process in China—State-Guided Transition Management

China's sustainable, low-carbon transformation has profited from past decisions made by the Chinese leadership, whose primary interest of maintaining the political legitimacy of its authoritarian regime has proven to have produced favorable conditions for China's low-carbon transformation. China's reforms and drive to open up have catalyzed a series of transformations in their society, economy and politics (Haifeng 2014). Unlike in democratic regimes, where governments often think that they can rely on the electoral process alone for legitimacy, authoritarian regimes depend on other means of legitimacy. After decades of seeing climate protection as something that undermines its economic development, or that emissions are merely a matter of international diplomacy rather than environmental sustainability (see Aden & Sinton 2006), China has begun to play a prominent role in reaching the Paris Agreement. With this shift in behavior, the Chinese leadership has finally acknowledged that by joining the global trend of low-carbon transition, it can further expand its political legitimacy (see Cao 2018).

Surprisingly, this change in China's behavior is made possible by its earlier decisions, which serve as necessary components of policy changes. For example, by changing its national development strategy in 2002, prioritizing economic efficiency between 1992–2002 by reforming its welfare policies, and by opting to prioritize economic efficiency while giving consideration to fairness (Li 2013), policies that aim to promote sustainable development and climate protection that were often perceived as undermining economic growth are now getting the attention of reformers. China's high economic growth was not translated into a 'trickle down' of wealth to a huge portion of the population, as income inequality has continuously increased, leading to popular unrest. The SARS crisis in 2003 further motivated the government and the urban Chinese population to expand its welfare system as the negative externalities of unaffordable healthcare became visible (Li 2013).

Additional concerns have emerged as the pace of China's economic growth, in terms of real growth of GDP, has slowed down since 2007 (from 14.2 percent in 2007, to 9.4 percent in 2009, to 7.9 percent in 2012, to 6.7 percent in 2016) (NBS 2017). In light of the 2007 financial crisis and the threat of economic recession in China, the Chinese leadership recognized the necessity of restructuring the economy to reduce dependency on exports and boost domestic demand. To achieve this, a whole range of policies have been designed and implemented that aim to support economic growth while at the same time producing benefits to social welfare (Li 2013). Massive investments were executed, including in the transport network and urban power supply. It can be argued that this massive investment in the transportation sector has subsequently promoted modes of transportation that are run by electricity. After almost ten years of investment and the upgrade of infrastructures, policies and decisions from that point on have tended to favor renewable energies, because renewables are, with the availability of appropriate infrastructures, more attractive than fossil fuels. The modernization of the urban power supply to major Chinese cities has defined a stable and promising domestic energy demand, which increasingly prefers renewable energies.

In addition, with the slowing of the GDP, the Chinese leadership has accepted the need of gradually defining economic growth with industrial quality and efficiency promotion to accelerate the adjustment of economic structures leading to the shift from a factor- and investment-driven economy into an innovation-driven one (He 2016). With huge investment and upgrades already having been conducted more than ten years ago, China is now determined to actively promote the transformation of its economic development pattern, its supply-side structural reform of the energy system, and its domestic consumption behavior to achieve a sustainable, low-carbon system while building and further expanding upon its core competitiveness. Moreover, the central government seeks to address the over-capacity practices of high-energy consuming industries (He 2016).

China is expected to overachieve the CO_2 reduction goals in its NDC, as well as its own national targets. China's CO_2 emissions may have peaked more than ten years ahead of its Paris Agreement commitment of hitting its peak CO_2 emissions before 2030. Around 2020, the terminal energy consumption and CO_2

emissions from the industrial sector are expected to peak. Nevertheless, as the following figure illustrates, its NDC is not ambitious enough to be consistent with holding warming to below 2 °C, let alone limiting it to 1.5 °C as required under the Paris Agreement, and is instead consistent with warming between 3 °C and 4 °C. Furthermore, the absence of comparable commitments regarding other, non-CO_2 gases could mean that China's total GHG emissions will continue to increase until at least 2030.

9.3.1 A comparison of the Ideal Type and an Empirical Case Study of China—Causal Mechanisms through Congruence Methods and Process-Tracing

China fits the primary condition of the ideal type of an authoritarian policy model. The Chinese regime is considered to be continually stable and robust. While democratic movements have gained significance in the country, these are generally limited to Hong Kong. The economic transition of China can be argued as evidence that a market-oriented economy can exist within the political parameters of an authoritarian regime by complementing market policies with social welfare reforms.

The following are the most relevant provisions of this ideal type in the context of transformation, where significant deviations in the Chinese case can be observed:

- The recruitment of new members of the political elite is structured and eidetic.
- The interaction between policy-makers and scientific communities often involves scientific and technocratic elites with long-standing relationships with the state.
- Issues are securitized, paving way to the "suspension" of some current rules and the adoption of new rules, which gradually leads to a "new normal", particularly in political agenda-setting.
- Because stable authoritarian regimes derive their (output) legitimacy primarily from their performance in achieving indicators of modernization, bureaucracies of authoritarian regimes will most likely play a very significant role in the planning and management of processes.
- Although authoritarian countries tend to be governed center-to-periphery and top-down, there is a predictability of institutional interactions (implying stability), as the character of historically dominant policies will define the policies taken in new areas.

- Persuasion interaction between elites and other social actors in authoritarian policy pathways tend to occur through informal and non-public channels, which are effective in channeling resistance towards constructive and cooperative relationships.
- Because authoritarian regimes will most likely influence all aspects of the transformation process, outcomes will require cooperation between different levels of state authority.

As in the case study of Mexico, the next step refers to the enumeration and analysis of the deviations, where theoretical and empirical explanations of these deviations will be introduced and explained.

9.3.1.1 The changing meaning of social connections in selecting the political elite in China

Authoritarian regimes are often defined by the exclusiveness of important political positions. Eidetic recruitment of the political elite is a major characteristic of their bureaucracies (e.g., a military regime with military personnel holding positions). Selection to the elite is usually defined mainly by political loyalty. While this is, in principle, also the case in China, where only members of the Communist Party can hold government positions, recruitment to the political elite in China has developed further than this. The criteria of selection now instead cater to efficiency, while pursuing the inclusion of ethnic minorities into the political elite. There are additional factors, which transcend party membership, that determine one's recruitment. In the last three decades, the Chinese leadership has instilled rules and norms into its elite selection process, prioritizing qualification and efficiency through nascent institutional mechanisms (see Cheng & Yiou 2017). Such mechanisms include the formal institutionalization of the inclusion of ethnic minority cadres among party-state elites through the Law of Ethnic Minority Autonomous Areas of the People's Republic of China. The Law stipulates that the top post in the local government in all ethnic minority autonomous areas (from the township level to the provincial level) should be held by a leader from the same ethnic minority background as the majority of citizens in that area (Cheng Li & Yiou Zhang 2017).

The academic literature on the selection of China's political elite identifies '*Guanxi*,' the network-based system of favor exchange, as the major principle that drives political, economic and social interactions (see Chen & Chao 2004). Nevertheless, in addition to formal rules, there are informal rules, particularly when selecting candidates for top positions that intend to circumvent *Guanxi*. For example, in the six CCP Central Committees that have formed since the 13th

Party Congress in 1987, ethnic minorities have been represented in the committee (between 10 to 11 percent of the membership). In addition, the seven-member Politburo, the most powerful body in the Chinese government, is itself responsible for selecting new members (Shirk 2012). Due to the informal rules adhered to by Politburo members, social connections and personal ties will instead reduce the likelihood of being selected to the Politburo. For example, officials will be required to recuse themselves from evaluating candidates from their own regions or those who have connections to them, like college ties (see Fisman et al. 2017).

Reforms in governance and other structural changes have further supported the creation of a new political elite. The concept of 'elite dualism' has defined the Chinese system of governance. The division of labor between the CCP and the government in governance has led to two distinctive career paths. While candidates for elite positions in the CCP are screened for technical qualifications and political credentials, those candidates for government positions are screened more rigorously for their human capital. In addition, promotion in the government system is more dependent on efficiency compared with promotions in the CCP hierarchy (Xiaowei 2004). This elite dualism can be identified as conducive to any transformation process that requires technical expertise from its policy-makers.

The selection of the political elite in China can be seen as similar to best 'practices' in democratic countries that aim to address corruption and red tape. While it can also be interpreted that these provisions in China are designed for propaganda purposes, they also promote efficiency, as social connections are increasingly limited by both formal and informal practices. In general, this development is not only beneficial when ensuring the long-term political legitimacy of the regime, but this also supports the low-carbon transformation process, as new recruits coming from other networks can provide much needed out-of-the-box thinking. China's new political elite has now a more integrated and pragmatic understanding of politics, economics, social issues and technologies compared with its past leadership (see Khan 2013).

9.3.1.2 Institutional Interactions through Partnerships—Urban Entrepreneurialism and Urban Clusters (Chengshiqun) in China

Authoritarian regimes dominate institutional, functional and bargaining interactions simply through their 'omnipresence' within government agencies, playing a very significant role in the planning and implementation of policies at all levels of governance. Past reforms have moved China significantly further away from a strict center-to-periphery and top-down style of governance. Rather than being a monolithic system, China's governance of science, innovation, and environmental decision-making has been characterized by 'fragmented authoritarianism,' with protracted bargaining between bureaucracy units, including ministries, advisory bodies and top-level 'National Leading Groups' (see Heggelund 2004; Tyfield et al. 2015) as well as fragmentation between levels of government. Partnerships between multiple stakeholders are reinforced by local networks, for example, between state-owned and private companies. These networks have been mobilized to implement the government's climate protection goals. Such networks include the Alliance of Peaking Pioneer Cities that aim to hit the peak of their city emissions in advance of national targets (see Hale 2017).

Another example of structural changes that are now unfolding refers to how local governments have re-invented themselves and how they have sought partnerships with business companies to promote local development. However, this development in China can also be understood as a measure of 'regaining' competencies that were increasingly outsourced by the state following the opening of markets to international business actors. Some scholars such as Jonas and Ward (Harrison & Hoyler 2014; see Jonas & Ward 2016) have claimed that the formation of city-region governance is a deliberate process of scale building, which involves both state and non-state actors. In addition, the re-emergence of city-region governance can be understood as a direct reaction to globalization, as Neil Brenner's (1999, 2004) research on 'state spatiality' describes, where the rise of regional governance can be broadly understood as a process of 'state reterritorialization', and the specific form of the city-region as 'state spatial selectivity', which means that a specific scale has been chosen or built by the state.

In many areas, such as Kunshan, a small city around 60 kilometers west of Shanghai, the formation and transformation of urban entrepreneurialism has facilitated economic devolution, paving the way for such areas to break out of the institutional constraints of state socialism and innovatively promote further devolution formally and informally from the state towards a development zone and town governance (Shiuh-Shen & Fulong 2011). Local and city governments started to transform themselves into market-friendly agents whose key goals are to form an alliance with more investors to promote local economic development. The functionality of city governments has changed from being mainly a social welfare deliverer to an economic development promoter. This change has further cemented the prioritization of economic efficiency at the grass-root levels.

Furthermore, as an indirect consequence of increased competition among cities, urban governance has become more cooperative, with other neighboring administrations under certain regional coordination by upper-level governments. The concept of urban clusters (*chengshiqun*) (Yao & Zhu 1992) has been revived and included as part of the agenda of government policies, either to build stronger coalitions for regional competitiveness or to solve the over-concentration of growth in large central cities (Wu 2016). Particularly because of the limits of economies of scale, local governments have opted to share and combine resources to maximize benefits. Interestingly, the resurgence of urban clusters in China has been highlighted as an effective policy, as China has sought to solve environmental problems. For example, in an effort to find solutions to the problems of smog and population over-concentration, the Chinese leader Xi Jinping proposed, in 2014, a regional approach to the future development of Beijing in the capital's region (*Jing-Jin-Ji*), which led to further discussions about city-region governance (Wu 2016). In March 2015, the central government approved the outline of the Jing-Jin-Ji Collaborative Development Plan, which indicated that the notion of the urban cluster had become an official term in governance and had become popularized. In May 2016, the State Council approved the Yangtze River Delta Urban Cluster Development Plan (Wu 2016).

This newly evolved state-led coordinative and collaborative urban entrepreneurialism is regarded as one of the most important principles of China's market transition. While many villages still adhere to strong local corporatism, where family and kin members control local enterprises, this trend demonstrates an increase in the leasing of collectively-owned enterprises to private actors (see Heggelund 2009; Shiuh-Shen & Fulong 2011). In addition, in contrast to the market logic, Chinese state-owned companies, which account for 80 percent of the stock market, tend to be more receptive to 'indigenous innovation' (*zizhu chuangxin*) mainly because of this state control (see Haifeng 2014).

As the central, regional, and local governments release new policy goals, such as moving up the value chain, state owned companies will tend to 'sacrifice' profit-making in order to internalize such policy goals. Furthermore, with the reform of elite selection (elite dualism) in place, government units are now technically able to effectively design and implement local development. With this new self-identification as an 'entrepreneurial state' (Mazzucato 2013), the Chinese central, regional, and local governments are not only driving research and development investment in strategic 'green' sectors, they are also constructing a market for innovation and building the skilled workforce required to serve emerging ideas of eco-innovation (see Tyfield et al. 2015) Furthermore, the asymmetrical transformation of the political and economic spheres in China involve the decentralization, in part, of economic decision-making, while the political system remains centralized and cadre promotion is based on the evaluation of the economic performance of their jurisdictions (Shiuh-Shen & Fulong 2011).

9.4 Chapter Conclusion—Theory Testing and the Implications of Case Findings for Theory and Practice

Of particular interest, in terms of the outcomes of the case studies, is how the gaps between theory and practice can be bridged. The case studies highlight how Mexico and China's deviation from the theoretical models of democratic and authoritarian policy models have captured interesting causalities that can be further conceptualized.

9.4.1 Lessons for Theory

The hypothesis that the successful implementation of sustainable, low-carbon policies is highly contingent on the capacity and autonomy of the State can be confirmed. However, as vindicated by the case studies, the terms 'capacity' and 'autonomy' require further concretization. State capacity, in the context of sustainable, low-carbon transformation, can be understood as how the State is able to accommodate different the perspectives of stakeholders affected by changes. As highlighted by Bruce Gilley (2012), China has the advantage of having relatively strong institutions that could manage the participatory process so as to ensure complementarities of top-down and bottom-up mechanisms (see Fraser et al. 2006; Stringer et al. 2007). Thus, as Gilley (2012) concludes, China had a potential advantage over more democratic regimes with weak states such as the Philippines and Thailand, as well as over more authoritarian regimes with weak states such as Myanmar (see Myint 2007).

As the Chinese leadership has linked inclusiveness with efficiency, formal and informal rules have been introduced and institutionalized to ensure representation in various decision-making processes. In contrast to China, Mexico seems to have more difficulties in engaging various stakeholders. In addition, autonomy, in the context of sustainable, low-carbon transformation, can pertain to how specific issues can be initially securitized to attract political attention and later on de-politicized to promote constructive collaboration. China is able to achieve a "new normal" in addressing emerging issues, because of structural reforms allowing the formal separation of political and non-political decision-making, where in some cases, non-political decision-making is outsourced to non-political actors for efficiency reasons. In Mexico, sustainable development and environmental issues are trapped in the political sphere, because of how the decision-making has been structured.

Moreover, a comparison of the case studies on Mexico and China confirms that a democratic policy model does not guarantee inclusiveness in decision-making. Because of Mexico's focus on the electoral process as the main legitimizing source of governance, there is a sense that this question of legitimacy has already been resolved. Thus, there seems to be less motivation to ensure the efficiency of policies, as legitimacy has already been covered by electoral victories. In addition, as the Council on Hemispheric Affairs (2011) points out, failure in implementing robust, democratic foundations has led and has reinforced structural imbalances that promote *clientelism* in Mexican politics. In the context of sustainable, low-carbon transformation, Mexico's focus on the electoral process has unintentionally framed sustainability and climate mitigation as mere problems of governance, instead of ones of social cohesion, long-term and inclusive economic development, and of environmental integrity. By tracing the process of legitimization, the *equifinality* of paths becomes evident, as different paths can produce both similar and different outcomes and as similar paths can also produce both similar and different outcomes.

Nevertheless, China's focus on output legitimacy and the introduction of a "new normal" have both led to the kind of structural changes that are supposed to only be observed in democratic regimes. With economic efficiency combined with social welfare as the main principles, new formal and informal rules in policy-making in various spatial levels have been established. For example, family, hometown, and college ties & connections are increasingly negatively affecting a person's selection to the Chinese political and economic elite. Therefore, elite recruitment has become more inclusive and fluid in China. Elite dualism and urban entrepreneurialism can be assessed as positively affecting sustainable, low-carbon transformation, because of wider participation in decision-making processes. While China cannot represent all existing authoritarian regimes, this case study demonstrates the normative traps of some theories (e.g., democratic peace) and how a case-to-case perspective can provide knowledge on the limitations of such theories.

In addition, while holistic approaches are needed as a basis for the comparison of cases which can be provided by "alternative settings" in order to generate useful knowledge, as the Ideal types suggest, additional subjects and additional ways of analyzing historical social processes for further research can allow a more integrated approach to problems and solutions. The introduced ideal type of transformation looks at the orchestration of various negotiation processes that are occurring at various levels within the system. The understanding of these different interdependencies in the various levels supports strategic planning in order to reduce transition costs and increase the political legitimacy of the outcome of the processes. Knowing that specific activities are aiming to come up with the agenda provides some time to prepare and manage conflicts that can be anticipated.

9.4.2 Lessons for Practice

The reasons why some climate protection measures are more successful in some countries than others cannot be fully explained, for example, by merely determining whether a country is democratic or authoritarian. It also depends on how "success" is defined. While China is often applauded because of its commitment to certain climate protection measures, it remains a question of whether it can still be considered as a success for climate protection when the motivations behind these decisions are not to protect the climate but, for instance, to combat air pollution. What happens when such goals have already been met before achieving long-term climate protection goals? Nevertheless, this question is only relevant when authoritarianism is understood as monolithic. For example, civil society groups and other stakeholders have more leverage over decision-making around environmentalism, climate change and innovation policies than in previous eras in China (Tyfield et al. 2015).

While governance structures have obvious and latent implications for societal consensus-building processes, consensus-building is dependent on the formal and material capacities of the relevant stakeholders to actually participate in the process. Effective management of transformation processes needs to effectively establish 'negotiative' mechanisms that allow the continuous revisiting of decisions that have been made in the past. The case study on Mexico's transformation process is merely a glimpse into the factors that are often neglected in the strategic planning of transformation to a low-carbon economy. Consensus-building is not self-perpetuating, especially not on countries with a government crisis related to the lack of transparency and accountability. Issues such as creating public space and empowering societal groups to be able to participate in orchestrated negotiation processes are often not adequately included or addressed in national strategies. As Raiza Pilatowsky Gruner (2016) argues, Mexico's lack of transparency and accountability at all levels of government will remain a major challenge and barrier to climate change national goals being enforced. This is reflected in a shortage of implementation and surveillance mechanisms and clear actions that will help to comply with the Paris Agreement pledges the country has made. With recent efforts of civil society groups to demand accountability and transparency from all levels of governance, climate policies can become 'collateral damage.'

The emergence of a bottom-up, green public space is crucial to the sustainable, low-carbon transformation process. By developing the capacity of societal actors to express and pursue their interests, decisions that are made will most likely become more effective. Inclusivity is an investment, because the costs of transition will not only be shouldered by more actors, but the total costs will also be limited, as individual stakeholders will limit the negative externalities that they are producing for the others, because they will also be paying for them.

The Philippines as a Case Study—Populism and Institutional Activism in Transformation Processes Towards Sustainability

10

The current resurgence and reinforcement of populists in many countries has profited not only from various real or imagined crises (e.g., 2015-present refugee crisis in Europe or the caravan of migrants in Latin America heading to the United States), but also from how established political parties and polities have addressed these crises, which have disenfranchised, in a *de facto* manner, a significant portion of the population (see White 2016). Former Greek finance minister and Professor of Economics at the University of Athens, Yanis Varoufakis, notes that President Trump's election, Brexit, and the resurgence of right-wing political parties in Germany, Austria & other countries are not new in history, but merely "*a post-modern variant of the 1930s, complete with deflation, xenophobia, and divide-and-rule politics*" (Varoufakis 2016). Populist movements have found and instrumentalized compelling issues, such as emission reduction, to gain political importance. For example, in an attempt to re-gain political importance, they have taken emission reduction as an example of a policy instrument that undermines national interests because they negatively affect job opportunities in various coal-dependent regions.

Many experts (see Storck & Stehr 2010; Stehr 2015; White 2016) argue that ambitious climate protection measures are also questions of governance and politics. As climate protection policies have become part of the "new normal" and of the mainstream socio-political and sociolinguistic narratives, they have also united and mobilized 'climate change deniers,' critics of the political 'establishment,' nationalists, xenophobes, alt-right groups, and fossil fuel interest groups to pose a coherent and effective political opposition. Because 'climate change policies' and 'climate science' have been mainstreamed or in some cases narrated as 'linked' with liberal ideas in the past few years, questions relevant to climate change have been unintentionally reduced to being only matters of political decisions and actions. With the rise of counter-movements including

A. M. Hernández, *Taming the Big Green Elephant*, Globale Gesellschaft und internationale Beziehungen, https://doi.org/10.1007/978-3-658-31821-5_10

anti-intellectualism and the emergence of the post-truth era, climate science, which has initiated political discussions on climate protection, is being delegitimized by actors in various directions, which is often not hard to do, due to the complexity and uncertainty of climate change as well as due to the conceptual and methodological limitations of scientific methods.

The Philippines and the United States (see Chapter 11) are two of the several countries wherein nationalists and right-wing populists have profited from such anti-intellectualist, anti-democratic, anti-establishment, anti-media, and post-truth movements as well as from the context of the political system. For example, with the absence of a run-off in the electoral system of the Philippines, as the official canvas of the Congress of the Philippines concluded, the populist President Rodrigo Duterte won the presidential election with the second-smallest mandate in Philippine history (Nery 2017), with just 39.01 percent of the counted electoral votes (16,601,997 votes). Rodrigo Duterte's campaign was based on hostility towards the 'West', the corrupt political establishment, the independent press, and on dehumanizing (real and alleged) criminals, including drug addicts.

With several similarities and the parallel development of the Philippines and the United States following the election of a populist leader, this chapter and the following chapter will provide important insights into understanding how a system can adapt to a regime hostile to many principles of sustainable development and climate protection. As a former colony of the United States, the Philippines has a political system that closely resembles that of the United States. A major focus is given to the role of social movements, including non-profits, advocacy groups, non-government organizations or NGOs, and other civil society groups, using an ideal type of the institutional activism-dominated policy model. In the case of the Philippines, populism and institutional activism have merged. Furthermore, the Philippine context challenges the existing 'right-left' dichotomy of political ideology with the 'textbook' right-wing Duterte regime debarring political opposition from the Left by 'subcontracting' certain policies to left-wing actors.

Finding compelling reasons for long-term climate protection under President Duterte is challenging, particularly because the Philippines is not a major emitter of greenhouse gases or GHG. In addition, the sociolinguistic narrative on climate protection in the Philippines is instead focused on climate adaptation. Because the country is one of the most vulnerable to the impacts of climate change, climate protection through emission reduction has not yet caught the attention of policy-makers and the Philippine society in general. The Paris Climate Agreement is generally linked with more international support of adaptation projects in the country. Upon ratification, the Philippines will have access to the Green

Climate Fund, which will be funded with USD 100 million annually by developed countries to support vulnerable and low-emitting countries confronted with climate change. Therefore, unlike in the United States, populist groups in the Philippines cannot draw more popular support by rejecting the Paris agreement. Despite previous negative comments about the Paris Climate Agreement, President Duterte approved the agreement through his signature and his submission of the instrument of accession to the Philippine Senate for ratification of the Paris Agreement on February 28, 2017 (Salaverria 2017).

An analysis of politics in the Philippines remains interesting, as President Duterte contains political opposition by dividing social movements. After his inauguration, he appointed three left-wing activists to his cabinet, including an environmental activist as Secretary of the Department on Environment and Natural Resources and a social activist as Secretary of the Department of Social Welfare and Development. As part of the social movement, the appointed environment Sec. Gina Lopez has typically used strategies common to advocacy groups in achieving goals.

Furthermore, another unique feature of the Philippine political system has led to the President's control of various social and environmental movements through the party-list system, through which, as mandated by the 1987 constitution (Article VI, Section 5 (i) and 2), 57 seats or 20 percent of the total seats in the House of Representatives are reserved for purportedly under-represented community sectors or groups, including labor, peasant, urban poor, senior citizens, indigenous, women, youth, and other such sectors (see Santos 1997). With elected social interest groups seeking collaboration with the newly elected president to increase the prospect of achieving their interests, social groups that are indifferent to specific issues are involved in 'tit-for-tats'.

While tolerating the appointment and presence of civil-group representatives who were linked with the military, several leftist house representatives, who were elected into the Philippine Congress through the party-list system, have declared their support of President Duterte and informally agreed to a 'truce' with the military. This co-option of various social movements through President Duterte can be interpreted as a strategy to stabilize his political control, as it prevents alliances between major social and environmental groups and the political opposition. With potential challengers, such as opposition politicians, court justices, and human rights commissioners currently in the defensive mode as most of them were removed from positions in important committees in the Senate and House of Representatives, and while some are currently facing impeachment trials or criminal charges or even imprisoned, no viable dissenters can mobilize popular support to the political opposition.

In addition, the current administration, like previous administrations, is profiting from the incapacities of political and legal constraints provided by state institutions, such as courts and the commission on human rights. This incapacity is further exacerbated by the 'weaponization' of congress' power to impeach (Nery 2017) and of the '*quo warranto*'- power of the Solicitor General, as manifested by the recent removal of the Supreme Court Chief Justice on grounds that she failed to submit a requirement prior to her appointment as Chief Justice, making her appointment by former President Benigno Aquino void (see Garcia 2018; Cabuenas 2018).

Further discrediting social movements, a legitimacy crisis within civil society groups emerged following the "pork barrel scam scandal", where politicians allegedly partnered with NGOs to divert and misuse their Priority Development Assistance Fund, popularly called "pork barrel," for personal gains (see Doronila 2013; Ubac 2013). In addition, many civil liberties and rights groups refuse to collaborate with current opposition politicians (or their families), whom they highly criticized when the latter were still in power. The current administration in the Philippines, after it has successfully co-opted major civil society groups represented in the House of Representatives, will most likely not expect a unified political opposition.

The goal of this chapter is to analyze and conceptualize the role of social movements, advocates, non-profits (and to a lesser degree profitable enterprises) and other civil society groups as agents of the transformation process towards sustainability in a political framework or a context that is partially or fully adversarial or hostile towards political deliberation. By understanding the resources and strategies available to these social actors when promoting or encountering policies that are conducive to sustainable, low-carbon development, best practices can be derived. In addition, the comparison of this case study with a theoretical model (ideal type) will be conducted. The Philippine case study will be analyzed using the ideal type of an institutional activism policy model.

Hypothesis 1: *Looking at the 'negotiative' requirement of transformation towards sustainability, the benefits and risks of institutional activism and social movements are highly contingent upon existing power relations and structures as well as on the level of capacity and autonomy of the State.*

Existing power relations and structures, as well as the level of capacity and autonomy of the state, motivate and alter utility values for advocacy groups and social movements who were embedded into the policy stream. Will the (liberal) normative concerns that often define social movements refrain them from instrumentalizing power asymmetries when they are in power? Will they deploy resources in strategic ways and compete with other stakeholders, including other NGOs and other social movements?

Hypothesis 2: *While institutional activism can facilitate rapid policy formulation, it can also reinforce existing inequalities in countries with low social capital.*

While institutional activists often present their interests and strategies as public interests, gaps between their interests and those of the general public can still exist. In addition, institutional activists may directly or indirectly reinforce existing structural imbalances and equalities when they find themselves in a more powerful position.

10.1 Context—Sustainable, Low-Carbon Development in the Philippines

10.1.1 The Paris Agreement and Responses From the Philippines

Climate change is evident in the Philippines. From 1951 to 2010, the Philippines' annual mean temperature increased by 0.65 degrees Celsius with a mean rate of 0.01 degree Celsius per year. Furthermore, records from 1951 to 2008 show increasing intensity and frequency of rainfall in most parts of the country. In addition, based on climate projections, the Philippines' annual mean temperature will increase by 0.9 to 1.1 degrees Celsius in the 2020s, and 1.8–2.2 degrees Celsius in the 2050s (see OML Center 2014).

Addressing climate change in the Philippines is mainly focused on adaptation to the adverse effects of climate change. One viable reason for this is the rather low contribution of the country to global emissions. According to the UNFCCC Secretariat, the Philippines was responsible only for 0.25 percent of global CO_2 emissions from fuel combustion (79.5 Mt CO_2 Eq.) in 2012, with its population comprising 1.38 percent of world total population in 2013 (98.39 million). Nevertheless, the Philippine Climate Change Assessment Report warns that if the Philippine power sector continues to depend on coal (which covers 39 percent of energy demand), emissions from the Philippines are likely to increase by around 400 percent by the year 2030, compared to 2007 levels (see OML Center 2014). The Philippine government will therefore need to cancel all 29 coal plants currently in the pipeline to stabilize the emission level.

The government's intention to reduce its carbon emissions by 70 percent by 2030 (DENR 2016) demonstrates a huge gap from the rise of emissions expected by the assessment report. In this regard, more ambitious mitigation measures will be needed. The government is not able to reconcile nor give any concrete means as to how it would mitigate the country's carbon emissions. The Department of Energy defined a policy goal as an energy mix of 30 (coal)—30 (renewables)—30 (natural gas)—10 (fuel oil), but without identifying concrete ways in which the government intends to achieve this goal. Moreover, as discussed earlier, as a weak state, the national government has low capacity and low autonomy to identify and implement projects to achieve this goal, especially in a country where power generation is not considered a public utility. The liberalization of the energy sector further limits the ability of the national government to achieve its mitigation policy goal, especially when the Philippines' largest electricity distributor and the sole provider in the National Capital Region, the Manila Electric Company (MERALCO), has so far only invested in coal power plants (Olchondra 2015; Flores 2017). There are also no clear government strategies as to how it intends to support solar and wind energy and enable new players to enter an energy market where coal is the baseload.

The main mitigation instrument foreseen by the government is increasing carbon sinks by reforestation, which is, in the context of rapid urbanization and the need for more land for agriculture, expected to be not enough. Hence, the mitigation strategy of the Philippines needs to be revisited. For example, there is still no comprehensive and integrated national strategy as to how this intention can be realistically enacted, for example, by linking climate mitigation goals to enhancing renewable energies and energy efficiency. The investments in renewable energies in the Philippines will need to be matched, for example, by investment in infrastructure, such as grid systems in order to address the intermittency challenges of renewable energies. In addition, there is a need to improve the business prospects of mitigation technologies in the country. Finally, a major hurdle that needs to be cleared refers to deficiencies in governance.

As the Philippines is one of the countries most vulnerable to climate change, political priority is instead focused on early-warning and post-disaster management. Furthermore, the country is still working on how to incorporate technologies and improving its disaster risk reduction and management capability. Information asymmetry is still apparent, particularly in cities and rural areas outside the capital region. While the country has significantly improved its disaster preparedness, it is still ranked by the 2016 Climate Change Vulnerability Index as the 13th most climate-vulnerable country (see Ranada 2015). This vulnerability is reflected in the issues pushed by the Philippines during climate negotiations.

For example, the Philippines led the Climate Vulnerability Forum of almost 50 developing countries in successfully pushing for 1.5 °C to be recognized as the aspirational target of the UN Paris Agreement, which the Philippines signed last April 2016.

10.1.1.1 Sustainable Development Policies in the Philippines

As one of the 193 member-states that adopted the 2030 Agenda for Sustainable Development in 2015, the Philippines is taking further steps in defining the country's roadmap towards sustainable development in the next 15 years. Together with the Philippine Statistics Authority, the National Economic and Development Authority (NEDA) is the main government body that steers the government's efforts to achieve the 2030 Agenda.

President Duterte has signed Executive Order (EO) No. 5, which provided for the adoption of ***Ambisyon Natin* 2040, as the Philippines 25-year, long-term vision and guide for development planning.** It describes the kind of life that people want to live, and how the Philippines will be by 2040. *Ambisyon Natin* 2040 is a product of a series of nationwide public consultations consisting of focus group discussions participated in by representatives from groups of youth, fishers, farmers, the urban poor, disaster survivors, indigenous peoples, people with disabilities, families of overseas workers, local migrants, and government workers, among others, and the administration of a survey led by NEDA, to determine the aspirations of the Filipino population. A number of technical studies were also commissioned in key thematic areas of development through the support of the Asian Development Bank to understand whether *Ambisyon Natin* 2040 is achievable and to determine what it would take to achieve the vision. It aims to triple per capita income to 11,000 USD in 24 years by sustaining at least 6.5 percent annual GDP growth alongside the implementation of policies that would make the Philippines a high-income country by 2040 with a "prosperous, predominantly middle-class society where no one is poor."

Nevertheless, the vision does not clearly include the energy sector as among the identified priority sectors, even though the energy sector was involved in the series of nationwide public consultations. While the PDP consists of the government's plans and programs for the energy sector geared towards achieving *Ambisyon Natin* 2040, the absence of the participation of energy-related stakeholders as well as societal groups addressing energy issues will most likely lead to gaps and missed opportunities. As expected, because of the country's focus on adaptation, it also fails to identify climate protection as an economic opportunity, for example, through energy efficiency technologies. The lack of political involvement in mitigation leaves the country outside the discourse on energy efficiency and renewable interests. This leads to the country not fully accessing all available opportunities to enhance energy security. The success of the vision's priority policies is highly contingent on energy supply security as sustainable, low-carbon energy systems can provide the instruments to achieve these goals.

In addition, the ***Philippine Development Plan*** (PDP) 2017–2022 foresees the reduction of poverty, especially in the provinces, and the reduction of unemployment from 5.5 percent at present to as low as 3 percent by 2022 through sustained, robust economic growth in the next six years in line with the vision to make the country a high-income country by 2040. It also aims to sustain 7–8 percent GDP growth in the medium-term, and slash poverty incidence to 14 percent by 2022 from 21.6 percent in 2015. In rural areas, the higher poverty rate of 30 percent in 2015 is expected to be cut to 20 percent in six years' time. Other targets include higher trust in government and society, more resilient individuals and communities, and a greater drive for innovation.

10.1.1.2 Energy Security Policies in the Philippines

Similar to many Asian countries, the GDP growth of the Philippines (average rate of 6.1 percent from 2011 to 2015) is highly contingent on energy-intensive industries, mainly manufacturing and retail (see Euromonitor International 2017). Accounting for 73.5 percent, the energy supply in the country is highly dependent on fossil fuels (coal, gas, and oil). In 2013, coal covered approximately 42.62 percent of electrical energy demand (75,266 GWh). While hydroelectric power accounts for 18 percent, geothermal covers 10 percent of total electricity production. Solar, wind and biomass account for 2 percent of the country's electricity production. Amid a significant increase in the global use of renewable energies, the Philippine government still intends to add 25 additional coal power plants to the current 32 coal-fired power generation facilities in the country (see Quismundo 2016), proving that the country is a laggard in adopting renewable energy technologies.

Energy supply security is also a political priority in the Philippines. The energy crisis in the country is usually at its peak in summer periods, when demand for electricity is high in order to cool and air condition, while the lack of rain reduces electricity generation from hydropower. According to Steven Rood (2015), the major challenge to effectively addressing the energy crisis in the country is its weak governance. Approval for permits could take years, especially when a certain set of applicants are being favored. He notes that the Department of Energy estimates that it takes 165 signatures and a minimum of three years to secure the necessary permits. In addition, Rood suggests that low trust among investors when financing the costs of new power plants is a direct reaction to the country's contractual and pricing insecurity. New administrations often renegotiate the terms of contracts made during previous administrations. Government administrations often seek emergency powers to address the energy crisis, but the political opposition often mistrusts such steps. This dependence on emergency powers to implement energy policies vindicates the low autonomy of the State. In addition, the constant need for emergency powers to implement energy policies may reinforce abuse of power, because emergency powers tend to discard guard-rails for accountability and transparency. As such, energy security tends to be a highly political issue in the country and is reduced to the subject of poor governance.

Immediately after his election, President Duterte promised a different and a more proactive approach to addressing the energy crisis in the country. DENR Secretary Lopez announced that she will prioritize the approval of permits for renewable energy projects over those of coal and other fossil fuels. Furthermore, as an environmentalist, she declared her opposition to the opening of the nuclear plant in Bataan, claiming that it will only contribute to less than 0.5 percent to the National Energy Grid with higher costs and risks (Cordero 2017). She suggested that waste-to-energy adoption can be tapped to address the energy crisis while solving waste problems in the country. Meanwhile, Energy Secretary Alfonso Cusi announced in July of 2016 that his team is about to review the country's energy mix, but in the same briefing he also declared that the Philippines "can't afford not to have coal" (Cordero 2017). The Climate Change Commission (CCC) of the Philippines has started its task of reviewing the government's energy policy. In cooperation with various government agencies, a comprehensive review of the government's energy policy involves a whole-nation approach to achieving a low-carbon development pathway, with national goals and targets for climate change mitigation and adaptation, disaster risk reduction, and sustainable development (Climate Change Commission 2016).

The Philippine Energy Plan (PEP) as well as the various sectoral roadmaps 2017–2040, which provide the framework for present and future energy policies, vindicate that the concept of energy security in the Philippines does not yet adequately address how the energy sector will contribute to the reduction of the country's GHG emissions. This is an implication, instead, of the adaptation-oriented narratives on climate change in the Philippines. While the Upstream Oil and Gas Roadmap 2017–2040 as well as the Coal Roadmap 2017–2040 provide concrete numbers demonstrating the increased usage of oil, gas and coal, the renewable energy roadmap does not provide any concrete targets in numbers or timelines, implying that energy security will be mostly covered by emission-rich energy sources.

10.1.2 Multiple Entry Points to Climate Mitigation and Sustainable Development in the Philippines

The entry points that will be discussed below do not comprise the complete list of all entry points to climate mitigation in the Philippines. This selection intends to highlight the most relevant ones in the context of system transformation as underscored by the theoretical models (ideal types).

10.1.2.1 Rural Development as an Entry Point to Sustainable, Low-Carbon Development

Because of the current narratives on climate change in the Philippines, additional efforts are needed to find entry points into climate mitigation. **Coupling emission reduction with rural development and good governance will most likely find more political and public support than if it would have been presented as a stand-alone issue.** For example, rural development will most likely involve the usage of agricultural waste products for bioenergy, as rural communities in the Philippines are highly agricultural. Nevertheless, the concept of waste-to-energy is highly contested in the country, because it is connoted merely with the burning of industrial and household waste. Environmental groups fear the release of toxins from the burning of household and industrial waste. Hence, using agricultural waste for biomass energy will first require its delinking from the current notion of waste-to-energy and waste-to-fertilizer.

Aside from the country's abundant supply of biomass resources (rice, maize, coconut, and sugarcane), agricultural crop residues, forest residues, animal wastes, agro-industrial waste, municipal waste (about 60 percent of which is biomass), and aquatic biomass among others remain unused. From the estimated total agricultural biomass waste in 2012 of 52,568.73 million metric tons, only 0.054 percent of it is being utilized (Cajes 2014). Merely 1.07 percent of the total biomass resources in the country is being used for energy production. Not only is this surplus waste agricultural biomass, it is a missed opportunity to increase the percentage of biomass, which was at 1.09 percent of the installed capacity (or, as older data shows, at 12.4 percent) of the country's total primary energy supply mix in 2011 (39.4 million tons of oil equivalent (MTOE) (DOE 2017). The estimated biomass required to produce such power is 566,092.8 metric tons, assuming that the biomass-powered plants run at full capacity (efficiency is 24 percent for large-scale biomass plants ranging from 15 to 60 megawatts). The biofuel roadmap 2017–2040 of the Department of Energy vindicates the peripheral role of bioenergy in the country.

With the highly underutilized resources and agricultural waste products for biomass, the Philippines' can afford to set higher targets for renewable energy's contribution to the country's installed generating capacity. Nevertheless, while the Philippines displayed a significant growth in power generation at 10 percent from 82,413,213 MW in 2015 to 90,797,891 MW in 2016, of this total generation, only 1 percent (or 725,906 MW) comes from biomass. Therefore, additional programs and strategies are needed to complement existing ones to realize higher production targets, to establish market-based industry involving biomass resources including agricultural waste, and to maximize the usage of available international financing schemes such as the Clean Development Mechanism (CDM). Furthermore, partnerships with local sugar producers and farmers are needed, as sugarcane waste covers most of the agricultural waste.

Several programs and projects to promote agricultural biomass waste have been carried out in the Philippines since the 1970s (with an estimated worth of USD 100 million). Based on experiences from previous agricultural waste to energy programs and projects, such efforts can only be successful if they can be adequately coupled with rural development. A significant portion of the efforts have been rated as 'less than successful' by audit reports due to institutional problems, a lack of stakeholder mobilization and beneficiary participation, a lack of human capital in rural areas, as well as due to financial problems such as high initial and maintenance costs (Cajes 2014). These factors indicate the existing gaps between such projects and rural development. Therefore, the success of future programs and projects is highly contingent upon how these deficiencies are properly addressed. Establishing new or promoting old cooperatives and other forms of traditional cooperation methods (e.g., *paluwagan*) can be beneficial in strengthening 'stakeholder and beneficiary' ownership. New forms of local governance can be identified and tested as these programs and projects are implemented.

10.2 Case Study—Institutional Activism and Sustainable and Low-Carbon Policy Goals in the 'Weak' Philippine State

This section pertains to a comparison of the current transformation process in the Philippines as an empirical or historical case and the ideal type of institutional activism. While the sustainable, low-carbon transformation is still at its beginning, it is significant to analyze the challenges of facilitating this transformation. While the low-carbon and sustainability policy goals have already been identified as political priorities, they are still predominantly perceived as isolated policy goals. The interlinkages and the resulting positive and negative synergies between them have yet to be recognized by the relevant policy-makers. The Philippines as a case study allows a practical outlook on a transformation process of country that has a very strong civil society which is both a direct result of and an implication of weak governance. The limitations of the state in providing expected services has prompted the state to "resign", and "forge" franchise-like partnerships with civil society groups (see Hernandez 2014a).

10.2.1 Institutional Activism in the Philippines—The Historical Context and the Party List System

Activism in the Philippines is connoted with confrontation with state authorities. The historical context of activism in the country links activism to the radicalization of mostly university students after certain violent actions or divisive policies of the government (see Weiss & Aspinall 2012). Patricio Abinales (1996) highlights the "enduring mark on Philippine society" on the "Philippine Left." Philippine activism is often linked with socialism or communism. The label of 'enemy of the state' during the Marcos military regime was used as political leverage to shame and justify the coercive actions of the state, as rural guerrillas, labor unions, community organizers, students and church activists were mobilized, and has become a major political force in the country (Abinales 1996), especially in rural areas. While the end of the military rule of Ferdinand Marcos has allowed activists to take positions in governments, other activists have opted to join the communist insurgency groups in the country.

Institutional activism is not a new phenomenon in the Philippines. As stated earlier, the Philippine political system allows representatives of marginalized groups to be elected to the Philippine Congress through the "party list system" in the House of Representatives of the Philippines. During the interim period from 1987 to 1998, sectoral representatives were appointed by the President and confirmed by the Commission on Appointments.

During the May 1998 elections, the first sectoral groups were elected. Currently, party-list representatives are indirectly elected when their groups win at least two percent of the national vote, where at least one seat and at most three seats are given, depending on a formula based on the number of votes garnered by the sectoral group. In the last elections in May 2016, eleven party-list groups made the two percent threshold. Winning groups include groups representing women, senior citizens, farmers, teachers, disabled people, overseas Filipinos and the poor (see Uy 2016). The party-list system has allowed activists to mobilize, gain public exposure & political experience, and, in some cases, these activists were afterwards regularly elected outside the party-list system.

However, with this "political space" provided to activists, institutional activism in the Philippines typically mainly addresses social capital, good governance and social policies. For example, the party-list system does not include any environmental groups, proving that environmental activism is still traditionally at the periphery of policy-making, and implying that these groups still need to catch up in terms of mobilization. Because of several competing interests with other social groups, environmental groups still need to find their own space which would allow proximity between environmental integrity and social justice.

10.2.1.1 Institutional Activism in the Philippines—The Appointment of Secretary Regina Lopez

The appointment of the activist Regina Lopez as Secretary of the Department of Environment and National Resources was highly contested. Her appointment, and her subsequent failure to acquire confirmation of her appointment from the Commission of Appointments of the House of Representatives, can be seen as a demonstration of the different negotiation processes that need to be adequately prepared for. Several business and industry groups, as well as local government units (LGUs), called her appointment "highly divisive", as she was said to ignore due process anytime it served her vested interests (see Simeon 2017). The Chamber of Mining opposed the claim of Sec. Lopez that she should be able to prohibit mining even in non-proclaimed watersheds (see Quismundo 2017). The Department of Finance, the Department of Labor, and Local Government Units claimed that they were not consulted by Sec. Lopez prior to the closure order (see Catoto 2017).

Eventually, the Commission on Appointments bypassed or deferred the confirmation of her appointment more than once, as many members of the commission expressed opposition to her appointment (Diaz 2016, 2017; Geronimo 2017). The so-called 'preference outliers' or those legislators who were most interested in mining issues actively sought membership in the relevant commission assessing the appointment of the DENR Secretary. Nevertheless, Sec. Lopez was confident that she would be reappointed by President Duterte.

The closure order of more than half of the country's mining companies through DENR and Sec. Lopez had mobilized popular support from various social justice and socio-environmental groups. More than 3,000 members of various anti-mining groups gathered to push for the confirmation of Sec. Lopez as Secretary of DENR (Alvarez 2017a). These groups reprimanded the mining industry by claiming that most Philippine mining operators do not view corporate social responsibility as a major concern. For example, it was argued that mine tailings as waste products without any financial value to the mining operators were merely addressed as a financial footnote in the reports of Philippine mining operators. In addition, the environmental group *Ibon Foundation* claimed that the mining industry does not contribute to local economic development, as regions with the biggest mining activities are among the poorest in the country (Altez 2017).

As expected, the mining industry as well as affected cities and municipalities opposed the cancellation of 'legitimate, large-scale mining projects' which were said to be backed by lawful contracts. The mining industry was also able to mobilize various social groups, which mainly represented local communities affected by the order. On February 16, 2017, some 5,000 workers from different mining companies operating in Surigao del Sur organized a protest urging Sec. Lopez and President Duterte to reconsider closing the mining operations in Surigao del Sur, as this will would have led to massive job loss (Catoto 2017). According to Artemio Disini, head of the Chamber of Mines in the Philippines, more than 219,000 people are directly employed by the mining industry and 1.2 million people indirectly affected. Because 13 of the 28 potentially closed or suspended mines were in Mindanao, this closure order would have mainly affected already poverty-stricken areas of the country (see Altez 2017; Dela Cruz & Serapio, JR. 2017). The orders to suspend or close down 28 mining operations would have cost local governments a total of more than PHP821.13 million (or ca. USD 15.8 million) a year, according to Finance Secretary Carlos G. Dominguez III (Vera & Domingo 2017), affecting 17 cities and municipalities in 10 provinces, three of them poised to lose revenues equivalent to more than half of their current operating incomes

In addition, Dindo Manhit (2017) is critical that decisions were made out of "emotional and dramatic harangue(s)" and were made by an environmental activist who sees social justice and environmental issues as "eternally contradictory with prosperity and economics." He adds that the activist politician, and those environmental activists supporting her decisions, were ignoring the USD 840 billion mineral revenues that can also be instrumental in financially achieving social justice and environmental integrity. He adds that while it is true that the mining industry represents only less than one percent of the economy, it should not be disregarded that there are only very few legitimate operating mines in the country, whose footprint reaches barely one percent of the landmass.

Sec. Lopez opted for a competitive negotiation strategy while underestimating the political resources available to the mining sector. Because Sec. Lopez removed the basic symmetry of the negotiatory situation with her mining policies, interest groups representing the mining sector and those local government units negatively affected shifted the bargaining to the hearings of the CA, where she could not eliminate procedural equality. In addition, she had no effective leverage in the CA hearings aside from the procedural power of President Duterte, who could re-appoint her any time the CA rejected her confirmation, until the end of his term in 2022. Confronted by this situation, Sec. Lopez brought the "negotiation" to the streets. This strategy is typically used by activists and social movements in the Philippines, usually organizing street protests as instruments for enforcing their influence in policy-making without participating in formal channels. She and her supporters mobilized street protests supporting her anti-mining policies. However, due to the divisive nature of the issues involved, the civil society was fragmented, and she failed to circumvent the polity structures (e.g., the Commission on Appointments) through street protests.

On May 9, 2017, after the rejection of her appointment, President Duterte decided not to reappoint her and instead appointed former military chief Roy Cimatu as the new Environment Secretary (Dizon et al. 2017). Secretary Cimatu eventually overturned the orders of former Sec. Lopez, such as her new policies on the issuance of environmental compliance certificates (ECC) (Gamil 2017). Furthermore, he expressed his intention to address misinformation and 'reverse' the negative publicity around the mining sector (Miraflor 2017).

10.2.2 An Ideal Type Analysis of Sustainable, Low-Carbon Development in the Philippines

The evaluation of the sustainable, low-carbon transformation in the Philippines will be conducted through ideal type analysis. The negotiation perspective allows an integrated outlook on the synergies and co-benefits, as well as risks intentionally or unintentionally created by institutional activism. As identified in the theoretical framework, a major assumption of institutional activism is that the results often legitimize the means. An additional assumption is that institutional activism may also seek procedures that are flexible, as defined by power relations, if these changes in procedures facilitate faster policy implementation.

While it is evident that institutional activism has been historically embedded in the political system of the Philippines, with the formalized political inclusion of marginalized sectors of the society into the legislation, there is still a need to understand how institutional activism defines decision-making in the context of weak governance. Similar to authoritarian states, countries with weak governance like the Philippines are often confronted by existing political structures that tend to sustain 'hegemonic' ideas or the dominance of one or several actors and exclude those who oppose the policies of these dominant actors. For example, the electoral system in the Philippines employs a 'winner-takes-all' principle, where losing parties are not provided with any formal means of representation. This principle is also reflected in policy-making and policy implementation, where public deliberation is only tolerated or even encouraged when it supports government policies. Opposing actors are put off and the reference to the rule of law is then highlighted. Furthermore, weak governance in the Philippines is expressed by 'franchising' various key government responsibilities to 'elite groups', including oligarchs and corporations (see Hernandez 2014a). Similarly, the presence of political dynasties, where one family has its members both in the political and business fields to ensure that their interests are always protected, hampers changes. In this context, regaining these responsibilities will first require revisions to the social contract.

The election of President Duterte has led to new and often paradoxical dynamics in Philippine politics. On the one hand, while the administration has employed authoritarian principles in implementing its policies, such as the concentration of state authority on executive institutions as well as penalizing representatives in the Congress and senators who do not support government policies by stripping them of key posts (see ABS-CBN News 2017; Morallo 2017), such moves are regarded as facilitating a more rapid formulation and implementation of policies. On the other hand, the government (including the DENR) has often resorted to the mobilization of citizen groups in order to support government policies which may not adhere to the rule of law and also to discredit political opposition. As the ideal type suggests, the relation between the policy-politics stream the and polity stream can be adversarial, especially when bureaucracy limits the pace of policy-making and policy implementation. Ironically, the Philippine government is not only instrumentalizing this bureaucracy to exclude opposition, but it also seeks to circumvent this bureaucracy when it is not beneficial to the government's interests.

Stream-alignment is defined by decisions reached more rapidly because of the exclusionary nature of agenda-setting. Although the confirmation of the appointment of DENR Secretary Regina Lopez was still pending, during her first months as secretary of the Department of Environment and Natural Resources she was inclined to dominate agenda-setting, and other actors were not formally given the chance to express their perspectives (see Cordero 2017; Alvarez 2017b). Looking at the ideal type of institutional activism, then, Sec. Lopez pushed her adversaries out of the policy-making sphere, allowing them no formal channels with which to dissent. What followed was that these opposing actors sought other bargaining avenues as they became aware that the "bargaining table" set by Sec. Lopez did not allow for bargaining at all, as former Sec. Lopez was not seen as being prepared to accept compromises. As Sec. Lopez had already employed a highly 'competitive' negotiation style, other actors sought to shift the forum and establish another 'bargaining table' that would have either excluded her or limited her prerogatives. Industry actors had already foreclosed on the possibility of working together with Sec. Lopez (see Simeon 2017). This led to the situation where a specific issue (here, mining) completely defined the course of the process (instead of the process defining the scope of the issues and how those issues should have been addressed), which produced negative-sum results, not only in mining policies, but also in other issues.

Former Sec. Lopez' actions confirmed that institutional activism focuses on issues and outcomes rather than on processes. In the context of key economic sectors 'franchised' to corporations and business groups, focusing on the process, for instance, would have witnessed Sec. Lopez first seeking to alter the playing field in order to change the rules of the game that had hitherto favored business and industry actors. Instead, she used the concentration of state authority in executive institutions to push for her environmental policies. In light of huge opposition, she used instruments typical of activist groups such as mass mobilization and aggressive rhetoric defaming mining groups as 'environmental rapists' and opposing politicians as 'killing mountains' (see Quismundo 2017; Simeon 2017). From the negotiation perspective, labelling other actors as the problem limits the sets of possible outcomes that are acceptable to all. The Philippine Business for Environmental Stewardship (PBEST), an environmental NGO advocating for the compliance of the country's businesses with al environmental rules and regulations, argued that 'responsible mining exists in the Philippines' (Business Mirror 2016). PBEST explained that instead of being branded as the enemy of the environment, the mining industry could be seen as the actor that could (and should) provide resources and a culture of innovation to solve environmental problems.

Furthermore, the role of science has been reduced to that of mere instrument. This gave groups opposing Sec. Lopez the possibility to claim that decisions made by her were merely based on ideologies rather than on scientific evidence (see Tria 2017; Alvarez 2017b). Carlos David argues that statements by Sec. Lopez may be understandable as claims from advocates, but it sends the wrong message when it comes from the head of the DENR (Business Mirror 2016), as it oriented the mining industry as part of the problem and not the solution. In addition, due to structural limitations, academic discourse in the Philippines tends to move outside the "typical channels" of scholarly debate such as peer-reviewed journals and conferences. As Filipino scholars are considered "periphery scholars" (Belcher 2009) with limited access to journals, debates are often conducted through opinion columns and sections of the newspapers, where academics and experts are able to quickly engage in public debate.

Looking at the case of institutional activism in the Philippines and how it compared to the ideal type, the context of (weak) governance in the country suggests that in order to facilitate sustainable, low-carbon transformation, major changes in governance structures are needed. The institutional activism of former Secretary Lopez elucidates that policy-making in the country focuses strongly on specific issues (rather than processes) that foreground negative-sum outcomes inhibiting possible synergies and trade-offs between issues. In addition, should Sec. Lopez have been successful in implementing her policies, it would have been a big question as to whether these policies would even have been institutionalized at all, especially after the administration of President Duterte when a new government administration comes into power in 2022. It is more likely that her policies would have been completely reverted, thus implying a return to default, further contributing to uncertainties and vacuums. In addition, as she was seeking to change the mandate of her government agency (from a regulatory to a development agency), she was also changing the internal functions and the qualifications needed for those placed in the agency. Doing so would have required her to deal with how to make a productive government office with people who may not have been in the right type of work due to the abrupt changes she made.

10.3 Conclusion—Lessons for Theory and for Practice

10.3.1 Lessons for Theory

The theoretical framework of the case study on the Philippines has provided an understanding of how institutional activism can both inhibit and promote sustainable, low-carbon transformation. Looking at the 'negotiative' requirement of sustainable, low-carbon transformation, the benefits and risks of institutional activism are highly contingent upon existing power relations and structures as well as on the level of capacity and autonomy of the state. While institutional activism can facilitate rapid policy formulation, it can also use bureaucratic leverage to reinforce existing inequalities in countries with low social capital. Because institutional activism uses the same structures that have created such inequalities in the first place, institutional activism may reinforce authoritarianism by excluding other interests and finding ways to legitimize such actions through means outside of the legal framework, such as social networks.

Institutional activism may also have negative implications for democracy and participation. It may, for example, further weaken social movements. Because satisfying all social groups is not possible, institutional activists may proactively seek to exclude other social groups that seek interests that oppose government policies. Therefore, institutional activism may unintentionally create new 'social elites' who will further weaken social movements, as disfranchised social groups will distance themselves from these social elites. In the case of the Philippines, environmental groups, for example, which are seeking to enhance the use of renewable energy will be easily labelled as 'ecological elites', delegitimizing the goals of these groups in the eyes of other disfranchised social groups. This development will most likely undermine the transformation process, especially because cooperation between these groups is inevitable. Furthermore, institutional activism may induce violence as adversaries are not given effective political channels, especially when decisions, such as the closure of mines, will be linked to the realm of the personal, such as livelihoods and incomes of households.

Furthermore, disfranchising (previously powerful) stakeholders such as business and industry groups is counterproductive, as this will provide these groups with additional resources to act as "spoilers" who, when outside the policy-making process, are not bounded by the norms and rules of negotiations or consensus-building. Labelling them as the problem is not helpful, as it will prevent them from contributing to solutions. Like authoritarian policy models, institutional activism may also cause poor policy formulation and poor policy implementation, as these policies will most likely be challenged or reversed after the administration changes. Furthermore, institutional activism may decrease the threshold for future political abuse, as it provides "undemocratic practices" in democratic political regimes with more resources to legitimize undemocratic actions through social networks and concentrated executive power. Especially in democratic countries with weak governance structures like the Philippines, institutional activism can motivate policy-makers addressing other issues to resort to similar authoritarian actions, especially when there is substantial opposition. Ignoring the principles of the "rule of the law" and due process as long as legitimizing factors can be found to support such actions creates precedents for future authoritarian practices. Therefore, environmentalism should also be subjected to formal and material democratic principles.

10.3.2 Lessons for Practice

The strategy of Sec. Lopez in eliminating the *negotiatory* or bargaining aspect of environmental policy-making was successful in eliminating reciprocity in this specific policy game. The absence of initial inequality in power motivated the mining and industry sector to shift the bargaining process to a forum where they could have procedural inequality. This was possible because of the monolithic architecture of policy-making frameworks. As Sec. Lopez adopted the strategy of "demonizing" the mining and industry sector, the latter reciprocated and provided arguments that saw Sec. Lopez as the problem. Sec. Lopez's appointment and her subsequent failure to acquire confirmation of her appointment from the Commission of Appointments of the House of Representatives can be seen as a demonstration of the different negotiation processes that need to be adequately prepared for.

Policies and polities should be separated from politics or, if not, should be above politics. While policies should reflect consensual processes, polities guarantee the rules of the game. Politics brings the dynamics in process, as new agendas are identified, or existing norms revisited following the emergence of system pressures due to incremental changes. Nevertheless, this can only function when those in power 'respect' the boundaries between streams. If this is not the case, the pragmatic approach is to 'go with the flow' and for those actors in the polities and politics stream to find ways of embedding themselves in the policies stream.

The Philippine case study demonstrates the importance of social movements, activists, and non-profits as advocates. It also shows that these groups are not resistant to existing structural privileges, particularly when these privileges allow them to purportedly achieve their goals. However, as Bass *et al.* (2014) claims, advocacy is about relationships and about changing power dynamics. These groups should not forget their initial mandate and should look at how existing structures are responsible for the inequalities that mobilized them in the first place. When in power, like in the Philippines, they should seek to alter relationships and change power dynamics.

The United States of America—Disruptive Governments, Social Movements and Technocrats in Transformation Processes Towards Sustainability

11

The election of the populist Donald Trump to the United States is argued to be a consequence of the fluke of the electoral college, the lackluster Democratic turnout, and the anti-establishment and populist sentiments in the population (see Atkins 2017). Through effective gerrymandering after the 2000 general elections, the Republican party and its presidential candidate Trump won the elections, even though he lost the popular vote by close to 3 million ballots. Another example of the flaw of the electoral system is shown by the 2018 midterm elections. Although the Democrats gained 56.9 percent of popular votes (or more than 12.5 million more votes than the Republicans), the Republicans still retained their control and even extended their majority in the Senate (Burns 2018). With the Republican Party controlling the executive, legislative (senate) and judicative branches, as Stephen Crowley (2016) notes, the checks and balances of the US political system will therefore need to come from social movements.

The goal of this chapter is to analyze and conceptualize the role of social movements, advocates, non-profits, profit-oriented/private sector enterprises, and other civil society groups in facilitating sustainable, low-carbon transformation in a political framework or context that is partially or fully adversarial or hostile to this transition. Best practices can be derived by understanding the resources and strategies available to these social actors in countering the actions of the state and government agencies which aim to reverse previous decisions that are conducive to low-carbon transformation. Can social movements provide genuine resistance dynamics to oppose new policies that aim to disrupt the transformation process towards sustainability? In addition, a comparison of these case studies to the theoretical models (ideal types) will be conducted. The United States will be analyzed using the technocratic/bureaucratic policy, as well as post-democratic model. Furthermore, the analysis of the United States will highlight how certain civil society

A. M. Hernández, *Taming the Big Green Elephant*, Globale Gesellschaft und internationale Beziehungen, https://doi.org/10.1007/978-3-658-31821-5_11

groups are intentionally or unintentionally promoting technocracy as the policy model that can resolve highly escalated bipartisan politics in the country.

After the election of President Trump, several experts and the media were quick in predicting 'system rupture.' There are several silver linings to these events and insights into the idea that the election of President Trump could actually promote sustainable, low-carbon transformation in the long run. For example, David Atkins (2017) of the Washington Monthly notes that the 2020 elections are far more important than those of 2016, as the Democrats were unlikely to win both. He explains that elections in every zero-year coincide with the Census. In this regard, those who win the governorships and legislatures in the zero-year have control over the district lines redrawn after the Census. He notes that this is the most important reason why Democrats continue to lose the House despite winning more overall popular votes, as the Republican electoral victory in 2010 allowed them to gerrymander Congressional and legislative district lines in the United States to the party's advantage. With the Republicans winning the 2016 elections, although losing more than 2.8 million of popular votes, the chance for the Democrats winning the 2020 elections becomes more likely and would allow Democrats to redraw those lines after an even more favorable census, potentially giving them a decade of dominance similar to that currently held by the Republicans. Nevertheless, this argument does not resolve the structural imbalances and deficiencies of the US political system. But from the perspective of sustainable, low-carbon development, this structural imbalance can help long-term transformation.

In addition, columnist Sophie Roth-Douquet (2016) suggests that one factor that made the election of President Trump possible was the apathy of millennials towards politics, which resulted in low voter turnout among voters under the age of 30, a cohort which mostly favored Sec. Hillary Clinton. She further explains that this election could be a wake-up call for millennials, reminding them of the importance of civic engagement. Months after the 2016 elections in the United States, the new term 'rage donations' emerged, describing an increase in contributions to non-profit and civil society groups (Pfeiffer 2016), particularly civil rights and environmental groups. For example, contributions to the American Civil Liberties Union of Massachusetts have increased by 500 percent. The Conservation Law Foundation in Boston witnessed a 222 percent increase in donations. The environmental group Sierra Club added 11,000 new monthly donors, while the Environmental Defense Fund raised USD 250,000 in the week after the election (Eckhouse 2016). Donations to EarthShare Washington and Forterra increased by 40 percent and 57 percent respectively (Ryan 2017).

Moreover, in terms of the improvement of the capacity of non-profits and civil society groups, the 2016 election of President Trump has led major corporations and business groups taking a clearer position on supporting climate protection and environmental integrity. On May 10, 2017, after the announcement of withdrawal from the Paris Climate Agreement by President Trump, the CEOs of 30 major companies, including Apple, Facebook, Google and Microsoft, bought full-page ads in major US newspapers to argue that remaining in the Paris Agreement is in everyone's best interests. Elon Musk, the founder of Tesla and SpaceX, and Robert A. Iger, the CEO of Disney, eventually left the economic advisory council for President Trump (Victor 2017). Jeff Immelt, the CEO of General Electric, expressed his disappointment and called for the industry to lead and not depend on the government (Victor 2017). The academic community joined the protests, with eighty-two presidents and chancellors of universities expressing their support for the Paris Climate Agreement (Tabuchi & Fountain 2017). In addition, several U.S. cities and states have announced that they will adhere to the climate agreement by looking at ways to reduce emissions, including negotiating contracts with local utilities to supply more renewable energy, building rapid transit programs, and other infrastructure projects like improved wastewater treatment. For example, the mayor of Salt Lake City, Jackie Biskupski, announced that her administration had brokered an agreement with a local utility to power the city by deploying 100 percent renewable energy by 2032 (Tabuchi & Fountain 2017).

The main hypothesis of this case study is the following:

Transformation processes have **self-adaptive capacities** through which disruptive governments and other actors will have lower leverage to reverse the transformation process.

A technocratic policy pathway is perceived as a short-term solution when addressing the ideological divide in the United States. The current inability of bipartisanship to achieve substantial policy goals promotes the rise of a new generation of technocrats. The current contestation over a general lack of adequate political representation in the United States further undermines public trust. Where there are no imminent solutions to such a legitimacy (representation) crisis, technocrats can provide other forms of legitimization. When technocratic stewardship can effectively encourage utilitarian outcomes that would ultimately generate the broadest benefits for the most number of Americans, a new social contract can be found.

11.1 Context—Sustainable Low Carbon Transformation Under Protectionism and Isolationism

11.1.1 The Paris Agreement and Responses from the United States

The U.S. federal government under President Trump is pursuing protectionist policies that have direct and indirect ramifications on climate protection, sustainable development, and energy security. This section contextualizes climate and environmental protection, sustainable development, and energy security as well as the interlinkages between these policy goals in the United States.

11.1.1.1 Climate Change Discourse in the United States Under President Trump and the U.S. Response to the Paris Climate Agreement

On 1 June 2017, President Trump announced the withdrawal of the United States from the Paris Agreement, which was followed by a formal communication to the United Nations of its intent to withdraw. This announcement aimed to fulfil an electoral promise of President Trump to eliminate 'burdensome' regulations on the energy industry in the country and to revive the coal industry, which he concretized in his 'America First Energy Plan.' Originally, the United States would have had to implement both the Clean Power Plan and the Climate Action Plan, which was forged by the administration of President Obama, in order for the United States to meet its 2025 Paris Agreement commitment or NDC, which means a reduction of emissions by 26–28 percent below 2005 levels including Land Use, Land Use Change and Forestry (LULUCF). With pre-Trump climate policies still in place, including the Clean Power Plan, this would only reduce emissions to 10 percent below 2005 levels by 2025 (Climate Action Tracker 2017c). With the suspension of the Clean Power Plan, emissions in 2025 are likely to be higher, at 7 percent below 2005 levels. Although, legally, the NDC remains in place as it is until at least 2019, the Trump administration has already stopped the implementation of the NDC at the federal level (Climate Action Tracker 2017c).

The 'America first' ideology of President Trump can also be translated as the withdrawal of the United States from its leadership role in global politics as it pursues national protectionism and isolationism (see Hardt & Mezzada 2016). This withdrawal can be used as leverage to demand more favorable terms, for example, in global trade. President Trump's USD 10 billion reduction of spending on diplomacy, foreign assistance, and contributions to international organizations, including 50 percent of US contribution to the World Bank's International Development Association, is seen as negatively affecting anti-poverty programs in (mostly) developing countries (see Simmons 2017; U.S. Department of State 2017; Morello 2017).

11.1.1.2 Economic Development and Energy Security Policies in the United States—The Return of a Fossil-Based Energy and Economy System

Immediately after the election, the Trump administration started to review all environmental and energy policies made not only during the term of former President Obama, but also during earlier terms. Energy security through fossil fuel production expects to gain political momentum as energy production security has been 'coupled' with job security, which has been highlighted as a major priority of the government. The Administration's 'America First Energy Plan' and the goal of U.S. 'Energy Dominance' are perceived as an encouragement of increased domestic production, reflected in the increased number of rig counts and drilling permit applications in the first months of 2017 (Blackmon 2017). The 'America First Energy Plan' does not mention renewable energy at all, which confirms the government's focus on fossil fuels. On several different occasions, President Trump complained about how expensive renewable energies are and about the subsidies renewable energy companies are receiving (Associated Press 2017). In a speech in the last week of June 2017, President Trump declared that this is the 'golden era' of U.S. energy, through which dominance will be asserted through the country's increased natural gas, coal, and petroleum exports, and identifying Eastern Europe and Asia as important markets for U.S. liquefied natural gas (LNG) exports (DiChristopher 2017).

In order to implement these plans, the Trump administration is reviewing linkages between energy production and environmental protection, where environmental protection measures that 'constrain' these plans are lifted. For example, Interior Secretary Ryan Zinke ordered a review of a conservation plan forged by the Obama administration to protect the greater sage grouse. The review aimed to determine if the plan interfered with the Trump administration's efforts to increase energy production on federal lands (Greshko et al. 2017). In addition, President Trump signed an executive order that ordered a review of bans on offshore oil and gas drillings in parts of the Arctic, Pacific and Atlantic Oceans, as well as a five-year oil leasing roadmap that excluded Alaska's Beaufort and Chukcho Seas. Moreover, the executive order also halts the designation or expansion of National Marine Sanctuaries, unless the move includes an Interior

Department estimate of the area's 'energy or mineral resource potential' (Greshko et al. 2017).

Expedited by the signing of the presidential memoranda to revive both the Keystone XL and Dakota Access pipelines on January 24, 2017, the U.S. State Department, on March 24, 2017, granted Transcanada Corporation a permit for the construction of the 1,200-mile (1,931-kilometer) Keystone XL pipeline, which will connect oil sands from Alberta, Canada to refineries in Texas (Mufson & Eilperin 2017; Greshko et al. 2017). This project is the fourth phase of the Keystone Pipeline System that was rejected by then President Obama due to environmental concerns and conflicts with Native American communities.

In addition to energy production based on an inclination towards coal, the Trump administration has announced the promotion of fossil fuels, particularly in the transport sector. President Trump appointed ExxonMobil CEO Rex Tillerson as Secretary of State. Furthermore, on March 25, 2017, EPA administrator Scott Pruitt and U.S. Secretary of Transportation Elaine Chao initiated the reconsideration of the emissions requirements for vehicles with model years between 2022 and 2025 by pursuing the rollback of the Corporate Average Fuel Economy (CAFE) standards, which aim to improve cars' fuel economy.

11.1.2 Multiple Entry Points to Climate Mitigation and Sustainable Development in the United States

As previous chapters suggest, entry points can be understood as problem-issues related to other policy priorities such as sustainable development and energy security, whose resolution can be coupled with climate mitigation in particular, that is, with emission reduction through renewables or through energy efficiency technologies. This section identifies two major entry points to climate mitigation and sustainable development in the United States that are driven by non-profits and social movements. Another entry point is driven by the business and financial sector as they seek to diversify and expand their global and domestic value chain.

11.1.2.1 Non-profits, Civil Rights & Liberties Groups, and Social Movements as Entry Points to Climate Mitigation

The resurgence of social movements in the United States can be a major entry point to climate mitigation and sustainable development goals. For decades, and especially after the 2016 US elections, coalitions and alliances between social movements have led to the process of knitting together horizontal relationships, and to the expansion of political consciousness and interests between groups, not only between groups within the United States, but also between movements from other countries in Europe, Africa, Asia, and South America with their U.S. counterparts. For example, the 'inextricable' link between addressing climate change and defending indigenous rights have placed the current environmental policies of President Trump in conflict with indigenous communities (Hardt & Mezzada 2016). Racial justice, as sought by the *Black Lives Matter* protests, is linked with gender, sexuality, and economic justice, which cover several elements of sustainable development. This 'venue shopping,' as borrowed from legal studies by Frank Baumgartner and Bryan Jones (1991), is an effective strategy of searching for a more receptive venue to achieve interests.

Meredith Rutland Bauer (2016) suggests that the current Trump protests could be the start of a new civil rights era. The election of President Trump has led to the enhanced capacities of social movements as donations and membership have risen by rates that were unimaginable before the 2016 elections (see above). Civil liberties and rights movements have expanded their demands by integrating other related issues. For example, defending indigenous rights now coincides with demands to adequately address the effects of climate change and of the fossil fuel-driven industry projects in indigenous communities. Racial justice now includes components of gender, sexuality, job security, and local community development, which are important pillars of sustainable development as summarized by the Sustainable Development Goals (SDGs). The 2011 Occupy movement included racial justice as a central component of its issues, as it is related to social inequality. In addition, as many groups see climate change as one of the major causes of migration from Mexico, empathy with illegal and undocumented Mexican migrants is easier to communicate (see Fox & Hernandez 1992; Rong 2010; Berrueta et al. 2015).

11.1.2.2 Urban Economic Development—The Emergence of Smart Cities and Smart Enclaves

With the expected reduction of federal funding for sustainability projects, the concept of 'smart cities', which has thrived in the past several years, will require a reconfiguration of local governance, because, particularly in the United States, the idea of 'smart cities' has been connoted with huge involvement from the federal government through funding (see Shelton & Clark 2016). Apart from the likely withdrawal of the Trump administration from promoting smart cities, revisiting the concept of smart cities calls for new questions on governance. Changes in federal policies will require new forms of partnerships, particularly between local governments and non-profits, to plan and deploy technologies linked to smart cities.

Smart cities can promote climate mitigation as they aim to reduce energy consumption through efficiency. However, as Shelton and Clark (2016) suggest, the idea of smart cities raises "questions about *techno centrism* in the reproduction of inequality and socio-spatial fragmentation." Therefore, while social movements are generally beneficial in pursuing climate protection goals, and the election of President Trump may paradoxically 'empower' social movements, smart cities and urban development, the entry point to climate change mitigation need to be carefully facilitated, because the vindicated involvement of social movements may further reinforce technocratic policy models, which may in the long-term undermine the quality of democracy.

Subsequently, as Jeffrey Berry and Kent Portney (2014) have identified, most non-profits are local in nature, serving the interests of local communities or even mere neighborhoods. As such, non-profits are often more successful in influencing local policies than federal policies. Apart from the way in which non-profits are behaving after the election of President Trump, the roles of social movements in urban or communal political systems in the United States have already been changing in the past several years. One example of changes in urban politics is the increasing importance of the 'politics of space' (Berry & Portney 2014), which refers to how non-profits and other social movements are more able to interact with local policymakers.

A major reason for failure in or the limitation of the environmental agenda being able to reach the majority of the US population is attributed to the historical development of environmental movements, where environmental movements traditionally concentrate on what is most visible in national politics. After the election of President Trump, there has been a shift of centers of environmental activism, from the federal capital of Washington D.C. to cities and local communities. As discussed above, compared with environmental groups, non-profits have focused on local issues. With this shift in environmental advocacy, the interlinking of interests between different non-profits can be more successful. Particularly because some cities are now opting for a 'stronger' environmental profile, new partnerships between environmental groups and other non-profits are more likely to occur. As more 'smart cities' and 'smart enclaves' are emerging in the United States, climate mitigation in the context of a federal government under President Trump will most likely continue to evolve around the kind of urban economic development that is highly dependent on social movements, local businesses, and industry sectors. Cities in the United States have already assumed a leading role in designing and implementing innovative policies to achieve sustainability (Portney 2013).

One interesting factor that has further promoted the emergence of these smart cities is the change in the political ecology of most cities. As Berry and Portney (2014) have observed, major companies and corporations have migrated to the suburbs or moved their headquarters to major U.S. cities such as New York City to reflect a new global focus. The diminished role of corporations in local politics has benefited leaders and representatives of non-profits, including citywide civic organizations, social service agencies, environmental groups, and neighborhood associations, as local politicians are seeking more interactions not only to win elections, but also to address various issues through consultations.

11.1.2.3 Private Investment—The Invisible Hand of Corporations and Business Entities

Another important entry into climate mitigation in the absence of federal support in the private and business sector. Before the election of President Trump, US domestic climate policies focused on state policies and federal incentives such as subsidies for renewable energy. On the day President Trump withdrew from the Paris Climate Agreement, the governors of California, New York and Washington announced the formation of the United States Climate Alliance, which is a coalition of states committed to meeting the objectives of the 2015 Paris Agreement on Climate Change. After many months, this coalition has now incorporated 14 states and Puerto Rico, and it also includes several states with Republican governors (Rogers 2017).

While these federal states, which emit 21 percent of U.S. carbon emissions, cannot make a significant difference in terms of global emissions, this coalition can act as a bandwagon, where, as path dependence theory argues, it is more expensive for non-members not to join, especially for Republican states like Iowa and Texas, which have a large wind industry. If leaders of non-member states can 'frame' the issue as supporting renewable energy rather than mitigating climate change, the coalition can expect to gain more political support and bipartisan endorsement at the state level. However, as past U.S. climate policies have depended heavily on federal subsidies, new agencies are needed to compensate for the absence of these federal incentives for renewable energy. Nevertheless, as many proponents of the 'free market' would argue, government subsidies can inhibit innovation as they may, for example, send wrong signals to the market (Wallsten 2000; see Brodwin 2013)

In a report published by Apex Clean Energy and the GreenBiz Group (see Abraham 2017), a survey of 153 major public and private U.S. corporations concluded that 84 percent of these companies are still "actively pursuing or considering purchasing renewable energy over the next 5 to 10 years." In addition, 43 percent of these companies intend to be more ambitious in their pursuit of renewable energy in the next two years. According to 87 percent of those actively pursuing renewable energy purchases, the election of President Trump had no impact on their decision, while 11 percent were more inclined to purchase renewable energy after the election. The major reason behind this preference is not political, but rather economical. Diversifying energy portfolios in terms of energy sources and geography through the inclusion of renewable energies is an important instrument against the rising and variable costs of fossil fuels. The surge of renewables is therefore something that will happen in a matter of time, because the tipping point that favors renewables may have already been passed.

With the investment behavior of corporations and business entities not significantly altered or hampered by the election of President Trump, infrastructure development, which is profoundly necessary to complement the deployment of clean energy technologies and the upfront costs of renewables are expected to decline. As several corporations and investors continue to develop digital security technologies (in terms of propriety technologies and digital information), the deployment of renewable energy becomes increasingly imminent, because, for example, digital technologies will further eliminate *caveats* for the deployment of renewables through smart technologies (e.g., smart grids, smart homes). With incremental learning already taking place, contributing to the maturity process of renewable energies, fossil fuel energies will most likely find it more difficult to compete in the future. The current U.S. administration will most likely further increase the dependence on the oil and coal sectors with federal government subsidies, making these sectors increasingly less attractive to new investors, particularly due to their volatility in upcoming years as new federal governments are elected, and upfront & maintenance costs for renewable energies are reduced due to new complementary technologies, innovation, and incremental learning.

11.2 Case Study—Social Movements and Technocracy as Agencies of Deterrence Against Disruptive Politics in the United States

Particularly in the first months after the election of President Trump, social protests experienced a renaissance in the United States. As social capital, that is, the perception that state institutions can be trusted, deteriorated, especially when President Trump has shown that he is implementing his electoral promises through executive orders and through 'tricks' (e.g., the fiscal budget) that were unimaginable, a 'new era' of social movements has emerged (see Rutland Bauer 2016; Cobb 2017). In addition to an increased attention to social movements, a growing community of proponents of technocracy is becoming louder in proposing that technocracy is the alternative governance system that can fix a 'broken' US political system (see Khanna 2017; Rohde 2017). Interestingly, as PayPal executive Peter Thiel argues, calling the United States a democracy is misleading, because a technocratic elite made up of career bureaucrats and appointed experts is already running the country, stealing governing authority away from citizens and their elected representatives (see Ferenstein 2015).

This section, however, argues that, after the election of Trump, the emergence of social movements, including non-profits and profit groups, may also further reinforce technocratic principles in a political system that is already technocratic in several of its core principles.

11.2.1 The Trump Administration and Social Movements—The Re-emergence of Technocratic and Post-democratic Governance Models in the United States

New and old forms of solidarity movements are being conceptualized and revived (e.g., total protest, civil disobedience). Interlinkages between issues have been rediscovered, paving the way for new alliances of non-profits, advocacy groups, etc. As Jelani Cobb (2017) notes, the Trump era may be reinforcing the conviction of the 1960s, that "democracy is in the streets." Nevertheless, social movements will need to evolve and reinvent themselves in order to pose effective resistance to a disruptive political leadership. For Micah White (2016), the difficult path of merging innovative protest, social movements and electoral parties is the only viable strategy that addresses disruptive political leadership. He highlights that fact that contemporary protest is 'broken' and that the dominant tactic of mobilizing citizens to protest on the streets, rallying behind a single demand, and raising awareness about an injustice will not lead to the desired social change. Street demonstrations as manifestations of the will of the collective will not shift sovereignty from the government to the protestors, unless such demonstrations create a movement-party. He concludes that the only viable way to transfer sovereignty back to the people is by winning elections. Social movements need to find ways to dominate elections. However, activism and advocacies are still far removed from social movements.

Since the Clinton administration, a series of conservative social movements in the United States, including the rise of the Tea Party and 'birther' movements challenging the legitimacy of the country's first Afro-American president, have emerged as a direct reaction to progressive and liberal policies. As Stephen Crowley (2016) continues to argue, the social movements after the election of President Trump will need to have a strategic vision, which will also connect with the justifiable anger that drove many voters to President Trump. The United States has had powerful social movements in the past: the organized resistance to British colonial rule, the underground railroad and the abolition movement, the strikes and labor organizing of the 1930s spurring the New Deal, and the civil rights movement (Crowley 2016).

Social movements, especially environmental and scientific groups, have been mobilized to show their opposition to President Trump's curbing of the enforcement of environmental regulations and reversal of climate policies. For example, on April 22, 2017, thousands of scientists and supporters marched through Washington D.C. to the US Capitol, voicing support for science's role in society. Other groups have dedicated themselves to fact checking in order to correct wrong information being circulated in the media and on social media. Other groups, such as the Environmental Integrity Project, published a report asserting that in the first six months of the Trump administration, the Environmental Protection Agency (EPA) has filed fewer lawsuits against companies breaking pollution control laws in comparison with the first six months of the agency under Clinton, Bush Jr. and Obama (Greshko et al. 2017), resorting to 'blaming and shaming' tactics. With this, social groups, especially epistemic communities, have re-visited and renewed their social mandate. In addition, as a response to the listed actions of the current US administration, some federal state governments and US cities have formed an alliance that reaffirms their commitment to the implementation of the Paris Agreement. This so-called 'green rebellion' might initiate a shift in transformative policy-making from the federal government to the state governments.

In addition to the re-emergence of social movements, profit actors from the business and industrial sectors may also fill the vacuum created by the resignation of the state as an agency of transformation towards sustainability. As several U.S. corporations stepped in to provide funding to renewable energy and energy efficiency technologies, they became 'first movers,' through which they were able to expand not only on their competitive advantages against other lagging corporations (e.g., by setting standards and introducing market barriers for non-conformists), they could also influence the agenda, methodologies, and interpretations of scientific studies in a way that was compatible with their interests. In the situation where profit actors are able to dominate more areas of social life, the United States could be heading towards post-democracy rather than technocracy.

11.2.2 A Comparative Analysis of the Ideal Type and the Empirical Case Study of the United States—Causal Mechanisms Through Congruence Methods and Process-Tracing

The comparison between the theoretical model (the ideal type) and the empirical case of the United States has proven to be highly insightful. In the context of low-carbon transformation in the United States, the disruptive leadership of President Trump has further complicated the process, where:

- This disruptive leadership has led to the mobilization of both profit-oriented and non-profit actors pursuing sustainable, low-carbon development.
- This disruptive leadership has motivated profit-oriented and non-profit groups to revisit and remodify their social mandate, put more attention on 'low-hanging fruits', and evaluate loose ends.
- As several aspects of sustainable, low-carbon transformation are to be materialized in local communities, non-profit groups have rediscovered their spatial advantages and recoupable resources.
- This disruptive behavior of the current federal government is not completely different from previous federal governments. For example, research funding through the federal government has been continually reduced, when compared with the 1960s and 70s.
- This disruptive leadership reinforces the existing technocratic and post-democratic qualities of the US political system.

11.2.2.1 An Ideal Type Analysis—Disruptive Political Leadership in the Context of Low-Carbon Transformation

Two scenarios will be analyzed when using the ideal types. The first scenario refers to the increased role of non-profit groups; as social movements overtake various competencies of the federal state. In this scenario, non-profit groups build *de facto* institutions, or **'shadow bureaucracies'**, that run various aspects of social life in the United States. For example, with the emergence of smart cities, local, non-profit groups are able to exert more influence on local policy-making. Through their increased relevance to local policy-making and policy implementation due to their purported technical expertise, non-profits are able to function as expert committees. This scenario will be analyzed through the technocratic policy model.

The second scenario refers to the increased role of profit-oriented groups following the withdrawal of federal state funding, for example, in research and development. As the federal state reduces its role in providing services, profit groups are given space to provide services such as in education, health, and in compliance with environmental protection rules, especially when such services can be linked with revenues. This scenario will be analyzed through the post-democratic policy model.

11.2.2.2 Low-Carbon Transformation in a Technocratic Policy Model

As discussed in Chapter 8 of this book, a (theoretical) technocratic policy model refers to a policy-making pathway where decision-making is initiated and executed solely or predominantly by expert committees. The technocratic model of governance often looks at Singapore as an example, where expert, bureaucratic committees use electoral feedback, big data, and other kinds of analytical tools to determine policies that reflect, in the long-term, the utilitarian interests of the society (Khanna 2017). The decisive element of the technocratic policy model is an actor finding legitimacy for its governing authority through its technical expertise.

As the following figure illustrates, in a technocratic policy model, the union of the policy and polity stream is the typical arrangement between policy-makers and the institutions managing or guiding the implementation of policies. The politics stream that reflects the low or limited participation of non-profits can contribute only indirectly to streams-alignment. Following streams alignment, further decisions are made in closed-door, expert committees, where non-profits will most likely assume an adversarial stance against these decisions (Fig. 11.1).

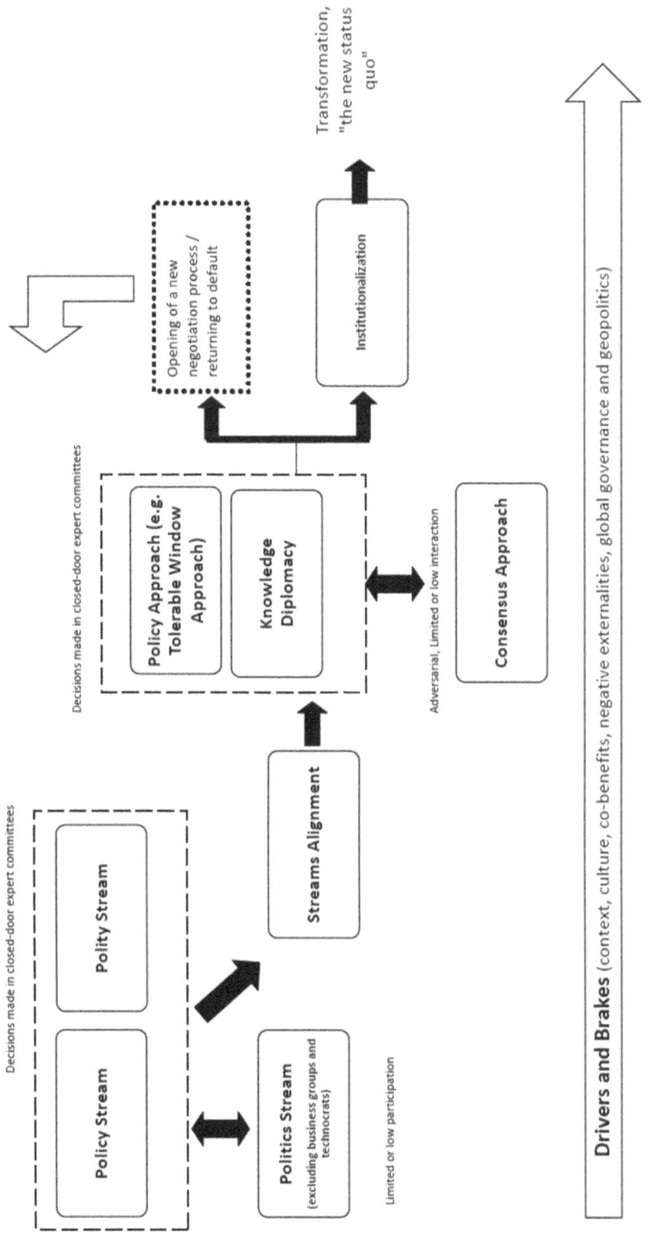

Figure 11.1 Technocratic/Bureaucratic Policy Pathway—An Ideal Type (own representation)

Comparing this theoretical model with the United States, non-profits can transform or at least 'package' themselves as the policy stream. The policy stream does not need to be represented solely by a government. When the government decides to abandon its leadership of the transformation process, others will emerge as viable alternatives. With the low-carbon transformation process already on its way, the process cannot be stopped, due to newly-established critical junctures and lock-ins as well as potential pay-offs. Due to the convergence of norms and values as well as surpassing of the tipping point, not even a disruptive federal government can deter other 'change agents'. The process is accompanied by a shift in policy-making towards the politics stream, and to a significant extent, to local policy-makers who are more likely to be pragmatic in their approaches. As the U.S. federal state increasingly withdraws from its various competencies in environmental protection and sustainable urban development, more social groups (both profit-oriented and non-profit), come into the picture, which will most likely legitimize their involvement through their technical expertise, forming de facto 'expert committees' that define technocratic policy models. Non-profits can determine and institutionalize various norms and standards that can serve as benchmarks of the low-carbon transformation process.

In the United States, due to the withdrawal of federal state institutions and the expected disruptive behavior of federal government agencies, expert-social groups will depend on norms and standards to build de facto polities or bureaucracies that will guide the transformation process. As the theoretical model suggests, technocratic policy pathways will be highly dependent on institutions, which implies a huge bureaucratic system. Nevertheless, with non-profits able and more willing to influence local electoral processes, bureaucracies that matter in terms of the transformation process, although more likely to be fragmented and dispersed, will still manage to provide the functions required of polities, such as verification and compliance. With non-profits forming verification measures, particularly when due to lock-ins, noncompliance will bring more competitive disadvantages and costs, and social and economic actors will still commit.

The theoretical technocratic policy model assumes a high level of social capital in the short term as the public will tend to tolerate a lack of inclusiveness and transparency for the sake of technical efficiency. Nevertheless, in the case of the United States, the lack of inclusiveness and transparency are major reasons for the emergence of the disruptive leadership. Therefore, non-profits need to constitute more inclusive bargaining interactions, especially at the local level.

11.2.2.3 Low Carbon Transformation in a Post-Democratic Policy Model

A post-democratic policy model refers to a policy pathway that is democratic in nature but has some features that are typical of pre-democratic political systems. The theoretical model highlights the important role of the finance, business and industry sectors in policy-making, not only in regard to how they are able to lobby their interests, often at the cost of other social actors, but also how the space has become conducive to the lobbying of these sectors, as market-based principles & logic have been instilled in the narratives that legitimize political actions. When arguing that not going against the interests of the business and industry sectors will lead to the unacceptable loss of jobs or the loss of economic competitiveness of a country, policy-makers are forced to accept their demands.

Comparing the post-democratic policy model to the United States, some elements of the US political system can confirm the post-democratic tendencies of the country. The current withdrawal of the federal state in order to pursue low-carbon, sustainable transformation reinvigorates the current devolution of state functions to private actors, particularly because privatization tends to be equated with rationalization and efficiency. With the various U.S. corporations still committing themselves to climate and environmental protection, monetary and economic values are increasingly defining the instruments of climate and environmental protection. As discussed earlier, one major entry point to climate mitigation has been identified through urban development (smart cities), which may further reproduce inequality among regions and cities as well as reinforce further socio-spatial fragmentation in the country.

As the following figure demonstrates, in a post-democratic policy model, business and industry actors can access the policy stream, either through direct influences or through the norms and standards being followed by policy-makers. The polity and the politics streams can contribute to the streams alignment. Nevertheless, with the state ceasing to monopolize authority and welfare services, as it has privatized most of its functions, the state will be most likely concentrating its activities on bureaucracy (the polity stream). Here, the state becomes predominantly a security provider (Fig. 11.2).

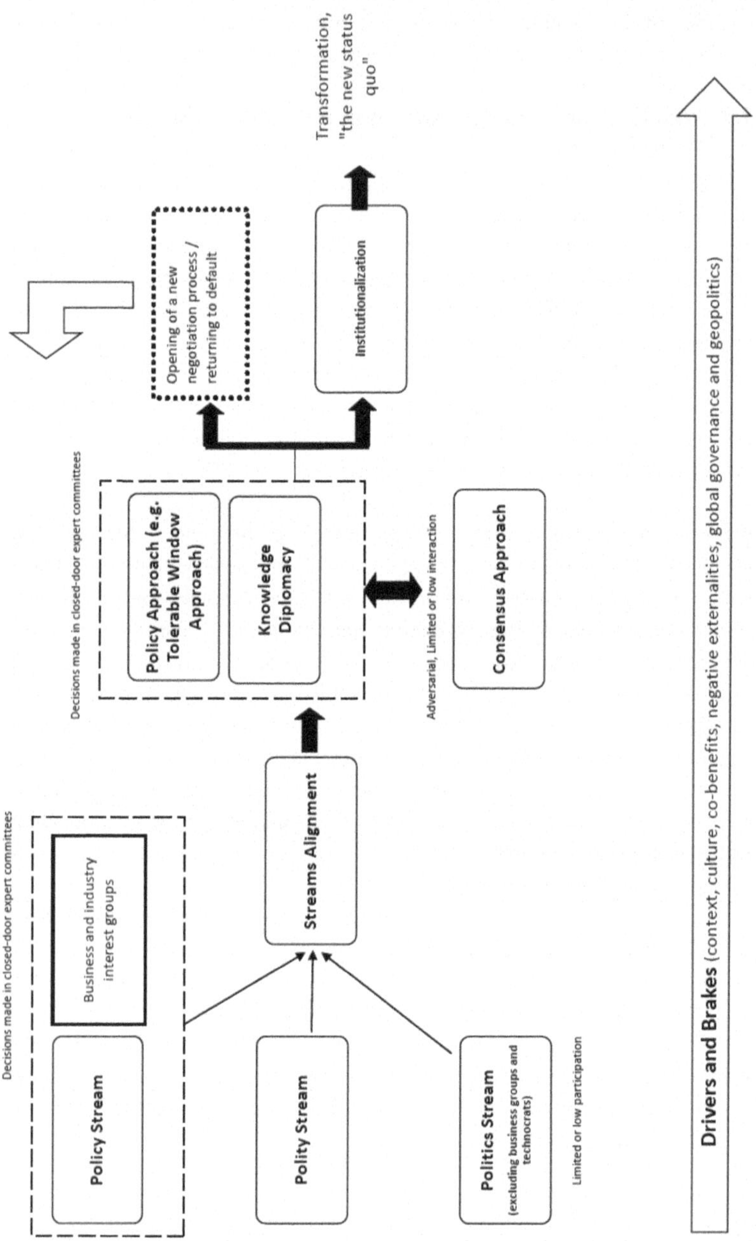

Figure 11.2 The post-democratic policy pathway—an Ideal Type (own representation)

Due to the privatization of most of public services of the state, the state will most likely have low autonomy and low capacity. This means that the state will depend highly on other actors when implementing policies. Because it merely functions as a regulatory body, should the government initiate and pursue more ambitious targets it will need more assistance and collaboration from other actors. The success of government-led programs will be highly dependent on how the economic actors will think they will profit from these programs. In addition, the tolerable-window approach will be highly de-politicized and commercialized, which will most likely lead to the dominance of the financial over the social aspects of public life. Maximizing benefits with the lowest possible costs will frame political actions, leading to non-monetary values being unable to compete against monetary values in terms of political decision-making.

Moreover, bargaining interactions follow the market-driven and market-defined framework for assessing the feasibility of policies. With the market logic defining the criteria for performance efficiency, the output orientation of legitimacy becomes the major driver of state actions. In a post-democratic policy model, as Hubertus Buchstein (in Crouch 2008) identifies, the re-definition of democracy through output-legitimacy opens the possibility of finding 'functional equivalents' to participatory legitimization, paving the way for dictatorial, aristocratic and technocratic policy models to be classified as democratic.

The imminent loss of federal funding for various environmental protection projects could create a vacuum, which will most likely be filled by the private sector, including profit-oriented and non-profit groups. The withdrawal of federal funding will further increase the privatization of knowledge and expertise in the country. As scientific communities become increasingly independent from government agencies, scientific knowledge can be further privatized, which can be beneficial on the meta-level, as scientists can maintain independence from political actors. Nevertheless, as is happening in the United States, the further privatization of this generation of scientific knowledge and technical expertise will be most likely accompanied by the federal government's increased resignation from various areas of societal life, which has been taken significantly into private hands (e.g., Ivy League universities). As such, the state will lose more of its competencies, which will be further assumed by profit-oriented and non-profit actors. This privatization of knowledge generation in the United States is not new, as the share of basic research funding provided by the federal government has been slipping in recent years, from around 70 percent in the 1960s and 1970s to an estimated 44 percent in 2015 (Science News 2017). In terms of non-profit groups that tend to pursue advocacy, some experts argue that government funding actually constrains advocacy (see O'Connell 1994; Reinelt 1994). For example, Steven

Smith and Michael Lipsky (1993) argue that non-profits that are dependent on government funds are less likely to engage in advocacy for fear of alienating government funders, driving away possible sources of new funding, or reducing the flexibility of funding.

Dispersed decision-making and factional politics in post-democratic policy models is complemented by a centralized concentration of power in the inner ellipsis of decision-makers, further reinforcing transparency deficits. The privatization of several state functions and the market-orientation of the remaining state policies will most likely lead to further shifts in power towards smaller membership of the elite, who are often referred to as the 'millionaires from Martha's Vineyard.' As the US federal government increasingly withdraws from various services, combined with increasing political opposition from within the Republican Party, President Trump will most likely resort to executive orders. As observed by Chris Cillizza and Sam Petulla (2017), President Trump is set to sign more executive orders than any other president in the last 50 years. With 49 executive orders already signed between assuming office in January 2017 and October 13, 2017, President Trump may resort to further executive orders after the possible loss of Republican control of the legislative branch, further limiting bargaining interactions in the United States. With this, decisions and policies will be less likely the results of bargaining and persuasion involving all relevant stakeholders.

11.3 Conclusion—Prescription and Lessons

11.3.1 Lessons for Theory

The case study on the United States has provided the theoretical underpinnings of disruptions within transformation processes. Through theoretical models, this case study has attempted to provide an understanding of the ramifications of the emergence of a disruptive political leadership to the transformation process. While the election of President Trump has mobilized and empowered social movements, both profit-oriented and non-profit, this empowerment can also further reinforce the existing technocratic and post-democratic tendencies of the U.S. governance system, which can further expand legitimacy deficits in the country. The very same legitimacy deficits held responsible for the electoral victory of a populist leader can further erode public trust in institutions.

As suggested by several examples in Greece and Italy, technocratic and post-democratic policy models are often sold as effective solutions to dysfunctional governance systems following various types of crises. However, as the U.S.

case study suggests, the transformation of profit-oriented and non-profit organizations into technocrats may further increase the gap between citizens and politics. The more the United States depends on the private sector, the more technocratic the country becomes, and the more exclusive policy-making becomes, the more inequality and socio-spatial fragmentation is reproduced.

11.3.2 Lessons for Practice

The implications of the election of President Trump for global climate protection can be analyzed through two perspectives—the implications 1) for the global order in general and 2) for global climate protection as a process. Without the intention of the current US federal government, it is paradoxically creating new opportunities for advancing global climate negotiations. Unlike with other global issues such as security and trade, the United States was, due to domestic pressure, not a leader in past climate negotiations. With the absence of U.S. leadership, there was a vacuum in climate negotiations, which European countries have tried to fill. Nevertheless, with the resignation of the country that, until recently, has emitted the most, European states are limited in their pursuit of an ambitious mitigation regime. They do not possess all the relevant resources to persuade or even coerce other states to support a mitigation regime that corresponds with the sort of climate integrity as proposed by epistemic communities. New major emitters such as China and India were reluctant to commit, because they calculated that the utility of committing was less than doing nothing (i.e. business-as-usual). This utility changed as the United States withdrew not only from climate negotiations, but also from other global regimes such as the UNESCO and TTIP.

The withdrawal of the United States from the Paris Climate Deal is symptomatic, as it vindicates a bigger picture of a global hegemony in showing gradual resignation from this role. This resignation is, however, seen as an opportunity for other states with the ambition to replace the United States as the *hegemon* and profit from 'hegemonic benefits', such as forging global narratives and setting standards relevant for coordination and collaboration strategies. The US withdrawal from the Paris Climate Deal as well as the reversal of almost all domestic climate policies forged not only by former President Obama, but also by earlier Republican and Democrat administrations, prevented the U.S. from any potential role in shaping future global climate regimes and institutions. Because of the linkages between climate protection and other issues, such as sustainable development and energy security, this resignation from the climate regime will also mean less 'Gestaltungsmacht' (shaping power) in other global regimes.

From the perspective of global climate protection as a process, there are new opportunities for advancing climate protection goals under the current US administration, which were not viable prior to the 2016 election of President Trump. As described above, the mobilization of social movements, the private sector, and state and local governments towards fulfilling the Paris Climate Deal is an unprecedented occurrence, and, if strategically used, can further advance climate protection as a process. However, embedding these actors into a global, climate-policy framework will need the resolution of several coordination and collaboration problems. It will, for example, require modifications of the norms and practices in global negotiations. Under which framework can the Federal Government of Germany, for example, negotiate with the City of Seattle without involving the US Federal Government? In this case, which frameworks are available for the city of Düsseldorf to directly collaborate and coordinate with the City of Seattle? If local governments cannot be signatories of international treaties, what alternative arrangements can be further supported? Should intra-city collaborations be the focal points of global climate negotiations? The answers to these questions will shed light on new agencies of global transformation towards sustainability.

12 Jamaica—The Transformation Towards Sustainability of an Island Economy Under Austerity Measures

This chapter diverges from the previous case studies. In addition to a literature review and qualitative interviews of local stakeholders, this chapter also contextualizes sustainable, low-carbon transformation by using an innovative experiment, where participants played the role of a decision-making government official committing to decisions under specific conditions (e.g., imposed austerity measures). When applied to Jamaica, the specific parameters of a scenario are assumed and through solution-oriented role playing, the process of decision-making is analyzed. The experiment employs a method, where a decision-making process is given a concrete space and time, which allows the identification of the main drivers and dynamics. These dynamics may be significant when tracing the course of the process.

The aim of this chapter is, as with the previous case studies, to provide an empirical basis for new or revisited theoretical concepts. As in the previous case studies, this chapter commences with the contextualization of the transformation process in Jamaica through literature review and interviews. What are the unique factors that drive the behavior of various actors? What challenges and caveats inhibit the kind of policy-making that embraces sustainable, low-carbon transformation? Which entry points to climate mitigation can be useful in disentangling Jamaica from its multi-layered and complex carbon lock-ins?

The simulation game was designed and conducted by the author within the framework of a collaboration project between the University of Technology (UTECH) in Kingston, the CARICOM, and the Deutsche Gesellschaft für internationale Zusammenarbeit (GIZ), where the author developed seven modules of the newly established master's Degree in Sustainable Energy and Climate Change, Innovation and Entrepreneurship. Participants of the simulation game were professionals from both the private and public sector, and who were enrolled

A. M. Hernández, *Taming the Big Green Elephant*, Globale Gesellschaft und internationale Beziehungen, https://doi.org/10.1007/978-3-658-31821-5_12

in the module on energy and environmental policies & economies. The professional background of the participants implies that they have significant (practical) knowledge of the issues involved. Most of the students are direct stakeholders in the low-carbon transformation process, which explains their enrolment in the master's program and allowing the simulation game to touch upon institutional memories and professional culture.

12.1 Context—Stumbling Blocks and Barriers to Sustainable, Low-Carbon Transformation

As the theoretical model (ideal type) demonstrates, the contextualization of Jamaica's transformation process will highlight the exogenous and endogenous factors that drive or hinder various processes relevant to the country's sustainable, low-carbon transformation.

12.1.1 Carbon Lock-Ins

Sustainable, low-carbon transformation is an elusive project in Jamaica (see Makhijani et al. 2013; UNFCCC 2015; GRICCE 2017). Political, social, technological, geophysical, and economic conditions are inauspicious to sustainable, low-carbon system transformation. Suitable policies to achieve sustainable and low-carbon growth are effectively inhibited by (carbon) lock-ins (Charvis & Heron 2016). For example, the decision to construct the Freedom Highway from Kingston to the Northern part of the Islands inhibits the development of the railway system, as provisions were made to avoid direct competition with the toll-collecting highway (Williams 2016). The country's high dependence on fossil fuels in terms of GDP/energy ratio and in almost all of its human activities is paradigmatic. Carbon lock-ins in Jamaica have limited the effectiveness of energy policies as stipulated by the *National Energy Policy* (2009–2030), the *Addendum on Energy Conservation and Efficiency* (2008–2022), the updated version of the *National Energy Conservation and Efficiency Policy* 2010–2030, and the *Vision 2030 Jamaica* (National Development Plan). These policies aim to promote energy conservation and efficiency. Such carbon lock-ins are complemented by an inability in effectively addressing the shortcomings of renewable energies, such as the intermittency of wind energy (Reynolds 2016; Willie & Morgan 2016)

Often labelled as a 'hostage' to oil, Jamaica's oil imports exceeded the value of its total exported goods by 118 percent in 2010 (Ahmed 2017). Imported oil provides approximately 95 percent of the country's primary energy services and accounts for over 90 percent of electricity production (MSET 2017), making Jamaica highly vulnerable to oil price volatility. Serious implications for the balance of payments, inflation, business competitiveness, and household poverty can be connected to Jamaica's energy insecurity. Exacerbating Jamaica's energy insecurity further, is its high energy intensity and high inefficiency in the use of energy resources. Due to the central role of the bauxite and alumina industries, Jamaica consumes an average of 4,800 kWh per US$1,000 of GDP, which is very high compared to other Latin American and Caribbean countries (MSET 2017). Electricity losses on the grid are high, at 22.3 percent, of which 10 percent are technical and the rest are from theft and illegal connections (MSET 2017). In addition, as Al Binger (2011) highlights, Jamaica wastes more than half of the available energy from imported fuels.

The transport sector of Jamaica is the largest consumer of petroleum, accounting for 42 percent of total petroleum consumption in 2008 (Binger 2011). Still, with the relatively expensive toll fees of the highway to sustain its operations, the Jamaican government cannot reopen its passenger train service, which may undermine the operations of the national highway. As the officials of the Jamaican Railway Corporation highlighted during an interview (Hernandez 2016), railway services are unable to compete with other modes of transport, because of high maintenance costs and the lack of investment in infrastructure. In addition, ambitious and eventually radical efforts are needed to allow the shift to a carbon-neutral transportation sector. However, with the country's electricity mainly being generated through oil-fired steam, combustion gas turbines, and combined cycle and diesel (Binder 2011), even the modernization of the railway system, which will be mainly powered through electricity, is expected to significantly contribute to Jamaica's de-carbonization. Therefore, the transport sector in Jamaica will remain a major source of carbon emissions in the long-term.

12.1.2 Social, Economic and Environmental Challenges to an Island Economy

As a small island state in the Caribbean, Jamaica is confronted by additional social, economic and environmental challenges typical to remote island economies (see Tisdell 2009). A major challenge is the interface between policies and an economy with limited competition. Due to scale economies, governments of small island economies tend to resort more often to regulation to control prices as business companies and industries seek higher revenues in a non-competitive market (Tisdell 2009). However, the political connections of company owners and managers as well as the low bargaining leverage of governments against multinational companies will more likely limit the effect of the 'political will' on regulating the market.

Small island states like Jamaica are highly vulnerable to imperfect market competition (see O'Sullivan 2003), particularly when trade commodities are involved. With imperfect competition, sellers are keen to influence the prices to earn more profits, particularly when limitations are unclear. The high prices of commodities are attributed not only to the limited number of sellers or traders, but also to *de facto* monopolistic competition, because sellers are selling highly differentiated products. Furthermore, Jamaica's supply chain of commodities requires additional intermediaries, which further increase the costs of trade, as large traders are unable to connect to all dispersed small markets from various areas in urban and rural Jamaica.

The high prices of commodities are also attributed to Jamaica's relatively high transportation costs, as the energy for transportation is provided almost solely by finite fossil fuels (Bedward & Simpson 2016). The limited number of inter-island transport options (McCalla 2016), as well as low frequency of transport connections in Jamaica, are responsible for the demand-supply imbalance following a situation where trade growth has outpaced the availability of transport services, leading to distorted signals about the demand for commodities (see Russell 2017). The carbon lock-in of Jamaica's economy sustains high transportation costs, as moving away from a carbon-intensive is inhibited by a complex set of other factors such as institutional barriers and high transition costs.

Like most small island countries, Jamaica has consistent trade deficits of around 20 percent of their GDP (Bank of Jamaica 2017). As of 2016, Jamaica had a negative trade balance of 3.55 billion USD in net imports (OEC 2017). Because trade accounts for around 50 percent of the GDP of Jamaica, lower demand of its bauxite used for aluminum production abroad will lead to significant losses in income. In addition, Jamaica is highly dependent on the United States as their main trading partner (52 percent of total trade), which undermines the resilience of the Jamaican economy. Related to these trade deficits, the negative capital flow in Jamaica is not only a sign of negative expectations with regards to economic growth, it also puts pressure on the economy. The −44.90 million USD capital flows in the second quarter of 2017 (−81.50 million USD in the first quarter of 2017) (Bank of Jamaica 2017) demonstrate the relative weakness of the Jamaican capital market and reflect the poor investment environment in the country, which further hamper economic development, as investors are reluctant to provide capital for operations and research & development.

Jamaica's trade deficits and negative capital flow are directly linked to the country's dependence on foreign aid and loans as well as on remittances from their citizens working abroad. Jamaica is one of the most indebted countries. It spends twice as much on debt repayment (1.2 billion USD) as it does on education and health combined (600 million USD) (Dearden 2013). Although Jamaica has repaid a total of 19.8 billion USD for its 18.5 billion USD debt, it still owes 7.8 billion USD as a result of high interest payments. In addition, Jamaica's debt is inhibiting income growth in Jamaica, due to austerity measures imposed by international lenders. For example, in exchange for an IMF loan of 1 billion USD in 2013, four years of austerity are responsible for a 20 percent real-term cut in wages (Dearden 2013). Huge debt has been a constant burden for Jamaica for four decades, where the economy has effectively not grown since 1990. Natural disasters, such as Hurricane Sandy in 2012, have further increased indebtedness, as Jamaica seeks foreign aid and loans for its rebook.

To summarize, Jamaica seems to be trapped by carbon lock-ins and the resulting unfavorable economic conditions undermining the country's attractiveness to foreign investors. While the tourism sector remains vibrant, partly due to austerity measures, Jamaica is lagging in improving infrastructure in non-tourist areas, further inhibiting economic growth (Durrant 2016). Although its energy demand is almost solely covered by imported fossil fuels, the country's efforts to expand the use of renewables are effectively hindered by the tendency of fossil fuel energy systems to be cheaper, better understood, and perceived as easier to employ.

A major factor that reinforces Jamaica's carbon lock-in is the behavior of the society as a whole (see Binger 2011). Carbon lock-ins are deeply embedded in the consumption behavior of the majority of the Jamaican population. Jamaica is confronted with a high-consumption society, in which the consumption of commodities (e.g., household appliances and motor vehicles) is hardly driven by efficiency considerations. While the Jamaican government has already initiated discussions aiming at giving energy efficiency and renewable energy more important roles in the country's energy system (Wood 2016), it has been lagging, due to gaps in the kind of policy that aims to effectively raise awareness of the connections between lifestyle and energy use (Binger 2011). Moreover, because political attention tends to be given to renewables, the country fails to address the improvement of energy efficiency, because of the inherent belief that savings in energy costs will mainly come from the deployment of renewable energy options.

12.1.3 Institutional Barriers

Functioning institutions are necessary for the successful deployment of sustainable energy, and ineffective institutions are a critical barrier to its growth (Knight 2016). While small island countries tend to have a high need of regulation leading to a higher share of public sector employees in total employment, Jamaica's public sector is relatively small, hinting at capacity deficits in providing services to citizens. As of July 2017, the public sector accounts for 59,400 employees, which is 4.88 percent of the total 1,216,200 employed labor force in Jamaica (SIJ 2017). For comparative purposes, Nordic countries Denmark, Norway and Sweden have higher public-sector employment levels, reaching nearly or over 30 percent of total employment between 2009 and 2013. The United Kingdom and Barbados have, respectively, 23.5 percent and 22.03 percent of its total labor force working in the public sector (see OECD 2011). The public sectors of Caribbean countries the Bahamas and the Dominican Republic employ 33.7 percent (2009) and 12.8 percent (2013) of the total labor force respectively.

Explanations as to the relatively small public sector in Jamaica are often linked to the country's constant exposure to rigid austerity measures through its high debt. As the public sector is unable to compete with the private sector in the labor market for hiring employees with the needed technical expertise, the technical competence of Jamaican public sector's employees is often questioned, inhibiting trust in state institutions. With the fast pace of technological advancement, regulatory bodies tend to struggle to catch up with regulatory provisions to ensure that other society priorities are not undermined. While the public sector is still perceived as a source of stable jobs, it is often the first affected by austerity measures imposed by creditors (e.g. hiring freeze).

In addition, some experts argue that a small public sector is partly responsible for the relatively low salary of private sector employees (see Malley & Moutous 1996; Algan et al. 2002; Burdett 2012). Nobel laureate in economics, Christopher Pissarides (2000), argues that the public sector competes with the private sector in attracting the best workers through so-called 'crowding out.' A small public sector like that in Jamaica cannot compete with the private sector. In addition, a larger public sector that can offer higher wages will most likely provide workers in the private sector more leverage when bargaining around salaries and additional benefits. Therefore, the public sector also influences the level of income in the private sector.

Sustainable low carbon transformation needs a public sector that is significantly capable of dedicating resources, for example, to address complex energy issues that are intertwined with other policy goals. Although government officials need to horizontally and vertically coordinate with colleagues from other government agencies and ministries, they will more likely find it difficult to collaborate in the context of competition for limited public resources following impositions of austerity. For example, sustainable, low-carbon transformation requires the exchange of updated information necessary for sustainable energy planning. The entanglement of various aspects of energy sector governance will bear witness to the cross-cutting of competencies of a vast array of agencies and government structures, which may lead to a lack of clarity about final decisions in the energy sector or unnecessarily prolong or complicate permitting processes. Such a long and complicated permit process may further hinder the entry of renewable energy technologies. Due to their wide-ranging and often cross-sectoral responsibilities, many government officials lack the detailed knowledge of sustainable energy technologies, their economic and financial requirements, and alternative mechanisms for their effective support.

With this contextualization of the various stumbling blocks to sustainable, low-carbon transformation, it is important that carbon lock-ins be identified, conceptualized and addressed through an integrated approach to make policy-makers understand and concretize missed opportunities. The next section aims to provide an integrated understanding of the requisites of Jamaica's sustainable, low-carbon transformation. What changes are needed to be implemented to effectively address lock-ins and related *caveats*?

12.2 The Agency and Audience of Sustainable, Low-Carbon Transformation in Jamaica

12.2.1 Jamaica's Response to the Paris Climate Agreement

Like many developing countries, Jamaica connotes climate change with vulnerability. As a small island developing state, Jamaica is particularly vulnerable to the impacts of climate change. Jamaica's economic development is at risk, because its major economic sectors such as tourism, agriculture, forestry and water are climate-sensitive (UNFCCC 2015). As such, like in the Philippines, political discourse and narratives on climate change in Jamaica evolve mainly around adaptation and seldom around mitigation. Nevertheless, Jamaica has announced that it intends to play its part in reducing GHG emissions through 'no regrets' emission measures (UNFCCC 2015). Emission reduction is also mainly framed from the perspective of energy security, as Jamaica seeks to resolve risks and threats to its energy supply system.

Jamaica became the 143rd country to ratify the Paris Climate Agreement on April 11, 2017 when the Minister without Portfolio of the Ministry of Economic Growth and Job Creation officially presented the instrument of ratification at the National Climate Change Conversation organized by the Ministry's Climate Change division (UNDP 2017). With Jamaica's ratification of the Paris Agreement, the INDCs have been adopted as NDCs, Jamaica will revise and update its NDCs by 2020 and will continue to update every 5 years thereafter.

The ratification was expected, because the agreement is aligned with Jamaica's existing domestic policies. Climate change has been 'mainstreamed' in Jamaica's policy-making, which will integrate mitigation and adaptation in present and future policies. Jamaica's National Development Plan, Vision 2030, which is the country's long-term, sustainable development program recognizes the need for a healthy, natural environment. Other key policies that support the ratification and implementation are the Second National Communication (2011), the Climate Change Policy Framework (2013) and the National Energy Policy 2009–2030 (2009). A major element of Jamaica's climate policy is, as mentioned, climate change adaptation. Jamaica has developed a Strategic Program for Climate Resilience (SPCR), as part of the Pilot Program for Climate Resilience (PPCR), to decrease Jamaica's vulnerability to the effects of climate change.

In terms of mitigation, Jamaica's intended nationally-determined contribution (INDC) will mitigate the equivalent of 1.1 million metric tons of carbon dioxide per year by 2030 or a reduction of 7.8 percent of emissions compared to the business-as-usual (BAU) scenario of growth without policy intervention, which uses 2005 as a base year (UNFCCC 2015). However, under this BAU scenario, GHG emissions from Jamaica would increase by 37 percent by 2030, which implies a massive gap between expected emission increase and INDC under the BAU scenario. In addition, Jamaica will conditionally increase its aim to a reduction of GHG emissions of 10 percent below the BAU scenario, subject to the provision of international support. The Jamaican government aims to significantly reduce emissions growth and achieve its NDCs through a program of modernization of energy infrastructure and diversification of energy sources towards cleaner and renewable fuels (20 percent by 2030), pursuing opportunities for energy conservation and incentivizing efficiency. The Climate Change Division of the Ministry of Water, Land, Environment and Climate Change will coordinate the actions of various ministries, departments and agencies in implementing Jamaica's INDCs.

12.2.2 Entry Points to Climate Mitigation, Energy Security and Sustainable Development

Entry points to climate mitigation, energy security and sustainable development in Jamaica can be identified through the contextualization of policy and market instruments.

12.2.2.1 Embedding the Informal Economy into Sustainable, Low-Carbon Transformation

The informal segment of the Jamaican economy is a significant issue when assessing sustainable, low-carbon transformation, because its size is estimated to be between 40 and 60 percent of the country's official GDP (Torero et al. 2006) (compared with 16.1 percent of GDP in OECD countries or 8.4 percent in the United States, see Schneider 2005). With the established connections between the informal economy and emission growth (see Abid 2015; Bento et al. 2017), sustainable, low-carbon transformation needs to include efforts not only to 'formalize' this segment of the economy, but also recognize the potential 'entrepreneurial spirit' of informal sectors (see Soto 1986) that could be conducive to sustainable, low-carbon transformation.

The informal economy a broad range of activities conducted in the informal sector can be condensed to identify several common characteristics that includes all employment that is not bound by contract or other legal regulations, small-scale operations, unregistered businesses, and all activities which generate revenue that is not reported to tax authorities (Graham 2016). While the informal economy in Jamaica is usually attributed to a loss of tax revenues, which is estimated to be around about 800 billion JMD in nominal terms per year, as well as to the evasion of environmental regulations and the vulnerability of workers due to a lack of government protection (70 percent of workers do not have legal contracts, see Torero et al. 2006), its impact on Jamaica's sustainable, low-carbon transformation remains a huge knowledge gap. If the informal economy is largely unaccounted for in sustainable, low-carbon modelling, policy approaches and scientific & policy analysis, the effectiveness of policy instruments can be a major source of uncertainty (see Benson et al. 2014). Nevertheless, including the informal economy in sustainable, low-carbon policy-making will be needed to fairly address the reasons why there is an informal economy in the country in the first place.

For example, one possible reason for the existence of the informal economy is the lack of political will to address this, because formalization will most likely further burden the poor. The informal economy is often seen as a major source of employment for those who do not have access to human capital. In addition, the informal economy is composed of various activities that are often reactions to fluctuations in the formal economy and provide 'cushions' in times of economic crises, as unemployed people are able to secure income through the informal economy (Benson et al. 2014). In addition, because the informal economy is largely unaccounted for, it is difficult to come up with categories or types of informal economic entities, especially as these entities cover different sectors such as energy, agri-food, trade, mining, housing and waste management. While some of these are not major emitters, such as street vendors, or are even are helpful to the environment, such as informal waste-picking (see Benson *et al.* 2014), others such as artisan mining, informal housing, and car repair shops, are contributing significantly to environmental degradation through uncontrolled and unmonitored pollution (see Abid 2015, Blackman and Bannister 1998; Lahiri-Dutt 2004).

Various studies and reports have identified microenterprises in wholesale/retail trade and agriculture as the main entities of Jamaica's informal economy by employing almost 60 percent of the workers in the informal economy, followed by manufacturing as a distant third (see Torero et al. 2006). These microenterprises contribute to the income generation of women in particular (57 percent of the total number of workers in the informal economy, see Torero et al. 2006) and supply various commodities particularly needed in the rural areas of the country. Nevertheless, while some of these entities are financially incapable of installing technologically advanced pollution control equipment, others refuse to install such pollution control, particularly when the government is most likely unable to monitor and control these entities (see Blackmann 2000).

Calculating the amount of emissions from the Jamaican informal economy can only depend on 'honest estimates.' Therefore, the potential benefits of engaging the informal economy for sustainable, low-carbon transformation will need to look beyond mitigation to innovation at the grassroots level. As possibly implied by the significant number of microenterprises in the informal economy of Jamaica run by tertiary graduates (around 33 percent), the informal sector in the country can be tapped as an important driver of sustainable, low-carbon transformation. However, engaging Jamaica's informal economy to commit to sustainable, low-carbon transformation will require the inclusion of non-state actors. The actors of the informal economy will most likely prefer the non-intervention of state actors, whose forms of formalization such as licenses, fees, and permits are linked to additional costs and limitations.

12.2.2.2 Sustainable Tourism—Efficient Hotel Buildings

As tourism is a huge source of revenue and employment in Jamaica, mitigation efforts that will affect the tourism sector will require careful implementation. The direct contribution of travel and tourism to Jamaica's GDP was 1.4 billion USD or 9.3 percent of total GDP in 2016 and is forecast to rise by 4.6 percent in 2016, and to rise by 5 percent per year from 2017 to 2027 to 13.4 percent of total GDP by 2027 (WTTC 2017). In addition, travel and tourism directly supported 97,000 jobs (8.4 percent of total employment), which is expected to rise by 4.1 percent in 2017 and by 4.4 percent per year to 155,000 jobs or 12.2 percent of total employment by 2027 (WTTC 2017). When jobs indirectly supported by the sector are included in the calculation, the total contribution of the travel and tourism sector in 2016 was 27.5 percent of total employment (318,500 jobs). It is furthermore expected that total employment will rise by 4.3 percent in 2017 and by 4.4 percent in 2027 to a total of 40 percent (WTTC 2017).

With the expected growth of the travel and tourism sector, without additional climate policies, the sector will be a major source of emissions. Nevertheless, the sector can benefit from mitigation policies by contextualizing (co-benefits and synergies) new investment and decision frameworks (including narratives). While government mitigation policies can, for example, focus on reducing electricity costs, particularly those needed for the cooling of hotels, through the gradual replacement of imported fossil fuels and the deployment of renewable energies for a long-term perspective, the sector can actively highlight investments in enhancing energy efficiency. Particularly with the expected warming in Jamaica, hotels burdened with the crippling effects of higher electricity costs can be supported through new policies on demand and supply. The tourism sector can be further motivated to address these challenges through policy and market instruments to promote efficient buildings that will significantly reduce energy consumption. Nevertheless, the tourism sector will need additional support to achieve energy efficiency while it addresses the effects of climate change such as sea-level rise, extreme weather events and erosion.

12.3 A Simulation Game—The Jamaican Energy Policy Under Austerity Measures

The energy policy game focuses on putting forward austerity measures which will **create 250,000 jobs** while **reducing its debts to 117 percent of GDP**, modernize the public sector by strengthening government capacity and effectiveness, enhance energy security and energy efficiency to reduce its dependence on oil, and generate additional income to stabilize government spending (25 percent of the 2016/2017 government budget) of **J$ 147.5 billion**. Emphasis is also placed on evaluating the risks and barriers of the chosen measures (*risks, unhappiness and ecological damage*).

12.3.1 The Background of the Game

The newly elected Prime Minister Andrew Holness of the Jamaican Labour Party (JLP) has promised to reverse the hard austerity measures dictated by the International Monetary Fund (IMF). In 2010, Jamaica needed the US$1.27 billion IMF loan to support its plan to recover from mounting government debt, weak economic growth, and the effects of the global financial crisis. While the government was able to restore economic stability, these measures are often regarded as unsustainable, because the reduction of budget deficits was primarily attributed to the effect of low oil prices which allowed the government to reduce its spending on oil imports. The current low oil price gives the government a reprieve, but if Jamaica wants to have sustainable economic growth, it cannot speculate solely on global oil prices, especially because of the political crisis in Venezuela which might lead to the cancellation of the agreement providing Jamaica with cheap oil. It needs to take on the program to break the cycle of high debt (currently about 140% of GDP) and low growth, trapping Jamaica in a cycle of debt service and borrowing for decades.

The new government cannot reverse the reforms stipulated by the IMF loan. The government understands that the obstacles to Jamaica's growth and job creation are numerous and severe. As identified by the IMF, the key problems for Jamaica are: crime, the cost and availability of credit, tax compliance costs, unreliable and expensive electricity, and a large informal economy. The IMF has also identified the need to address the large size of the public sector that has also stifled private sector dynamism and places too much emphasis on government as the engine of growth and employment.

12.3.2 The Game—Goals and Instruction

The new government has tasked an expert panel with making recommendations to improve the fiscal standing of Jamaica. The expert panel has produced a list of possible measures. The cabinet of the government conducts a meeting to evaluate the austerity measures suggested by the panel. Furthermore, the government has tasked this panel with recommending measures to meet the following goals **while meeting the austerity goals set by the International Monetary Fund**:

- Create more than 250,000 jobs while reducing its debt to 117% (debt to GDP ratio) in 2017.
- Modernize the public sector by strengthening government capacity and effectiveness
- Create an enabling environment for the private sector by fostering investments in high-potential sectors,
- Build social and climate resilience by strengthening social safety nets and by supporting the development of a comprehensive framework for disaster and climate risk management
- Enhance energy security and energy efficiency to reduce dependence on oil imports.

As members of the government cabinet, participants need to evaluate the measures presented and choose which measures are to be implemented to meet these political goals. This should be done while considering the social, economic, and environmental sustainability of these specific measures. Furthermore, participants should identify possible conflict cleavages, conflict parties, issues and other negative externalities and provide "compensatory measures" (including the costs of these measures).

The participants should follow the following steps:

The first step is to generate additional sources of income to allow much-needed investment and to finance the increase of the income tax rate threshold (from J$592,800 to J$1,000.272). The assumed amount of needed additional income to stabilize government spending is 25 percent of the 2016/2017 government budget or **J$ 147.5 billion**.

The second step after generating additional sources of income is to choose and evaluate measures that would implement the goals mentioned above. The expert panel have identified additional sources of funding available to developing countries under the framework of various development funds such as the climate fund or the clean development mechanism. The participants need to check Jamaica's eligibility for this additional funding.

The third step is to evaluate the risks and barriers of the chosen measures. For this game, each option shows the expected costs and expected revenues. Costs are shown as: *Risk Points (RPs), Unhappiness Points (UPs) and Ecological Damage Points (EDPs)*

Some measures are linked with risks (the probability that the measure will not work as well as externalities, trade-offs and co-benefits), public discontent or public resistance (leading to street protests and more social unrest), and ecological damage points (leading to environmental damages). Aside from the goal of generating or saving **J$ 147.5 billion, no set of austerity measures is allowed to have more than 10 RPs, 10 UPs and 2 EDPs.**

Participants may decide to alter a specific value. For example, in suggesting measure no. 4, a tax may be introduced with a 20 percent increase (instead of 10 percent as the expert committee suggested). This will lead to an additional 75 percent of the initial value to reflect the marginal benefits of values. In turn, the RPs and UPs will be doubled, and EDP tripled. Some measures cannot be altered or doubled (marked with *).

12.3.3 Results and Interpretation

The three groups have produced a set of decisions as summarized by the following three figures:

Group 1 (PHMEL) was able to come up with actual budget cuts totaling **127.043 billion JMD**. Adjusting this number to consider the marginal benefits, the group achieved a budget cut of a total of **106.84 billion JMD**. Marginal benefit adjustment refers to some measures that were doubled (or tripled) compared to the figures given by the expert panel. Group 1 decided to double the figures of the selected austerity measures (2a, 2b, 2c, 13, 14, 16, 17, and 20). Nevertheless, a doubling the provision on increasing income tax will not lead to a doubling of the savings, because of the expected marginal benefit of factor 0.75. Both numbers are short of the required **147.5 billion JMD.** In comparison, Group 2 (HVSP) achieved budget cuts of a total of **125.804 billion JMD**. Interestingly, the group decided to bridge the remaining amount through additional foreign loans and grants. Group 3 (AGBPB) on the other hand achieved cuts of a total of **150.854 billion JMD**, which surpasses the required 147.5 billion JMD goal. When asked how the group was able to negotiate savings with such relative ease,

the group claimed they focused on the direct and indirect benefits of each austerity measure. When it became apparent that 'harsh' austerity measures would later yield to additional benefits, negotiations became less contested.

In terms of limitations to the Risk Points (RPs) (10), Unhappiness Points (UPs) (10) and Ecological Damage Points (EDPs) (2), group 1 met the limitations on UPs and EDPs with −9 and −27 points respectively. However, with 14 RPs, group 1 surpassed the allowed RPs. Group 2 managed to meet all the limitations on points. With 10 RPs, 0.5 UPs and −14 EDPs, it is expected that the budget cuts will not face fierce political and social resistance. Group 3 produced a set of austerity measures with the most favorable points. With 10 RPs, −2.5 UPs and −24.5 EDPs, group 3 vindicated the pattern of the usefulness of linking environmental protection with other policy priorities. When environmental benefits of economic and political measures are 'concretized,' the linkages become clear and are easier to embed in their decisions. Furthermore, with the surprisingly 'good EDPs' of all groups, **discussions were made whether a 'points trade' should be made possible following a similar principle of carbon trading, with RPs to be substituted by UPs and EDPs. This 'trade' can be further pursued in real life to facilitate decision-making.**

Due to time constraints, groups 1 and 2 were not able to discuss the other aspects of the game, such as the identification of relevant stakeholders as well as the expected co-benefits and synergies, which could have provided them with additional resources to legitimize the austerity measures or to even bargain for further budget cuts. It was difficult for them to connect austerity measures with the creation of more than 250,000 jobs while reducing its debt to 117 percent (debt to GDP ratio). A possible explanation for this difficulty is that they did not completely understand the rationale behind the 'points.'

On the other hand, Group 3 was able to initiate the assessment of budget savings using the imposed conditions, because the group tried to understand why a specific austerity measure was too risky to implement. For example, when a measure was expected to lead to job cuts, this measure was combined with discussions about contingencies such as additional policy instruments for job creation. This linkage made contextualization possible. In addition, by identifying the ministries and other related government agencies, group 3 was able to have an overview of the required government capacity that is needed to ensure the effectiveness of the implementation of the austerity measures, while maximizing their co-benefits and minimizing the risks (Table 12.1).

Table 12.1 Example: The Results of Group 1 (PHMEL) (own representation)

No	Measure	Benefit(Jmd) Billion		RP	UP	EDP	Modified
		Generate	Save				
		139,0425714	-20,2	13	-9	-26	
		118,8425714					
2	a	0,525		0	0	0	Doubled
	b	0,7		-1	-1	0	Doubled
	c	0,75		-2	-2	0	Doubled
3		0,5		-1	-1	0	
4		0,6		0	0,5	0	
5	a	0,3		0,5	1	0	
	b	0,55		0,5	0,5	0	
	c	0,8		0	-1	0	
6	a	0,3		0	-1	0	
7	b	1,628571429		0,5	1	0	
	c	4,375		1	-1	0	
8	a	4		0,5	1	0	
9		1,8		1	1	-1	
10		3		1	0	-1	
11	c		-0,2	-2	-2	-2	
12	b	6,489		1	0,5	-2	
	c	3		0,5	0,5	-2	
	e	12		1,5	1	-4	
13		3,5		1	2	-4	Doubled
14		7,05		1	1	-8	Doubled
15		3,6		0	0,5	0	
16		9,275		4	-2	0	Doubled
17		7		2	0	-2	Doubled
18		5,3		2	-1	0	
19		4		0,5	0,5	1	
20		3,5		2	-4	0	Doubled
23		3		0	0,5	0	
25		5		1	2	0	
26		8		0,5	1	0	
27		4		0,5	0	0	
28		10		3			
29		3			1		
30		1		1	0,5	-2	
31		8		0,5	1		
32	a		-1	-2	-2	0	
	b		-2	-1	-2	-1	
	c		-4	-2	-2	0	
	d		-3	-1	-2	2	
33			-10	-2	-3	0	
34	a	0,5		1	1	-1	
	c	7		0	1	-1	
36		5		-1	-1	2	
Actual		127,0425714	-20,2	14	-9	-27	
Target		36,375	111,125	10	10	2	
		106,8425714					

12.3.4 Observations from the Behavioral and Negotiation Point of View

The author of this book/game designer added and highlighted some game parameters that would test the negotiation behavior of the participants. As noticed by the participants (and written in the questionnaire), the need to negotiate with other stakeholders (other ministries) made decision-making very complex.

The following is a selection of observations made by the game master during the game:

Group 1

- Group 1, which consisted of all male participants, spent a significant amount of time (around 60% of time) discussing the procedures that were to be followed. However, after the group was able to find consensus about the procedures, the bargaining interactions became easier to conduct.
- There was a general impression that the participants were 'territorial,' because the discussions were often about the limitations of what they could accept as representative of a specific ministry. Because of this, it was difficult for a participant to assume the role of a facilitator in the negotiations. Often, a participant who was indifferent to a specific issue intuitively mediated between participants who were obviously unable to move forward because of differences.
- Interestingly, on various occasions, humor (use of jokes) was used to 'deflate' some tensions between parties.
- Group 1 used all possible technical tools to make the visualization of values easier, such as the projection of an excel table showing all the measures that they have already reached. This visualization gave the group additional motivation to work together as they become solution-oriented.

Group 2

- Group 2, which consisted of all female participants, focused on the fairness aspects of the provisions. The deliberations were often framed by concepts of fairness and equity. Interestingly, the participants apparently had a similar definition of fairness and equity, as one session of the module was dedicated to understanding the concept of fairness and justice. This gives the idea that it is important for participants of any negotiation to have a basic understanding of such concepts, as this will effectively facilitate negotiations.

- Group 2 consisted of four participants who applied different negotiation styles (competitive, collaborative, cooperative, avoiding). One participant was highly competitive, two were rather collaborative and the remaining one was an avoider.
- The two collaborative participants were able to 'contain' the competitive participant by highlighting benchmarks and objective standards. Because of this, the deliberations became highly analytical.

Group 3

- Group 3 consisted of both male and female participants. There were no clear gender-based implications of this composition.
- Interestingly, one participant connected to the group through Skype. Nevertheless, as expected, the internet connection was difficult, and he was disconnected most of the time. During the times he was briefly connected, he tried to unilaterally dictate the course of the negotiation until the connection failed again. This can be explained by his motivation to compensate for his absence. Nevertheless, the connection difficulty significantly delayed the negotiations, because the discussion was constantly repeated for the sake of the missing participant. This experience implies the importance of 'institutional memory' and 'personal connections' during deliberations. A participant that is new to the group will need additional time to catch up with the obvious and latent information and the related signals needed to agree on decisions.
- All (except for the skype participant) were collaborative during the negotiations.

12.4 The Ideal Type of Democratic Policy-Making Under Low Capacity and Low Autonomy—The Role of Austerity Measures and Carbon Lock-Ins in Jamaica

Jamaica has developed into one of the most stable democracies in the Caribbean region. While some election periods, such as the 1980 general elections, which was marked by over 800 casualties, have witnessed sporadic violence, Jamaica has never experienced a successful coup attempt since its independence in 1962, and although elections were often delayed by the incumbent government, elections have been regularly conducted and the opposition party is regularly able to win elections.

12.4.1 The Material Value of Democracy in Jamaica

As identified in chapter 8, the manner in which political actors are able to align their political interests with public opinion or how they can shape public opinion is an important subject of analysis of policy-making in democratic countries. Jamaica's "dumb" democracy is currently challenged by legitimacy deficits as implied by the downward trend of voter turnouts since 1944 (The Gleaner 2016). The perception of disconnect between politics and societal interests fuels political apathy, especially among the youth, which weakens civil society engagement. In turn, political apathy further reinforces legitimacy gaps. For example, approximately 28 percent of the votes from the eligible electorate was enough to give a two-thirds majority in the House of Representatives to the People's National Party (PNP) in the 2011 elections. This was slightly improved in the following elections. In 2016, the Jamaica Labour Party (JLP) won the General Elections held on 25 February 2016 with 50 percent of votes (or 32 out of 63 seats) with only 47.7 percent voter turnout, which was the lowest since 1983, the year when the PNP boycotted the election.

Because many democratic countries tend to rely solely on elections as source of political mandate, input legitimacy is often taken as 'default,' evident and given. As such, some governments and state institutions do not see the need to build up their capacities to effectively engage and facilitate persuasive interactions. As long as their decisions are within the boundaries set by the constitution, no additional efforts are identified and implemented to build the capacities of other stakeholders to actually and effectively participate in persuasion and bargaining regimes. In Jamaica, while there is a stable democratic regime, state institutions are often overwhelmed by several lock-ins and structural impediments. For example, Jamaica's dependence on fossil fuels and bargaining interactions that are allowed to define how the country will achieve sustainable, low-carbon transformation is not creating enough new impulses for the necessary changes.

As the ideal type of the democratic policy model suggests, the transformation process is not only dependent on the interactions between the three streams, but also on the drivers and brakes. In Jamaica's case, carbon lock-ins have impeded stream alignments. In addition, local conditions, such as 'brain drain', have inhibited consensus-building, as important stakeholders have limited technical capacity to actually contribute to consensus-building.

Carbon lock-ins limit the perceived available and feasible sets of decisions (and policies) in many ways, which constrain efforts to promote sustainable, low-carbon transformation. State institutions are confronted by its low autonomy and low capacity in facilitating functional, institutional, and bargaining interactions among relevant stakeholders. The low autonomy of Jamaican institutions pertains to the multiple dependencies of these institutions on designing, implementing and monitoring policies. Jamaica's high dependence on foreign loans and remittances, as well as the related imposed austerity measures limit the ability of Jamaican policy-makers to make independent decisions without undermining its access to future loans. Low autonomy (translated to the 'tolerable window') is, for example, not being determined through streams alignment, but by foreign lenders and carbon lock-ins. Therefore, existing guard-rails tend to favor non-sustainable and high-carbon policies.

Jamaica's low capacity can be significantly attributed to its relatively small size (around 4 percent of the total labor force). This and the paradoxical public perception that the Jamaican public sector is 'too big,' implying legitimacy deficits, limiting its institutional capacity to address complex and intertwined issues in order to pursue sustainable, low-carbon transformation. Jamaica's low capacity is further reinforced by 'brain drain', as the country lacks policy entrepreneurs with both technical expertise and knowledge of the local context. Knowledge diplomacy is therefore a huge challenge as technical and academic studies relevant to Jamaica's sustainable, low-carbon transformation is not able to catch up with emerging necessities. As such, Jamaican policy-makers, for example, often resort to studies and reports published by international bodies with limited (local) contextual value.

In addition, the rather weak social movement or civil society working on sustainable development and environmental/climate protection in Jamaica pave way for certain (business) actors that represent the fossil fuel sector to over-proportionately influence policy entrepreneurship (also called lobbying). Nevertheless, there are several environmental NGOs such as the Nature Conservancy which helped to create the Blue and John Crow Mountain National Park for which it brokered a Debt for Nature Swap (see GRICCE 2017) that are actively engaged with international donors to support environmental and climate protection in Jamaica. However, there are significant missed opportunities that can be adequately addressed with a more empowered Jamaican civil society. The general civic discontent and political apathy of a significant part of the population are symptoms both of the low autonomy and low capacity of state institutions, which further induce limitations to any transformation process in Jamaica, as potential partners for transformation are effectively alienated and disenfranchised (see Campbell 2016).

12.5 Conclusion—Capacity-Building as Key to Jamaica's Sustainable, Low-Carbon Transformation

12.5.1 Lessons for Theory

The ideal type analysis of Jamaica's policy model has led to some theoretical challenges. The simulation game highlighted the co-benefits of various austerity measures. The identification of these co-benefits and other synergies was made possible through the contextualization of each measure. As the positive and negative externalities of each measure were identified, it became evident that negative externalities, when properly addressed by compensatory measures, may create new values, for example for climate protection or job creation. A lesson for theory is that 'empathy' can be the key to any transformation process, as addressing multiple perspectives can actually expand the value of a specific measure. Nevertheless, expanding the value might require additional investment, which requires a long-term outlook.

12.5.2 Lessons for Practice

Jamaica lacks local scholars who have the methodological and scientific expertise to produce studies that meet high academic validity standards. Because epistemic communities play a huge role in understanding the complexities of climate change and of how climate protection, energy security, and sustainable development interplay, Jamaica's sustainable, low-carbon transformation will necessitate an unprecedented upgrade of its pool of experts. In addition, Jamaica's pool of technical experts should not only come from government agencies, but also from independent research institutes that are able to pursue both basic and applied research without depending on either the government or the business/industry sectors.

Moreover, the capacity-building of scientific communities in Jamaica will need to find a balance between propriety and access to public goods. Through various interviews of local experts and scientists, it became apparent that Jamaican universities tend not to share information and data with other scholars (both within the same organizations and between organizations) for propriety reasons. This outlook can be attributed to the dependence of research on private funding.

There is a need to address the 'angst' of researchers and research institutes, because a sustainable, low-carbon transformation will require more inter- and intra-disciplinary collaboration to effectively address complex issues that supersede disciplinary boundaries. As one institute produces a set of data, other institutes may be in a better position to assess the meaning and implication of these data. Another policy-oriented institute may be better at transforming the data and its assessment into policy recommendations as other contextual factors are embedded into the analysis. The Jamaican government needs to ensure access to relevant knowledge to support the maturation process and the adaption of knowledge to Jamaican specificities.

In the same manner, Jamaica needs to upgrade the capacity of its civil society to participate in consensus-building processes. Linked to this is the need to effectively address the latent disconnect between policy-making and the societal mandate. This can be done, for example, by initiating ambitious consultations on structural reforms. Effective consultations are, however, contingent on social actors that are able to formulate and advocate for various societal priorities such as environmental protection, civil rights and liberties, equity, and social innovation. Jamaica needs to improve its social capital if it wants to achieve sustainable, low-carbon transformation.

13 Lessons for Theory: A Conceptual Framework of Transformative Pathways

A major objective of this book is to provide theoretical and practical knowledge on how sustainable, low-carbon transformation can be facilitated. As a creative and a rational process, transformation can be managed. However, the management of transformation necessitates an integrative and process-oriented outlook to grasp the various issues, dynamics, causalities, associative relations, lock-ins, critical junctures, tipping points, interactions, behavior, and analytical levels that drive any transformation process. Chapters 2 to 6 have contributed to the theoretical framework or scope of the book, followed by chapters 7 and 8, which presented the knowledge and decision tools as methodologies (the ideal types as theoretical models, case studies and simulations). These tools guided the analysis of the case studies in chapters 8 to 12. These case studies offered the empirical foundation by providing the context, agency, and audience relevant to the transformation process of selected countries. This chapter delivers the next step, which introduces a conceptual framework to better understand and explain 'stratified' transformative pathways from the 'negotiative' perspective.

A. M. Hernández, *Taming the Big Green Elephant*, Globale Gesellschaft und internationale Beziehungen, https://doi.org/10.1007/978-3-658-31821-5_13

The Conceptual Framework of Transformative Pathways (CFTP) attempts to provide an important understanding necessary to grasp the complexity of shifting from the initially chosen or assumed pathway ('business-as-usual') to other pathways, which in this book are referred to as sustainable, low-carbon (transformative) pathways. As a framework, the CFTP will provide an **explanation of causality** (referred to here as 'congruence'). This explanation will be **substantiated** using previous works in relevant fields including well-established theories, as well as the case studies (including the simulation game) presented in this book. Afterwards, the assessment of the congruence (or explanation)'s **ability to predict** will be assessed, testing its possible reoccurrence in future events as well as its applicability to other contexts. Another possibility of testing the ability to predict is to provide insights into which conditions this congruence can occur. The testing will be ended by discussing its limitations and analyzing to what extent this congruence can be **falsifiable**. An important disclaimer of this chapter is that this conceptual framework is still being developed and will eventually reach maturity as time passes.

13.1 The Parameters of the Conceptual Framework of Transformative Pathways—The Negotiation Outlook

The following figure mirrors the integrated stream of transformation. Before introducing the various phases of transformative pathways, there is a need to discuss some important characteristics of the illustration (Fig. 13.1).

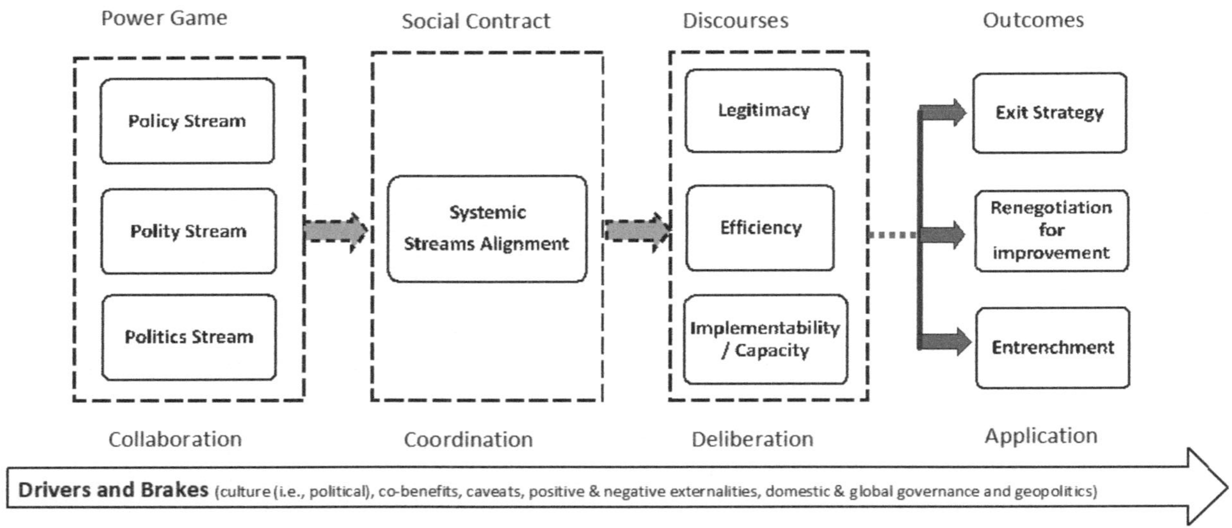

Figure 13.1 The Conceptual Framework of the Transformative Pathway—the Negotiative Outlook on Decision-making (own representation)

The **non-linear process** projects decision-making at both the **global** and **domestic** levels, where there are evident deviations, particularly because of the varying types of exogenous interventions, the varying implications of public goods in terms of exclusion, as well as the diversity in the range of capacities. It cannot be automatically assumed that the global/domestic is merely a question of scaling or abstraction, because while these two rationales are interrelated, they can also influence each other. For example, the global can limit the ability of the domestic to shift its energy system. Nevertheless, the 'vertical' hierarchy between the 'global' and the 'domestic' needs to be assumed as an explanatory variable of distinct dynamics. For example, Anthony Bogues (2011) argues that the national is the self and the global is the other, which posits a hierarchical process that distances the self from the other. In this sense, the domestic is the self and the global is 'everyone else on the international stage.' There is a need to highlight the fact that the boundary between the global and the domestic is diffuse, as conflicts, vulnerabilities, value systems, institutions, and technologies are conflated. As the politics of Jawaharlal Nehru represented, there cannot be *an internationalist who is not a nationalist* (Chacko 2011).

Moreover, while the 'domestic' indicates the concept of citizenry following the norms bestowed by state sovereignty, the 'global' is itself still in the process of exploring the possibility of a world citizenship (see Roscrance 1998; Dunne 2008). A huge barrier to this is the somewhat exclusive nature of public spheres, in which a public sphere is connoted to exist only through **the mobilization of an identity**. If the European Union is to be taken as the best example of the possibility of a 'post-national constellation' (see Calhoun 2002; Zürn 2002, 2009), the limitations of extending 'European Union citizenry' have become evident. Jürgen Habermas' (2006) suggests that the new, European public sphere, while previously offering hope of a true world citizenship, has becomes bleaker, as social movements in many European countries have emerged, demanding the reversal of this outward extension of European citizenry. To address the gap between the global and the domestic, this proposed conceptual framework assumes that the 'global' professes to be a certain degree of citizenry that can be decoupled from the principles of state sovereignty, **a citizenry based on human solidarity** (Arendt 1958; see Bogues 2011). This concept of citizenry based on solidarity can be compared with the idea of an 'internationalist nationalism' initially introduced by Priya Chacko (2011 p. 181).

The stages of interaction serve as spaces for the three types of interactions: functional, institutional, and bargaining interactions. As described in the previous chapters, because spheres and interests often overlap, interactions are necessary to address common vulnerabilities. Functional interactions highlight the overlap of mandates or visions. Institutional interactions refer to interactions between polities, where each represents 'embodied' distinct norms, principles, and practices, which are often self-enforcing. Bargaining interactions refer to interactions between actors that have the main goal of building alliances and partners through changes in the others' preferences and dispositions. They also refer to interactions between stakeholders, with the main purpose of exchanging values with or without changing the preferences of their counterparts.

The analysis of the different outcomes of functional, institutional, and bargaining interactions allows the integrative understanding of (domestic) collective actions that will be reflected by the behavior of this collectivity (or state) at the international and domestic level. At the international level, similar interactions occur, leading to another set of collective actions; however, the 'global' collectivity can deviate significantly from the 'domestic' collectivity (and vice versa), primarily because of the possibility of several types of interventions that are often defined in terms of sanctions and rewards. The 'prisoner's dilemma' game has a different meaning, for example, for global relations when confronted by *Realpolitik* in global relations or by low social capital than it does for intra-state relations.

In addition, because interactions are influenced by drivers and brakes (e.g., culture, co-benefits, and externalities), the transformation process can only be conceptualized through its contextual relevance and is therefore historical. Going back to the global/domestic juxtaposition, the contextualization of the global and the domestic can be transferred using two directions. The global context can be translated to the national context and the national context to the global context, where gaps can be evident, as some elements get 'lost in translation.' The global context is not the aggregation of all national contexts, because it is also an outcome of various unique interactions (that cannot be repeated), where some actors or issues can dominate the various processes under present conditions, leading them to dictate the parameters of the global context (of that time). In the same manner, some elements of the global context can be instilled back into the domestic level, where additional elements emerge as counter-reactions, particularly when conflicts of values, ideologies, and relationships become evident.

Decision-making requires some basis or points of reference for orientation. This highlights the cognitive, hence, human character of the transformation processes. As the illustration above suggests, the process is divided into four cognitive frames: *social contract, power game, discourses,* and *outcomes*. These cognitive frames are stable constructs that provide a lens that allows individuals to see and understand the situation and to create a context for complex behavioral responses (Walsh 1995; see Smith & Tushman 2005). These frames promote the development of mind-sets useful to processing information and to engaging learning. For example, in the 'social contract' frame, actors are most likely keen on maximizing their influence when drafting the provisions (e.g., standards) of the social contract, as this social contract will later determine rewards and sanctions. Actors may therefore employ distinct competitive strategies, creating a coordination problem. Furthermore, actors require useful information to allow them to anticipate the consequences of each provision. In most cases, an inability to assess the provisions inhibits participation and increases the probability of defection in those cases where the social contract is implemented. As the process unfolds, the same actors will change and adapt their strategies, depending on the frames.

Corresponding with the cognitive frames are the stages of (cooperative) interaction: collaboration, coordination, deliberation, and application. These are derived from the four categories of cooperation problems (Stein 1983; Martin 2010; see Snidal 2010), which are here taken as **stages** or **phases** that are useful in conceptualizing the various related problems of collective actions: *collaboration problems, coordination problems, deliberation problems,* and *application problems.* While the cognitive frames pertain to the constitution of collective action, the stages of interaction concur in the relationships among actors, between issues, and between structures & actors. For example, when actors assume and experience asymmetrical interests, they are confronted with an equilibrium outcome that leaves at least one actor dissatisfied. As institutions facilitate cooperation, coordination problems can be resolved, promoting the integration of interests in the deliberation and application stages.

13.2 A Conceptual Framework of Transformative Pathways—The Congruence and Theorization of Causalities and Associations

As described earlier, this section will introduce and discuss relevant 'congruence', which pertains to the explanations of causalities as identified in the previous chapters.

A congruence can be expressed through one of the following formulations:

1) **If X ... then Y**
   In this case, X is the explanatory variable for Y.
2) **X is associated with Y, Z ...**
   In some cases, X can only be partly or indirectly explained through the occurrence of Y and Z, or only in conjunction with certain factors.

In addition, a congruence will be theorized by the following steps:

1) **Validation through substantiation:** This involves an analysis using existing theories and empirical evidence collected from both the case studies & simulation games, and from empirical data, models, & expert judgment. The challenge is to find the explanatory value without losing substantive meaning as the value is generalized.
2) **An analysis of the ability to predict:** This pertains to the analysis of the possibility of reoccurrence in the future as well as its applicability to other contexts (or under which conditions it can occur in other contexts)
   - The ability to predict also refers to the level of confidence based on expert judgment, data, and theory. This project uses the IPCC's likelihood scale in describing this level of confidence (see Moss & Schneider 2000; IPCC 2005), as summarized in the following Tab. 13.1:

Table 13.1 Likelihood Scale (see Moss & Schneider 2000; IPCC 2005)

Term	Likelihood of the Outcome
Virtually certain	99–100% probability
Very likely	90–100% probability
Likely	66–100% probability
About as likely as not	33 to 66% probability
Unlikely	0–33% probability
Very unlikely	0–10% probability
Exceptionally unlikely	0–1% probability

3) **Falsifiability**: an analysis of the limitations and scope of the explanations and under which conditions the explanation will not be viable
   - Variable y will very likely not occur if z.

Congruence 1: At the domestic level, if the levels of capacity and autonomy of the state facilitating the transformation process are low, then defection from the state-sponsored transformative pathway will be *very likely.*

Most literature on statehood refers to state capacity and state autonomy as indicators of state power (see Krasner 1984; Kreuzer & Weiberg 2005; Chernillo 2007; Back & Hadenius 2008). A state with high capacity and high autonomy is one that can provide basic tasks (including welfare services and security) and that is able to do so with a minimum of intervention from the public. A state with low capacity and low autonomy is one that lacks the ability to fulfil basic tasks and is subject to direct public control and interference. It is also one where power is highly decentralized among state and non-state actors. It needs to be highlighted that both democratic and authoritarian states can have high capacity and high autonomy, whereas having high autonomy tends to undermine democracy, as participation is limited. In the context of sustainable, low-carbon transformation, a state with high capacity and high autonomy will *very likely* find it easier to design sustainable, low-carbon transformation policies. Nevertheless, it needs to be asked how this high capacity and high autonomy has been achieved. Is it because of high social capital, where the public opts not to intervene, because it sees no reason to do so as the state can be generally trusted to seek policies that benefit all? Or is it because the public is completely excluded from decision-making?

The case study on China suggests that even an authoritarian country can find ways to balance efficiency and legitimacy. *In lieu* of the normative bias favoring democratic regimes, explanations are often sought as to how an authoritarian regime such as that in China can still manage to 'survive.' A likely explanation as to how China found a way to legitimate its institutions without requiring the 'concordant' process of deliberative decision-making can be offered by the possibility of strategically facilitating (or even manipulating) the approval process in front of the designated audience. Understanding this approval process is key to the success of the Chinese regime in achieving its audience's approval. In his book "The English Constitution," Walter Bagehot (1867) contended that the principles of the division of power (between legislature, executive, and judiciary) and of checks and balances (between the different elements of the constitution) are 'erroneous.' He identified the two elements of state institutions in the United Kingdom as the "dignified" and the "efficient." These two elements can explain how this approval process can be facilitated. The "dignified" parts played the essential role of winning and sustaining the loyalty of the public (input legitimacy) and the "efficient" parts were responsible for the technical aspects to ensure that goals were reached (output legitimacy). Using the general logic of these two elements, China's institutions have evolved to reflect a dualism of governance in terms of its institutions. China has developed state institutions that not only allow but are also dependent on the coexistence of the 'efficient' and the 'dignified.' The 'dignified' pertains to the parts that represent the political elite, whose members are recruited from the communist party cadre. The 'efficient' pertains to the technical elite whose members are recruited based on their technical expertise. With the integration of these two parts, China can fulfil both the political as well as the technical requirements of the transformation process.

Meanwhile, as the Mexican and Philippine case studies confirm, democracy, when confronted by deficiencies, cannot guarantee to promote transformation process towards sustainability. The dominance of institutional activists and social movements in the country indicates a Philippine State with low capacity and low autonomy. The low capacity and low autonomy of the Philippine State are both a cause and an effect. In the case of Mexico, the lack of venues or channels for the effective participation of societal groups can be held responsible for the states low capacity. These societal groups could have contributed important inputs to the effective implementation of relevant energy projects. On the one hand, this situation reinforces the ability of dominant **actors to disconnect various bargaining games from policy games**. For example, as institutional activists willingly or unwillingly opt to reinforce existing structural imbalances and use privileges previously reserved for the dominant actors, the transformation process is *very likely* inhibited, because this disconnect will *very likely* mobilize 'preference outliers' leading to the proliferation of fractal systems. The disconnection of various bargaining games will *very likely*, on the other hand, lead to further limitations in the Philippine State's autonomy. Because sustainable, low-carbon transformation will *virtually certainly* touch on various interconnected issues, the State will *virtually certainly* need insurmountable resources to integrate the dispersed fractal systems of decision-making.

In addition, as the case study and simulation on Jamaica suggest, the level of capacity and autonomy of the state can also be associated with **existing lock-ins**. Jamaica's carbon lock-ins limit the set of possible decisions aiming at implementing sustainable, low-carbon transformation, implying both the low capacity and low autonomy of the Jamaican state. Such lock-ins create, among other things, institutional barriers, which further limit the synergies emerging from functional, institutional, and bargaining interactions. For example, Jamaica's dependence on international loans is associated with the country's rather small public sector, preventing the state from effectively facilitating and participating in various functional, institutional, and bargaining interactions, which would have introduced much needed impulses to resolve such lock-ins. Due to the wide-ranging and often cross-sectoral responsibilities of many government officials in Jamaica, they likely lack the detailed and integrated knowledge of sustainable energy technologies, their economic and financial requirements, and alternative mechanisms for their effective support.

Nevertheless, the level of capacity and autonomy of the state is highly contingent on **how the state can 'depoliticize' and 'securitize' certain issues**. The securitization of certain issues will *likely* initiate "emergency powers", allowing change agents to tap "exemptions" to the "normal" set of rules and regulations, in order to better address the existing constraints caused by lock-ins. The case study on China exemplifies how China was able to do a complete turn-around on its environmental and climate protection policies. Through the effective securitization of environmental and climate protection, China was able to revise its socio-linguistic narratives and justify the establishment of a "new normal." These narratives that, for example, link the need to address climate change with China's economic competitiveness, provided the regime with important capital to establish the "new normal" within limited constraints from many types of carbon lock-ins.

Congruence 2: The increasing relevance of fractal decision-making systems in the context of sustainable, low-carbon transformation at both the global and domestic level is *virtually certainly* associated with the frequent occurrence of disconnections between various bargaining and policy games. Fractal decision-making *likely* imposes a polycentric order, both at the global and domestic level.
As more bargaining games are disconnected from policy games, **decision-making becomes *virtually certainly* polycentric**. Furthermore, as each issue is separated from other issues, where the state encourages public participation in one issue but limits or excludes another issue, governance will *likely* become polycentric (see Ostrom 2010). The autonomy of the state decreases as more fractal decision-making systems (with each of these fractal systems seeking its own specific equilibrium) emerge, due to the increased polycentrism of governance. This means that the state becomes less capable of constituting and implementing policies by itself. The state will need to address multiple **competitions within each of these fractal systems**, which strain the state's capacity. The state will likely prioritize certain issues and delay or even resign in others, leading to individual vacuums in certain issues. These vacuums will *likely* further reinforce fractal systems. In such a situation, in facilitating and managing sustainable low carbon transformation, the State will *virtually certainly* be dependent on multiple fractal decision-making frameworks, which *will virtually certainly* exacerbate both the collaboration problem (e.g., the emergence of more equilibria) and the coordination problem (e.g., an increase in problems related to communication).

In the case study of the United States, the emergence of 'smart' cities and 'smart' enclaves as well as the re-emergence of social movements following the state's increased outsourcing of welfare services to the private sector will *likely* further undermine the autonomy of the state through the reinforcement of technocratic and post-democratic governance principles in the country. As the private sector and social movements continue to set the standards, benchmarks, and norms in various sectors and establish *de facto* 'expert committees' that compete with state institutions in terms of authority and expertise, the state will *very likely* be more dependent on the private sector and other non-state actors when implementing a wider range of policies, which will *virtually certainly* further exacerbate legitimacy deficits. These *de facto* 'expert committees' are informal conglomerates of technical experts that compete with experts within state polities. In addition, the dependence on *de facto* 'expert committees' will *likely* aggravate polycentric decision-making, because these de facto 'expert committees' will *likely* be sectoral in nature. Cross-cutting expertise is *likely* limited due to the corporate nature of accountability. For example, members of *de facto* 'expert committees' on financial issues will *very likely* come from the finance sector and have limited exposure to related social issues. In addition, because they are accountable to the stakeholders of the finance sector, there will *very likely* have limited motivation to encompass, for example, human rights concerns.

Therefore, the success of the transformation process depends *virtually certainly* on how the objectives of the transformation process can be aligned with the objectives of these *de fac*to 'expert committees.' In addition, the increased importance of these *de facto* expert committees will *virtually certainly* lead to further legitimacy gaps in the transformation process. Hence, new forms of accountability and transparency are needed to address new types of structural imbalances.

Congruence 3: The diffusion of norms, principles, and standards within a system is *very likely* associated with the identity-based concept of citizenry, both at the global and national level, because citizenry underpins the flow of social practices among actors.

As implied earlier, the convergence of norms and values that resolve coordination and collaboration problems professes a certain degree of identity-based citizenry. Nevertheless, there is a need to consider an understanding of citizenry that is decoupled from the principle of state sovereignty, because this is often used as a pretext for exclusion. Several authors have called for similar concepts (see Arendt 1958; Bogues 2011). For example, Priya Chacko (2011 p. 181) introduced the idea of an "internationalist nationalism." When analyzing any transformation process, there is a need to identify the various categories that can unify actors, including both the change and status quo agents. For convergence to be initiated, respective norms, values, and principles need to be diffused to the value systems of the others, without causing ruptures in these systems. However, this diffusion presumes one or more entry points. Another idea about diffusion is contributed by David Strang and John Meyer (2010 p. 150), who argue that diffusion is shaped and accelerated by culturally-analyzed similarities among actors, and by theorized accounts of actors and practices. They continue by suggesting that when social entities belong to a common social category, diffusion should be rapid. As convergence moves one step forward, the next step will require less than the resources needed to make the previous step.

In the context of sustainable, low-carbon development, the diffusion of new norms, principles and standards that reinforce sustainability rationales in collective actions is *very likely* to occur in a homogenous system rather than in a fragmented one. However, there is a need to analyze what makes the system homogenous, particularly when actors will *virtually certainly* be diversified. Even in classical 'nation' states such as France and Germany where the population is generally perceived as homogenous, there are differences, depending on which category (language, religion, level of income) is considered. The difference between homogeneity and heterogeneity depends significantly on the socio-technical and socio-linguistic narratives used. These contend which similarities and differences are deemed relevant and which elements of these similarities or differences (*us against them*) will *likely* mobilize identity-building. Therefore, there is a need to find a set of categories that highlight similarities without linking differences with threats—a citizenry based on human solidarity.

Congruence 4: At the domestic and global level, power asymmetries *need to* define the asymmetries of privileges. As power shifts during the transformation process, if structural arrangements and institutions (including norms and practices) are preventing corresponding changes in the distribution of privileges, and status quo agents are successful in maintaining or even expanding old privileges, then individual incentives to defect from the transformation process will *likely* outweigh the incentives of continued cooperation/collaboration.

Shifts in the underlying structure of power are reflected, sometimes gradually rather than abruptly, by changes in social institutions like regimes at the global level (see Young 2010 p. 175) and in state institutions at the domestic level. While actors accept that power asymmetries are a given, they take the distribution of privileges seriously and contest it, should they find themselves in an unfavorable position. Nevertheless, they will *very likely* accept the distribution of privileges according to power asymmetries, particularly when this power status is achieved and maintained by costs shouldered by the powerful. However, as soon as power configurations shift, the distribution of privileges is *virtually certainly* expected to shift as well. If not, the distribution mechanism will be contested and if status quo agents are able to instrumentalize their old privileges to inhibit change in the distribution of privileges, then defection is *virtually certain* to occur.

Asymmetries in power are knowledge-intensive. Therefore, the system is *very likely* to witness an intensive exchange of information. Further, additional 'convening' power can be generated through capacities to introduce indicators and benchmarks that are needed to assess power relations. Therefore, another challenge lies in the empirical and conceptual problems of measuring power, assessing when and how power is shifting, and differentiating paradigmatic shifts from mere one-time, coincidental deviations. In addition, as Oran Young (2010 p. 176) contends, while it is easy to recognize major shifts in power, it is difficult to pin down the preliminary stages of significant shifts, or to monitor them closely as they unfold. The ability of early identification is important, as it allows more time and resources to counter emerging shifts or to adapt to their implications as first movers.

Another challenge is linked with the self-reinforcing characteristic of power, often sustained by privileges, with or without active intervention from the actors. In addition, some privileges are latent, which requires addition effort to be properly conceptualized and resolved. Other privileges are symptomatic. These privileges can be caused by variables that are systems-related, which cannot be resolved without causing additional paradoxes. For example, the underrepresentation of scholars from developing countries in the generation of academic knowledge is not always a result of the intended marginalization of these scholars but can also be attributed to differences in orientation or mandate (e.g., the teaching mandate of professors). This underrepresentation is rather a symptom of 'biased' indicators of the 'performance quality' of scholars, which tend to focus heavily on publications in peer-reviewed journals.

Looking at the international system, emerging powers such as China and Mexico will *virtually certainly* seek access to privileges enjoyed by contemporary powers, and when confronted by an inability to do so due to existing structural constraints, these emerging powers will *very likely* evaluate whether defection (and the establishment of competing systems) will bring more benefits. In some cases, emerging powers will establish competing regimes or institutions that will *very likely* be open only to selected actors. This behavior will *likely* be interpreted by established powers as rule-breaking and therefore as a threat to international stability and order. In addition, emerging powers will *very likely* 'shop for forum,' which means that in addressing one issue they will *very likely* prefer to participate in a specific global institution, but in another issue, they will participate in a competing global or regional institution. This behavior will *likely* be seen negatively by established parties, because this undermines the predictability and consistency of foreign policies. Therefore, power shifts in transformation processes will *very likely* lead to an international order that is *likely* more fragmented and therefore polycentric.

Congruence 5: At the global level, if the states are experiencing increased convergence, then the motivation to defect *virtually certainly* decreases. In other words, the convergence of norms, principles, and practices is both a requirement and an outcome of cooperation.
Convergence refers to the similarities in experiences between actors in terms of lock-ins, standards, and norms. The increased *rapprochement* of the policies and actions of countries will *very likely* promote cooperation or collaboration. As convergence increases, the immediate pay-offs of defection *likely* decreases, because convergence resolves the 'prisoner's dilemma' in collaboration games (see Layer 1980; Snidal 2010). The *rapprochement* of multiple equilibria in the context of convergence implies that the suboptimal equilibrium's pay-offs will *very likely* become minimal. Furthermore, it needs to be highlighted that convergence does not automatically mean the elimination of asymmetries between actors. Asymmetries in power or privileges can even promote cooperation. As Duncan Snidal (2010 p. 11) contends, asymmetries increase the likelihood of some cooperation. However, the distribution of benefits from cooperation will *very likely* reflect this asymmetry, and the discrepancy between the asymmetry and the benefits will *virtually certainly* lead to contestation. As the distribution of costs and benefits can also favor weaker parties, weaker states will *likely* perceive that this probability of benefits outweighs complete exclusion.

The negotiation outlook on collective decision-making suggests that cooperation in the context of an unequal distribution of privileges is *likely* tolerated when the actors are confronted with similarities in terms of lock-ins, standards, and norms, implying that the degree of convergence among actors offsets the legitimacy gaps that resulted from asymmetries in power and privileges. Because convergence implies the ability to reciprocate the behavior of the others, actors expect that they can also profit from the privileges of powerful actors without shouldering the costs of achieving and maintaining power. Therefore, because convergence constitutes the anticipation of spill-over effects, asymmetries become tolerable. In this sense, it can also be argued that the incentives to defect from a transformation process in the context of asymmetries are *very likely* concretized through convergence.

In addition, it can be argued that actors will *very likely* allot more time to negotiations with those actors with similar lock-ins compared to those which are perceived as being significantly different. This means, for example, that while countries with the same type of policy pathways (democratic, authoritarian, etc.)

are expected to prefer negotiations among each other, the *caveat* to negotiating will likely disappear when the policy pathway taken by the counterparts does not reflect the various lock-ins one is confronted with. In addition, further convergence is achieved as actors explore additional potentials of cooperation, cementing shared values and establishing new capacities, which eventually pave the way for more exclusive membership. Therefore, while convergence promotes further cooperation, it can also limit the scale of cooperation, as actors outside the fractal system (convergent system) will *very likely* be excluded.

A possible limitation of this congruence is when a specific public good relevant to the transformation process debars the exclusion of non-members, or that the multiple memberships of one actor to more than one 'convergent club' is possible. In addition, countries that are attempting to combine various transformative pathways with contradictory norms and values will *very likely* be difficult to address. For example, when a country pursues multiple policies that are in their essence contradictory with each other, like aiming to reduce emissions but granting new concessions to coal mining companies, other countries that still intend to engage in cooperation will need to look beyond convergence as orientation. Another limitation to this congruence refers to a situation where information on the other's behavior is limited or can be easily manipulated, because relevant issues are highly politicized or securitized, which compel exceptions to existing rules and practices.

Congruence 6: If critical junctures (and lock-ins), in the context of sustainable, low-carbon transformation, create conflicts in social mandates, then there is *very likely* a need to find a concept of 'conversion' for the relevant values through a 'common currency.'

Several collaboration and coordination problem-issues were resolved in the last few years as confirmed by the Paris Climate Agreement. The first signs of payoffs from mitigation policies made in the past have already occurred. Examples of these signs include the gradual decrease of upfront costs and the market price of renewables. In addition, the slowing growth in the global CO_2 emission level was recorded despite continued economic growth, hinting at stabilization and a slower global growth in fossil fuel consumption (see Jackson et al. 2015; IEA 2016a; Löfken & Martin 2017). While it is still premature to claim that the critical juncture that favors sustainable, low-carbon seems to have already arrived, signs indicate that this critical juncture is only a matter of time.

This critical juncture is expected to be further reinforced, eventually establishing self-driving lock-ins, as the effects of investments in renewables are realized in the next few years. Since 2015, there have been more energy power plants using wind, water, and solar power than those using energy from fossil fuels and nuclear power (IEA 2016a). In addition, 70% of new investments made (or 288 billion USD) in the electricity sector are attributed to renewables (IEA 2016a) and a significant chunk of these investments were made in China, which is the primary source of emission growth. When this critical juncture is established, distortions, such as the election of President Trump, as the case study on the United States shows, are *unlikely* to cause major reversals of the transformation process or even a system rupture. On the contrary, there are important silver-linings to such distortions that will *very likely* further reinforce the transformation process. The relevant climate and sustainability initiatives coming from the private sector and civil society under President Trump, which were not available during previous administrations, are *likely* promising signs that after the term of President Trump, the sustainable, low-carbon transformation of the United States or even of many developing countries will *very likely* accelerate. New climate leaders such as China have emerged. Because the Chinese regime has recognized that the decrease of coal use in China was largely responsible for CO_2 stabilization, China has garnered the 'moral legitimacy' needed for its leadership.

The road towards this critical juncture is long. Additional efforts and time are needed to promote the required convergence of norms, standards, and values, also due to marginal benefits. This road will *virtually certainly* demand the further relinquishing of personal rights, liberties, and freedoms at the domestic level and sovereignty at the global level. As new lock-ins emerge, more rights and freedoms may be undermined, which may alter preferences, particularly when benefits remain 'theoretical' and 'collective' while the costs are 'practical' and 'personal'. Because sustainable, low-carbon transformation involves cutting across issues, jurisdictions, and mandates, conflicts of rights and liberties will *virtually certainly* be inevitable. The failure to adequately address emerging conflicts will *very likely* further motivate the creation of additional fractals in an already fragmented system.

As hinted at earlier in this book, conversion is inevitable, because identifying benchmarks as well as the contingents of transformation require the comparability of values and, later, of the 'inventories' of a policy that need to be replaced without undermining the overall effectiveness of this policy. The resolution of both coordination and collaboration problems are *virtually certainly* dependent on benchmarks and contingencies, which will *likely* cross-cut several issues, rights, and mandates. Therefore, social contracts will *very likely* need to include mechanisms of conversion to diminish the self-enforcement of existing structural biases. Using the conflict between the German wind energy sector and environmental groups, under current conditions, the offshore wind energy sector will *very likely* produce more compelling arguments to persuade policy-makers and public opinion. The reason behind this is that this sector can easily 'convert' its current and future values into more tangible 'currencies' that are welcomed by policy-makers and the public. For example, the number of jobs that are created and will be created by the sector are compelling. For the environmental groups, it will be difficult to convert 'environmental integrity' into currencies that can equally compel political and public acceptance as much as the arguments of the offshore wind energy sector. How many jobs can one unit of environmental integrity create? Answering this question is not only difficult from the methodological perspective, but it is also difficult because the answer will *very likely* imply that the others should relinquish rights and liberties and undermine the social mandates of other actors. For example, hypothetically speaking, if one can answer with certainty that one unit of environmental integrity will create 100 jobs, this will *very likely* mean that the reduction of 100 jobs in the energy sector will be tolerated or demanded, then additional compelling values can be presented by the energy sector such as the economic competitiveness of the city or country. For environmental groups, converting environmental integrity into economic competitiveness may be more difficult to achieve.

The simulation game on the Jamaican austerity measures hinted at the possibility of 'trading' values: risk, unhappiness, and ecological damage points (see the case study on Jamaica). This idea came into the discussion as the participants quantified the risks, unhappiness levels and ecological damage. As the participants focused on the co-benefits and synergies of selected austerity measures, some provisions produced positive externalities for the environment. What if this 'conversion' could be produced in reverse? This would, however, require further theoretical underpinnings.

Congruence 7: If the deliberation over the factors relevant to legitimacy, efficiency, and capacity focus mainly on 'big bang' situations, then it will *very likely* lose count on the importance of 'low' politics for systemic and social integration.

An upcoming debate about transformative pathways will raise the question of whether a certain transformative pathway can be best achieved through voluntary or binding commitments. An intuitive answer to that is that this pathway needs to be binding to all or to none. Binding commitments can be designed in such a way that non-participation brings less pay-offs or even unacceptable disadvantages. However, as argued earlier, a sustainable, low-carbon transformative pathway will *very likely* demand limitations and constraints on liberties and freedoms, which also includes the freedom to decide 'unwisely'. Relinquishing certain individual rights and liberties to achieve collective sustainable, low-carbon goals will *very likely* necessitate tedious deliberation, as individual actors will assess the values behind their preferences in terms of incentives. Further inhibiting deliberation is the uncertainty of the future outcomes of present decisions, which motivates actors to agree on commitments that allow exit-strategies.

At the global level, attaining a single, global-wide, sustainable, low-carbon transformation is, under current conditions, perceived to be merely theoretical or academic. A specific unknown threshold needs to be identified, conceptualized and achieved first, through which it would eventually become unbearable to be in an unsustainable, high-carbon system. What can be currently observed, is that one or a small group of states have chosen a 'contextualized', sustainable and low-carbon transformative pathway that addresses local conditions while accommodating global visions. As such, their pathways are contingent upon different 'flexibility' measures, as well as requiring varying bridging technologies that enable transition without less unacceptable sacrifices and steep cuts in their utility values. Nevertheless, the contextualization of pathways *virtually certainly* demonstrates the diversity of individual 'high' and 'low' politics, which refer to the level of securitization of issues. Securitization implies the willingness to employ coercive measures. Nevertheless, differences in political priorities and indifferences can be tapped to expand values.

The simulation game on Jamaica demonstrated how some participants, who were representing various stakeholders, were able to gain additional pay-offs through issues they were initially indifferent to. Because the issues they were indifferent to were considered to be 'high' politics by the others, they had nothing to lose when they supported the interests of these others. As they were in a bargaining game, their indifferences became integral to the achievement of their 'high' politics. Indifference can therefore provide additional leverage. In the same manner, participants, whose 'high' politics became obvious to the others through their behavior and rhetoric, experienced increased resistance and bargaining intensity, as the others perceived that they could gain more from the participants with clear, 'high' politics. Therefore, if given the chance to repeat the process, these participants will *very likely* hide their 'high' politics the next time around, increasing the need for ambiguities and further increasing the complexity of interactions.

In addition, appropriate attention needs to be given to the anti-functionalist effect of 'high' politics. Functional interactions imply the systemic and social integration of various utilities, which can be distorted if these interactions involve 'high' politics. In the case study on the Philippines, it was a game-changing event when the appointed Environment Secretary elevated the mining issue as 'high' politics, which in turn transformed her confirmation into 'high' politics, in which she had no jurisdiction or bargaining leverage. While the confirmation was initially a formality of appointment, its importance as leverage for her opponents became evident. This demonstrates that policy-makers need to consider how turning an issue into high politics will be *very likely* translated into other issues, and that one should assess his or her own bargaining leverage in those other issues, including those issues one is indifferent to. Therefore, 'low' politics and 'high' politics should receive equal attention from both policy-makers and academes, as they both offer opportunities and weaknesses when engaging in functional and bargaining interactions. Focusing mainly on 'high' politics will *likely* imply an underestimation of 'low' politics, which can be easily turned into 'high' politics as the negotiation process unfolds.

Lessons for Practice: Reflexivity and Stakeholder Engagement for Transformations Towards Sustainability

14

This chapter intends to present a practical approach to strategically facilitating sustainable, low-carbon transformation. The recommendations that can be made are presented while using a Weberian understanding (*Verstehen*) of various variables and dynamics that has been crystalized through this book's theoretical foundation (chapters 2 to 6), methodological tools (chapters 7 and 8), case studies (chapters 9 to 12), simulation game (part of chapter 12), and the theoretical claims through the conceptual framework (chapter 13). A major contribution of this book is a set of recommendations that aim to support an inquiry-based, reflective, collaborative, and integrative facilitation of the transformation process. Reflexivity is itself a form of intervention that allows systems to adapt while preventing ruptures. An analysis of reflexivity can help better structure institutional, functional, and bargaining interactions from the negotiative perspective on context, agencies, and audiences of transformation towards sustainability. **Reflexivity analysis is a matrix or collection of concrete questions that resonate at the (meta-level) theoretical/conceptual, methodological, and practical challenges relevant for each analytical level** (actors, issues, structures, processes, and outcomes).

Serving as a roadmap, the stakeholder engagement plan is furthermore introduced in this chapter. As a practical example of application the engagement plan, this chapter looks at the transformation of the transport sector towards sustainability in Germany. The matrix is a decision tool that equates the typical 'hypothetical' analysis in legal studies. Hypothetical analysis pertains to the use of fictional

A. M. Hernández, *Taming the Big Green Elephant*, Globale Gesellschaft und internationale Beziehungen, https://doi.org/10.1007/978-3-658-31821-5_14

but still realistic and feasible accounts when analyzing the potential actions of protagonists. The matrix demonstrates, for example, how narratives are tailored to make points without being burdened by doubts about the incompleteness of information. Hypothetical accounts can answer some questions that are unanswered by real-life case studies, because these accounts, including motivations and interactions, are described in an imaginary fashion (Green 2000 p. 991). Fictional vignettes may be useful to help identify situations where particular rules may apply and explore the ambiguity of rules (Green 2000 p. 995). Finally, unlike real-life case studies, hypothetical accounts can recognize the sensitivity of decision-making towards moral nuances and complexity.

14.1 Reflexivity Analysis—Developing Perspectives for Stakeholders' Engagement

The reflexivity analysis of the multi-level and polycentric sustainable, low-carbon transformation towards sustainability can be conducted using the five different analytical levels (actors, issues, structures, processes, and outcomes). The use of these levels highlights the systems analytical approach. For this purpose, concrete questions and elaborating questions are formulated to help identify the conceptual (theoretical), methodological, and practical issues that need to be addressed when facilitating the transformation process. The questions summarize the insights and impulses gained from the previous chapters. The theoretical assumptions, knowledge tools such as theoretical models (ideal types), case studies, simulation, as well as the conceptual framework have not only contributed to the meta-level conceptual understanding of sustainable, low-carbon transformation and to explaining complex issues and dynamics, they have also identified methodological and practical issues that should be concretized and elaborated when facilitating sustainable, low-carbon transformation. These questions constitute the strategic approach that needs to be pursued by each stakeholder when preparing their strategies and when participating in various functional, institutional, and bargaining interactions (Table 14.1).

Table 14.1 Reflexivity Analysis—Questions and Issues

Actors:

Questions	Elaborating Questions	Meta-level theoretical and conceptual Issues	Methodological Issues	Practical Issues
Power How does power define actors' preferences and collective actions?	How can power and which type of power can compel or prevent actions? How can power asymmetry prevent or enhance cooperation? How can weaker actors maintain leverage against stronger actors? How can powerful actors be motivated to participate and honor agreements? How can weaker parties achieve their goals and refrain from challenging the same outcomes once they become more powerful? How is power related to rational choice? How can actors adapt to the changing sources of power as well as the changing meanings and implications of power asymmetry?	Conceptualization of power asymmetry; the linkage between power asymmetry and behavioral preference; a pronouncement of the linkage between power (asymmetry) and cooperation; a conception of power-based decision-making; an extrapolation of issue complexity in power assessments; the ascertainment of power in terms of vulnerability (and vice-versa); an explication of the linkage between power and the status quo/change	An assessment of power structures vis-à-vis the potential behavior of actors; the predictability of actions using the analysis of power structures; the adaptation to the impacts of power asymmetry and to preferences and negotiation strategies; the calculation of one's power leverage and that of the others; the designation of power relations vis-à-vis the emergence of more powerful actors	Designing the appropriate strategy management of power games; the establishment of communication channels; the facilitation of negotiations; the identification and constitution of the mandates of chairs and conveners; the identification of different types of leverages; the adaptation of accountability mechanisms to changing power relations
Rationality and interests What are the interests and targets of both state and non-state stakeholders?	How are these interests defined and driven and by which factors? How can these interests be concretized and fulfilled? Which shared interests can be bundled together? Which interests are indifferent to whose interests? Which interests are incompatible with the others? How can interests be modified and made compatible? How are these interests aligned or adversarial to the principles and requirements of sustainable, low-carbon transformation? Are there third parties whose interests should be considered?	An analysis of the impacts of the ontological and epistemological baggage of the concepts and principles of targets and ambitions; affirmation of linkage between targets/ambitions and interests; the conception of interests based on rationality functions; an explication of the link between targets/ambitions and sustainability principles; the contemplation of purposive rationality (*Zwecksrationalität*); a pronouncement of the linkage between rationality and reference frames	An assessment of zones of possible agreements between multiple targets and ambitions; the identification and evaluation of appropriate targets and ambitions based on interests; the reference of targets and ambitions to local conditions (the local context); designing and measuring benchmarks & milestones; the qualitative and quantitative valuation of the human factor in rational choice; the costing out or converting of different values to make them relevant or quantifiable and therefore comparable	The establishment of mechanisms of generating, maintaining, implementing, modifying, and verifying targets and ambitions; the enhancement of the capacity to identify efficient, reliable, and realistic targets & ambitions; the improvement of interest-based bargaining; overcoming information asymmetry; designing decision tools to identify and concretize targets; designing and implementing a game plan based on reference frames

Actors:

Questions	Elaborating Questions	Meta-level theoretical and conceptual Issues	Methodological Issues	Practical Issues
Leadership and facilitation Which actors can act as leaders or facilitators/mediators to support various deliberation processes?	Are leaders necessary for transformation processes? What are the responsibilities of leaders? How can biased actors with clearly vested interests still be able to facilitate agreement-building processes? What are the intentions and possible pay-offs for potential leaders and facilitators? How can the intentions of leaders and facilitators be aligned with sustainable, low-carbon transformation? Which strategies are available to motivate other parties to accept leadership and facilitation?	The ascertainment of the procedures and process-related impacts of impartiality and neutrality; the weighing of effects of facilitation and mediation against power asymmetries; the affirmation of links between interests and actions; an understanding of the role of reciprocity	The measurement of asymmetry; a performance assessment of facilitation and mediation; the valuation of conflicts of interest and bias; the valuation of the pay-offs of facilitation and mediation; the evaluation of existing conflicts of interest	The enhancement of mechanisms of identifying, mandating, and verifying leadership and facilitation; the determination of appropriate profiles for leaders, facilitators and mediators; establishing procedures for empowering leaders; the improvement of accountability and transparency; the demonstration of leadership by mobilizing strengths and addressing weaknesses
Cooperation with partners, allies and spoilers Which actors can be valuable partners or allies? Who are the potential spoilers?	What are the motivations behind cooperation? How are potential cooperation partners identified, chosen and tested? Is a cooperative partnership emergent or purposive? Which actors are potential spoilers to the outcome and adversaries to the process/procedure? Is there a third or further category of actors (e.g., non-aligned)? Which existing networks can serve as pools of partners?	An analysis of reciprocity and cooperation; a conception of the balance of power and power equalization through strategic partnerships; the extrapolation of links between strategic partnerships and outcomes, particularly between partnerships and transformations towards sustainability; the development and trajectory of emergent and purposive cooperation; the re-visitation of simplistic and misleading dichotomies; the pronouncement of the meaning of multilateralism and bilateralism for cooperation	The performance assessment of partners; the performance and impact assessment of spoilers; the operationalization and exposure of sociotechnical and sociolinguistic narratives on partners and spoilers; the prediction of the future behavior of partners and spoilers; the evaluation of networks	The identification of dependable patterns of cooperation; the validation of the role of emotionality when working with spoilers; the establishment of communication channels with partners and spoilers; the establishment of discourse with opposition and spoilers; the management of networks

Actors:

Questions	Elaborating Questions	Meta-level theoretical and conceptual Issues	Methodological Issues	Practical Issues
Contestation between change agents and status quo agents Which actors are relevant to the realization of transformation towards sustainability? Who are the change agents? Who are the status quo agents?	How is relevance defined or not defined by proximity to stakes? Are epistemic communities and knowledge experts relevant? If yes, are they pay-off seeking stakeholders? Does relevance automatically constitute stakeholder status? How can stakeholders influence decision-making in authoritarian regimes? Is the inclusion of stakeholders a prerogative of democratic regimes? How can excluded or non-relevant actors still assist in realizing goals? How can they help achieve sustainable developmental goals without distorting the transformation process? How can an actor be relevant to the procedure but not to the process (and vice-versa)? Which frontlines represent which conflict cleavages?	The re-conceptualization and contextualization of policy models; the examination of the link between goal implementation and system cohesion; understanding the symbiotic relationship between change and status quo agents; the contemplation of the demonization tendencies in mutual relations between change and status quo agents	An integrated impact assessment of epistemic communities, technologies, and bargaining strategies; the process-tracing of policy models and policy outputs; a diffusion assessment of the innovative, market-based, political, ecological, socio-cultural, and technological drivers of transformation; the evaluation of conflict cleavages between change and status quo agents	The engagement of change and status quo agents; the establishment of new rules conducive to transformation towards sustainability; the attribution of changes in collective actions and interactions to technologies, particularly to knowledge tools and information technologies; the constitution of new forms of the (de) legitimation strategies of lock-ins; the establishment of reliable knowledge management
The representation of collective groups and constituents How can collective groups be effectively represented and by whom in joint decision-making?	How is a mandate given by constituents to representatives at bargaining tables? Who should be chosen as a representative? Are these representatives really pursuing the interests of the constituents? How can a conflict of interests be identified? How can genuine representation be guaranteed? How can representatives be monitored and if needed replaced during the process? How do NGOs represent collective interests? Which governance structures can best promote the representation of constituents? Is representation inherent to democratic structures? Can authoritarian regimes come up with appropriate representation?	The conceptualization of collective decision-making; the conception of the collectivity; the explication of the link between deliberation and effective decision-making; the anticipation of consensus-building according to policy models; an analysis and weighing up of the different local modes of collective decision-making; grasping with the cultural aspects of representation; the resolution of the representation of spoilers and counter-movements; the conceptualization of agencies and agents	A performance assessment of representation and agency; the consolidation of the link between legitimacy and representative authority; the measurement and evaluation of the material, expressive, and solidarity benefits of NGO engagement; an assessment of social change through NGO participation	The establishment and maintenance of communication and network channels; the verification of performance of representatives; the identification of required benchmarks for effective representation; the design and organization of managerial mechanisms of representation; the attribution of changes in collective actions and an intervention into effective representation

Actors:

Questions	Elaborating Questions	Meta-level theoretical and conceptual Issues	Methodological Issues	Practical Issues
The monitoring and verification of commitments Which actors are eligible and credible enough to conduct monitoring and verification of commitments and compliance?	Should monitoring and verifying actors be neutral and/or impartial? Can biased actors be impartial to the process/procedure? What standards and indicators are available and relevant to assess compliance? Who have developed these standards and indicators? Are these standards reproducing or reinforcing structural imbalances? How should outside intervention into monitoring and verification be evaluated? Under which authority are commitments made?	An analysis of the link between process and implementation; an affirmation of the link between compliance and verification; the conceptualization of neutrality and impartiality; the ascertainment of the mandate/justification for external intervention	The assessment of neutrality and impartiality; the evaluation of bias; the measurement and assessment of the performance of monitors and controllers; the impact assessment of verification methods	Due diligence in terms of the potential monitoring and verifying of actors; the management of monitoring and verification; the identification of acceptable actors as monitors; the identification and formalization of benchmarks and indicators; improving the evaluation of monitory and verifying actors
The keepers of data, information and knowledge How do expert decision-makers gather, distribute and interpret data, information, and knowledge?	What qualifications are needed for these actors? With which instruments should these actors manage and process data and knowledge? How are attitudes and preconceived values affecting the gathering and selection of data and information? Which values need to be resonated in the assessment? Which indicators lead to which judgments? How much flexibility and how long a 'grace period' should and could be given to actors? How is bias affecting the assessment of data and information? How can actors adequately provide value assessment and data interpretation? How can a heavy reliance on one form of information (anchoring or focalism) when making decisions affect the efficiency of decision-making? How can this be addressed?	The examination of human capital and the required skills/competencies; the attribution of the achievement of anticipated outcomes through skills; the affirmation of a link between normativity and data processing; the conceptualization of relevant biases and distortions; the grasping of links between knowledge and reality and an understanding of the link between flexibility and outcome; an analysis of the link between ambiguity in assessments and the validity criteria (objectivity, reliability and applicability)	The assessment of required qualifications; the performance evaluation of knowledge intermediaries; a causality assessment between values and data management; the evaluation of data management tools; an impact assessment of value orientation/normativity; a performance assessment of the recipients of flexibility and ambiguity in assessments; the calibration of theoretical models and projections to ensure the applicability of resulting knowledge	The enhancement of reliability and the availability of data; the improvement of data management; the selection of appropriate data management tools; the establishment of the management of data collection, data processing, and data interpretation; the calibration and application of theoretical knowledge; the management and verification of first and second opinions; the identification and resolution of gaps between and misjudgments of interpretations; the accountability of management; the drafting of political mandates and actions from empirical data

Actors:

Questions	Elaborating Questions	Meta-level theoretical and conceptual Issues	Methodological Issues	Practical Issues
Relationships Which relationships between actors matter for sustainable, low-carbon transformation?	What type of relationship is needed for a long-term transformation process? Which types of relationships are conducive to achieving sustainable, low-carbon policy goals? How can relationships positively and negatively influence institutional designs and agreement-building processes?	The conceptualization of social trust (social capital); the ascertainment of conduciveness; an analysis of the link between cohesion and agreements; the grasping of a link between institutional designs and agreements	The performance assessment of actors according to given relationships; an impact assessment of relationships; the process-tracing between relationships and the achievement of sustainable development	The establishment of personal relationships between actors; the enhancement of evidence-based decision-making; the recognition of cultural differences
Choice and behavioral change How can actors' behavior and preferences be influenced and, if needed, shifted?	How does emotion affect behavior and behavioral change? How can behavior be changed? How can ideology-based opposition to transformation towards sustainability be reverted and persuaded? How can narratives empowering carbon lock-ins be refuted? Can behavioral change be initiated without "pain" and "shocks"? Through which tools and premises can choices be made, altered or maintained? How conducive or detrimental are the human factors to transformation?	The ascertainment of the utility of behavioral change; the pronouncement of the trajectory of paradigm shifts; the affirmation of regressions from changes; an examination of the pay-offs of structural changes; an analysis of the link between behavioral change and system ruptures; an explication of linkages between behavior and the view of human nature (Menschenbild) and of the world (Weltbild)	The operationalization of methods of analysis of policy instruments and of behavioral change; the assessment of the effects of structural changes to behaviors; a narrative analysis of lock-ins; an integrated impact assessment of the potential shocks leading to behavioral change; the measurement of distortions or the manipulation of choices	The promotion of changes to routines and habits to address contingencies; the organizational and institutional management of shifts; the revision of social mandates following shifts; the establishment and revision of compensatory mechanisms during transition periods; the establishment of flexibility measures and adaptation; the improvement of compensatory actions to ideology-driven opposition
Interactions and participation How do policy-makers interact with policy entrepreneurs, including the private sector?	How do actors constitute collective actions? Which types of collaborations between policy-makers and non-state actors, including the private sector, are needed and are feasible when advancing sustainable developmental goals? How can communication channels be established? How can jurisdictions be clarified when dealing with diffuse and cross-cutting issues?	The examination of the social mandate of policy entrepreneurs, including profit and non-profit entities; the conceptualization of policy entrepreneurship; the identification of existing power asymmetries; the conceptualization of public ownership of collective ownerships; an understanding of the political, economic, socio-cultural, and environmental barriers and caveats to and for policy entrepreneurs; the ascertainment of trade-offs between participation and efficiency	An interaction analysis; a policy analysis and comparative policy analysis; an impact assessment of inclusive participation; an analysis of the organizational characteristics of individual policy entrepreneurs; an assessment of political instruments to entice certain behavior from policy entrepreneurs	The determination of the practical implications of change in the routines and habits of policy entrepreneurs; the management of policy entrepreneurship; the equalization of the distorted asymmetry of resources among policy entrepreneurs; the identification and management of the actions and behavior of change and status quo agents; the establishment of a dialogue space between policy-makers and policy entrepreneurs

Issues:

Questions	Elaborating Questions	Meta-level theoretical and conceptual Issues	Methodological Issues	Practical Issues
Relevance How is the relevance of issues determined and by whom?	Is relevance a concept that can only be determined under normativity? Does relevance change over time? How can relevant components of non-relevant issues be adequately addressed? How can non-relevant components of relevant issues be sorted out? How can relevance be objectively measured and evaluated? How does the coupling and decoupling of issues promote transformation?	The conceptualization of relevance; the affirmation of the effects of the coupling and decoupling of issues; an understanding of the impact of advocacy in the determination of relevance; the ascertainment of indifference; the pronouncement of linkages with circumstantial relevance to outcomes; the assertion of the relevance of audience	An integrated assessment of the relevance of the issues; an analysis of non-relevant issues; the exposition of interdependences between issues; the evaluation of double–counting, which could distort the degree of relevance; the measurement and evaluation of indifference; the evaluation of the interdisciplinarity of issues and its effects on measuring the relevance of data	The identification and formalization of indicators and benchmarks of relevance; fact-checking on relevant issues; accountability management; the monitoring of the emerging relevance of up-to-date non-relevant issues; the identification and evaluation of key strategic issues; addressing the immeasurability of some stakes
Prioritization How do different ranges of the definition of 'sustainability' determine and guide the significance and prioritization of issues?	How are the ontological and epistemological conceptions of relevant issues aligned with the overarching principles of sustainability? How is this conception creating or reinforcing existing inequalities? How are variations and discrepancies between concepts and connotations among developed and developing countries inhibiting cooperation? How can hyperbolic discounting (or the tendency for people to have a stronger preference for more immediate pay-offs) distort prioritization? How can it be contained?	The conceptualization of sustainability; the resolution of distortions; the explication of the linkage between disruptions and system rupture; the extrapolation of the linkage between global visions and local concretization; the postulation of the implementation of sustainability principles; the affirmation of the role of rationality in prioritization; the explication of the relations between prioritized and non-prioritized issues; the explication of the relevance of time frames	An assessment combining modernist approaches and sustainable technology studies; an evaluation of the importance of the issues for prioritization; the weighing of policy instruments in terms of their effectiveness in achieving sustainable development goals; the quantification of sustainability; an integrated performance assessment of sustainability measures; an impact assessment of sustainability policies; an understanding and the resolving of methodological obstacles to analyzing technology and modernity	An appraisal of the specificities of the local context; the management of sustainability indicators; the attribution of prioritization to individual issues vis-à-vis collective sustainability goals; the empirical substantiation of transformations and the sustainability debate; the embedding of non-Western notions of sustainability; the establishment and improvement of knowledge management; the monitoring of non-priorities that can potentially change
Entry points Which issues can be identified and operationalized as entry points for sustainable, low-carbon transformation?	How can these entry points be identified? How is the securitization of issues effective in pushing relevant issues onto the political agenda of policy-makers? At what point can securitization inhibit sustainable, low-carbon transformation? Can de-securitization help unlock stalemates? How does the interconnectivity of issues result from assorted problems? Which issues of a policy can be altered or even taken out without undermining the overall effectiveness of this policy?	The conceptualization of capacity-building and policy transfer; the pronouncement of network effects; an understanding of the impacts of securitization on norms and norm diffusion; the justification and elaboration of the role of agents, the audience and its context in securitization; the contemplation of the generation of political agendas for political contestation; an examination of the link between lock-ins and stalemates	Process tracing and causality testing between entry points and the achievement of sustainability; an integrated impact assessment of individual and a combination of entry points for sustainable development; the measurement of the securitization of issues; a performance evaluation of selected processes; a causality assessment between securitization and policy implementation; an evaluation of synergies, feed-backs, co-benefits, and trade-offs between entry points	The translation of sectoral knowledge into sustainable development; the identification and preparation of entry points to the achievement of individual goals, leading to a transformation towards sustainability; integrated and systematic management of entry points; the verification and monitoring of entry points; advocacy for data-driven SD policies; the identification of champions of change (change agents) and spoilers for each entry point; dispute resolution between trade-offs; the management of negative synergies from interconnectivity issues

Issues:

Questions	Elaborating Questions	Meta-level theoretical and conceptual Issues	Methodological Issues	Practical Issues
Agenda-setting How is agenda-setting initiated and by whom?	How is the ability to set the agenda a source of power leverage? Should agenda-setting be inclusive or exclusive? Which items on the agenda are non-acceptable, to which actors, and why?	An understanding of the power behind agenda-setting; the conceptualization of agenda-setting as a process and a procedure; the assertion of agenda vis-à-vis legitimacy	The process tracing of how adequate agenda-setting promotes adequate outcomes; data collection; a performance assessment of agenda-setting, an impact assessment of the agenda; the measurement of shifts in power leverage through agenda-setting	The management of agenda-setting, logistics, and the organization of implementation; the elaboration and execution of monitoring and verification; the establishment of accountability management
Collective actions How does the definition, understanding, concretization, and evaluation of each issue compel collective actions?	How does an issue elicit action and/or inaction? Which issues lead to stalemates? How should 'toxic' issues be addressed and by whom? Should the participation of actors be restricted depending on the issue, where indifferent actors should be prevented from using their indifference to gain leverage in other issues? Under which conditions might individuals cooperate to pursue common goals? Are collective actions emergent or purposive?	An understanding of rationality systems for value judgment; the conceptualization of epistemological borders and crossings between relevant issues; an understanding and a pronouncement of the processes and structures of assessing issues; an examination of distortions of realities resulting from one-sided narratives and discourses; the conception of structural and process-related imbalances against "invisible" periphery actors when addressing issues; the extrapolation of mechanisms of self-reflexivity	An assessment of the impacts of adequately addressing issues; an evaluation of data and the information defining prioritization; evaluation methods; the determination of priorities; the process tracing of prioritizing and the success of implementation and the achievement of goals; an evaluation of the precariousness and distortions in an understanding of the issues; an evaluation of opportunity costs resulting from misleading prioritization	A collection of perceptions, value judgements and narratives related to the issues; the monitoring of changes in the perceptions of issues; the establishment and maintenance of communication mechanisms related to the exchange of perceptions; the deconstruction of existing discourses and narratives; the allocation of resources corresponding with prioritization; the promotion and facilitation of empowerment and capacity-building
Bargaining and policy games How are the issues being processed in various bargaining and policy games?	Are the issues connecting actors or dividing them? Which issues provide incentives and opportunities? How are cross-cutting issues addressed, by whom, and under which jurisdiction & mandate? How do bargaining games influence the behavior of actors in policy games?	An understanding of the dynamics of bargaining processes; the assertion of linkages between bargaining procedures and outcomes; the conceptualization of a "*Weitsicht*" (long-term view) as a strategic approach; an explication of incentives and containment; an examination of the bargaining and policy mandate; a position analysis	An impact assessment of individual issues on policies; the calculation of the aggregation of issues to policy design and implementation; a performance evaluation of bargaining actors vis-à-vis policy promotion; the critical evaluation of bargaining and policy performance under the terms of the mandate; the evaluation of the cross-cutting elements of bargaining and policy-making; the quantification of benefits and opportunities resulting from linking issues	The validation of regressions as learning tools for future decisions; the translation of the meaning of bargaining issues to policies; the revision and adaptation of mandates; the formulation and distribution of incentives and sanctions; an analysis of competitors; the development of bargaining and policy-making strategies that emphasize resources, skills, and collective competencies

Issues:

Questions	Elaborating Questions	Meta-level theoretical and conceptual Issues	Methodological Issues	Practical Issues
The relevance of data and information Which data and information are relevant for each issue?	How are data and information filtered and validated? How are optimality and equilibrium determined? How can decisions be made based on incomplete and/or unreliable information? How is uncertainty to be addressed when assessing the meaning of data and information? How can access to information be ensured to guarantee fair playing fields? How can social science respond to the challenges of providing useful future scenarios?	The conceptualization of optimality and rational choice; an understanding of the meaning of data and information for collective actions; the pronouncement of uncertainty and its effects on decisiveness; the conception of "equitable access" to information; an understanding of the social embeddedness and social utility of models and scenarios	An assessment of optimality and equilibrium; the evaluation of real-world conditions using optimality approaches; the measurement of identified benchmarks and indicators of optimality; the evaluation of the completeness of data and information; the evaluation of access to information and performance	The design and implementation of filtering and validating data and information; a comparison between optimality and real-world conditions, the management of data collection and the interpretation of resulting information; the improvement of qualifications and capacity of data providers
Confidentiality, complexity and uncertainty How can stakeholders deal with confidentiality, complexity and uncertainty when addressing issues?	How should complicated and complex issues be addressed where substantial expertise is difficult to develop? How are visions or scenarios of the future embedded in discourses? Which mechanisms can help actors cope with uncertainty? How are lies and deceptions to be prevented? What constitutes a lie or a deception? Can lies and deceptions be acceptable, particularly when concealing data and information would prevent self-incrimination and other disadvantages in various bargaining and policy games? How do confidentiality measures in agreements lead to abuses and structural imbalances?	The conceptualization of confidentiality vis-à-vis deliberation and agreements; the understanding of complexity; an examination of tolerance towards lies and deceptions in the context of collective decision-making; the pronouncement of learning potentials; grasping the link between dystopian or utopian thinking and decision-making or policy-making	The measurement of the degree of complexity and uncertainty; an assessment of the adherence to the confidentiality of the stakeholders; an impact assessment of the lies and deceptions; an evaluation of the barriers to confidentiality; an evaluation of the impact of uncertainty when effectively addressing issues; an impact assessment of confidentiality measures for accountability and inclusive consensus-building	The management of the audience's approval or rejection of the outcomes emerging from confidential measures; the forging of tolerable areas of lies and deceptions; the management of complexity and uncertainty; the design and implementation of contingency measures to address complexity and uncertainty; the differentiation between the issues and processes of complexity/uncertainty

Issues:

Questions	Elaborating Questions	Meta-level theoretical and conceptual Issues	Methodological Issues	Practical Issues
Incrementalism and leapfrogging How are issues re-defined by its incremental value?	How is incrementalism creating direct and latent caveats for decision-making? How are these caveats preventing the implementation of effective policies? Which elements of the incremental value is a lock-in? When capacity-building in sustainable, low-carbon transformation depends on incremental values (e.g., best practices), should these values be a public good? How can incrementalism allow the formal protection of intellectual property rights? Should institutions such as supreme courts seek to end structural bias at once, or should they opt for a strategic course, taking aim at one issue at a time? Which specific stages of trajectories can be circumvented in leap-frogging without sacrificing technological and social maturity in different subsystems (e.g. the education system)?	The conceptualization of incrementalism and of incremental value; the measurement of the degree of the manifestation of increments; an understanding of lock-ins that can be useful for or detrimental to the transformation towards sustainability; a definition of emerging issues using existing knowledge; an explication of the different phases of trajectories; the pronouncement of the linkage between learning and risk-aversion	The evaluation of increments; an impact assessment of incremental learning; the quantification and measurement of caveats; an impact assessment of lock-ins; an assessment of incremental values such as best practices; the measurement of the benchmarks and indicators of leapfrogging; the optimization of incrementalism; the regulation of leap-frogging; the evaluation of missed opportunities due to leap-frogging and incrementalism	The identification and collection of incremental values and knowledge; a comparison between increments and new knowledge; the implementation of effective policies using incremental knowledge; the verification of incremental values; the strategic management of corrective measures; the coordination between complementary and competing subsystems
Knowledge gaps Are there knowledge gaps preventing an integrated outlook on issues?	Which gaps can be bridged at low cost and risk and how? How can actors identify knowledge gaps when they are not conscious of missed knowledge? How can these knowledge gaps be bridged and by whom, both in the short- and long-term? What are the effects of these gaps on the overall objectives and the achievement of sustainable, low-carbon transformation? How can information asymmetry between actors be addressed to allow the creation of contracts covering all necessary contingencies?	An understanding of knowledge gaps and their causes; the link between knowledge gaps and trade-offs/co-benefits; the conceptualization of uncertainty; the conceptualization of precautionary principles (decision-making under uncertainty); the rumination on the unknown; the ascertainment of contingencies; the postulation of information asymmetry and its effects on transformation processes	The evaluation of material and intangible loss & harm resulting from knowledge gaps; an integrated impact assessment of knowledge gaps; the quantification of the unknown; an evaluation of the distribution of information; process tracing of the causes of information asymmetry	The identification and monitoring of knowledge gaps; the bridging of knowledge gaps; the adaptation to new knowledge that can bridge gaps; the verification of new knowledge that aims to bridge knowledge gaps; the implementation of actions and decisions in the context of the precautionary principle; the management of institutional memory

Issues:

Questions	Elaborating Questions	Meta-level theoretical and conceptual Issues	Methodological Issues	Practical Issues
Trade-offs and co-benefits Which trade-offs, synergies, and co-benefits between relevant issues can be useful in achieving the necessary outcomes?	Which linkages are fatal? How do trade-offs and negative externalities increase the complexity of issues and processes? How can trade-offs be resolved? How can trade-offs lead to distortions of perceptions? How can trade-offs and co-benefits reduce or increase the zone of possible agreement in negotiations? How are processes able to transform trade-offs into stumbling blocks, and co-benefits into enabling factors to delay/block or achieve necessary outcomes? How can trade-offs (e.g., energy efficiency for emissions reduction) be addressed by flexibility and creativity?	The conceptualization of the emergence of new bargaining leverage through resulting trade-offs and co-benefits; an understanding the role of agency in determining trade-offs and co-benefits; the pronouncement of the linkage of trade-offs and co-benefits with behavioral change; the conceptualization of 'fatality' in the context of system ruptures; the extrapolation of the dynamics behind synergy effects; the prediction of the course of the negotiation process with trade-offs and co-benefits defining leverage and zones of possible agreement	The evaluation of material and intangible loss and harm resulting from trade-offs as well as from material and intangible gains from co-benefits and synergies; the measurement and identification of pay-off redistribution mechanisms and compensation for losses as well as "equalizing" contributions for others negatively affected; the collection of relevant data and information on trade-offs and co-benefits; the attribution and valuation of "guilt" into compensation; process-tracing to analyze causalities, leading to trade-offs, co-benefits, and synergies	The identification and verification of the practical impacts of multiple trade-offs, co-benefits, and synergies; data and evidence-supported determination of equalizing or compensatory mechanisms; the management of compensations contingent upon additional responsibilities; the verification of compensation payments; ensuring the clarity of institutional and formal jurisdictions on issues

Structures:

Questions	Elaborating Questions	Meta-level theoretical and conceptual Issues	Methodological Issues	Practical Issues
Standards and reference frames Which objective standards are available to allow credible and reliable decision-making?	How are objective standards reached and by whom? Does objectivity guarantee acceptability? Are these standards open to political negotiations? If yes, how is their optimality undermined? Which flexibility measures and compensation payments can be tapped to bridge the gaps between optimality and the political acceptance of standards? Which reference frames (e.g., power, rationality, democracy, or adaptability) are needed to promote the transformation towards sustainability?	The conceptualization of objectivity as validity criteria; the understanding of structural imbalances that prevent or distort credible data and information collection; the pronouncement of the linkage between flexibility measures and policy implementation; the understanding of standardization as a contingency measure; the conceptualization of credibility	A performance assessment of objective standards; scoping for information; an assessment of available data; the formulation and impact assessment of standards and benchmarks; the evaluation of objective standards vis-à-vis policy implementation and the achievement of goals; an assessment of credibility	The verification of mechanisms and objective standards; the formalization of objectivity as the standard; accountability management and due diligence; the identification and justification of flexibility measures; the convergence management of standards; data management; the logistical management of information scoping and collection

Structures:

Questions	Elaborating Questions	Meta-level theoretical and conceptual Issues	Methodological Issues	Practical Issues
Decision Frameworks Under which frameworks can multiple decision-making levels or fragmented decision-making in modular sub-systems be integrated and facilitated?	How do multiple decision-making levels enhance polycentrism? How does polycentrism promote or prevent cooperation? How can the differing mandates for each level or subsystem be integrated? How can 'forum shopping' in decision-making be prevented? How should actors create alliances to enhance their capacity to participate in relevant sub-systems? Which regimes are better suited in forging and implementing multi-level decisions? How are rules and norms established in each decision framework?	The conceptualization of an integrated approach to assessing multi-level decision-making; the examination of the linkage between diversity and polycentric decision-making; an analysis of the linkage between polycentrism and cooperation; decision analysis; an explication of the integration and coordination of coherent actions at various levels and subsystems	An impact assessment of polycentrism; a performance evaluation of partners and allies; the tracing of causalities and interdependencies between modular sub-systems; the measurement of synergies arising from linking decision (sub)frameworks; a critical outlook on policy frameworks	The enhancement of adaptive strategies to polycentrism; the monitoring and verification of polycentric cooperation; the allocation of tasks and accountability at relevant levels; the establishment of coordination mechanisms; addressing the historicity of decision frameworks
Institutions and organizations Which organizational structures can best support the transformation process towards sustainability?	Which institutional arrangements can ensure participation and compliance? How big or lean should the organization be to ensure functionality? How can the works of the organization be checked without hindering the organization from achieving their goals? What kind of mandate is needed to ensure the legitimacy of the organization? How can this mandate adapt to changes without causing ruptures? How can the organization equalize the leverage of strong parties and build the capacity of weaker parties? How can organizations and institutions effectively respond to ecological changes (feedbacks)?	The conceptualization of participation; an examination of the linkage between mandate and legitimacy; an understanding of the role of power in designing organizational structures; an explication of the linkage between social mandates/contracts and organizational settings; an understanding of the role of organizations and institutions as formative spheres; an analysis of the classification and typologies of institutions and organizations; the creation and maintenance of institutional and organizational identities	A performance evaluation of organizational design; an impact assessment of organizational reforms and changes; an impact assessment of mandates; the evaluation of organizational dynamics as power leverage	The establishment of effective quality management; the implementation of accountability management; monitoring and verification; the management of the self-defense mechanisms of organizations; bridging organizations and paradigms; the verification of mandates and social contracts; the management of linking citizen forums with scientific assessment; the management and verification of the outreach activities of institutions and organizations; the management of the opening of organizational and institutional structures to deliberation; the democratization of deliberation across different types of expertise, experts, and politics (the democratization of experts)

Structures:				
Questions	**Elaborating Questions**	**Meta-level theoretical and conceptual Issues**	**Methodological Issues**	**Practical Issues**
Regimes and policy models Which political regime/system is best suited to implementing sustainability policy goals?	How are democratic regimes in a better position than authoritarian and totalitarian regimes to produce significant environmental and sustainable developmental commitments? Which ideal types of democracy (liberal, deliberative, socio-liberal) can most effectively pursue environment policy stringency (e.g., an environmental tax, environmental standards)? How do hybrid regimes deviate from ideal types in terms of policy implementation?	The definition of democracy and authoritarianism; an understanding of social welfare in the context of policy models; the conceptualization of legitimacy in various policy models, including hybrid types; an understanding of the historical and cultural contexts of regimes and policy models	The measurement of input and output legitimacy; a comparative analysis of policy design and implementation according to policy models; a narrative analysis; a performance assessment of the principles of democracy and authoritarianism; the evaluation of innovation according to policy models	Regime transition management; the implementation of due diligence; the improvement of accountability management; the attribution of outputs to individual principles (e.g., the authoritarian elements of a democratic regime and vice-versa)
Risks, threats and coincidences (luck) How do perceptions of risk, threats, and luck constitute responsibilities, accountabilities, and commitments?	How do emerging risks and threats lead to changes in governance? How can risks lead to system ruptures? Which preventive and contingency measures can be effective in reducing risks? Which risks are unacceptable? How are threats changing the dynamics and rules of the system? Are the costs of preventive measures justifiable as intangible and theoretical risks? How can risks be attributed to perpetrators to determine responsibilities and remedial actions? Which moral responsibilities can result from coincidences and luck? How can threats and sanctions initiate escalation? How do threats constitute legitimacy gaps? How do threats change relationships and interactions? Are blaming and shaming effective strategies for persuading laggards and spoilers?	The conceptualization of risks and volatility; the pronouncement of linkages between risk reduction and the quality of collective decision-making; the conceptualization of behavioral change when averting risks; the explication of the linkage between luck and moral responsibilities; an understanding of acceptable and unacceptable risks; an examination of the possibilities of reversing past decisions	A performance assessment of structures and mechanisms; the evaluation of opportunity costs resulting from both the failure of preparing for risks and from risk-aversion; the measurement of the value of preventive and contingent measures; the definition of scenarios of the future; the evaluation of self-fulfilling prophecies in actions; the evaluation of the acceptability of risks and threats	The anticipation of potential risks; accountability management; the verification of risks; the attribution of risks to factors, actors, and dynamics; the management of compensatory actions resulting from risks and coincidental misfortunes; the diversification of activities and measures to spread risks and promote system stability
Dispute management Which mechanisms are viable when resolving disputes over time?	Which mechanisms are needed to resolve future disputes? How can mechanisms of dispute resolution be modified over time to adapt to changes in the nature and intensity of disputes? How should inevitable disagreements be handled?	An understanding of the reasons behind disputes; the conceptualization of disputes as spheres of deliberation and consensus-building	An assessment of mechanisms; a performance assessment of procedures; an impact assessment of conciliators; the evaluation of dispute settlements; a comparative analysis between scenarios of settlement and non-settlement	The management of disputes; the selection of conciliators; the identification of relevant stakeholders; the management of institutional memory; the verification and accountability of management; the inclusion of dispute resolution measures in agreements; the anticipation of potential dispute issues

Structures:

Questions	Elaborating Questions	Meta-level theoretical and conceptual Issues	Methodological Issues	Practical Issues
Paradigm shifts How can paradigm shifts be initiated and executed?	Which paradigms require shifting? Why are paradigms shifting? Which paradigms need to be maintained to ensure sustainable, low-carbon transformation? Why do most SDG mechanisms lack representation from non-state actors? Are paradigm shifts emergent or purposive? How can legislation and social norms adjust to paradigm shifts? Are paradigm shifts technologically, norm, or actor-driven?	The conceptualization of paradigms; an understanding of the processes behind paradigm shifts; an explanation of triggers and points of no return; an extrapolation of linkages between critical junctures and lock-ins to individual decisions or policies; a conception of complacency and an aversion to change	An integrated impact assessment of paradigm shifts; the evaluation of opportunity costs resulting from the failure to achieve paradigm shifts; process tracing and the assessment of causalities; the designing of benchmarks and indicators; the measurement of convergences between sub-systems	The attribution of shifts to individual policies and decisions; the management of risks; the establishment of compensatory mechanisms; accountability management
Policy instruments Which policies, including market instruments, are needed and are available to achieve concrete goals (e.g., local community development, innovation, usage of waste materials) and commitments?	How can incentive and sanction systems produce the appropriate behavior and actions? How can policy-makers retract or revise existing policies to further advance sustainability policy priorities without losing political credibility?	Linkage between incentives/sanctions and behavior/actions; the attribution of functionality to policy instruments; the conceptualization of a social mandate to institutions and agencies designing and implementing policies; the conceptualization of deliberation and consensus-building	The measurement of pain/pay-offs leading to specific decisions and actions; the measurement of system tolerance; the evaluation of missed opportunities resulting from the non-existence of policy instruments; the impact and performance evaluation of policy measures; an integrated assessment of policy instruments	The monitoring and verification of policy instruments; accountability management; the inclusion of non-state actors when designing and implementing policy measures; the establishment of compensatory mechanisms; the design of membership in policy and decision-making bodies

Structures:

Questions	Elaborating Questions	Meta-level theoretical and conceptual Issues	Methodological Issues	Practical Issues
Structural constraints Which structural and systemic constraints can influence the transformation process?	Is the geopolitical context a crucial factor in decision-making? How does polycentrism and the monolithic architecture of the system promote or inhibit sustainable, low-carbon transformation? What are the determinants of success and failure of non-state groups such as NGOs when promoting sustainable development? How can structural and systemic inefficiencies be bypassed, if not corrected? How can the inability of existing institutions to resolve structural and systemic problems be effectively addressed?	The conceptualization of latent and evident structural bias; an understanding of contextual elements; an explanation of the self-suffocation of systems; the pronouncement of the linkage between polycentrism and low-carbon development	The measurement of influence; an impact assessment of constraints; the evaluation of missed opportunities due to the self-engagement of the system; the quantification and justification of claims of structural bias; the evaluation of context; the design and measurement of benchmarks and indicators	Verification management, the implementation of due diligence and accountability; the interpretation of local conditions defining the geopolitical context; the identification of constraints and explanations of their causes; the attribution of constraints to individual structures; the differentiation of constraints caused by structures and actors' misjudgment
Drivers, triggers and tipping points What drives decisions (e.g., technology, market, culture)?	What are the triggers of actions? Which factors obstruct or delay actions? Can decisions driven by technology, market, or culture be aligned with the principles and goals of sustainable, low-carbon transformation? If not, which adjustments are needed? If yes, how can technological and societal innovation be supported and by which policy instruments and social capital? How can technology utilities provide values beyond their products and services (e.g. a car company providing mobility impulses, such as car sharing)? Which tipping points are relevant for transformation? Which factors and events are game changers?	An understanding of the role of pioneers, first movers, multipliers, and champions; linking technological, market and cultural innovation with societal change and human well-being; linkages between drivers of decisions and procedures; the conceptualization of disruptive events or agencies; an understanding of the role of recipients' lifestyles on the emergence of innovation	An assessment of realistic and speculative scenarios; the determination of relevant indicators and benchmarks; impact assessments; process tracing; the evaluation of complementary and competing technologies; the assessment of required complementary infrastructures (e.g. digitalization) and policy instruments (e.g. fiscal policies)	The promotion of social acceptance of technologies; the adaptation of technologies to structural changes; purpose planning for drivers; the management of technological, societal, market, and cultural trade-offs, co-benefits, and synergies; the identification of tipping points

Structures:

Questions	Elaborating Questions	Meta-level theoretical and conceptual Issues	Methodological Issues	Practical Issues
Self-enforcement How can structures promoting a transformation towards sustainability reinforce themselves?	How can self-enforcement promote or inhibit sustainable, low-carbon transformation? How can self-driving dynamics be predicted and controlled? Who is to be held accountable for the negative externalities brought by self-reinforcing structures? Who can take credits over the positive contribution of self-driving dynamics vis-à-vis rewards and entitlements? Should structures be independent from human cognition? If yes, how? Which structures can be (re) developed to reduce risks and volatility in decision-making? How can decision frameworks be resilient and adaptive?	An understanding of relationships between resilient and adaptive capacities; the conceptualization of self-enforcement; the conceptualization of accountability over self-enforcement; an explication of apparent contradictions; the pronouncement of the linkages between self-driving dynamics and free-will	An impact assessment of self-enforcement; the measurement of resilience and adaptation through benchmarks and indicators; an assessment of the adaptive capacity of the system; the measurement and attribution of accountability converted into sanctions and moral responsibilities	The accountability management of effects resulting from self-enforcement; the establishment of early warning and response systems; monitoring and verification; the attribution of rewards and sanctions; the improvement of reaction time for self-enforcement
The nexus of global-local Are there local, regional and/ or international frameworks or agencies that can be tapped to advance capacity-building?	How is the global interconnected with the national and local spheres? How is learning across the levels of analysis helpful to transformation? How can regional powers or middle powers assume a regional leadership role in sustainable development? Can regional bodies such as the APEC or ASEAN play a more pronounced role in advancing sustainable developmental policy goals? Can regional "champions" of sustainable development be identified to serve as catalysts of transformation? How can regional success stories be useful for other regions? How can local/regional issues be effectively addressed globally (and vice-versa)? How can the inability of local actors to participate in global decision-making be effectively addressed and resolved?	An understanding of the meaning of locality in globalization; the postulation of a connection between local, regional, and international bodies and a conceptualization of their relationships; an understanding of the links between global and local; conceptualization of "glocalization"; an explication of the core-periphery dichotomy in the context of global-local relations; the pronouncement of norm diffusion across the levels of analysis; an analysis of the linkage between "glocality" and legitimacy	A performance assessment of "glocalized approaches"; the differentiation between indigenous and exogenous interventions; the evaluation of global visions for local actions; an assessment of the inclusion of local actors in global decision-making; an evaluation of local impulses (e.g. aboriginal water governance, the Taloana concept for climate negotiations); the quantification of the benefits of the scaling up and scaling down of best practices	The justification of global decisions vis-à-vis local audiences (and vice-versa); the management of social mandates; accountability and transparency management; the addressing of NIMBY and free-drivers; the bridging of global visions with local actions; the coordination of distinct processes and dynamics at various governance levels; the integration and coordination of coherent actions at various levels

Processes:

Questions	Elaborating Questions	Meta-level theoretical and conceptual Issues	Methodological Issues	Practical Issues
Inclusion and exclusion How can inclusive processes strengthen patterns of justice and fairness?	Does inclusion promote predictability in decision-making? How is justice relevant to sustainable, low-carbon transformation? How do inclusive processes affect the extent of other processes? How does the opening of deliberations promote the achievement of goals? How do the reactions of other processes further influence the course of one process? How can feedbacks be identified and measured? Which feedbacks between processes need to be properly addressed? How are "political subjects" identified and embedded in specific contexts? How do processes mobilize agents and audiences? Which rebound effects require attention? What prevents accountability? How does the maintenance of patriarchal values create structural imbalances, or are these patriarchal values themselves symptoms of structural imbalances? How does the promotion of women's rights promote other societal goals? How does culture define practice? How does addressing gender gaps promote environmental and climate protection as well as other sustainable development goals? How are gendered injustices the outcomes of changes in institutions?	The conceptualization of rewards and sanctions for injustices; an understanding of the mechanisms of bestowing respectability; an explication of inclusiveness and exclusiveness in decision-making processes; an analysis of the linkage between change and status quo processes; an understanding of feedback; the conceptualization of silence and complicity; an explication of free-riding and the public good dilemma	An assessment of relevance; an impact assessment of processes; the measurement of feedback, the rebound effect and its externalities; the methodological instruments used to study (in)justices, including gender-related abuses; the measurement and prediction of the possibility of being excluded; the evaluation of counter-movements and other responses to change; the evaluation of the competitive advantage of being "in" and the competitive disadvantage of being "out"	The formalization of atonement; the monitoring and verification of benchmarks and indicators; the attribution of outcomes to processes; accountability management; the distribution of the costs and pay-offs of inclusion and exclusion; the establishment of capacity-building measures to promote inclusion; the determination of strategies of exclusion; the prevention of free-riding

Processes:

Questions	Elaborating Questions	Meta-level theoretical and conceptual Issues	Methodological Issues	Practical Issues
Discourses and Perspectives How can different perspectives in each process be addressed and used to expand value?	Do the positions of stakeholders depend on which processes they are participating in? Which positions are developed a fortiori during the bargaining processes? How are multi-level perspectives reflected in decision-making processes? Which opportunities are available through sectoral approaches? How can the coherence of various relevant levels and modular subsystems be achieved? How can the convergence of principles and norms be facilitated? How can all levels of governance be designed so that they include the perspectives of the most vulnerable? How do discourse entrepreneurs communicate and interact with each other and with norm entrepreneurs? How can an actor not only understand the perspectives of the others but also make one's perspective be understood by the others (the reverse perspective)? How should public spheres be constituted to promote public discourse? Which agencies (e.g. the church, NGOs, universities) can serve as hosts of public discourse? Can effective public discourse occur in authoritarian states?	The conceptualization of relationships between discourse entrepreneurs; an understanding of the importance of consensus-building and deliberation to transformation processes; an affirmation of the linkage between diversity and value; an examination of participation; an understanding of sectoral perspectives; the conceptualization of the convergence and diffusion of norms and principles	An impact assessment of diversity in perspectives; the evaluation of perspectives; the measurement of opportunity costs in monolithic decision-making processes; the operationalization of reverse perspectives; an assessment of appropriate actions that are locally rather than universally approved by the audience	The identification, creation and management of agencies or spheres that connect perspectives; the empowerment of weaker actors; the establishment of new norms; accountability management; the development and concretization of principles for common but differentiated responsibilities; the translation of access to perspectives into empathy; the overcoming of barriers and caveats for societal dialogue; the integration and coordination of coherent actions at various levels
Process legitimacy Which factors can provide legitimacy to the transformation process?	How important is the approval of the audience? How and why is legitimacy inevitable? What constitutes an audience? Which external audiences can be relevant? What happens when the audience disapproves of policies? How can the outcome of collective decision-making be justified in front of constituents? How can social mandates frame collective actions or prevent certain actions? How does legitimacy ensure compliance? How is climate skepticism linked with right-wing populism? How can legitimacy be made more culturally pluralistic?	The conceptualization of internal and external transparencies and accountabilities; the conception of the linkage of process legitimacy to outcome legitimacy; an explication of the audience and its leverage against agents; an understanding of social mandates and their ramifications for social cohesion	The quantification and measurement of approval; an impact assessment of process legitimacy on the effective implementation of policy goals; the optimization of processes vis-à-vis goals; the measurement of the adaptability of those processes on unravelling changes	The formalization of legitimacy; verification and accountability management; the establishment of reconciliatory mechanisms between audiences and agents; the management of diversity and the complexity of processes (branching points); the implementation of corrective and compensatory mechanisms

Processes:

Questions	Elaborating Questions	Meta-level theoretical and conceptual Issues	Methodological Issues	Practical Issues
Communication How can communication among actors, between representatives and constituents as well as between agents and audiences be established?	Which structural conditions are needed to allow communication? What is the role of language as a tool of communication? How is language a barrier or a bridge to sustainable development? Which communication mechanisms can provide opportunities for collaborative exchanges? How does power define the communication process? How can communication resolve coordination problems? How does communication resolve the prisoner's dilemma? Are there limitations on the need for communication? How does communication enhance or inhibit bargaining? How can the dependence on the English language as the dominant carrier of scientific knowledge be addressed? Which problems in communication can inhibit cooperation?	The conceptualization of language as the carrier of information and knowledge; an understanding of the role of sociolinguistic narratives in the transformation processes; an assertion of the link between capacity-building in communication and participation in decision-making processes; the conceptualization of coordination and coordination problems; an explication of the linkage between communication and bargaining, as well as between communication and deliberation	An impact assessment of communication channels; the measurement of communication skills; an analysis of collaborative exchanges; an evaluation of the effects of communication on coordination and collaboration; an assessment of communication skills; an analysis of rhetorical preferences, depending on power-base reference frames	The management of exchanges of knowledge; the fact-checking of sociolinguistic narratives; a comparison of the meanings and interpretations of terminologies; the improvement of translation and the use of communication and information technologies; the improvement of listening skills
Learning How does the learning of actors and agencies resolve which challenges to transformation towards sustainability?	How does experiential learning constitute practice and define actions? How do actors assess information and use it to modify their behavior and decisions? How can learning lead to pragmatic decisions? Is learning possible for all relevant actors? How does learning promote cooperation? How does learning resolve coordination and collaboration problems? How can actors learn from bridging the gaps between discourse and materiality? How can regressions and set-backs lead to learning? How is it possible to reverse learning and unlearn erroneous learning materials?	An explication of the linkage between learning and incrementalism; the conceptualization of experiential learning; an assertion of the linkage between learning and cooperation; an understanding of the value of regressions and set-backs (discriminative constraints) to decision-making; the grasping of learning from big bangs and/or incremental changes	The measurement of learning among actors and agents; a comparison between learning goals and learning outcomes; an analysis of regressions and their impacts; causality tracing between learning and the resolution of the indecisiveness dilemma; the assessment of experiences as inputs for learning; the measurement of the usefulness of learning outputs for transformation towards sustainability	The management of learning institutions; the verification of learning materials; the orientation of learning to policy goals; the sharp-edging of multi-disciplinary profiles of global transformations towards sustainability; the translation of learning into shorter thinking and reaction times

Processes:

Questions	Elaborating Questions	Meta-level theoretical and conceptual Issues	Methodological Issues	Practical Issues
Persuasion and advocacy How can actors achieve their goals through persuasion and advocacy?	How does persuasion change behaviors and utility preferences? Which persuasion techniques can be used in a highly competitive environment? How can decision-makers, confronted by high uncertainty, be persuaded? How are persuasions creating more value for transformations? How does the demonization of others inhibit persuasion? From where do advocacy groups derive their social mandate? How do policy entrepreneurs resolve power asymmetries between them and their target actors? Which types and venues of cooperation among policy entrepreneurs can promote a transformation towards sustainability?	The conceptualization of changes in beliefs and value systems due to persuasion; an understanding of advocacy as a means of fulfilling interests; an examination of policy change due to advocacy; the presumption of the connection between advocacy and larger public policy concerns; an understanding of the opportunities and limitations of advocacy with regards to the reversal of past decisions; a rumination on social mobilization; the grasping of the significance of venues and platforms (public spheres); the conceptualization of codes of conduct and rules for policy entrepreneurs	The evaluation of arguments made for persuasion; an impact assessment of persuasive measures; an assessment of the tactics of advocacy groups; a performance analysis of NGOs and other policy entrepreneurs; a measure of advocacy that covers a broad range of actions; a comparison of viable venues for advocacy (courts, the streets); the measurement of policy changes due to advocacy; the evaluation of the game plan of policy-making and policy implementation	The accountability of advocacy groups and interest surrogates; the verification of promises; the accountability and transparency of the audiences and constituents of policy entrepreneurs; the development of appropriate game plans and competitive gambits
Morality and Normativity How does morality and normativity define functional, institutional, and bargaining interactions?	How can 'good' intentions produce 'bad' results? How can valuable silver linings be identified and enhanced? What is the role of luck, coincidences and circumstance in determining moral responsibilities? How do luck and coincidences define individual preferences, decisions, and actions? How can individual actions that fall within social norms like driving cars or having a big family be blamed for aggregated values that are detrimental to environmental integrity? How do power relations define responsibilities? How can the naming, blaming and shaming of the divergent actors from the norms resolve the prisoners' dilemma? Are value-free trajectories of sustainability possible?	The conceptualization of remedial actions; an understanding of the attenuation of blame; an understanding of the complex and neglected aspects of moral responsibility judgments; an explication of the shifts in moral understanding and responsibility; the definition of a political interpretation of responsibility; an understanding of cumulative effects; an analysis of the acceptance of normativity in decision frameworks; an explication of the reproduction of the frames of reference in reinforcing accepted beliefs and norms	The evaluation of regret; the measurement of fault and guilt; an assessment of the impacts of guilt on actions; a comparative analysis of narratives on moral responsibility; the evaluation of power in determining blame and guilt ("history is written by the winners"); culpable causation; the evaluation of the value adaptiveness of agencies and audiences	The justification of interventions using moral principles; the attribution of commitments and contributions to circumstantial luck; accountability management; the justification of sanctions and compensatory measures; the attribution of blame to perpetuators in complex issues; the attribution of blame and responsibilities based on uncertainty; engagement in arguments and fights over moral responsibilities

Processes:

Questions	Elaborating Questions	Meta-level theoretical and conceptual Issues	Methodological Issues	Practical Issues
Identity and ownership How can the consolidation of identity and ownership of sustainable development further advance the transformation process?	How can ownership promote transformation processes? How can the recipients of technological transfer and capacity-building efforts entail process ownership? What does ownership mean to international assistance efforts? How are intellectual property rights addressed in collaboration efforts? How does identity provide rallying points for collective actions? What can mobilize "eco-identity"? How are identities, ideas and narratives being (re)produced, and in which ways?	The conceptualization of policy transfers vis-à-vis norm diffusion; an understanding of mobilizing processes leading to identities; the pronouncement of the linkage of changes to the loss of identity; the adjudication of identity narratives; the conceptualization of ownership; an explication of the linkage between ownership and transformation processes	The quantification of ownership; an impact assessment of identity-based measures; the evaluation of process ownership vis-à-vis the achievement of policy goals; the scoping of the boundaries between identities; the consolidation of identity-building measures	The identification of champions; the formalization of rallying points for transformation; the institutionalization of measures promoting the ownership of the recipients of technology transfers; the modification of narratives; the translation of ownership into responsibility and commitment; the prevention of polarization tendencies

Outcomes:

Questions	Elaborating Questions	Meta-level theoretical and conceptual Issues	Methodological Issues	Practical Issues
Post-agreement opposition How can agreements effectively address post-agreement opposition and challenges?effectively address post-agreement opposition and challenges?	Who are the potential post-agreement challengers and opposing actors? What are the motivations of these actors? Which arguments are typically used by former participants to discredit the agreements? Why did they initially support the agreement but later withdraw support? How can post-agreement opposition be an accepted part of the process?	The promotion of opposition as an accepted norm of deliberation; the conceptualization of "evolving deterrence"; an understanding and promotion of the credibility of agreements	The evaluation of process resilience; an impact assessment and the measurement of preference functions in collective decision-making; a comparative analysis of different interpretations of the same issues	The establishment of early warning and response management; the promotion of the reliability of outcomes; an improvement in dialogue and communication management with stakeholders; compensation for emerging contingencies

Outcomes:

Questions	Elaborating Questions	Meta-level theoretical and conceptual Issues	Methodological Issues	Practical Issues
Alternatives Which outcomes can improve the 'best alternative to a negotiated agreement' (BATNA) of all actors?	Which alternative outcomes are available and feasible for each actor? How can the BATNA be aligned with the principles and goals of sustainable, low-carbon transformation? How can the clarification of alternatives prevent actors from cheating? How can tangible outcomes be compared to theoretical alternatives? How can judgements about acceptable risks be made? How could potentially unrealistic expectations be tested? What are some ways to use differing interests to create value?	The conceptualization of BATNA; an examination of the narratives and a romanticizing of the alternatives; an understanding of one's reservation value and that of the others; an analysis of utopian/dystopian thinking; the conception of the idealization of theoretical alternatives	A comparison between real outcomes and hypothetical alternatives; a comparison of BATNA and outcomes; the modelling of alternative scenarios; the measurement of acceptability of alternative outcomes; the calculation of the risks of the alternatives; an assessment of options to enhance value-creating performance	The reliable comparison of options; the establishment of fact-checking and correction management related to a nostalgic memory of past regimes; fact-checking in the post-truth era; the identification of strategic alternatives in response to issues; the establishment of analytical frameworks to assist the creative development of alternatives
Ambiguity and flexibility Which ambiguities are useful for ensuring the implementation of negotiated outcomes?	Which ambiguities are embedded in outcomes? How do ambiguities constitute the flexibility and acceptability of agreements? Which types of ambiguities are detrimental to the long-term transformation process? How do ambiguities affect relationships and interactions? How does ambiguity promote trust and cooperation? Are ambiguity and flexibility the prerogatives of powerful actors? How much ambiguity can be achieved without sacrificing efficiency? How does ambiguity promote participation and inclusion? How can creativity and imagination be sustained?	The extrapolation of the linkage between complexity and ambiguity; an explication of the linkage between ambiguity or flexibility and efficiency; the pronouncement of the linkage between ambiguity or flexibility and power; an understanding of the difference between ambiguity and entitlement	The conversion of principles of justice and fairness into ambiguity and flexibility; the evaluation of ambiguity vis-à-vis system shocks; the differentiation of ambiguity from free-riding; an assessment of creative solutions in terms of them being realistic; the evaluation of improvisation skills drawn on (life) experience and institutional memory	The attribution of vulnerabilities to compensatory mechanisms through ambiguities and flexibilities; accountability and verification management; bridging ambiguity and reciprocity in cooperative relationships; the collection and implementation of creativity in agreements

Outcomes:

Questions	Elaborating Questions	Meta-level theoretical and conceptual Issues	Methodological Issues	Practical Issues
Interests What possible agreements or pieces of an agreement (outcomes) could satisfy the interests of all actors and audiences?	How far is the negotiated agreement from the (technically) optimal solution? How can the resulting gaps be compensated to ensure the efficiency of agreements? How can the integrity of negotiated agreements be established when they are far from optimal? How can multiple, individual, optimal solutions be aligned or aggregated to resolve coordination and collaboration problems? How can short-term interests be made compatible with long-term interests? How useful is the use of power in coercing the reconciliation of interests?	An understanding of biases that distort interests; the justification of compensatory measures; an understanding of the role of emotions; the conception of interests based on the context of power asymmetry	The depiction of short-term and long-term interests; the modelling of interests; the anticipation of others' interests; the evaluation and measurement of interests for comparison purposes	Access to information about one's interests and those of the others; setting up objective standards and indicators to elaborate interests
Divergence How can the divergence of interests be used to create additional value in outcomes?	How are differences be tolerated or addressed in the outcome? How can diversity be useful in expanding the value of agreements? How can differences be connected, and by which social mandate? How can gaps between technically optimal solutions and negotiated agreements be addressed? While the convergence of principles and norms can promote transformation, how can divergence resolve the locality and contextuality of various problem issues? Can divergence promote expert specialization? Which political skills are needed to reconcile divergent interests?	The conceptualization of reactive devaluation (devaluing proposals only because they originated from an adversary); the pronouncement of the linkage between divergence and convergence; an explication of the linkage between divergence and flexibility; an understanding of divergence in the context of cooperation	A critical assessment of the variations among sectors and technologies; the evaluation of best practices; an impact assessment of diverging norms and principles; an evaluation of sub-optimal compromises resulting from the reconciliation of divergent interests	The delegitimating of counterfactual claims on global transformation towards sustainability; the establishment of the connection between divergence and the application of solutions; the design of interventions to reconcile interests; the creation of balance between harmony and dissent; the establishment of mechanisms to combat polarization tendencies; the integration and coordination of coherent actions considering divergent principles and mandates
Expectations and pay-offs How can present behavior be framed by expectations of future outcomes?	Which expectations are inhibiting or promoting which outcomes? How do self-fulfilling prophecies affect the present behavior of actors? How do too optimistic and too pessimistic expectations limit the real potentials of the achieved agreement? How can potentially unrealistic expectations be tested and corrected?	The conceptualization of expectations; an understanding of self-fulfilling prophecies; an explication of cognitive lock-ins	An assessment of the ontological and epistemological baggage of ideas and principles; an evaluation of methods of coupling and decoupling; the conversion of collective pay-offs to individual pay-offs (and vice-versa)	The collection, attribution and distribution of pay-offs from outcomes; the bridging of individual and collective pay-offs

Outcomes:

Questions	Elaborating Questions	Meta-level theoretical and conceptual Issues	Methodological Issues	Practical Issues
Outcome legitimacy How do the negative externalities of the outcome or individual elements of the outcome affect the legitimacy of the whole outcome?	How can externalities be fairly distributed to the actors causing them? How can the value of the externalities be converted to become significant to policy-makers? Are all relevant negative externalities properly addressed? How do negative externalities affect cooperation? How do these affect one's utility function? What external criteria might plausibly be relevant? How can outcomes be justified to constituents?	An explanation of causalities between outcomes and legitimacy; an explication of narratives vis-à-vis legitimacy; the presumption of system adaptation and latency; the pronouncement of implementation and verification as tools of outcome legitimacy	The evaluation and measurement of transition costs vis-à-vis transition pay-offs; the assessment of the verification systems in place; the evaluation and measurement of public acceptance	The management of heterogeneous and fragmented public opinion; fact-checking management; the application of outcomes to local conditions; the elaboration of the details of the outcome; the management and improvement of information campaigns
Contract regimes and implementation How are outcomes logistically and materially implemented?	Which organizational resources are needed to support implementation? Which roadmap or timeline can be used to implement policies? Does the process require mediation through an impartial third-party? Which additional roles can stakeholders take on as the outcomes are implemented? Which benchmarks and indicators can be used to monitor and, if needed, correct the implementation of outcomes? Should contract regimes be centralized or decentralized?	A conception of system ruptures; an understanding of the degree of institutionalization associated with contract regimes	An assessment of the benchmarks behind critical junctures; the evaluation of alternative regime arrangements; an assessment of the adaptive capacities of contract regimes; the optimization and calibration of benchmarks and indicators; the evaluation of implementation plans and roadmaps	The distribution of the costs and benefits of implemented policies; the adjustment of contracts and mandates; the concretization and elaboration of stipulations in contracts; action planning and implementation

Outcomes:

Questions	Elaborating Questions	Meta-level theoretical and conceptual Issues	Methodological Issues	Practical Issues
Post-agreement modifications How can provisions in the negotiated outcome be modified without endangering the implementation of the outcome?	How can unpopular outcomes be retrospectively justified? How can new provisions and stipulations be added into the agreement without requiring a default on negotiations? How can shifts and changes in power resources during the course of negotiations and after settlements be addressed in anticipation? How can the outcome be stable enough to allow minor modifications?	An understanding of the sources of stability; an explication of the link between system stability and outcome stability; the conceptualization of flexibility and creativity in responding to new conditions; the conception of system ruptures	An assessment of the adaptive capacities of implementing regimes; the measurement and evaluation of system ruptures and disruptions; an impact assessment of disruptive governments	The establishment and verification of rules on post-agreement modifications; the management of early-warning and rapid-response mechanisms; transparency and accountability management

14.2 The Stakeholder Matrix and Engagement Plan

The insights and lessons gained from the theoretical, methodological, and empirical chapters of this book are used to come up with a stakeholder matrix and engagement plan that can help decision-makers structure their strategies and adapt to the various dilemmas and self-driving dynamics when making important decisions. The previous section empowers stakeholders to understand the questions that need to be asked to "master" the transformation process towards sustainability. The identification of meta-level theoretical, methodological, and practical issues allows integrated and systems analytical thinking that promotes the expansion of values. This expansion of values promotes collective decision-making by highlighting the 'positive sum' character of the transformation process.

The following figure illustrates an empty template of a matrix that summarizes and applies the outputs of all the chapters of this book. The stakeholders are first categorized according to their role in the policy-making process. Tier 1 are the direct agents that directly come up with policy instruments that could promote or inhibit transformation towards sustainability. Tier 2 refers to context-related policy entrepreneurs that include both enablers and spoilers which are not directly involved in policy-making but can enable or hinder (delay or obstruct) decision-making. Tier 3 (audience) pertains to entities that bestow different types of legitimacy on the transformation process through their direct or indirect approval or disapproval not only of the whole transformation process, but also of different (sub)processes (Table 14.2).

Table 14.2 The Stakeholder Matrix and Engagement Plan. (Source: own representation)

Stakeholders		Roles		Power base	Negotiation analysis		Conflict analysis		Engagement		Entry points to transformation	Caveats to support transformation	Position for further actions
		System role	Role in the process		Interest	Negotiation style	Definition of conflict	Understanding of methodology of resolution	Type of engagement	Output of engagement			
Tier 1 (Agents)													
Tier 2 (Context-related policy entrepreneurs)													
Tier 3 (Audience)													

The different aspects of the matrix include the system and process-related role of these stakeholders, conflict analysis (how these stakeholders define conflict and how they see this conflict being resolved), and the type of engagement that can be utilized to produce specific outputs from this engagement. In addition, the matrix highlights the entry points to transformation towards sustainability, the caveats to support this transformation process, as well as the possible positions of stakeholders for further actions (which type of actions are most likely to be pursued).

To demonstrate the use of the matrix, a preliminary draft of the stakeholder analysis and engagement plan for the transformation process towards sustainability of the German transport sector (*Verkehrswende*) will be introduced. Some impulses were taken from current discussions among relevant stakeholders participating in various public discourses on sustainable transport in Germany. The draft suggests, for instance, how asking appropriate reflexive questions can explain why some stakeholders are ambivalent to sustainable transport. This highlights why one stakeholder or even a policy-making agent produces a series of actions that are contradictory. This is not necessarily an argument for the unpredictability or irrationality of this actor, but rather suggests existing entry points and *caveats* or barriers.

The Tier 1 agents refer to the different relevant government bodies as stipulated by the federal system, as well as Germany's membership in the European Union. While the federal ministries tend to be the major agenda-setting actors in the negotiation process, the state governments (*Bundesländer*) employ other venues of participation. The city governments and local councils (*Gemeinde*) are also involved through various means and are considered the policy-makers nearest to the citizens. The Tier 2 agents are the policy entrepreneurs who have varying degrees of influence over Tier 1 agents. They also contribute different types of inputs that allow Tier 1 agents to efficiently address certain issues while maintaining legitimacy. They include the different "advisory councils" (*Beiräte*) such as the *Deutsches Ethikrat* (German Ethic Council), the *Rat für nachhaltige Entwicklung* (Advisory Council for Sustainable Development), the *Sachverständigenrat zur Begutachtung der gesamtwirtschaftlichen Entwicklung* (Advisory Council of Evaluators for the Evaluation of Total Economic Development) and the *Wissenschaftlicher Beirat für globale Umweltveränderung* (the Scientific Advisory Council for Global Environmental Change). These councils have become important pillars of policy-making in Germany. Other Tier 2 agents include research institutions, businesses and industry agents (either individually or as proponents of *Verbände* (associations)), the public transportation sector (represented by either individual entities or by associations) and labor unions. Foundations are considered Tier 2 agents, because they influence power relations between Tier 2 agents through their capacity-building activities. The media is considered here as a policy entrepreneur, because it often pursues its own interests, such as the accountability of policy-makers and the capacity-building of other policy entrepreneurs, and even of the audience by providing information. Political parties have been categorized as Tier 2 agents. Although they set the pace and direction of government policies and are often even political parties building the government or its coalition, as the German political party culture demonstrates, they can pursue other interests. In addition, government ministries can pursue policies that are the results of compromises with coalition partners, which can be unacceptable to the political base of the party. Furthermore, groups within a political party that control different levels (federal, state and local) may pursue contradictory views. Moreover, referring back to the "the efficient" and "the dignified"-dichotomy presented in the previous chapters, in this context, Tier 1 represents the "efficient" while Tier 2 the "dignified." Finally, Tier 3 refers to the different audiences that assess the interplay between the efficient and the dignified. It includes the German audience, the EU audience, the global audience, as well as the distinct constituents of Tier 2 agents.

The matrix also demonstrates the system and process roles of Tier 1 and Tier 2 agents in the transformation process towards sustainable transport. While some agents can either push for change (change agents), others are more interested in ensuring stability by minimizing change (status quo agents). For example, the transportation ministry can be regarded as a change agent. Responding to structural changes in the transport sector, which may include new technological innovation that favors the sustainable development of the sector, it sets the agenda for different negotiations with other Tier 1 agents. Other Tier 1 agents, such as the Finance Ministry, may be keen on ensuring that the propositions of the change agents will not undermine the fiscal health of the country, thus initially acting as a brake to changes, at least until uncertainties about the future costs of transformation can be calculated and managed. In addition, some agents can be both a change and a status quo agent due to the complexity of the issues involved, where in some issues they seek change and in some they resist. For example, the Ministry of Economy and Energy can both **push** and **pull** the process depending on the issues involved. This might be initially seen as contradictory or even irrational behavior on behalf of the agent. In this situation, this ministry is dependent on how issues can be decoupled. For example, the Ministry of Economy and Energy on the one hand limit the pace of fuel switch from diesel to electric cars to protect the German car industry (pull), but on the other hand implement policy instruments to unlock carbon lock-ins in the car industry (push).

Moreover, the process roles of the agents refer to how each agent from every tier can contribute or inhibit the transformation process. For example, scientific communities as Tier 2 agents can provide inputs for evidence-based decision-making that ensure the effectiveness of transport policies and thus the legitimacy of relevant procedures. Other agents, such as the car industry, can be learners in the process, which, once persuaded through interactions with other agents, will be important game changers in the process. Scientific communities and think tanks can accelerate this learning process through partnerships and networks. Agents such as foundations and think tanks are relevant to the process, as providers of resources and proponents of capacity-building. They can, for example, increase funding to universities and research institutions that focus on public acceptance of public transportation systems.

The power base identifies the different sources of leverage for each agent. Some agents, through their access to expert knowledge, depend on procedural power to pursue their interests when interacting with the others. For example, the credibility of the Ministry of Economic Cooperation and Development *vis-à-vis* foreign partners is defined by the know-how it can provide to other countries. Few agents can employ leverage through negative power, which can successful increase the costs and efforts needed to implement certain policies. For example, individual federal states (*Bundesländer*) can decide to block bills proposed by the federal government irrespective of their political party affiliations. Citizen groups that believe that building new train stations in their communities could attract criminals, drug addicts, and "cheap" tourism have different ways of blocking decisions or increasing the costs of implementing projects.

The negotiation analysis refers to the interests and anticipated negotiation style of agents when engaging in various levels of bargaining. The interests reflect the social mandate of these agents. Understanding these interests promotes flexibility and creativity in forging agreements. For example, in understanding that consumer protection will most likely be in the interests of the Ministry on Justice and Consumer Protection when it comes to sustainable transport, other agents wishing to achieve its support will need to include proposed stipulations ensuring consumer protection. Other interests of this ministry may include ensuring security and safety in transit infrastructures. Moreover, agents are anticipated to employ specific negotiation styles, which often depends on the agents' role in the transformation process. For example, the European Commission might be highly competitive in the process to compensate for its position of merely responding or reacting to decisions made in Berlin (or Bonn). Other agents, such as federal state governments and local governments that employ negative power, will very likely be competitive in negotiating with the federal government, because veto power has the initial logic of preventing something. Agents such as the Ministry of Economy and Energy may tend to employ an avoidant negotiation style, because of its ambivalence to sustainable transport. With uncertainty, these actors will very likely be trapped in an indecisiveness dilemma. Thus, they will very likely avoid agreeing to much-needed, immediate commitments.

The conflict analysis pertains to the definition of conflict cleavages or the threshold where confrontation becomes more acceptable or desirable than inhibition. The conflict can refer to issues, processes, and procedures. In addition, conflict analysis summarizes each agent's understanding of viable methods to achieve resolution of conflicts. For example, labor groups may see the conflict as resulting from inequitable procedures due to hierarchical relationships in the context of mutual dependence. For these labor groups, resolving procedural inequities will very likely employ context-sensitive approaches and will specifically target compensatory mechanisms for specific imbalances. The Federal Ministry of Employment and Social Affairs may see the conflict arising because of unclear jurisdictions, which can be resolved through deductive approaches through which acceptable principles are initially achieved, and then applying these principles to concrete issues. For example, this Ministry will very likely focus first on reconciling workers' rights for employees of both the public transport sector and the car industry to the principles of sustainable transport.

'Engagement' refers to the ways in which agents can be mobilized in a process from the perspective of Tier 1 agents. Engagement is highly differentiated, depending on their role and their potential inputs into the transformation process. Tier 1 agents can empower, collaborate, consult, involve, or inform Tier 2 agents. For example, Tier 1 agents may choose to collaborate with selected Tier 2 agents such as scientific communities and think tanks. These selected agents can provide policy briefs and policy recommendations during consultations, or even appoint Tier 2 representatives to various expert committees. Others Tier 2 agents can be empowered through capacity-building measures (e.g., funding, access to information), because the fulfilment of their interests is to the benefit of Tier 1 agents. This empowerment can vindicate the social mandate of Tier 2 agents and help reinforce their identities as policy entrepreneurs are eventually able to reciprocate, which further legitimizes the process.

Tier 1 agents might also decide to limit or prevent the participation of certain Tier 2 agents due to a number of political and logistical reasons. These Tier 2 agents are merely informed. Nevertheless, those policy entrepreneurs who are merely informed will very likely still seek other means of influencing Tier 1 agents, depending on the capacity and autonomy of state institutions—from producing position papers to mobilizing street protests and boycotts through the media. Some will seek to influence public opinion and deliver sociolinguistic narratives to the audience which might be successful in gaining the attention of Tier 1 agents. For example, the Stuttgart 21 movement in Germany targeted the German railway corporation (*Deutsche Bahn*), leading not only to a loss for the *Christian Democratic Union* (CDU)-led conservative state government in Baden-Württemberg, but also to the massive increase in the costs of re-building the central station in the city of Stuttgart. The costs increased from 4 billion euros to 9 billion euros due to delays and additional provisions stipulated by later court orders that were successfully demanded by citizen groups. The Stuttgart 21 case proves that public acceptance can be a huge barrier in pursuing the *Verkehrswende*.

Entry points to transformation towards sustainable transport reflect the opportunities for each agent during and after the transformation process. These entry points may result from positive externalities, co-benefits and synergies. Some entry points are purposive, and others are emergent. Purposive entry points refer to benefits for each agent from additional measures to support sustainable transport that are in anyway planned to achieve other developmental goals. For example, the German Environmental Ministry (*BMU*) seeks to mitigate climate change through emission reduction. Because *Verkehrswende* seeks to decouple transport emissions from GDP growth, the BMU will most likely be motivated to support the *Verkehrswende*. Another example is the Ministry of Finance (*BMF*), which will most likely support the introduction of new taxes, such as fuel taxation and carbon pricing, needed to implement the *Verkehrswende*, because these new taxes could help the *BMF* maintain the fiscal health of the government. Emergent entry points are the direct, positive effects of sustainable transport that could motivate the support of agents. For example, the expectation that the *Verkehrswende* will very likely lead to the reduction of massive public investment in road infrastructure construction and maintenance will persuade the *BMF* to support the *Verkehrswende*.

Caveats to support transformation are the reasons behind the agent's reluctance or opposition to sustainable transport. Most *caveats* refer to perceived future disadvantages as direct results of redistribution, double contingencies, political risks or even redundancy. For example, because of the redistribution for the EU Community (as an audience), the German *Verkehrswende* might further constrain EU wide electricity transmission lines, as well as put vehicles from other EU countries transiting in Germany in a disadvantageous position should fees for road use be introduced on German highways to motivate the use of public transportation (redistribution). As an example of double contingencies, the Media as a Tier 2 agent might be confronted with additional uncertainties and credibility problems due to its lack of technical expertise in issues relevant to *Verkehrswende*. Political parties might estimate the political risks of the *Verkehrswende* and refrain from pursuing unpopular measures such as the introduction of road use fees or the increase of a car tax and of a speed limit on all parts of the German *Autobahn*. In addition, private households might be indifferent to the sentiments of other private households in other areas directly affected by the construction of necessary infrastructure, the limitation of parking spaces, or the closure of city centers to car use. They are, in this case, essentially redundant and will most likely be supportive when they have direct benefits or be adversarial when personally confronted by negative effects (the '*not-in-my-backyard, but yes if in the backyard of the others*' mentality).

Positions for further actions are demanded of agents to materialize their purpose as the transformation process unfolds. These positions have direct implications for the various levels of functional, institutional, and bargaining interactions. Some positions will call for more **generic outcomes, which might enable different understandings of guiding principles and formulas**. For example, some agents will look at the impact of the *Verkehrswende* on the egalitarian public space. Will the *Verkehrswende* promote interactions between citizens from different backgrounds or will it further reinforce segregation? Policy-makers will need to revisit and, if necessary, modify the compatibility of the principles of the *Verkehrswende* to those existing local narratives that frame principles. Will the construction of new rail networks be compatible with local identities (and traditions), particularly when gentrification through suburbanization arises? Will the increased property value and accessibility of real estate eventually drive out vulnerable, poor households?

Other positions may call for **more time and flexibility to find technical solutions within the problem frame**. For example, creating more opportunities for interdisciplinarity and systems thinking might allow the improvement of the intermittency problems of renewable energies that are significant for electric and hybrid cars. In addition, improving access to modern forms of transportation depends on income levels and income distribution. However, levels of income are also dependent on access to affordable and reliable transportation technologies. This 'vicious cycle' reiterates the limitations of technical solutions. Therefore, technology-driven policies need to work in concert with other development policies such as employment, income, institutional structures, social objectives, environmental integrity, and regional or local development.

Some positions might demand the targeting of the **development of relations and communication channels**, while others may focus on **policy and bargaining games**. Dialogue processes have wide applicability in *Verkehrswende*. Not only can they support the maturity of relevant technologies through provider-user support systems, they can also enhance input and output legitimacy. Through mechanisms for feedback and flexibility in programs and projects, dialogue becomes an investment and not a cost. The establishment of networks and cooperation bodies can help create and maintain various centers of excellence as spaces for knowledge-sharing on different issues that cut across policy priorities.

As a disclaimer, the example of the matrix and stakeholder engagement plan for the German *Verkehrswende* is, to date, merely conceptual, but still useful in many ways. While assumptions of the profiles of the stakeholders were made based on interpretations of the existing literature and on anecdotal analysis, there are still open issues that require further research. Nevertheless, it demonstrates how emerging coordination and collaboration problems, as well as planning issues can be anticipated. In addition, it identifies the areas of the German *Verkehrswende* that may not yet be fully understood (Table 14.3).

Table 14.3 Stakeholder Matrix and Engagement—Transformation towards Sustainable Transport (source: own representation)

Stakeholders		**Roles**		**Power base**	**Negotiation analysis**		**Conflict analysis**		**Engagement**		**Entry points to transformation towards sustainable transport (selection)**	**Caveats to support transformation towards sustainable transport**	**Positions for Further Actions**
		System role	Role in the process		Interest	Negotiation style	Definition of conflict	Understanding of the methodology for resolution	Type of engagement	Output of engagement			
Tier 1 (Agents)	BMU (Environment)	change agent	decision-maker; leader	procedural power through expert reviews, agenda-setting); positional power; negative power (refusal of permits)	environmental integrity	collaborative	conflict arising from diffuse jurisdictions and mandates challenging the *Ressortprinzip or principle of ministerial autonomy* (structure) as well as from variation in rationales (processes)	move directly toward what seems to them most significant; use of the principle of joint cabinet decision-making	collaborate	strategy paper, position paper, workplan, implementation plan; draft bill	reduction of air pollution; finding how transport emissions can be strongly decoupled from GDP growth; reduction of fuel, waste, chemical, oil spill, and other hazardous particulates discarded from aircrafts, cars, trucks, ships, and trains or from port and airport terminal operations that can contaminate hydrographic systems.	new environmental concerns through the importation of raw materials for batteries; expansion of grid systems needed for electric cars; some biofuels being environmentally poor and causing inequalities by inducing increases in food prices; political costs due to perceived political opposition of constituents; negative transport-related impacts of the development on areas of designated landscape importance; transport-related impact of the development on areas of nature conservation or biodiversity and Earth heritage interests (such as geology) where they interact with roads; loss of fertile lands due to transportation infrastructure constructions; endangered animal species as a result of changes in their natural habitats and the reduction of ranges	prevention of harm to biodiversity; inclusion of sustainable transport into sustainable urban environment planning; understanding the key environmental barriers to effectively identifying, managing and implementing equitable, affordable, low-carbon and innovative transportation systems; the consolidation of mitigation efforts in the transport sector; revalidation of new vehicle and fuel standards *vis-à-vis* environmental integrity;

Stakeholders		Roles		Power base	Negotiation analysis		Conflict analysis		Engagement		Entry points to transformation towards sustainable transport (selection)	Caveats to support transformation towards sustainable transport	Positions for Further Actions
		System role	Role in the process		Interest	Negotiation style	Definition of conflict	Understanding of the methodology for resolution	Type of engagement	Output of engagement			
	BMVI (Transport & Digital Infrastructure)	change agent	decision-maker; leader; agenda-setter	power through the control of resources (transportation as service); information power; procedural power (expert knowledge)	mobility	collaborative	conflict arising from diffuse jurisdictions and mandates challenging the *Ressortprinzip or principle of ministerial autonomy* (structure) as well as from variation in rationales (processes)	inductive approach by dealing pragmatically with encountered difficulties and underlying principles may become discernible only in the end; use of the principle of joint Cabinet decision-making	collaborate	strategy paper, position paper, workplan, implementation plan; draft bill	reduction of traffic congestion; decrease of upfront costs; elimination of barriers to market entry for electric vehicles (especially those related to range anxiety)	high costs of immediate construction of infrastructures such as the expanding grid systems and rapid construction of charging stations; political costs due to perceived political opposition of constituents	strategic partnership between BMU and BMVI; reduction of complexity; clarification of mandates and jurisdictions in the context of cross-cutting issues; improvement of security of transport infrastructures; addressing inherent weaknesses of the transport planning processes—national or urban (basically have remained "technical processes"

Stakeholders		**Roles**		**Power base**	**Negotiation analysis**		**Conflict analysis**		**Engagement**		**Entry points to transformation towards sustainable transport (selection)**	**Caveats to support transformation towards sustainable transport**	**Positions for Further Actions**
		System role	Role in the process		Interest	Negotiation style	Definition of conflict	Understanding of the methodology for resolution	Type of engagement	Output of engagement			
	BMJV (Justice & Consumer Protection)	status quo agent	decision-maker; guardian of tolerable window; reminder of existing norms and principles	sanctioning power; power through control of (human) resources; procedural power (agenda-setting); power through association ("in the name of the law")	consumer protection	collaborative	conflict arising from diffuse jurisdictions and mandates challenging the *Ressortprinzip or principle of ministerial autonomy* (structure) as well as from a variation in rationales (processes)	scoping for precedent cases and interpretation; normative activation by appealing to fairness, procedural and substantial justice; use of the principle of joint cabinet decision-making	collaborate	strategy paper, position paper, workplan, implementation plan; draft bill	change in lifestyle and consumer behavior among the youth	opening of new precedents for compensatory mechanisms (e.g., compensation for loss of property value in near proximity to new infrastructures such as transmission lines); political costs due to perceived political opposition from constituents	behavioral/lifestyle change; demand reduction through behavioral change

Stakeholders		**Roles**		**Power base**	**Negotiation analysis**		**Conflict analysis**		**Engagement**		**Entry points to transformation towards sustainable transport (selection)**	**Caveats to support transformation towards sustainable transport**	**Positions for Further Actions**
		System role	Role in the process		Interest	Negotiation style	Definition of conflict	Understanding of the methodology for resolution	Type of engagement	Output of engagement			
	BMBF (Education & Research)	change agent	decision-maker; mediator; enhancer of the negotiation capacities of other stakeholders	procedural power (expert knowledge); referent power (connector); information power	legitimacy through evidence-based policy-making	collaborative	conflict arising from diffuse jurisdictions and mandates challenging the *Ressortprinzip* (structure) as well as from variation in rationales (processes)	division of labor and scoping for experiences from various stakeholders; use of the principle of joint cabinet decision-making	collaborate	strategy paper, position paper, workplan, implementation plan; draft bill	need for evidence-based decisions; technological spill-overs	lack of trust in expert knowledge; political costs due to perceived political opposition from constituents	strategic partnerships between research communities and BMVI; reduction of contingency and complexity; identify the knowledge gaps responsible for barriers and caveats; improvement of institutional capacity and incentives to translate good knowledge into effective actions

Stakeholders		Roles		Power base	Negotiation analysis		Conflict analysis		Engagement		Entry points to transformation towards sustainable transport (selection)	Caveats to support transformation towards sustainable transport	Positions for Further Actions
		System role	Role in the process		Interest	Negotiation style	Definition of conflict	Understanding of the methodology for resolution	Type of engagement	Output of engagement			
	BMF (Finance)	status quo agent	decision-maker; learner; spoiler; brake; controller of socio-linguistic narratives	power through the control of resources; negative power; formal power	improvement of fiscal health	competitive	conflict arising from diffuse jurisdictions and mandates challenging the *Ressortprinzip or principle of ministerial autonomy* (structure) as well as from variation in rationales (processes)	inductive approach by dealing pragmatically with encountered difficulties and underlying principles may become discernible only at the end; use of the principle of joint cabinet decision-making	collaborate	strategy paper, position paper, work-plan, implementation plan; draft bill	introduction of new taxes such as fuel taxation and carbon pricing; financial profitability of mass transit options; reduction of regressive car use that requires massive public investment for road infrastructure construction and maintenance	high upfront costs for new infrastructures; austerity measures; *Schuldenbremse* (debt ceiling); political costs due to perceived political opposition from constituents	market incentives and finance instruments; fuel taxation and carbon pricing; elimination of vehicle subsidies; de-linkage between planning and financing

Stakeholders		**Roles**		**Power base**	**Negotiation analysis**		**Conflict analysis**		**Engagement**		**Entry points to transformation towards sustainable transport (selection)**	**Caveats to support transformation towards sustainable transport**	**Positions for Further Actions**
		System role	Role in the process		Interest	Negotiation style	Definition of conflict	Understanding of the methodology for resolution	Type of engagement	Output of engagement			
	BMWi (Economy and Energy)	change agent/ status quo agent	decision-maker; learner; spoiler; brake; controller of socio-linguistic narratives; focal point of interests of economic groups	power through the control of resources; negative power; formal power; reward power; coercive power	economic competitiveness of Germany (e.g., through energy security)	avoiding	conflict arising from diffuse jurisdictions and mandates challenging the *Ressortprinzip or principle of ministerial autonomy* (structure) as well as from variation in rationales (processes)	inductive approach by dealing pragmatically with encountered difficulties and underlying principles may become discernible only at the end; use of the principle of joint Cabinet decision-making	collaborate	strategy paper, position paper, workplan, implementation plan; draft bill	increase in demand for energy; impulses for battery technologies and their technological maturity; enhanced energy security; decreased dependence on fossil-fuels	existing carbon lock-ins in industries; concerns about increased import dependence on Asia for batteries; large unmanageable redistributive consequences leading to distorted market signals; political costs due to perceived political opposition from constituents	sectoral approaches; coupling sustainable transport and economic development

Stakeholders		Roles		Power base	Negotiation analysis		Conflict analysis		Engagement		Entry points to transformation towards sustainable transport (selection)	Caveats to support transformation towards sustainable transport	Positions for Further Actions
		System role	Role in the process		Interest	Negotiation style	Definition of conflict	Understanding of the methodology for resolution	Type of engagement	Output of engagement			
	BMZ (Economic Cooperation & Development)	change agent	decision-maker; mediator; enhancer of capacities; monitor and verification agent; focal point of German interests in other countries	expert power; procedural power (agenda-setting); referent power	protection of economic well-being	collaborative	conflict arising from diffuse jurisdictions and mandates challenging the *Ressortprinzip or principle of ministerial autonomy* (structure) as well as from variation in rationales (processes)	inductive approach by dealing pragmatically with encountered difficulties and underlying principles may become discernible only in the end; use of the principle of joint Cabinet decision-making	collaborate	strategy paper, position paper, workplan, implementation plan; draft bill	increased pool of inputs for Germany's international development assistance projects; increased partnership with foreign governments; finding how transport emissions can be strongly decoupled from GDP growth	lack of clarity around jurisdiction; political costs due to perceived political opposition of constituents	clarification and improvement of technology transfer schemes; inclusion of sustainable transport into sustainable economic development planning; assessment of the key economic barriers to effectively identifying, managing and implementing equitable, affordable, low-carbon and innovative transportation systems; formulation of integrated policies reflecting the multi-sectoral nature of transport and the necessity of the vertical and horizontal coordination of actions

Stakeholders		Roles		Power base	Negotiation analysis		Conflict analysis		Engagement		Entry points to transformation towards sustainable transport (selection)	Caveats to support transformation towards sustainable transport	Positions for Further Actions
		System role	Role in the process		Interest	Negotiation style	Definition of conflict	Understanding of the methodology for resolution	Type of engagement	Output of engagement			
	BMAS (Employment and Social Affairs)	status quo agent	decision-maker; reminder of existing norms and principles related to social issues and workers' rights	negative power; referent power; expert power; power through control of resources	labor protection	avoiding	conflict arising from diffuse jurisdictions and mandates challenging the Ressortprinzip (structure) as well as from variation in rationales (processes)	deductive approach by looking first for acceptable principles and then applying them to concrete issues; use of the principle of joint cabinet decision-making	collaborate	strategy paper, position paper, workplan, implementation plan; draft bill	decrease of travel time from home to work; increase of employment in the transportation and energy sectors	labor interests of workers in the car industry; political costs due to perceived political opposition from constituents	protection of labor rules and norms; pronounce the key social barriers to effectively identifying, managing and implementing equitable, affordable, low-carbon and innovative transportation systems; addressing the gender-related challenges of sustainable transport

Stakeholders		Roles		Power base	Negotiation analysis		Conflict analysis		Engagement		Entry points to transformation towards sustainable transport (selection)	Caveats to support transformation towards sustainable transport	Positions for Further Actions
		System role	Role in the process		Interest	Negotiation style	Definition of conflict	Understanding of the methodology for resolution	Type of engagement	Output of engagement			
	BMG (Health)	change agent	decision-maker; focal point of possible co-benefits	referent power; expert power; negative power	health protection	collaborative	conflict arising from diffuse jurisdictions and mandates challenging the *Ressortprinzip* or principle of ministerial autonomy (structure) as well as from variations in rationales (processes)	inductive approach by dealing pragmatically with encountered difficulties and underlying principles may become discernible only at the end; use of the principle of joint cabinet decision-making	collaborate	strategy paper, position paper, workplan, implementation plan; draft bill	savings from prevented health costs due to lower air pollution and dust (*Feinstaub*) as well as savings from avoided sickness related absences of employees; promotion of personal physical activities leading to increased public health benefits from more physical activities	health risks arising from complementary technologies and infrastructures; political costs due to perceived political opposition from constituents	improvement of measurement of savings for public health

Stakeholders		Roles		Power base	Negotiation analysis		Conflict analysis		Engagement		Entry points to transformation towards sustainable transport (selection)	Caveats to support transformation towards sustainable transport	Positions for Further Actions
		System role	Role in the process		Interest	Negotiation style	Definition of conflict	Understanding of the methodology for resolution	Type of engagement	Output of engagement			
	EU Commission	status quo agent/ change agent	brake; accelerator; reminder of existing norms and principles (e.g. EU norms on subsidies)	negative power; positional power (hierarchy)	protection against unfair subsidies	competitive	conflicts arising from differences on procedures of implementation of directives	cognitive approach by moving directly toward what seems to them most significant (for example the interaction itself)	collaborate	workplan, implementation plan; directives	setting the pace for other EU countries in sustainable transport; elimination of vehicle subsidies	dominance of Germany in the EU electricity market; volatility of electricity prices in certain EU countries; *Maut* fees in German highways causing disadvantages to other EU countries; political costs due to perceived political opposition of constituents	guarding against national subsidies; implementation of EU-wide standards on vehicle emissions; formulation of integrated policies reflecting the multi-sectoral nature of transport and the necessity of vertical and horizontal coordination of actions
	Bundesländer (Federal States)	status quo agent	decision-maker; implementing body; brake; agenda-setter; discourse entrepreneur	negative power through veto (*Bundesrat*); positional power; procedural power (implementing bodies of policies)	fiscal health	competitive	conflicts arising from top-down interventions (process and procedure) as well as from structural imbalances and privileges (structure)	inductive approach by dealing pragmatically with encountered difficulties and underlying principles may become discernible only at the end	collaborate	strategy paper, position paper, workplan, implementation plan	sustainable mobility solutions resolving problems of economies of scale in rural areas; equitable mobility access between federal states	high upfront costs for new infrastructures; austerity measures; *Schuldenbremse* (debt ceiling); political costs due to perceived political opposition of constituents	ownership of sustainable transport; formulation of integrated policies reflecting the multi-sectoral nature of transport and the necessity of vertical and horizontal coordination of actions; decentralization of powers and responsibilities

Stakeholders		Roles		Power base	Negotiation analysis		Conflict analysis		Engagement		Entry points to transformation towards sustainable transport (selection)	Caveats to support transformation towards sustainable transport	Positions for Further Actions
		System role	Role in the process		Interest	Negotiation style	Definition of conflict	Understanding of the methodology for resolution	Type of engagement	Output of engagement			
	Gemeinde (Local governments)	status quo agent	decision-maker; implementing body; direct contact for citizens; discourse entrepreneur	negative power; positional power (implementing bodies); informational power; control of resources	fiscal health	competitive	conflicts arising from top-down interventions (process and procedure)	inductive approach by dealing pragmatically with encountered difficulties and underlying principles may become discernible only in the end	collaborate	strategy paper, position paper, workplan, implementation plan	sustainable mobility solutions resolving problems of economies of scale in rural areas; sustainable transport can curb tourism in their areas; reduction of the conversion of scarce pedestrian spaces to car parking; bringing communities together/social inclusion	space problems due to need for 36,000 public charging stations and 7,000 public fast charging stations; NIMBY dilemma; political costs due to perceived political opposition from constituents; negative transport-related impact of the development of the townscape; severing of social and economic cohesion through new transport facilities that cut across an existing urban community	ownership of sustainable transport; highlight and expand the benefits of sustainable transport to local community development; addressing ~~of~~ existing urban patterns as lock-ins; formulation of integrated policies reflecting the multi-sectoral nature of transport and the necessity of the vertical and horizontal coordination of actions; decentralization of powers and responsibilities

Stakeholders		Roles		Power base	Negotiation analysis		Conflict analysis		Engagement		Entry points to transformation towards sustainable transport (selection)	Caveats to support transformation towards sustainable transport	Positions for Further Actions
		System role	Role in the process		Interest	Negotiation style	Definition of conflict	Understanding of the methodology for resolution	Type of engagement	Output of engagement			
Tier 2 (Context-related Policy Entrepreneurs)	Think Tanks (e.g., AGORA)	change agent	providers of scientific inputs; discourse entrepreneur	procedural power (expert knowledge and expertise)	evidence-based decision-making, establishment of sustainability principles	collaborative	diverse: lack of structure (e.g., demand for sustainability principles)	systemic and integrated approaches	consult	policy briefs; policy recommendation; side-events; informal events; publications; reports	increase of demand for analyses resulting from cross-cutting issues	example of diverse *caveats*: loss of social mandate for think tanks either rejecting transformation in general or specific issues	examples of diverse positions: appraisal of a range of transport policies and instruments for promoting sustainability at national, regional and local levels; decoupling car segment purchase from income (circumventing status symbol of luxury cars); investment in quality transit infrastructure; promotion of the use of ICTs for sustainable transport that support travel substitution, efficiency movements, organizational structure, retail structure, and location flexibility

Stakeholders		**Roles**		**Power base**	**Negotiation analysis**		**Conflict analysis**		**Engagement**		**Entry points to transformation towards sustainable transport (selection)**	**Caveats to support transformation towards sustainable transport**	**Positions for Further Actions**
		System role	Role in the process		Interest	Negotiation style	Definition of conflict	Understanding of the methodology for resolution	Type of engagement	Output of engagement			
	Science Platforms and Beiräte (advisory councils) representing Universities and Research organizations	change agent/ status quo agent	providers of scientific inputs; discourse entrepreneur	procedural power (expert knowledge and expertise)	evidence-based decision-making	collaborative	conflict arising through knowledge gaps on issues	both inductive and deductive approaches	consult	Public joint declaration, inputs in expert committees; policy briefs	diverse entry points for scientific communities: adequate calibration of models through application; solution-oriented research through solution-seeking research funding	diverse caveats: loss of scientific independence due to research mainly catering to in-demand issues; loss of credibility due to mainstreaming; accountability issues due to participation in closed-door meetings; lack of maturity of scientific results due to orientation towards the cycles and time frames of policy-makers	examples of diverse positions: critical analyses of sustainable transportation planning with an outlook to the future, aspects of e-mobility; infrastructure for e-mobility like solar charging stations and renewable fuel opportunities; full accounting of life cycle assessment (LCA) emissions from a transport-perspective requires the inclusion of emissions from the construction and maintenance of infrastructures such as bridges, tunnels

Stakeholders		Roles		Power base	Negotiation analysis		Conflict analysis		Engagement		Entry points to transformation towards sustainable transport (selection)	Caveats to support transformation towards sustainable transport	Positions for Further Actions
		System role	Role in the process		Interest	Negotiation style	Definition of conflict	Understanding of the methodology for resolution	Type of engagement	Output of engagement			
	ÖPNV (Bus, tram, taxi, car-sharing)	change agent	provider of best practices; agenda-setter; discourse entrepreneur	power through control of resources; referent power	mobility	collaborative	conflicts arising from structural imbalances and privileges (structure)	context-determined approaches	consult, empower	position paper	increased importance of public transport in urban development policy; reduction of exposure to oil price volatility and shocks	high upfront costs; low public acceptance of car-sharing; theft and vandalization of infrastructures; diffuse legislation; dependence on state subsidies	Revalidation of new vehicle and fuel economy standards; ensuring public safety within the premises of public transportation (train stations, bus stops); improvements to the local public transport network, walking, and cycling facilities; elimination of under-pricing of car use which distorts consumer choices (most road infrastructure is subsidized as it is considered a public service)

Stakeholders		**Roles**		**Power base**	**Negotiation analysis**		**Conflict analysis**		**Engagement**		**Entry points to transformation towards sustainable transport (selection)**	**Caveats to support transformation towards sustainable transport**	**Positions for Further Actions**
		System role	Role in the process		Interest	Negotiation style	Definition of conflict	Understanding of the methodology for resolution	Type of engagement	Output of engagement			
	Car Industry (both through *Verband* or as individual companies)	status quo agent	spoiler; brake; learner; agenda-setter; discourse entrepreneur	referent power; power through control of resources; procedural power (technical expertise)	revenues	competitive	conflicts arising from top-down interventions (process and procedure)	context-determined approaches	consult	position paper	electric mobility and new technologies as drivers for growth; prognosis of decreasing costs through improved battery technologies; less accidents due to improved efficiency of the vehicle fleet with more stringent standards adopted along with improved efficiency standards	decrease of revenues from conventional vehicles, particularly from cars with diesel motors; prices of electric vehicles and batteries still high (although reducing); lack of infrastructure, and recharging standards not uniform; vehicle range anxiety; lack of capital and electricity in some areas	improvement of the protection of intellectual property rights; incentives and market instruments to important transport technologies such as exhaust heat recovery systems; creative regulation and policy instruments that allow changes without excessive costs in emission standards
	Political Parties (*CDU/ CSU, SPD, Die Linke, Die Grünen, AfD*)	change agent/ status quo agent	focal point in various types of antagonism; agenda-setter; discourse entrepreneur	power through associations (in the name of justice etc)	electoral victory	competitive	conflicts arising from procedure and differences in ideologies (issues, processes)	deductive approach by looking first for acceptable principles and then applying them to concrete issues	inform	position paper	electoral gains through resolution of traffic congestion and mobility constraints	electoral loss due to unpopular measures such as speed limitations; political costs due to perceived political opposition from constituents	mixed positions due to the diversity of political parties such as universal access provided for the elderly, children, and people with disabilities; noise reduction; including transportation in planning the of egalitarian public spaces

Stakeholders		**Roles**		**Power base**	**Negotiation analysis**		**Conflict analysis**		**Engagement**		**Entry points to transformation towards sustainable transport (selection)**	**Caveats to support transformation towards sustainable transport**	**Positions for Further Actions**
		System role	Role in the process		Interest	Negotiation style	Definition of conflict	Understanding of the methodology for resolution	Type of engagement	Output of engagement			
	Energy Utilities (predominantly conventional energy (both through Verband or as individual companies))	status quo agent	provider of resources; discourse entrepreneur	referent power; power through control of resources; procedural power (technical expertise)	revenues	competitive	conflicts arising from top-down interventions (process and procedure); deficits or overproportioned outcomes of rules	context-determined approaches	consult	position paper	Revenues from electric cars; new legislation; increased flexibility and resilience	lagging of battery/storage technologies; grid management for mobility technologies	Gradual transition from fossil fuels to renewable energy; improvement of intermittency problems of renewable energies; improvement of grid infrastructures; supply differentiation
	Renewable Energy Sector (both through *Verband* or as individual companies)	change agent	provider of resources; discourse entrepreneur	referent power; power through control of resources; procedural power (technical expertise)	revenues	competitive	conflicts arising from structural imbalances and privileges (structure); deficits from unequal playing fields	context-determined approaches	consult, empower	position paper	Revenues from electric cars; new legislation	intermittency problems; cultural barriers; lack of appropriate infrastructure; speculation of investors; lack of public acceptance	fair playing field in the energy sector; support of technological breakthroughs in car batteries and energy storage

Stakeholders		Roles		Power base	Negotiation analysis		Conflict analysis		Engagement		Entry points to transformation towards sustainable transport (selection)	Caveats to support transformation towards sustainable transport	Positions for Further Actions
		System role	Role in the process		Interest	Negotiation style	Definition of conflict	Understanding of the methodology for resolution	Type of engagement	Output of engagement			
	Business & Industry Companies, Investors (banks) and Employers (including the freight and shipping industry) (both through *Verband* or as individual companies))	status quo agent	spoiler; brake; learner; agenda-setter; monitoring and verification; discourse entrepreneur	referent power; power through control of resources; procedural power (technical expertise)	revenues	competitive	conflicts arising from top-down interventions (process and procedure); deficits in rules	context-determined approaches	consult	position paper	savings from avoided sickness-related absences of employees; increased revenues from tourism; savings from decreased costs of transport; increased distribution activities through sustainable transport supporting e-commerce; new business opportunities	levies to equalize playing fields between conventional and sustainable transport providers; slow and unreliable or volatile policy-making; lack of appropriate infrastructure; relatively low risk-return profile of sustainable transport infrastructure; lack of opportunities relative to fossil-fuel based alternatives, due to market and government failures that fall short of accounting for the full costs of carbon-intensive transport modes (externalities, public goods dilemma); public investment still skewed towards carbon-intensive road transport modes (including infrastructures) discouraging private investment's shift towards sustainable transport; lower investment opportunities for private companies; lower returns on investment, high upfront costs for rail and metro investments and long development timelines and payback periods relative to road projects; larger-scale carriers operating on extensive networks that often need to be managed on a network basis; high risks or perception of risks faced by private investors throughout the life of projects	exemption of business and industry players from potential levies to promote sustainable transport; addressing the aversion of consumers to new types of vehicles with significantly different attributes such as size, range, length of refuelling or recharging time;

Stakeholders		**Roles**		**Power base**	**Negotiation analysis**		**Conflict analysis**		**Engagement**		**Entry points to transformation towards sustainable transport (selection)**	**Caveats to support transformation towards sustainable transport**	**Positions for Further Actions**
		System role	Role in the process		Interest	Negotiation style	Definition of conflict	Understanding of the methodology for resolution	Type of engagement	Output of engagement			
	Foundations	change agent/ status quo agent	provider of resources	power through control of resources; referent power	social legitimacy	collaborative	conflicts arising from imbalances in resources available to interest groups (agenda-setting)	context-determined approaches as implied by distinct interests	inform	position paper; funding of chosen projects deemed relevant	diverse	diverse *caveats* such as a lack of public acceptance and cultural barriers; negative impacts to the heritage of historic resources where they interact with development-generated transport measures	diverse positions: coherence of policies to achieve sustainable transport
	Media (conventional)	change agent/ status quo agent	provider of communication; maker of sociolinguistic narratives; keeper of institutional memory; accountability and transparency manager	annoyance and inconvenience power; referent power; coercive power (naming, blaming and shaming)	public access to information; accountability	competitive	conflict arising through gaps in communication (process)	context-determined and inductive approach	inform	newspaper articles; commentaries both in print and live; journals; blogs	diverse entry points: coverage of best practices, examples of personalities	diverse *caveats*: coverage of worse practices; sensational journalism with a tendency towards exaggerating problem issues; lack of technical expertise from journalists claiming absolute knowledge	diverse positions: transparency of various decision-making processes and consultations; access to information and data about measures

Stakeholders		**Roles**		**Power base**	**Negotiation analysis**		**Conflict analysis**		**Engagement**		**Entry points to transformation towards sustainable transport (selection)**	**Caveats to support transformation towards sustainable transport**	**Positions for Further Actions**
		System role	Role in the process		Interest	Negotiation style	Definition of conflict	Understanding of the methodology for resolution	Type of engagement	Output of engagement			
	Citizen Groups (including neighbourhood associations)	change agent/ status agent	direct contact with private households, recipients of programs/ policy instruments; discourse entrepreneur	negative power (boycott)	protection of properties; protection of liberties	competitive	conflicts arising from top-down interventions (process and procedure); deficits or over proportional outcomes of rules	context-determined approaches as implied by distinct interests	inform/ consult	protests, boycott, electoral results, support of alternative political groups	creation of new jobs, access to more opportunities; decrease of travel time; improvement of physical health; improvement of traffic congestion, noise and air pollution	increase of conventional transport expenses due to levies; unsafe infrastructures; cultural barriers such as the lack of a culture of walking; electric vehicle range anxiety; increase of price and accountability gaps due to privatization and diffuse private-public partnerships	safety; reduction of costs for private households; prevention or adequate compensation for displacement (e.g. expansion of train tracks, transmission lines); appropriate consultation of citizens; prevention of gentrification resulting from increased values of real estate after investment in public transportation
	Labor Unions	status quo agent	reminder of existing norms and principles; spoiler; brake;	negative power (strikes); referent power; procedural power (expert reviews, agenda-setting)	protection of workers' rights and safety	avoiding	conflicts arising from hierarchical relationships (actors and processes)	context-determined approaches	consult	position paper	creation of new jobs from public transport; promotion of far-reaching opportunities, reduced access time, travel costs and trip uncertainty	job loss in the car industry sector; political costs due to perceived political opposition from constituents	transition schemes for workers moving from one sector to another; adaption of working hours scheme to transport realities (work from home); affordability (percentage of income used to pay for transport) of transitions in the transport sector

Stakeholders		**Roles**		**Power base**	**Negotiation analysis**		**Conflict analysis**		**Engagement**		**Entry points to transformation towards sustainable transport (selection)**	**Caveats to support transformation towards sustainable transport**	**Positions for Further Actions**
		System role	Role in the process		Interest	Negotiation style	Definition of conflict	Understanding of the methodology for resolution	Type of engagement	Output of engagement			
Tier 3 (Audience)	EU Community	n.a.	approving body (legitimacy)	reward power	stability and economic progress	n.a.	n.a.	n.a.	inform	declaration; legal challenges	reduction of upfront costs due to Germany's pioneering role in sustainable transport; access to best practices; contribution of Germany's transport sector to EU-wide emission reduction	Germany's *Verkehrswende* as further accelerator of the deployment of renewable energy further straining the energy security of other EU countries; further constraints on EU wide transmission lines; further competitive advantage of Germany's car industry through German policy instruments that benefit local car sector	*vis-à-vis* Germany: demands that most likely relate to subsidies from the German State to the German car industry as well as to the hasty deployment of renewables, further reducing the price of renewables and pressuring EU countries that depend on fossil fuels
	German Public	n.a.	approving body (legitimacy)	reward power	human well-being	n.a.	n.a.	n.a.	inform	protests (demonstrations or election of protest parties; participation in consultation events	reduction of traffic congestion; decrease of upfront costs for public transportation; reduction of costs of hybrid and electric vehicles; elimination of range anxiety due to the development of technology; decrease of barriers to opportunities; more time for other activities	similar to those of the *Energiewende*, additional levels merely forwarded to private consumers; loss of space due to the need to construct charging stations; lack of participation and accountability	diverse positions: transparency of various decision-making processes and consultations; access to information and data about measures

Stakeholders		Roles		Power base	Negotiation analysis		Conflict analysis		Engagement		Entry points to transformation towards sustainable transport (selection)	Caveats to support transformation towards sustainable transport	Positions for Further Actions
		System role	Role in the process		Interest	Negotiation style	Definition of conflict	Understanding of the methodology for resolution	Type of engagement	Output of engagement			
	Global Community	n.a.	approving body (legitimacy)	reward power	human well-being	n.a.	n.a.	n.a.	inform	declaration; legal challenges	diverse entry points to sustainable transport	diverse caveats	diverse positions
	Investors and shareholders	n.a.	approving body (legitimacy)	power through control of resources; referent power	revenues	n.a.	n.a.	n.a.	inform	further investment or pull-out	diverse entry points to sustainable transport	diverse caveats	diverse positions
	Stakeholders of Interest Groups	n.a.	approving body (legitimacy)	power through control of resources; referent power	diverse interests including protection of public goods including cultural goods	n.a.	n.a.	n.a.	inform	intergroup dialogues or pull-out	diverse entry points to sustainable transport	diverse caveats	diverse positions
	Base of Political Parties	n.a.	approving body (legitimacy)	negative power; referent power; information power	achievement of societal well-being according to their ideologies and principles	n.a.	n.a.	n.a.	inform	interparty dialogue; change of leadership	diverse entry points to sustainable transport	diverse caveats	diverse positions

Conclusion—Creating Momentum for Transformation Through Purpose 15

Many experts and pundits from the popular media often depict sustainable, low-carbon transformation as a revolution (see Sawin & Moomaw 2009; Pan 2016a, 2016b). For example, Tom Delay (2009) of The Guardian sees "*a new revolution that fast tracks the deployment of a new set of technologies.*" He continues that the new low carbon economy is "*poised to be the mother of all markets and will be as transformative in its impact as the first industrial revolution.*" Delay sees this revolution as an opportunity for countries to re-establish themselves as major global competitors. For Janet Sawin and William Moomaw (2009) the 'renewable revolution' of the entire global energy system is a matter of preventing catastrophic climate change. In addition, for Claus Leggewie and Dirk Messner (2012), the 'Great Transformation towards a global low-carbon economy,' which can be compared to the Neolithic Revolution and the Industrial Revolution, is not self-perpetuating (*Selbstläufer*). They argue that while the main technological, economic, and social elements that will permit the transformation are already in motion, additional changes (behavioral change, social mandates, paradigm shifts, and structural changes) are still necessary to allow the transformation to unfold. **The momentum of transformation needs constant 'spurring.'**

Throughout this book, I have cautioned against labelling sustainable, low-carbon transformation as a revolution, because a revolution connotes a system that has collapsed, that has drastically realigned relationships, and that has created new winners and losers. As sustainable, low-carbon transformation is a process, linking it to a revolution is misleading if not useless, **because transformation needs to build not only through leapfrogging but also incrementally, with learning curves and consensus-building, while effectively absorbing new game-changing impulses that modify the equilibrium of policies/decisions.** A revolution produces anxieties through vacuums and 'surprises' that often justify

A. M. Hernández, *Taming the Big Green Elephant*, Globale Gesellschaft und internationale Beziehungen, https://doi.org/10.1007/978-3-658-31821-5_15

drastic and Draconian measures, including the suspension of hard-fought principles such as fairness, human rights and social equality. Because of the uncertainty of revolutions, potential losers attempt and are often successful at 're-mobilizing' support from various societal groups and organizing counter-movements, which further creates instability. In some cases, counter-revolutions as historical examples, such as the counter-reformation or even the current state of post-truth politics, might employ coercion that often surpasses the boundaries of what is acceptable, particularly when these movements assume the emotional narrative of struggle. This remobilization initiates self-enforcing dynamics that further increase complexity. Some of these dynamics may be successful in shattering negotiation processes and increasing the threshold for renegotiations. Finally, because sustainable, low-carbon transformation is a non-linear process, it can be strategically facilitated. In this case, the management of procedures needs both conceptual and empirical underpinnings to understand and adapt to challenges. Strategic planning means persistence and creativity. In addition, the reflexivity of the transformation can be useful in determining *ad hoc* strategies to resolve challenges at various levels of joint decision-making through the possibility of differentiating impacts and purposes. Reflexivity helps to achieve measurable, specific and credible results. It identifies what it takes to help focus emotions and energy by knowing which questions need to be asked and by thinking about the answers of questions around power, purpose, and success, which can mobilize individual and collective actions. What specific actions are needed to achieve a transformation towards sustainability?

The ultimate goal of this book is to provide a comprehensive and integrated **understanding** of sustainable, low-carbon transformation that is both global and domestic in its scope and that broadens the theoretical and methodological capacity of scholarly disciplines to analyze underlying concepts, ideas, principles, and notions relevant to **explaining** why and how distinct collective actions are reached as well as how functional, institutional, and bargaining interactions influence collective actions. I have integrated the 'understanding' and 'explaining' approaches to 'grasp' complex processes and dynamics that are often observed by stakeholders. 'Understanding' identifies the purpose and 'explanation' determines the necessary action.

Studying transformation processes is challenging. Possibly the most important question when analyzing transformation is to **estimate how much change or intervention (assuming that transformation is initiated by revisions of the status quo) can be tolerated by the system without causing system ruptures, without initiating fragmentation, without reproducing inequalities that made the transformation necessary in the first place, and without creating**

fractures as negative externalities to other systems. Interestingly, the most prominent reason why certain actors can (successfully) resist change is the claim that changes that are 'sold' as solutions may *de facto* lead, directly or indirectly, to more problems that could easily escalate into system ruptures. Particularly when changes are understood as threats to system stability, coercion (including physical violence) can be easily justified. I have argued that what is missing in the current discourse on the transformation towards sustainability is that there is the need for the transformation to stop, reflect upon, and modify processes.

As sustainable, low-carbon transformation deals with multiple processes, the analysis needs to grasp the connection between the departure point of the process and the point at which process goals are achieved. Studying transformation also implies the need to look at both the past and the future, as well as what the past means for the future and what the future means for the present. Although, in general, the past can be captured using historical analysis, assessing the meaning of a past event for the future is constrained by the fact that not all significant data and information can be found or is accessible when connecting, with absolute certainty, causes to effects in order to justify corrective interventions (including positive and negative externalities caused by actors to other actors, and causes by one modular sub-system to another sub-system). In addition, because studies in transformation also look at trajectories and development pathways, they need to address the specificities of making sense of the future. Is it possible to acquire the ability to predict future events or to predict how behavior will change when certain parameters have been or can be altered? Hence, uncertainty becomes an inevitable condition of transformation and major attention should be given to early warning and quick response mechanisms when implementing transformative goals. Decision-makers will also need to find ways to 'manage' uncertainty, not only to justify their decisions, but also to ensure that the most efficient decision can be made, even with incomplete information. Moreover, as a non-linear process, sustainable, low-carbon transformation will very likely witness self-driving dynamics and self-enforcing processes that have gained independence from agents due to the emergence of lock-ins.

A comprehensive and integrated understanding of sustainable, low-carbon transformation is established by the research approaches used in this book. After resolving the ontological and epistemological baggage of various concepts, ideas and notions relevant to sustainable low-carbon, gaps and trade-offs have been identified to analyze the proximity between the analytical value of sustainable, low-carbon transformation and its actual practical value for decision-makers. For example, by understanding the implications of the conflictive nature of transformation, strategies can be forged for stakeholders to allow them to benefit from several functional, institutional, and bargaining persuasive, and bargaining interactions. With this understanding, measures can be better explained to stakeholders, resolving credibility gaps resulting from the complexity of the issues involved and the diffuseness of the jurisdictions. By understanding that power refers to creating dependence on the monolithic architecture of the world system, collaboration and coordination problems can be resolved. The calculative meaning of connecting basic bargaining and policy games provides a new explanation for how weaker parties can effectively interact with stronger parties.

In this project, I have defined **transformation as shifting from the initially chosen (or taken) pathway to another pathway, as goals have been revised for the system to adapt to changes**. Pathways are sets of critical junctures and lock-ins that frame decisions and actions. With this definition, **sustainable, low-carbon transformation is then depicted as shifting from one pathway to another by shouldering transition costs, that is, the costs of detaching a system from existing unsustainable and carbon lock-ins**. The methodologies employed in this book follow a storyline to resonate the complexity of transformation processes. After identifying the theoretical parameters for the theoretical models (ideal types) presented in chapters 2 to 6 and chapter 8, an assessment of the case studies was conducted in chapters 9 through 12 to give context to sustainable, low-carbon transformation. The theoretical models (ideal types) used the negotiation perspective in understanding and explaining how interactions are managed in different policy models (authoritarian, democratic, etc.) as well as in different variations of policy models (institutional activity, post-democracy, and technocratic). In addition, chapters 9 to 12 'unmasked' sustainable, low-carbon transformation and demanded clear proximity to normativity. Functional, institutional, and bargaining interactions were highlighted, through which collective actions were made. In addition, data assessment through process-tracing and congruence methods has led to theory development (theoretical claims) (chapter 13) and a reflexivity analysis & engagement plan (chapter 14). A check-list of questions was presented to assist stakeholders when strategically preparing their engagement.

15.1 Theoretical Claims: A Theory of Transformative Pathways (TTP)

As the theoretical models were contextualized to test their empirical value, chapter 13 introduced a Conceptual Framework of Transformative Pathways (CFTP). This CFTP attempted to provide additional theoretical inputs to better grasp the complexity of shifting from the initially chosen or assumed pathway ('business-as-usual') to other pathways. As a framework, the CFTP provided an explanation of causality, which was substantiated using existing theories and empirical data. This explanation was supported by the case studies presented. Afterwards, an assessment of their ability to predict congruence was further evaluated, exploring its possible re-occurrence in future events as well as its applicability to other contexts.

The theory problematized how studies of transformation processes need to deal with normative and narrative bias when analyzing interactions within transformation systems, which are mainly attributed to the cognitive challenges brought by emotions, empathy (or the lack thereof), and biases. Because sustainable, low-carbon transformation requires justifications and legitimacy, implying that an additional analysis is needed to understand how social mandates and (input/output) legitimacies are achieved, normativity is inevitably a fundamental pillar of transformation. Furthermore, the theory addresses various methodological challenges brought about by the complexity of transformation, such as the difficulties of scaling up, identifying benchmarks, assessing tipping points, externalities & synergies, and evaluating boundaries.

Moreover, the CFTP argues that decision-making requires a basis or some points of reference for orientation. It introduces the four cognitive frames: *the social contract, the power game, discourses* and *outcomes*. These cognitive frames are stable constructs that provide a lens to see and understand the situation and to create a context for complex behavioral responses. Corresponding with the cognitive frames are stages of interaction: ***collaboration, coordination, deliberation, and application***, which address the various related problems of collective actions: ***collaboration problems, coordination problems, deliberation problems,* and *application problems***. While the cognitive frames pertain to the constitution of collective action, the stages of interaction concur within relationships among actors, between issues, and between structure & actors.

15.1.1 To Summarize, the Theory has made the Following Concrete Arguments:

- At the domestic level, if the levels of capacity and autonomy of the state facilitating the transformation process are low, then defection from the state-sponsored transformative pathway will be very likely.
- The increasing relevance of fractal decision-making systems in the context of sustainable, low-carbon transformation at both the global and domestic level is associated with the frequent occurrence of disconnections between various

bargaining and policy games. Fractal decision-making is likely to impose a polycentric order, both at the global and the domestic level.
- The diffusion of norms, principles, and standards within a system is associated with the concept of citizenry both at the global and national level, because citizenry underpins the flow of social practices among actors.
- At the domestic and global level, power asymmetries define the asymmetries of privileges. As the transformation process unfolds, if structural arrangements and institutions (including norms and practices) are preventing changes in the distribution of privileges and are actively seeking the reproduction of old privileges in previously powerful actors, then individual incentives to defect from the transformation process are likely to outweigh the incentives of continued cooperation/collaboration.
- At the global level, if the states are experiencing increased convergence, then the motivation to defect decreases. In other words, a convergence of norms, principles, and practices is necessary for cooperation.
- If critical junctures (and lock-ins) in the context of sustainable, low-carbon transformation create conflicts in social mandates, then there is a need to find a concept for the 'conversion' of relevant values through a 'common currency.'
- If the deliberation over the factors relevant to legitimacy, efficiency, and capacity focuses mainly on 'big bang' situations, then it will lose count of the importance of 'low' politics for systemic and social integration.

15.2 Further Recommendations for Facilitating the Transformation Towards Sustainability

Facilitating sustainable, low-carbon transformation to become the 'Great Transformation towards a global low carbon economy' (Messner 2015), and one that is comparable to the Neolithic and Industrial Revolutions, is not only necessary to concretize and make use of the lessons of past transformations to prevent or limit the occurrence and effects of vacuums and externalities, but also to ensure that human systems are able to develop adaptive mechanisms to ensure that aggregated changes will not lead to system ruptures.

15.2.1 Actors

The targets and ambitions of both state and non-state stakeholders should be aligned with the principles of sustainable, low-carbon transformation. This book has highlighted the elusiveness of motives and the fact that decisions are no longer merely about the facts. The elusiveness of motives remains a huge challenge for policy-making in the context of sustainable low-carbon, because deviancy is not always rational and predictable, making efforts to understand it highly complicated. Nevertheless, while these motives are a riddle, they can still be controlled. The convergence of the utility preferences of individuals and collective groups can be achieved and controlled through cooperation, where reciprocity is enhanced by learning curves and incremental values.

For the alignment of targets and ambitions to occur, appropriate data and information are needed for actors to adequately reflect upon their interests, and for them to recognize that fulfilling the interests of others is necessary to achieving one's own interests. Appropriate data and information do not mean completeness, as this is impossible. What is possible, however, is for actors to have genuine access to available information and for them to find ways of handling incomplete information, even when they need to make immediate decisions. In addition, as interactions are hosted by a system that is monolithic in its architecture, cooperation is the only viable way to address linkages of interests. As 'power' is understood by this book as the capacity to deter dependence, actors can develop strategies to make them indispensable to the others, giving them some level of leverage even though the others have evident financial and institutional advantages.

15.2.1.1 The Identification of the Appropriate Capacity of Stakeholders

In addition, there is a need to assess which size of the polities or of the public sector is preferable when facilitating the long-term integration of these sustainability projects. The case studies presented in this book have provided insights into the effects of the low capacity and low autonomy of the state. For example, as demonstrated by the case study of Jamaica, the success of sustainable, low-carbon transformation is also contingent upon the human resources capacity of the state to monitor and evaluate the transformation process. Is the state able to provide the technical expertise on various issues related to the transformation process? Is this 'lagging behind' of the state responsible for inefficient legislation and other policy instruments? When a state such as Jamaica is subjected to austerity measures as imposed by international donors, can the state really develop a 'healthy' capacity? Therefore, the facilitation of sustainable, low-carbon transformation will also need to assess the effects of international donors and creditors in terms of capacity-building. The dilemma of a state that is subjected to austerity measures is that the 'butterfly effect' of small provisions is inhibited, such as investments that are deemed to have small effects on the present but could lead to bigger effects in the medium- and long-term.

Nevertheless, the size of state apparatus is also determined by existing lock-ins, which, as shown by the case study on Jamaica, are causes that are maintained by a dependence on specific stakeholders. Carbon lock-ins will very likely lead to goals and actions from government agencies and state resources that will resonate these lock-ins, in terms of government subsidies and market incentives for example, which will most likely put further non-carbon technologies in a disadvantageous position. Therefore, there is a need to find an ideal size for the public sector, based on needs and not on lock-ins.

15.2.2 Issues

Sustainable, low-carbon transformation will involve a multitude of issues. Each issue will call for a different set of actors, structures, knowledge, and temporal & spatial contexts, as well as ontological and epistemological conceptions. Each issue will very likely produce externalities and feedbacks, which further complicate the planning of collective actions. In addition, issues will be prioritized differently by actors depending on how these issues are perceived as relevant problems. Further, addressing specific issues can create a demand for decisions that require efforts that cut across different modular sub-systems, each of which will very likely have distinct mandates, jurisdictions, senses of equality & 'fairness tolerable' windows, and sense of urgency.

With this complexity of issues, the facilitation of sustainable, low-carbon transformation will need to be able to 'detach' issues from all types of baggage to allow new ideas and concepts as well as paradigm shifts, and to eventually identify additional entry points for sustainable, low-carbon transformation. Such entry points can serve as departure points for collective actions. In addition, these entry points can be used to define various basic bargaining and policy games as multiple processes (e.g., consensus-building, state-building, economic transition, and de-colonization) unfold.

15.2.2.1 Revisit Public Discourses and Debate

Developing countries need to assess the relevance of the roots and origins of sustainable, low-carbon discourse, particularly, regarding sustainability. Many scholars suggest that the environmental roots of sustainability discourse in most European countries have created a basic asymmetry between the environment and the social (see Kapoor 2001; Agyeman & Evans 2004; Davidson 2009; Boström 2014). Davison (2009) and Kapoor (2001) argue that, as the concept of sustainability resulted from discourses on environmental forums, it carries a particular 'ontological and epistemological baggage', which creates a conservative bias towards how sustainability issues are defined and addressed. This bias causes, for example, the prioritization of environmental integrity over social justice.

Magnus Boström (2014) contends that while conservation of the environment is desirable, it is usually less important than the conservation of certain social sustainability aspects. He explains that environmental aspects generally take precedence over social aspects, because of the diffuse and multitudinous nature of social sustainability, which may refer to social welfare, quality of life, social justice, social cohesion, cultural diversity, democratic rights, gender issues, workers' rights, broad citizen participation, and the development of social capital & individual capabilities, among others (Boström 2012). This bias was demonstrated by the policies introduced and implemented by former Philippine Environmental secretary Gina Lopez during her brief tenure, when she prioritized environmental conservation over the livelihood of the thousands of individuals who lost their jobs. As a result, participatory opportunities were deliberately restricted by not inviting numerous stakeholders, as Gina Lopez did not see their relevance due to her narrow framing. As a result, these excluded actors (business groups, local government units, and community development groups) sought other forums to address their concerns. Although she attempted to reframe public discourse by equating social justice with environmental integrity, it became apparent that the 'ontological and epistemological baggage' of her environmental advocacy conflicted with the livelihood concerns of those affected by the closure of the mines.

The ontological and epistemological pretext of sustainable, low-carbon discourse is inevitably derived from the contemporary political priorities of the national government, as well as from tangible problem-issues. As most developing countries with medium-income levels demonstrate, their development trajectory is mainly driven by the process of consolidating power as these countries undergo state-building. The consolidation of power will likely define functional, institutional, and bargaining interactions, as stakeholders seek to maximize their individual utility before lock-ins are established. With various insurgencies controlling parts of several developing countries as well as boundary conflicts with neighboring countries, issues relevant to state-building will be virtually certainly inherent to the discourse on sustainability.

Without the historical environmental discourse that occurred in developed countries, the connotation of sustainability in these countries will very likely deviate from the connotation prevalent in the political and academic discourse. As highlighted by Mikael Klintman (2012), the dichotomy between local and global is often simplistically framed as a duality of social versus environmental concerns. Therefore, for many developing countries, the distance between the global and the local can be explained by this difference in discourse. What if the *caveats* for developing countries against embracing similar commitments to sustainable, low carbon exist because of the conditions wherein environmental sustainability is exogenous to them, as this concept was instilled in them by developed countries? If the Eurocentric discourse on sustainability is expected to be of value in developing countries from the 'South,' will this exacerbate the already existing gaps between the 'global' and the 'local,' where **the global is driven by environmental sustainability and the local by social sustainability**? Furthermore, assuming that the Eurocentric discourse on sustainability is inevitable, because of existing power asymmetries, how can climate policies in developing countries still achieve legitimacy, where gaps between the intangible global climate goals and the tangible social realities are evident?

The conflicts between developed and developing countries in terms of climate mitigation can be partly explained by the ontological and epistemological differences in the concepts of climate mitigation among countries. As climate policies were initiated by environmental scientists and advocacy groups, binding emission reductions are not inherent to the public discourse on sustainability in developing countries, preconceived as issues around state-building. In this regard, sustainable, low-carbon transformation in many developing countries will be framed by a concept of sustainability that is different to the concept framing the behavior and actions of most developed countries, where the dominance of environmental sustainability has defined concrete objectives, measurable indicators, and universal applications, and has elevated an approach based on the 'technocratic, top-down expert culture in environmental management' (Kapoor 2001) regarding deliberations on social and economic sustainability.

With the clarification and understanding of the ontological and epistemological differences of concepts related to sustainable, low-carbon transformation, how can 'frame-bridging' efforts be made to support sustainable, low-carbon transformation? How can frame-bridging lead to mutual learning experiences between actors as they engage in functional, institutional, and bargaining interactions? Can this frame-bridging also facilitate a different notion of politics and the *political* (see Davidson 2009)? Asymmetries resulting from ontological and epistemological differences between concepts of sustainable, low-carbon transformation can be effectively addressed by promoting the capacities of stakeholders.

15.2.3 Structures

The facilitation of sustainable, low-carbon transformation is also defined by the integration of multiple structures, which may both promote and inhibit the pace of transformation. While these structures are mutually complementing, others are mutually contradicting. Transformation is not unitary and encompasses transformation within multiple modular sub-systems, which may be converging or diverging. Structures are entities that have been intentionally and unintentionally established to manage various processes and can both drive and inhibit decisions and actions. The comparative analysis of structures across different modular sub-systems can provide insights into why a specific structure, for example, promotes transformation in one sector but inhibits another. How are these structures interconnected, and what happens when they are disconnected? Can actors effectively use this connectedness as a strategy to pursue their interests, as was demonstrated in the case study on the Philippines, where mining groups were successful in disconnecting from basic bargaining and policy games?

In addition, the effective integration of structures will also depend on the institutional designs and arrangements of each sub-system as well as of the whole system. Institutions require the careful planning of organizational design, checks & balances, legitimacy, and social mandates. Of equal importance to facilitation is the understanding of how structures can be self-reinforcing. As institutions and mechanisms become separated from the behavior of humans, additional resources are needed to ensure that these institutions and mechanisms comply with the principles of sustainable, low-carbon transformation.

15.2.3.1 Promoting Mobility and Global Networking

As Magnus Boström (2014) contends, some actors are entangled in a local context, whereas other actors move more freely between different levels (from local to global and vice versa) and can mobilize and combine various resources from their global networks. The precedence of environmental sustainability in public discourses on sustainable, low-carbon transformation is reinforced by the mobility of environmental groups as compared to that of social groups, which tend to be entangled at the local level, because of the local nature of social issues, as well as because of the structural limitations on global networks when addressing social sustainability, such as civil rights and gender equality.

The strategic use of new technologies to advance and promote innovative organizational structures and communication channels is inevitable. It can further improve the capacities of local stakeholders to forge useful partnerships and attract global attention to local concerns. The careful deployment of technologies needs to be complemented by improvements in the ability to monitor and intervene in institutional, functional, and bargaining interactions occurring at various levels to enable the identification of gaps and learning from best practices. Technologies should not be the only drivers of transformation, because by allowing this, other societal goals will very likely become secondary.

Moreover, additional resources are needed to help stakeholders to refrain from perceiving, framing, and representing a 'global view' or a universal interest that is too distant from local conditions (see Boström & Tamm Hallström 2010). As Eurocentric claims of universality are formalized, standardized, and institutionalized, improving the capacity of local stakeholders to interconnect and link local problems to global matters will very likely reduce the 'context blindness' and 'local uselessness' of these universal principles and standards. When theoretical knowledge (global), which tends to be abstracted and detached from the local context (see Cheyns 2011), ceases to subordinate practical knowledge (local) through improved interconnectedness, asymmetries resulting from ontological and epistemological differences in concepts of sustainable, low-carbon transformation will be less likely to define interactions between stakeholders.

As demonstrated by the case study on Mexico, the emergence of a bottom-up, public sphere is crucial to the sustainable, low-carbon transformation process. By developing the capacity of actors and their ownership of the process to highlight social sustainability, decisions that are made will most likely be more effective. As discussed, inclusivity is an investment that is often underestimated, because the costs of transition will not only be shouldered by more actors, but the total costs will also be limited, as individual stakeholders will limit the negative externalities that they are producing for the others, because they will also be paying for them.

15.2.4 Processes

Sustainable, low-carbon transformation is driven by the accumulation and orchestration of multiple processes, which can be both self-driving and managed. The growing numbers of actors relevant for the required paradigm shifts and behavioral changes as well as the types (including hybrids) of policy regimes imply the co-existence of multiple processes that are co-evolving. Transformative pathways involve processes that converge as lock-ins are established. Therefore, any facilitation of sustainable, low-carbon transformation will need to grasp the drivers of each of these relevant processes, including how and where these processes are inter-connected and how they are affecting each other. The pace of transformation of each sub-system also affects the pace of transformation of the others. When the transformation of a sub-system is 'too fast' or 'too slow,' it may send wrong or distorted signals to others. Rebound effects can also emerge in certain sub-systems, off-setting the gains made by the others.

Furthermore, any facilitation needs to effectively link these processes to contexts and collective actions to address mutual feedbacks. As an analysis of a process is often done by looking at its application to a specific context, it is a huge challenge to completely grasp the different cause-and-effect relationships that drive processes. As such, it is recommended that this analysis of processes be complemented by innovative methods of scientific inquiry that allow the detaching of processes from contexts to better understand causalities.

15.2.4.1 Highlighting the Long-Term Aspects of Interactions

Effectively abrogating carbon lock-ins will require a long-term outlook on interactions. As changes in the utility preferences of stakeholders will very likely require time, facilitating sustainable, low-carbon transformation will require additional resources to establish and maintain long-term platforms and incentive systems. As suggested by Nicolas Faysse (2006), establishing long-term multi-stakeholder platforms means better opportunities for capacity building. As entry points for sustainable low carbon transformation are identified, stakeholders can focus on synergies and co-benefits that will alter their utility preferences. Synergies and co-benefits require the linking of issues, where the realization of benefits will occur after a given set of time. As these synergies and co-benefits materialize, these long-term platforms and incentive systems will need to be documented and assessed, constituting a 'memory' that will ensure that these benefits are properly documented and therefore useful.

Nevertheless, because many sustainability projects have a limited time-frame, they use a 'project mind-set' (Casula Viffel & Thedvall 2012 p. 26). As such, there are missed learning opportunities resulting from the failure to connect these sustainability projects, assess impacts and feasibility, and modify future projects. As argued by Magnus Bostöm (2014), the integration of the social, economic, and environmental aspects addressed by these sustainability projects necessitates a learning period characterized by multiple communications and interactions. Therefore, the success of sustainable, low-carbon transformation is dependent on incrementalism.

15.2.5 Outcomes

Each modular sub-system has its own set of interactions, which include the resolution of problem-issues. Many types of agreements are produced, which can be both binding or non-binding. Most cooperation frameworks aim at producing binding agreements, as social trust is still elusive. However, reality shows that it is often better to achieve non-binding agreements than having no agreement at all. Furthermore, non-binding agreements often produce additional impulses for future agreements as learning unfolds. In addition, from the negotiation perspective, these outcomes can be relevant for agenda-setting, but not for the clarification of interests or the concretization of solutions. The outcome of interactions in one sub-system can either complement or compete with the outcomes of the others. Outcomes can be limited in their temporal validity or can be perpetual in their consequences. In addition, outcomes can be the means to an end or can be an end in themselves. Furthermore, the success of outcomes in achieving predetermined goals will depend highly on established compliance systems that can be dependent upon other outcomes. Ambiguities and flexibilities can be both useful and detrimental elements of outcomes.

15.2.6 Gaps in Knowledge and Future Research

While conducting this book, several gaps in the knowledge have been identified and collected. While some gaps were addressed, others were not, because they needed further theoretical and empirical analyses that could not be accommodated by this project. Some of them are presented in this section as suggestions for further future research.

This book attempted to introduce a conceptual foundation to the study of sustainable, low-carbon transformation. Major gaps in the knowledge refer to the methodological shortcomings of future studies, as the enormous variety of processes and technologies adds to the complexity of assessment (see Tanaka 2008; Siitonen et al. 2010). New systematic approaches and underlying methodologies are further needed to avoid double-counting, for example, due to the many different ways of attributing emissions (see Fischedick et al. 2014) or externalities.

The collection and assessment of data and information is confronted with a lack of globally standardized and homogenized data. An analysis of sustainable, low-carbon transformation involves multiple sectors, such as the private and public sectors as well as the sectors representing industry, energy, agriculture, etc.

There is a diversity in practices within and among sectors, leading to uncertainty, a lack of comparability, incompleteness, and doubts about the quality of available data. While some sectors are keen to produce data, others, such as the informal sector, refuse to cooperate. Sector data tend to be collected by the private sector, which is highly aggregated and gives little information about individual processes.

The availability and quality of data in the public domain is often subjected to political the calculations of authorities. In many cases, an improved understanding of the mitigation potentials, interplay, and costs, as well as environmental and socio-economic consequences of policies are desirable, but there are some situations where this improvement is linked with a fear of being compelled to decide in a specific direction, which may be contrary to the ideological stance of the policy-makers. Furthermore, an improvement in knowledge does not automatically mean a change in behavior, because this knowledge may not be aligned with one's identity or may not be useful, as the assessment of mitigation potentials on a global and national scale may fail to address the boundaries of global and national jurisdictions. Particularly when addressing trade-offs between many sustainable, low-carbon policy goals requires cross-cutting actions from competing and cooperating institutions, government agencies, and societal groups, the boundaries between them may be 'too high' to overcome. Addressing trade-offs will not only require an understanding of the net impacts of different types of policies, it also requires concretizing the linkages between them. As these linkages are very likely process-driven, mutual feedback can change over time, making it difficult to attribute effects to causes. In addition, the quantification and monetization of both positive and negative externalities are difficult to achieve, and, if done at all, are often not well-integrated into the decision-making processes.

Further gaps in knowledge refer to governance issues on sustainable, low-carbon transformation. There are questions around how partnerships of sectors, government bodies, civil society, and private governance for climate governance can overcome *caveats* brought about by existing ontological and epistemological baggage.

15.2.7 Final Message

A significant factor that hinders sustainable, low-carbon transformation is the establishment and use of 'false dichotomies' in understanding and explaining collective decisions and actions that are driven by elusive motives. These false dichotomies abuse gaps between rationality and preferences. Gideon Lasco (2018) problematizes the wide use of false dichotomies in political discourses where narratives such as "*stupid people with good intentions*... (are better)... *than smart people with bad intentions*" are offered and compel people pick between two options as if these were the only choices. As such, the analysis of sustainable, low-carbon becomes a matter of choice between rejection and support, where criticisms are easily branded as rejection of the entire transformation. Sustainable, low-carbon transformation involves issues that are complex, making it impossible to be either 'pro' or 'anti' sustainable, low-carbon transformation. For example, criticizing the wind energy projects of Danish companies in Mexico because they are causing irreversible social problems does not mean that one is anti-sustainability. In the same manner, when someone is 'eco' friendly, it does not mean that this person needs to stop using planes and cars as a means of transportation or stop printing out journal articles to read manually. As each one of us experiences sustainable, low-carbon transformation in different ways, we need to be open and empathic. We should not be chained to political correctness.

References

Abell, P. (2004) Narrative explanation: an alternative to variance-centered explanation? *Annual Review of Sociology* **30**, 287–310.

Abers, R. N. & Tatagiba, L. (2014) Institutional Activism: Mobilizing for Women's Health from Inside The Brazilian Bureaucracy: GT14 – Entre as Ruas e os Gabinetes: institucionalização e contestação nos movimentos sociais latino-americanos. *38º Encontro Anual da Anpocs.*

Abid, M. (2015) The close relationship between informal economic growth and carbon emissions in Tunisia since 1980: The (ir)relevance of structural breaks. *Sustainable Cities and Society* **15**, 11–21.

Abinales, P. (ed.) (1996) *The Revolution Falters. The Left in Philippine Politics After 1986.* Southeast Asia Program Publication, Ithaca, NY.

Abraham, J. (2017) Despite Trump, American companies are still investing in renewable energy. *The Guardian,* October 11. https://www.theguardian.com/environment/climate-consensus-97-per-cent/2017/oct/11/despite-trump-american-companies-are-still-investing-in-renewable-energy. Accessed 10/18/2017.

ABS-CBN News (2017) LP senators removed from key posts in Senate reorg. *ABS-CBN News,* February 27. https://news.abs-cbn.com/news/02/27/17/lp-senators-removed-from-key-posts-in-senate-reorg.

Aden, N. T. & Sinton, J. E. (2006) Environmental implications of energy policy in China. *Environmental Politics* **15** (2), 248–270.

Adger, W. N., Barnett, J., Chapin III, F. & Ellemor, H. (2011) This Must be the Place: Underrepresentation of Identity and Meaning in Climate Change Decision-Making. *Global Environmental Politics* **11** (2), 1–25.

Adler, E. & Haas, P. (1992) Conclusion: Epistemic Communities, World Order, and the Creation of a Reflective Research Program. *International Organization* **46** (1), 367–390.

Adorno, T., Frenkel-Brunswick, E., Levinson, D. & Sandof, N. (1950) *The Authoritarian Personality.* Hapres and Brothers, New York.

Aguayo Quezada, S. & Parra Rosales, L. P. (1997) *Las Organizaciones No Gubernamentales en Derechos Humanos: Entre la Democracia Participativa y la Electoral: Serie ONG de los Sesenta.*

A. M. Hernandez, *Taming the Big Green Elephant,* Globale Gesellschaft und internationale Beziehungen, https://doi.org/10.1007/978-3-658-31821-5

Aguilera Portales, R. E. (2010) La relación de una triada compleja: entre el derecho, la moral y la política. *Anuario de la Facultad de Derecho* **28**, 455–491.

Aguilera Portales, R. E. (2011) Educación Ciudadana para una Cultura de la Legalidad: Ejemplar dedicado a: Homenaje al Profesor Dr. Ferrando Montovani. *Letras jurídicas: revista electrónica de derecho* **12**.

Aguilera Portales, R. E. & Gonzáles Cruz, J. (2010) Estado democrático, sistemas de legalidad y corrupción en América Latina. *Revista telemática de filosofía del derecho (RTFD)* **13**.

Aguilera Portales, R. E. & Sánchez Garcia, F. R. (2010) Cultura política, sociedad civil y gobernabilidad democrática. *Letras jurídicas: revista electrónica de derecho* **10**.

Agyeman, J. & Evans, B. (2004) Just sustainability: the emerging discourse of environmental justice in Britain? *Geographical Journal* **170** (2), 155–164.

Ahmed, A. (2017) *Jamaica's Electricity Mix in 2030: The Role of Renewables and Natural Gas*.

Algan, Y., Cahuc, P. & Zylberberg, A. (2002) Public employment and labor market performances. *Economic Policy* **17** (34), 7–66.

Allison, G. & Zelikow, P. (1999) *Essence of Decision: Explaining the Cuban Missile Crisis*, 2nd Edition. Longman, New York, Reading, Menlo Park, Harlow, Don Mills, Sydney, Mexico City, Madrid, Amsterdam.

Altemeyer, B. (2006) *The Authoritarians*. University of Manitoba, Winnipeg.

Altez, J. A. L. (2017) Making mining work. *Philippine Daily Inquirer,* March 07. https://opinion.inquirer.net/102230/making-mining-work. Accessed 3/7/2017.

Alvarez, K. C. (2017a) Anti-mining groups clamor for Gina Lopez confirmation as DENR chief. *GMA News Online,* March 01. https://www.gmanetwork.com/news/story/601484/news/nation/anti-mining-groups-clamor-for-gina-lopez-confirmation-as-denr-chief. Accessed 3/2/2017.

Alvarez, K. C. (2017b) DOF chief: Gina Lopez failed to observe due process in shutdown of mines. *GMA News Online,* March 14. https://www.gmanetwork.com/news/story/603124/money/companies/dof-chief-gina-lopez-failed-to-observe-due-process-in-shutdown-of-mines. Accessed 3/17/2017.

Anderman, M. (2007) *Status and Prospect of Battery Technologies for Hybrid Electric Vehicles, including Plug-in Hybrid Electric Vehicles*.

André, C. (2008) Développement personnel: À la recherche du bonheur. *Sciences Humaines* **7**, 72–73.

Andresen, S. & Gulbrandsen, L. (2003) *The Role of Green NGOs in Promoting Climate Compliance*, Oslo.

Anstey, M., Avenhaus, R. & Faure, G. O. et al. (2009) Science in International Policymaking. *PINPoints* **33**, 1; 31.

Arendt, H. (1958) *The Human Condition*. University of Chicago Press, Chicago.

Arias-Maldonado, M. (2007) An imaginary solution? The green defence of deliberative democracy. *Environmental Values* **16** (2), 233–252.

Armitage, D. (2005) Adaptive Capacity and Community-Based Natural Resource Management. *Environmental Management* **35**, 703–715.

Arnstein, S. R. (1969) A ladder of citizen participation. *Journal of the American Planning Association* **35** (4), 216–224.

Aron, W. (2001) Science and the IWC. In: Friedheim, R. (ed.) *Toward a Sustainable Whaling Regime*. University of Washington Press and Canadian Circumpolar Institute, Seattle, London and Edmonton, pp. 105–123.

Arthur, B. (1988) Self-enforcing Mechanisms in Economics. In: Anderson, W. P. & Arrow, K. (eds.) *The Economy as an Evolving Complex System*. Addison Wesley, Redwood City, CA, pp. 9–31.

Arthur, B. (1994) *Increasing Returns and Path Dependence in the Economy*. University of Michigan Press, Ann Arber.

Aspinall, E. (2002) Sovereignty, the Successor State, and Universal Human Rights: History and the International Structuring of Acehnese Nationalism. *Indonesia* **73**, 1–24.

Associated Press (2017) U.S. utilities seek solar power as Trump sides with coal, fossil fuels. *Los Angeles Times,* February 04. https://www.latimes.com/business/la-fi-solar-power-20170204-story.html. Accessed 10/18/2017.

Atkins, D. (2017) The Silver Lining of Trump's Win: 2020 is More Important than 2016. *Washington Monthly,* January 14. https://washingtonmonthly.com/2017/01/14/the-silver-lining-of-trumps-win-2020-is-more-important-than-2016/. Accessed 10/9/2017.

Avritzer, L. (1995) Transition to Democracy and Political Culture: An Analysis of the Conflict between Civil and Political Society in Post-Authoritarian Brazil. *Constellations* **2** (2), 242–267.

Axelrod, R. (1984) *The Evolution of Cooperation*. Basic Books, New York.

Baber, W. F. & Bartlett, R. V. (2005) *Deliberative environmental politics: democracy and ecological rationality*. MIT Press, Cambridge, MA.

Back, H. & Hadenius, A. (2008) Democracy and state capacity: Exploring a J-shaped relationship. *Governance* **21** (1), 1–24.

Bagehot, W. (1867) *The English Constitution*. Chapman and Hall, London.

Baldwin, R. E. (2016) *The great convergence: Information technology and the new globalization*. The Belknap Press of Harvard University Press, Cambridge, Massachusetts.

Bank of Jamaica (2017) *Jamaica Balance of Trade*. https://tradingeconomics.com/jamaica/balance-of-trade. Accessed 11/17/2017

Barbier, E. (2009) *A Global Green New Deal: Report prepared for the Green Economy Initiative of UNEP*.

Bardhan, P. (2010) *Awakening Giants. Feet of Clay. Assessing the Economic Rise of China*. Oxford University Press, Oxford.

Barett, B. & Chambers, W. B. (1998) *Primer on Scientific Knowledge and Politics in the Evolving Global Climate Change Regime: COP3 and the Kyoto Protocol*. United Nations University, Tokyo.

Baron, J. (1994) Thinking and deciding.

Barr, N. (2012) *The relevance of efficiency to different theories of society: Economics of the Welfare State*. Oxford University Press, Oxford.

Barrett, S. (2003) *Environment and Statecraft*. Oxford University Press, Oxford.

Bass, G., Abramson, A. & Dewey, E. (2014) Effective advocacy. Lessons for nonprofit leaders from research and practice. In: Pekkanen, R., Smith, S. R. & Tsujinaka, Y. (eds.) *Nonprofits and Advocacy: Engaging Community and Government in an Era of Retrenchment*. Johns Hopkins University Press, pp. 254–293.

Baumgartner, F. & Jones, B. (1991) Agenda dynamics and policy subsystems. *Journal of Politics and Law* **53** (4), 1044–1077.

Bazerman, M. H., Magliozzi, T. & Neale, M.A. (1985) Integrative bargaining in a competitive market. *Organizational Behavior and Human Decision Processes* **35** (3), 294–313.

Bazerman, M. & Shonk, K. (2005) The Decision Perspective to Negotiation. In: Moffitt, M. & Bordone, R. (eds.) *The Handbook of Dispute Resolution*. Jossey-Bass, San Francisco, CA, pp. 52–65.

BBC News (2001) China's Great Green Wall. *BBC News,* March 03. https://news.bbc.co.uk/2/hi/world/monitoring/media_reports/1199218.stm. Accessed 9/27/2017.

BBC News (2016) Australia senator Malcolm Roberts calls climate change a UN conspiracy. *BBC News,* August 05. https://www.bbc.com/news/world-australia-36972449. Accessed 11/30/2016.

Bedward, T. & Simpson, V. (2016) Sustainable transport in Jamaica, Ministry of Transport and Mining, Kingston, Jamaica.

Beeson, M. (2010) The coming of environmental authoritarianism. *Environmental Politics* **19** (2), 2726–294.

Belcher, W. L. (2009) *Writing your journal articles in 12 weeks*. SAGE Publications, Los Angeles, London, New Delhi, Singapore, Washington DC.

Benson, E., Best, S. & del Pozo-Vergnes, E. et al. (2014) *Informal and Green? The forgotten voice in the transition to a green economy,* Discussion Paper March, London, UK.

Bento, A., Jacobsen, M. & Lui, A. (2017) Environmental Policy in the Presence of an Informal Sector. *UC Center for Energy and Environmental Economics*.

Berrueta, V. M., Serrano-Medrano, M., García-Bustamante, C., Astier, M. & Masera, O. R. (2015) Promoting sustainable local development of rural communities and mitigating climate change: The case of Mexico's Patsari improved cookstove project. *Climatic Change* **140** (1), 63–77.

Berry, J. & Portney, K. (2014) The Group Basis of City Politics. In: Pekkanen, R., Smith, S. R. & Tsujinaka, Y. (eds.) *Nonprofits and Advocacy: Engaging Community and Government in an Era of Retrenchment*. Johns Hopkins University Press, pp. 21–46.

Bessette, J. (1980) *Deliberative Democracy: The Majority Principle in Republican Government: in How Democratic is the Constitution?* AEI Press, Washington, D.C.

Beyerlin, U. (2006) Bridging the North-South Divide in International Environmental Law. *Heidelberg Journal of International Law* **66**, 259–296.

Bibby, W. (2012) Technologies of the Clean Development Mechanism: Neoliberal Barriers to Carbon Offsetting. *Human Welfare* **1**, 105–116.

Biersteker, T. & Weber, C. (eds.) (1996) *State Sovereignty as Social Construct*. Cambridge University Press, Cambridge, UK.

Bijker, W. (1995) *Of Bicycles, Bakelites and Bulbs. Toward a Theory pf Sociotechnical Change*. MIT Press, Cambridge, MA.

Bijker, W. (2010) How is technology made? That is the question! *Cambridge Journal of Economics* **34** (1), 36–76.

Bijker, W., Bal, R. & Hendriks, R. (2009) *The paradox of scientific authority: the role of scientific advice in democracies*. MIT Press, Cambridge, MA.

Bijker, W., Hughes, T. & Pinch, T. (1987) *The social construction of technological systems: new directions in the sociology and history of technology.* MIT Press, Cambridge, MA.

Binger, A. (2011) *Energy efficiency potential in Jamaica: challenges, opportunities and strategies for implementation*, United Nations, Santiago de Chile.

Birkeland, T. A. (2005) *An introduction to the policy process: theories, concepts, and models of public policy making*, 3rd. M.E. Sharpe, Armonk, NY.

Birnie, P. & Boyle, A. (1992) *International Law and the Environment*. Oxford University Press, New York.

Blackmann, A. (2000) Informal sector pollution control: What policy option do we have? *World Development* **28**, 2067–2082.

Blackmon, D. (2017) The Trump Energy Policy Revolution Creates Its Own Set Of Challenges. *Forbes,* July 10. https://www.forbes.com/sites/davidblackmon/2017/07/10/the-trump-energy-policy-revolution-creates-its-own-set-of-challenges/#515de01d4123. Accessed 10/18/2017.

Blair, T. (2011) Who, What, Why: What can technocrats achieve that politicians can't? *BBC News,* November 14. https://www.bbc.com/news/magazine-15720438. Accessed 8/17/2017.

BMZ (2015) Klimaschutz ist nachhaltige Entwicklungspolitik. https://www.bmz.de/de/presse/aktuelleMeldungen/2015/november/20151118_Klimaschutz-ist-nachhaltige-Entwicklungspolitik/index.html. Accessed 1/20/2017.

Boavida, N. F. F. G. (2017) *The role of indicators in decisions of technology innovation*. KIT Scientific Publishing, Karlsruhe.

Bodansky, D. (2010) The Copenhagen Climate Change Conference: A Postmortem. *The American Journal of International Law* **104** (2), 230–240.

Boden, T., Andres, R. & Marland, G. (2017) *Global, Regional, and National Fossil-Fuel CO2 Emissions*. Oak Ridge National Laboratory (ORNL), Oak Ridge, TN (United States).

Bogues, A. (2011) Radical anti-colonial thought, anti-colonial internationalism and the politics of human solidarities. In: Shilliam, R. (ed.) *International relations and non-Western thought: Imperialism, colonialism and investigations of global modernity*. Routledge, London, pp. 197–214.

Bolton, R., Lagendijk, V. & Silvast, A. (2018) Grand visions and pragmatic integration: Exploring the evolution of Europe's electricity regime. *Environmental Innovation and Societal Transitions*.

Bonaiuti, M. (2014) *The Great Transition*. Routledge, London and New York.

Booth, W. C., Colomb, G. G. & Williams, Joseph, M. (1995) *The Craft of Research*. University of Chicago Press, Chicago.

Boström, M. (2012) A missing pillar? Challenges in theorizing and practicing social sustainability. *Sustainability: Science, Practice, and Policy* **8** (1), 3–14.

Boström, M. (2014) Sustainable development by the multi-stakeholder model? In: Fitzpatrick, T. (ed.) *International handbook of social policy and the environment*. Edward Elgar, Cheltenham, pp. 349–375.

Boström, M. & Tamm Hallström, K. (2010) NGO power in global social and environmental standard setting. *Global Environmental Politics* **10** (4), 36–59.

Boyle, A. (1999) Some Reflections on the Relationship of Treaties and Soft Law. *International and Comparative Law Quarterly* **48**, 901–913.

Bradford, G. (1989) *How Deep is Deep Ecology?* Times Change, Ojai, CA.

Brand, F. (2009) Critical Natural Capital Revisted: Ecological Resilience and Sustainable Development. *Ecological Economics* **68**, 605–612.

Braudel, F. (1958) Histoire, science sociales. La longue durée. *Annales Economies Societés Civilisations* **XIII** (4), 723–753.

Brembs, B., Button, K. & Munafò, M. (2013) Deep impact: unintended consequences of journal rank. *Frontiers in human neuroscience* **7**, 291.

Bremmer, I. (2018) *Us vs. Them: The Failure of Globalism*. Portfolio/Penguin, New York.

Brenner, N. (1999) Globalisation as Reterritorialisation: The Re-scaling of Urban Governance in the European Union. *Urban Studies* **36** (3).

Brenner, N. (2004) Urban governance and the production of new state spaces in western Europe, 1960–2000. *Review of International Political Economy* **11** (3), 447–488.

Brewer, G. & Stern, P. (2005) *Decision Making for the Environment: Social and Behavioral Science Research Priorities*. National Research Council of the National Academies, Washington, D.C.

Brodwin, D. (2013) The Double-Edged Subsidy Sword. *US News,* September 05. https://www.usnews.com/opinion/blogs/economic-intelligence/2013/09/05/how-government-subsidies-both-help-and-hurt-taxpayers. Accessed 11/1/2017.

Brooks, T. (2006) Knowledge and Power in Plato's Political Thought. *International Journal of Philosophical Studies* **14** (1), 51–77.

Bruckner, T., Petschel-Held, G. & Toth, F. (eds.) (1998) *The Tolerable Window Approach to Global Warming*. World Congress of Environmental and Resource Economists, Venice, Italy

Bruckner T., I. A. Bashmakov, Y. Mulugetta, H. Chum, A. de la Vega Navarro, J. Edmonds, A. Faaij, B. Fungtammasan, A. Garg, E. Hertwich, D. Honnery, D. Infield, M. Kainuma, S. Khennas, S. Kim, H. B. Nimir, K. Riahi, N. Strachan, R. Wiser, and X. Zhang (2014) *Energy Systems*, Cambridge University Press, Cambridge, UK.

Bunker, B. & Rubin, J. (eds.) (1995) *Conflict, Cooperation, and Justice*. Jossey-Bass Publishers, San Francisco.

Burdett, K. (2012) Towards a theory of the labor market with a public sector. Elsevier. *Labor Economics* **19** (2), 68–75.

Burns, A. (2018) A Week after the Election, Democratic Gains Grows Stronger. *New York Times*, 13 November. https://www.nytimes.com/2018/11/13/us/politics/midterm-results-democratic-gains.html. Accessed 10/21/2020.

Business Mirror (2016) Environmental NGO: Responsible mining exists in the Philippines. *Business Mirror,* July 02. https://www.businessmirror.com.ph/environmental-ngo-responsible-mining-exists-in-the-philippines/. Accessed 3/19/2017.

Buzan, B. & Lawson (2015) *The Global Transformation: History, Modernity and the Making of International Relations*. Cambridge University Press, Cambridge, UK.

Byrne, J. & Glover, L. (2002) A Common Future or Towards a Future Commons: Globalization and Sustainable Development Since UNCED. *International Review of Environmental Strategies* **3**, 5–25.

Cabacungan, G. C. (2013) Superior berates 'crying' climate exec Saño. *Philippine Daily Inquirer,* November 19. https://globalnation.inquirer.net/91553/superior-berates-crying-climate-exec-sano. Accessed 5/26/2019.

Cabuenas, J. V. (2018) Quo warranto can also be used against President, VP–Supreme Court. *GMA News Online,* May 13. https://www.gmanetwork.com/news/news/

nation/653237/quo-warranto-can-also-be-used-against-president-vp-supreme-court/story/. Accessed 7/2/2018.
Cadman, T. (2013) *Climate change and global policy regimes: Towards institutional legitimacy*. Palgrave Macmillan, Basingstoke.
Cajes, A. (2014) *Philippine waste agricultural biomass: Prospects and opportunities: Sub-Regional Dissemination Workshop on Waste Agricultural Biomass to Energy in South East Asia*.
Calhoun, C. (2002) Imagining Solidarity: Cosmopolitanism, Constitutional Patriotism, and the Public Sphere. *Public Culture* **14** (1), 147–171.
Campbell, W. (2016) Jamaica's jostle with democracy. *Jamaica Observer*, February 22. https://www.jamaicaobserver.com/columns/Jamaica---s-jostle-with-democracy_52123. Accessed 11/21/2017.
Candeal-Haro, J. C. & Induráin-Eraso, E. (1995) A note on linear utility. *Economic Theory* **6** (3), 519–522.
Cao, J. (2018) Recalibrating China-U.S. Climate Cooperation Under the Trump Administration. *China Quarterly of International Strategic Studies* **4** (1), 77–93.
Carbon Tax Center (2017) *What about China?* https://www.carbontax.org/what-about-china/ Accessed 9/28/2017.
Carraro, C., Eyckmans, J. & Finus, M. (2006) Optimal Transfers and Participation Decisions in International Environmental Agreements. *Review of International Organizations* **1**, 379–396.
Carraro, C. & Sgobbi, A. (2008) Modelling negotiated decision-making in environmental and natural resource management: A multilateral, multiple issues, non-cooperative bargaining model with uncertainty. *Automatica* **44** (6), 1488–1503.
Carraro, C. & Siniscalco, D. (1994) Technical Innovation and Environmental Protection. Environmental Policy Reconsidered: The Role of Technological Innovation. *European Economic Review* **38** (3–4), 545–554.
Casula Viffel, A. & Thedvall, R. (2012) Organizing for social sustainability: governance through bureaucratization in meta-organizations. *Sustainability: Science, Practice, and Policy* **8**, 50–58.
Catoto, R. (2017) 5,000 mine workers protest closure of mining firms. *Minda News*, February 16. https://www.mindanews.com/top-stories/2017/02/5000-mine-workers-protest-closure-of-mining-firms/. Accessed 3/2/2017.
CCICED (2015) *Final Report–National Governance Capacity for Green Transformation*, Beijing.
CDIAC (2017) *Mexico Fossil-Fuel CO2 Emissions*.
Cede, F. (2009) The Settlement of International Disputes by Legal Means—Arbitration and Judicial Settlement. In: Bercovitch, J., Kremenyuk, V. & Zartman, I. W. (eds.) *The SAGE Handbook of Conflict Resolution*. SAGE Publications, Los Angeles & London, pp. 358–375.
Cede, F. (2012) Evolving International Law of Intervention and Prevention. In: Anstey, M. & Zartman, I. W. (eds.) *To Block the Slippery Slope: Reducing Identity Conflicts and Preventing Genocide*. Oxford University Press, New York.
Chacko, P. (2011) The internationalist nationalist: pursuing an ethical modernity with Jawaharlal Nehru. In: Shilliam, R. (ed.) *International relations and non-Western*

thought: Imperialism, colonialism and investigations of global modernity. Routledge, London, pp. 178–196.
Charvis, M. & Heron, H. (2016) Energy System of Jamaica, Office of the Utilities Regulations, Kingston, Jamaica.
Chasek, P. (2001) *Earth Negotiations: Analyzing Thirty Years of Environmental Diplomacy*. UNU Press, Tokyo.
Chasek, P. (ed.) (2006) *Global Environmental Politics*. Westview Press, Boulder, CO.
Chen X. & Chao, C. (2004) On the intricacies of the chinese guanxi: A process Model of guanxi development. *Asia Pacific Journal of Management* **21** (3), 305–324.
Cheng Li & Yiou Zhang (2017) Assessing institutional rules in China's elite selection: The case of ethnic minority leaders. *Brookings,* April 19. https://www.brookings.edu/opinions/assessing-institutional-rules-in-chinas-elite-selection-the-case-of-ethnic-minority-leaders/. Accessed 10/5/2017.
Chernillo, D. (2007) *A Social Theory of the Nation-State. The Political Forms of Modernity beyong Methodological Nationalism*. Routledge, London & New York.
Chesterman, S. & Mahbubani, K. (2010) The Asian Way of Handling the World. *The Guardian,* March 04. https://www.theguardian.com/commentisfree/2010/mar/04/global-problem-solving-asian-way. Accessed 5/22/2018.
Cheyns, E. (2011) Multi-stakeholder initiatives for sustainable agriculture: limits of the inclusiveness paradigm. In: Ponte, S., Gibbon, P. & Vestergaard, J. (eds.) *Governing through Standards, Origins, Drivers and Limitations*. Palgrave, Basingstoke, pp. 210–235.
Chrisholm, M. (1982) *Modern World Development: A Geographical Perspective*. Hutchinson, London, Melbourne.
Christensen, C., Bauman, J., Ruggles, R. & Sadtler, T. (2006) Disruptive innovation for social change. *Harvard Business Review,* **December**, 94–101.
Christie, I. & Warburton, D. (2001) *From Here to Sustainability*. Earthscan, London.
Churchman, D. (1995) *Negotiation. Process, Tactics, Theory*. University Press of America, Lanham, MD.
Cillizza, C. & Petulla, S. (2017) Trump is on pace to sign more executive orders than any president in the last 50 years. *CNN,* October 13. https://edition.cnn.com/2017/10/13/politics/donald-trump-executive-orders/index.html. Accessed 11/2/2017.
Ciuta, F. & Klinke, I. (2010) Lost in Conceptualization: Reading the New Cold War with Critical Geopolitics. *Political Geography* **29** (6), 323–332.
Clarke, L., Jiang, K. & Akimoto, K. et al. (2014) *Assessing Transformation Pathways: Climate Change 2014: Mitigation of Climate Change. Contribution of Working Group III to the Fifth Assessment Report of the Intergovernmental Panel on Climate Change Schlömer, C. von Stechow, T. Zwickel and J.C. Minx (eds.),* Cambridge University Press, Cambridge, UK.
Climate Action Tracker (2017a) *China – Rating, 18 September 2017*, https://climateactiontracker.org/countries/china.html. Accessed 09/22/2017.
Climate Action Tracker (2017b) *Mexico – Rating*. https://climateactiontracker.org/countries/mexico.html. Accessed 09/22/2017.
Climate Action Tracker (2017c) *USA*. https://climateactiontracker.org/countries/usa.html. Accessed 09/17/2017.

Climate Change Commission (2016) *PHL begins comprehensive energy policy review*, Climate Change Commission, Office of the President of the Philippines, Manila. https://climate.gov.ph/15-press-release/121-phl-begins-comprehensive-energy-policy-review. Accessed 03/17/2017.

Climate Links (2017) *Greenhouse Gas Emissions Factsheet: Mexico*. May 2017, https://www.climatelinks.org/resources/greenhouse-gas-emissions-factsheet-mexico. Accessed 09/28/2017.

Cobb, J. (2017) The Return of Civil Disobedience. *The New Yorker*, January 09. https://www.newyorker.com/magazine/2017/01/09/the-return-of-civil-disobedience. Accessed 11/1/2017.

Cobham, A. (2014) Uncounted: Power, inequalities and the post-2015 data revolution. *Development* **57**, 320–332.

Cogley, G. J., Kargel J.A., Kaser, G. & van der Veen, C. J. (2010) Tracking the source of glacier misinformation. *Science* (327), 522.

Cohen, J. & Arato, A. (1992) *Civil Society and Political Theory*. MIT Press, Cambridge, MA.

Collier, D. & Collier, R. (1991) *Shaping the Political Arena: Critical Junctures, the Labor Movement and Regime Dynamics in Latin America*. Princeton University Press, Princeton, NJ.

Colman, A. (2003) *Oxford Dictionary of Psychology*. Oxford University Press, New York.

Corbett, J., Grube, D. C., Lovell, H. & Scott, R. (2018) Singular memory or institutional memories? Toward a dynamic approach. *Governance* **31**(3), 555–573.

Cordero, T. (2017) DENR chief Gina Lopez orders cancellation of 75 mining contracts. *GMA News Online*, February 14. https://www.gmanetwork.com/news/story/599487/money/companies/denr-chief-gina-lopez-orders-cancellation-of-75-mining-contracts. Accessed 2/18/2017.

Correa d'Almeida, A. & Poon, J. (2015) Making Chinese Cities Smarter: Leapfrogging Intra-city Transport Development with 'Big Data'. *The World Post*, October 01. https://www.huffingtonpost.com/andre-correa-dalmeida/chinese-smartercities-lea_b_8223530.html. Accessed 8/11/2016.

Costa, L., Rybski, D. & Kropp, J. P. (2011) A Human Development Framework for CO2 Reductions. *PloS ONE* **6** (12), e29262.

Council of Councils (2018) *2018 Report Card on International Cooperation*. https://www.cfr.org/interactive/councilofcouncils/reportcard2018/#!/. Accessed 05/28/2019.

Council on Hemispheric Affairs (2011) *Democracy in Mexico: The Past, Present and Future*. https://www.coha.org/democracy-in-mexico-the-past-present-and-future/. Accessed 05/28/2019.

Cozzens, S. E. & Kaplinsky, R. (2009) Innovation, poverty and inequality: Cause coincidence or co-evolution? In: Lundvall, B.-A., Josepj K.J., Chaminade, C. and Vang, J. (ed.) *Handbook of innovation systems and developing countries: Building domestic capabilities in a global setting*. Edward Elgar, Cheltenham, UK.

Crone, P. (2005) *Medieval Islamic Political Thought*. Edinburgh University Press, Edinburgh.

Cross, J. (1996) Negotiation as Adaptive Learning. *International Negotiation* **1**, 153–178.

Crouch, C. (2008) *Postdemokratie*, 1. Auflage der deutschen Übersetzung. Suhrkamp Verlag, Frankfurt am Main.

Crowley, S. (2016) If our protests against Donald Trump aren't strategic, they will fail. *The Guardian,* December 16. https://www.theguardian.com/commentisfree/2016/dec/16/trump-protest-strategy-march-washington. Accessed 10/12/2017.

Crump, L. & Zartman, I. W. (2003) Multilateral negotiation and the management of complexity. *International Negotiation* **8** (1), 1–5.

Cullet, P. (1998) *Equity and Flexibility Mechanisms in the Climate Change Regime: Conceptual and Practical Issues*, Geneva. https://www.ielrc.org/content/w9801.pdf. Accessed 05/28/2019.

Dahl, R. (1957) The Concept of Power. *Behaviorial Science* **2** (2), 201–215.

Dai, X. (2007) *International institutions and national policies,* 1st ed. Cambridge University Press, Cambridge.

Darby, M. (2014) Korolec: Poland is a climate policy success story. *Climate Change News,* August 18. https://www.climatechangenews.com/2014/08/18/korolec-poland-is-a-climate-policy-success-story/. Accessed 12/12/2016.

Davenport, T. H. & Prusak, L. (2000) *Working Knowledge: How Organizations Manage What They Know*. Harvard Business School Press, Boston, MA.

David, P. (1988) *Path-dependence: Putting the Past into the Future of Economics*. Stanford Institute for Mathematical Studies in the Social Sciences, Stanford, CA.

Davidson, M. (2009) Social sustainability: a potential for politics? *Local Environment* **14** (7), 607–619.

Dearden, N. (2013) Jamaica's decades of debt are damaging its future. *The Guardian,* April 16. https://www.theguardian.com/global-development/poverty-matters/2013/apr/16/jamaica-decades-debt-damaging-future. Accessed 11/13/2017.

Dedeurwaerdere, T. (2014) *Sustainability Science for Strong Sustainability*. Edward Elgar, Northampton, MA.

Dela Cruz, E. & Serapio, M., JR. (2017) Embattled Philippine minister may win reappointment if Congress defers decision. *Reuters,* March 09. https://www.reuters.com/article/us-philippines-mining-idUSKBN16G0EB?il=0. Accessed 3/14/2017.

Delay, T. (2009) Low carbon economy will transform world like the first industrial revolution. *The Guardian,* July 02. https://www.theguardian.com/environment/cif-green/2009/jul/02/low-carbon-economy. Accessed 1/10/2018.

DeMint, J. (2016) *Obama Sidesteps Senate Approval of Paris Agreement*. https://www.heritage.org/environment/commentary/obama-sidesteps-senate-approval-paris-agreement. Accessed 05/28/2019.

DENR (2016) PH determined to cut emissions of carbon, other greenhouse gases. *Department of Environment and Natural Resources, Philippines,* 2016. https://www.denr.gov.ph/news-and-features/latest-news/2529-ph-determined-to-cut-emissions-of-carbon-other-greenhouse-gases.html. Accessed 3/11/2017.

Depledge, J. (2005) *The organization of global negotiations: Constructing the climate change regime*. Earthscan, London & Sterling, VA.

Diaz, J. (2016) CA bypasses 15 Duterte appointees. *Philstar Global,* October 27. https://www.philstar.com/headlines/2016/10/27/1637793/ca-bypasses-15-duterte-appointees. Accessed 3/17/2017.

Diaz, J. (2017) Gina, 3 others bypassed by CA. *Philstar Global,* March 12. https://www.philstar.com/headlines/2017/03/12/1680323/gina-3-others-bypassed-ca. Accessed 3/17/2017.

DiChristopher, T. (2017) Trump wants America to be 'energy dominant.' Here's what that means. *CNBC,* June 28. https://www.cnbc.com/2017/06/28/trump-america-energy-dominant-policy.html. Accessed 10/18/2017.

Dicken, P. (2015) *Global shift: Mapping the changing contours of the world economy,* Seventh edition. Sage, Los Angeles, California.

Die Bundesregierung (2016) *Was bringt, was kostet die Energiewende*, Berlin.

Diehl, P. F. & Gltsch, N. (eds.) (2001) *Environmental Conflict.* Westview Press, Boulder, CO.

Dizon, N., Canivel, R. S., Gamil, J., Aurelio, J. & Avendano, C. (2017) Cimatu appointed DENR secretary. *Philippine Daily Inquirer,* May 09. https://newsinfo.inquirer.net/895312/cimatu-appointed-denr-secretary. Accessed 10/17/2017.

DOE (2017) *2016 Philippine Power Situation Report.* Department of Energy, Republic of the Philippines. https://www.doe.gov.ph/electric-power/2016-philippine-power-situation-report. Accessed 05/28/2019.

Dong Wei (2010) NGOs Play a 'Constructive Role' In Climate Change. *China Daily.* October 8. https://www.chinadaily.com.cn/china/2010-10/08/content_11386672.htm. Accessed 05/28/2019.

Doronila, A. (2013) Money Trail of Fugitive Napoles. *Philippine Daily Inquirer.* August 19. https://opinion.inquirer.net/59151/money-trail-of-fugitive-napoles. Accessed 05/28/2019.

Doyle, T. & Simpson A. (2006) Traversing more than speed bumps: green politics under authoritarian regimes in Burma and Iran. *Environmental Politics* **15** (5), 750–767.

Drori, G., Meyer, J. & Hwang, H. (eds.) (2006) *Globalization and Organization: World Society and Organizational Change.* Oxford University Press, Oxford.

Drösser, C. (1994) Fiktive Versuche. *Zeit Online,* February 11. https://www.zeit.de/1994/07/fiktive-versuche. Accessed 12/25/2017.

Druckman, D. (ed.) (1977) *Complexity in International Negotiations.* Sage, Beverly Hills.

Dryzek, J. (2010) *Foundations and Frontiers of Deliberative Governance.* Oxford University Press, Oxford.

Dubreuil, B. (2010) *Human Evolution and the Origins of Hierarchies: The State of Nature.* Cambridge University Press, New York.

Dupont, A. (1996) Is there an ' Asian way'? *Survival. Global Politics and Strategy* **38** (2), 13–34.

Dupont, C. (1994) Coalition Theory: Using Power to Build Cooperation. In: Zartman, I. W. (ed.) *International Multilateral Negotiations.* Jossey-Bass Publishers, San Francisco, pp. 148–177.

Dupont, C. & Faure, G. O. (2002) The Negotiation Process. In: Kremenyuk, V. (ed.) *International Negotiation. Analysis, Approaches, Issues*, Second Edition. Jossey-Bass, San Francisco, pp. 39–63.

Durrant, R. (2016) Sustainable development in Jamaica, Jamaica Promotions Corporation (JAMPRO), Kingston, Jamaica.

Easterly, W. (2007) Was Development Assistance a Mistake? *American Economic Review* **97**, 328–332.

Easton, D. (1975) A Reassessment of the Concept of Political Support. *British Journal of Political Science* **5**, 435–457.

Eckhouse, B. (2016) Money Pours into Sierra Club at Frantic Pace After Trump Victory. *Bloomberg,* November 16. https://www.bloomberg.com/news/articles/2016-11-16/environmental-donors-pledge-cash-at-frantic-pace-after-trump-win. Accessed 10/9/2017.

Ehnert, F., Kern, F., Borgström, S., Gorissen, L., Maschmeyer, S. & Egermann, M. (2018) Urban sustainability transitions in a context of multi-level governance: A comparison of four European states. *Environmental Innovation and Societal Transitions* **26**, 101–116.

EIA (2016a) *Mexico: International Energy Data and Analysis*. 06 October. https://www.eia.gov/beta/international/analysis.php?iso=MEX. Accessed 05/28/2019.

EIA (2016b) *Mexico Energy Profile: Among Largest Source Of US Oil Imports – Analysis*. December. https://www.eurasiareview.com/10122016-mexico-energy-profile-among-largest-source-of-us-oil-imports-analysis/. Accessed 05/28/2019.

Eichengreen, B. (2011) Global Shifts. In: Bank of Finland (ed.) *Anniversary Symposium*, Helsinki.

Eichengreen, B., Wyplosz, C. & Park, Y. C. (eds.) (2008) *China, Asia, and the New World Economy*. Oxford University Press, Oxford.

Elder, G., Johnson, M. K. & Crosnoe, R. (2003) The Emergence and Development of Life Course Theory. In: Mortimer, Jeylan, T. & Shanahan, Michael, J. (eds.) *Handbook of the Life Course*. Springer, Heidelberg, pp. 3–19.

Elkington, J. (1994) Towards the Sustainable Corporation: Win-Win-Win Business Strategies for Sustainable Development. *California Management Review* **36**, 90–100.

Elkington, J. (1997) *Cannibals with Forks: The Triple Bottom Line of 21st Century Business*. Capstone, Oxford, UK.

Elliott, J. (2013) *An Introduction to Sustainable Development*. Routledge, New York.

Energy Transition (2014) *The role of Latin America in global emissions*. https://energytransition.org/2014/12/the-role-of-latin-america-in-global-emissions. Accessed 05/28/2019.

Epstein, C. (2005) Knowledge and Power in Global Environmental Activism. *International Journal of Peace Studies* **10** (1), 47–67.

ESMAP (2016) *Low-Carbon Development for Mexico*, Energy Sector Management Assistance Program, the World Bank, Washington, D.C. https://www.esmap.org/sites/esmap.org/files/P108304_MX_Low-Carbon%20Development%20for%20Mexico_Briefing%20Note003-10.pdf. Accessed 05/28/2019.

Etcheverry, J. (2011) New Climate Protection, Energy Security, and Employment Creation Strategies for Latin and North America based on Renewable Energy Collaboration. *Latin American Policy* **2**, 43–57.

Euromonitor International (2017) *Economy, Finance and Trade*. https://www.euromonitor.com/economy-finance-and-trade. Accessed 05/28/2019.

Eyerman, R. & Jameson, A. (1989) Environmental Knowledge as an Organizational Weapon: The Case of Greenpeace. *Social Science Information* **28** (1), 99–119.

Farzin, Y. H. (1996) Optimal Pricing of Environmental and Natural Resource Use with Stock Externalities. *Journal of Public Economics* **62**, 31–57.

Fawcett, W., Hughes, M., Krieg, H., Albrecht, S. & Vennström, A. (2012) Flexible strategies for long-term sustainability under uncertainty. *Building Research & Information* **40** (5), 545–557.

Faysse, N. (2006) Troubles on the way: an analysis of the challenges faced by multi-stakeholder platforms. *Natural Resources Forum* **30**, 219–229.

Feinberg, R., Waisman, C. & Zamosc, L. (eds.) (2006) *Civil Society and Democracy in Latin America*. Palgrave Macmillan, New York.

Feinstein, C. (1998) Pessism Perpetuated: Real Wages and the Standard of Living in Britain during and after the Industrial Revolution. *Journal of Economic History* **58** (3), 625–658.

Feng Wang & Haitao Yin, S. L. (2010) China's renewable energy policy: Commitments and challenges. *Energy Policy* **38**, 1872–1878.

Ferenstein, G. (2015) Peter Thiel Says America Is A Technocracy, Not A Democracy. Here's 1 Graph That (Sort Of) Proves His Point. *The Ferenstein Wire,* April 02. https://medium.com/the-ferenstein-wire/peter-thiel-says-america-is-a-technocracy-not-a-democracy-here-s-1-graph-that-sort-of-proves-2d7ef06aff8a. Accessed 11/2/2017.

Fischedick M., J. Roy & Abdel-Aziz, A. et al. (2014) *Industry: In: Climate Change 2014: Mitigation of Climate Change. Contribution of Working Group III to the Fifth Assessment Report of the Intergovernmental Panel on Climate Change*, Cambridge, UK.

Fisher, D. R. & Green, J. F. (2004) Understanding Disenfranchisement: Civil Society and Developing Countries' Influence and Participation in Global Governance for Sustainable Development. *Global Environmental Politics* **4** (3), 65–84.

Fisman, R., Jing Shi, Yongxiang Wan & Weixing Wu (2017) Connections and the Selection of China's Political Elite. *STICERD*.

Fitzpatrick, T. (ed.) (2014) *International handbook of social policy and the environment*. Edward Elgar, Cheltenham.

Flores, A. M. (2017) Meralco building modern coal plant. *Manila Standard,* March 03. https://thestandard.com.ph/business/power-technology/230830/meralco-building-modern-coal-plant.html. Accessed 4/21/2017.

Fogel, C. (2002) *Greening the Earth with Trees: Science, Storylines and the Construction of International Climate Change Institutions*. University of California, Santa Cruz.

Fox, J. & Hernandez, L. (1992) Mexico's Difficult Democracy: Grassroots Movements, NGOs and Local Government. *Alternatives* **17** (2).

France, N. (2013) Editorial: Challenges of the transition to a low carbon, more electric future: From here to 2050. *Energy Policy* (52), 1–9.

Franco, R. C., Wang, L. & O'Rourke, P. et al. (2010) Civil Society and Social Capital in Mexico and Central America. In: Anheier, H. K., Toepler, S. & List, R. (eds.) *International encyclopedia of civil society*. Springer, New York, pp. 262–268.

Franklin, R. L. (1968) *Freewill and determinism: a study of rival conceptions of man*. Routledge and K. Paul.

Fraser, E.D.G., Dougill, A. J., Mabee, W. E., Reed, M. & McAlpine, P. (2006) Bottom up and top down: analysis of participatory processes for sustainability indicator identification as a pathway to community empowerment and sustainable environmental management. *Journal of Environmental Management* **78** (2), 114–127.

Fredericks, S. E. (2012) Justice in sustainability indicators and indexes. *International Journal of Sustainable Development & World Ecology* **19** (6), 490–499.

Freistein, K. (2016) Effects of indicator use: a comparison of poverty measuring instruments at the World Bank. *Journal of Comparative Policy Analysis: Research and Practice* **18** (4), 366–381.

French, H., Renner, M. & Gardner, G. (2009) *Toward a Transatlantic Green New Deal*, Berlin.

Friedman, T. (2007) The Power of Green. *The New York Times,* April 15. https://www.nytimes.com/2007/04/15/opinion/15iht-web-0415edgreen-full.5291830.html?pagewanted=all. Accessed 5/23/2018.

Friedrich, C. (1963) *Man and His Government: An Empirical Theory of Politics*. McGraw Hill, New York.

Fücks, R. (2011) *The Great (Green) Transformation*. Heinrich-Böll-Stiftung, Berlin. https://ecosummit.net/uploads/eco11_fuecks_boell_slides.pdf. Accessed 05/28/2019.

Gale, D. (1976) The linear exchange model. *Journal of Mathematical Economics* **3** (2), 205–209.

Galtung, J. (1990) Cultural Violence. *Journal of Peace Research* **27** (3), 291–305.

Gamil, J. (2017) Cimatu overturns Gina Lopez's order on ECC issuance. *Philippine Daily Inquirer,* July 10. https://newsinfo.inquirer.net/912696/cimatu-overturns-gina-lopezs-order-on-ecc-issuance. Accessed 10/17/2017.

Ganzach, Y. & Karsahi, N. (1995) Message framing and buying: A field experiment. *Journal of Business Research* **32**, 11–17.

Garcia, P. (2018) Experts discuss possible outcomes of quo warranto case vs. Chief Justice Sereno. *CNN Philippines,* May 11. https://cnnphilippines.com/opinion/2018/05/11/quo-warranto-petition-maria-lourdes-sereno-votes.html. Accessed 7/2/2018.

Gauthier, D. (1969) *The Logic of Leviathan*. Clarendon Press, Oxford.

GEA (ed.) (2012) *Global Energy Assessment—Toward a Sustainable Future*, Cambridge University Press, Cambridge, UK and New York, NY, USA and the International Institute for Applied Systems Analysis, Laxenburg, Austria.

Geels, F. (2005) The Dynamics of Transitions in Socio-technical Systems: A Multi-level Analysis of the Transition Pathway from Horse-drawn Carriages to Automobiles (1860–1930). *Technology Analysis & Strategic Management* **17** (4), 445–476.

Geels, F. & Schot, J. (2009) The dynamics of socio-technical transitions: A socio-technical perspective. In: Grin, J., Rotmans, J. & Schot, J. (eds.) *Transitions to sustainable development—New directions in the study of long term transformative change*. Routledge, London, pp. 11–104.

Geels, F. W. (2011) The multi-level perspective on sustainability transitions: Responses to seven criticism. *Environmental Innovation and Societal Transitions* **1**, 24–40.

Geels, F.W. & Schot, J.W. (2007a) Typology of sociotechnical transition pathways. *Research Policy* **36**, 399–417.

Geels, F.W. & Schot, J.W. (2007b) Typology of sociotechnical transition pathways. *Research Policy* **36**, 399–417.

Genus, A. & Coles, A.-M. (2008) Rethinking the multi-level perspective of technological transitions. *Research Policy* **37**, 1436–1445.

George, A. L. & Bennett, A. (2007) *Case studies and theory development in the social sciences*. MIT Press, Cambridge, MA.

Geronimo, Jee, Y. (2016) What drives Gina Lopez? *Rappler,* August 01. https://www.rappler.com/newsbreak/in-depth/141535-environment-gina-lopez-profile. Accessed 2/18/2017.

Geronimo, Jee, Y. (2017) CA to bypass Gina Lopez as environment chief—Pacquiao. *Rappler Philippines,* March 14. https://www.rappler.com/nation/163562-commission-appointments-gina-lopez-confirmation. Accessed 3/17/2017.

Gibbons, D. E. (2007) *Communicable Crises: Prevention, Response, and Recovery in the Global Arena*. IAP.

Gibson, R. (2005) *Sustainability Assessment*. Earthscan, London.

Gilbert, N. & Troitzsch, K. (2005) *Simulation for the social scientist,* 2nd ed. Open University Press, New York.

Gilley, B. (2012) Authoritarian Environmentalism and China's Response to Climate Change. *Environmental Politics* **21** (2), 287–307.

Giupponi, C. & Sgobbi, A. (2013) Decision Support Systems for Water Resources Management in Developing Countries: Learning from Experiences in Africa. *Water* **5** (2), 798–818.

Godet, M. (2000) The Art of Scenarios and Strategic Planning: Tools and Pitfalls. *Technological Forecasting and Social Change* **65**, 3–22.

Goldberg, M. L. (2013) Samantha Power's First Week: When Activists are Diplomats, and Diplomats are Activists. United Nations News and Commentary Global News—Forum. *UN Dispatch,* August 12. https://www.undispatch.com/samantha-powers-first-speech-when-activists-are-diplomats-and-diplomats-activists/. Accessed 3/2/2017.

Goldemberg, J. (1998) Leapfrogging Energy Technologies. *Energy Policy* **2**, 729–741.

Goldin, I. & Winters, L. (eds.) (1995) *The Economics of Sustainable Development*. Cambridge University Press, Cambridge, UK.

Graham, L. (1993) *The Ghost of the Executed Engineer: Technology and the Fall of Soviet Union*. Harvard University Press, Cambridge, MA.

Graham, N. (2016) From the womb to the tomb via Jamaica's $800 million informal enonomy. *The Jamaican Gleaner,* November 01. https://jamaica-gleaner.com/article/news/20161101/womb-tomb-jamaicas-800-million-informal-enonomy. Accessed 11/21/2017.

Grant, R. & Keohane, R. (2005) Accountability and Abuses of Power in World Politics. *American Political Science Review* **99**, 29–44.

Green, B. (2000) There but for Fortune: Real-Life vs. Fictional Case Studies in Legal Ethics. *Fordham Law Review* **69** (3).

Green, M. J. & Self, B. L. (1996) Japan's changing China policy: From commercial liberalism to reluctant realism. *Survival. Global Politics and Strategy* **38** (2), 35–58.

Green New Deal Group (2008) *A Green New Deal*, London.

Greshko, M., Parker, L. & Howard, B. C. (2017) A running list of how Trump is changing the environment. *National Geographic,* August 23. https://news.nationalgeographic.com/2017/03/how-trump-is-changing-science-environment.html. Accessed 10/17/2017.

GRICCE (2017) *Jamaica—Approach to Climate Change*. Grantham Research Institute on Climate Change and the Environment. https://www.lse.ac.uk/GranthamInstitute/country-profiles/jamaica/. Accessed 05/28/2019.

Grießhammer, R., Brohmann, B. & Bauknecht, D. et al. (2015) *Wie Transformationen und gesellschaftliche Innovationen gelingen können. Transformationsstrategien und Models of Change für nachhaltigen gesellschaftlichen Wande,* 1. Auflage. Nomos Verlagsgesellschaft, Baden-Baden.

Grin, J., Rotmans, J. & Schot, J. (2010) *Transitions to Sustainable Development. New Directions in the Study of Long Term Transformative Change*. Routledge, London.

Grin, J., Rotmans, J. & Schot, J. (2011) On patterns and agency in transition dynamics: Some key insights from the KSI programme. *Environmental Innovation and Societal Transitions* **1** (1), 76–81.

Grubler, A., Bai, X. & Buettner, T. et al. (2012) Chapter 18—Urban Energy Systems. In: *Global Energy Assessment—Toward a Sustainable Future*, Cambridge University Press, Cambridge, UK and New York, NY, USA and the International Institute for Applied Systems Analysis, Laxenburg, Austria, pp. 1307–1400.

Grundle, S. & Parker, S. (eds.) (2012) *The new Italian Republic: from the fall of the Berlin Wall to Berlusconi*. Routledge, London.

Guehenno, J. M. (1994) *Das Ende der Demokratie. Aus dem Französischen von Rainer von Savigny*. Artemis & Winkler, München.

Gumport, P. (2000) Academic restructuring: Organizational change and institutional imperatives. *Higher Education* **39**, 67–91.

Guo, C., Bond, Craig, A. & Narayanan, A. (2015) *The Adoption of New Smart-Grid Technologies, Incentives, Outcomes, and Opportunities*, Santa Monica, CA.

Gutmann, A. & Thompson, D. (2002) *Why Deliberative Democracy?* Princeton University Press, Princeton.

GWEC (2010) *Global Wind Power 2009 Report*, Global Wind Energy Council, Brussels, Belgium. https://www.tureb.com.tr/files/bilgi_bankasi/dunya_res_durumu/8.gwec_global_wind_2009_report.pdf. Accessed 05/28/2019.

Haas, P. (1992) Introduction: Epistemic Communities and International Policy Coordination. *International Organization* **46** (1), 1–35.

Haas, P. (2010) Introduction: Epistemic Communities and International Policy Coordination. In: Goldstein, J. & Steinberg, R. H. (eds.) *International Institutions*. Sage, Los Angeles, London, New Delhi, Singapore, Washington DC, pp. 185–220.

Habeeb, W. M. (1988) *Power and Tactics in International Negotiation: How Weak Nations Bargain with Strong Nations*. John Hopkins University Press, Baltimore, MD.

Habermas, J. (2013) *Im Sog der Technokratie*. Suhrkamp, Frankfurt am Main.

Häfele, W., Anderer, J., McDonald, A. & Nakicenovic, N. (1981) *Energy in a Finite World: Paths to a Sustainable Future (Volume 1)*. Ballinger, Cambridge, MA.

Haifeng, H. (2014) The road to green transition in China. *PHBS Working Papers, Peking University HSBC Business School* (No. 2014001).

Haley, B. (2017) Designing the public sector to promote sustainability transitions: Institutional principles and a case study of ARPA-E. *Environmental Innovation and Societal Transitions* **25**, 107–121.

Hardin, G. (1968) The Tragedy of the Commons. *Science* **162**, 1243–1248.

Hardt, M. & Mezzada, S. (2016) The power of the movements facing Trump. *Resilience,* November 22. https://www.resilience.org/stories/2016-11-22/the-power-of-the-movements-facing-trump/. Accessed 10/12/2017.

Harrison, J. & Hoyler, M. (2014) Governing the new metropolis. *Urban Studies* **51** (11), 2249 – 2266.

Hartwick, J. (1977) Intergenerational Equity and the Investing of Rents from Exhaustible Resources. *The American Economic Review* **67** (5), 972–974.

Haukkala, T. (2017) A struggle for change—The formation of a green-transition advocacy coalition in Finland. *Environmental Innovation and Societal Transitions*.

He, J.-K. (2016) Global low-carbon transition and China's response strategies. *Advances in Climate Change Research* **7** (4), 204–212.

Healy, M. E. (1947) Le Play#s Contribution to Sociology: His Method. *The American Catholic Sociological Review* **8** (2), 97–110.

Heggelund, G. (2004) *Environment and Resettlement Politics in China: The Three Gorges Project*. Aldershot, Ashgate.

Heggelund, G. (2009) China's climate change policy: domestic and international developments. *Asian Perspective* **31** (2), 155–191.

Heilbroner, R. (1974) *An Inquiry into the human prospect*. Norton, New York.

Hekkert, M. P., Suurs, R. A.A., Negro, S. O., Kuhlmann, S. & Smits, R.E.H.M. (2007) Functions of innovation systems: A new approach for analysing technological change. *Technological Forecasting and Social Change* **74** (4), 413–432.

Hennicke, P. & Welfens, P. J. J. (2012) *Energiewende nach Fukushima: Deutscher Sonderweg oder weltweites Vorbild?* Oekom Verlag, München.

Hernandez, A. (2014a) *Nation-building and Identity Conflicts. Facilitating the Mediation Process in Southern Philippines*. Springer VS, Wiesbaden.

Hernandez, A. M. (2014b) *Strategic Facilitation of Complex Decision-Making. How Process and Context Matter in Global Climate Change Negotiations*. Springer International, Cham, Heidelberg, New York, Dordrecht & London.

Hernandez, A.M. (2016) Interview od 12 Representatives from the Jamaica Railway Services, 12 September, Jamaica, Kingston, Jamaica.

Heyward, M. (2007) Equity and International Climate Change Negotiations: A Matter of Perspective. *Climate Policy* **7**, 518–534.

Hirschmann, A. (1974) *Abwanderung und Widerspruch: Reaktionen auf Leistungsabfall bei Unternehmungen, Organisationen und Staaten*. VS Verlag für Sozialwissenschaften, Tübingen.

Hobsbawm, E. (1965) *The Industrial Revolution: From 1750 to Present Day*. Weidenfeld & Nicolson, London.

Hoefer, C. (2008) Causal Determinism. In: Zalta, E. (ed.) *The Stanford Encyclopedia of Philosophy*, Winter 2008 edition. Stanford University Press.

Holden, B. (2002) *Democracy and global warming*. Continuum, London.

Hopmann, P. T. (1996) *The Negotiation Process and the Resolution of International Conflicts*. University of South Carolina Press, Columbia, SC.

Hopmann, P. T. (2002) Negotiating data: Reflections on the Qualitative and Quantitative Analysis of Negotiation Processes. *International Journal of Environment and Sustainable Development* **7** (1), 67–85.

Hopwood, B., Mellor, M. & O´Brien, G. (2005a) Sustainable Development: Mapping Different Approaches. *Sustainable Development* **13**, 38–52.

Hopwood, B., Mellor, M. & O'Brien, G. (2005b) Sustainable development: Mapping different approaches. *Sustainable Development* **13** (1), 38–52.

Hsu, C. L. (2001) Political Narratives and the Production of Legitimacy: The Case of Corruption in Post-Mao China. *Qualitative Sociology* **24** (1), 25–54.

Hughes, N. (2009) *A Historical Overview of Strategic Scenario Planning, and Lessons for Undertaking Low Carbon Energy Policy: A Joint working paper of the EON/EPSRC Transition Pathways Project (Working paper 1) and the UKERC*. https://www.researchgate.net/publication/238111229_A_Historical_Overview_of_Strategic_Sce-

nario_Planning_A_Joint_Working_Paper_of_the_UKERC_and_the_EONUKEPSRC_Transition_Pathways_Project. Accessed 05/28/2019.
Humphrey, M. (2007) *Ecological politics and democratic theory: the challenge to the deliberative ideal*. Routledge, London.
ICLEI (2018) *Local Governments for Sustainability—Who we are*. https://www.iclei.org/iclei-global/who-is-iclei.html. Accessed 05/28/2019.
IEA (2011) *World Energy Outlook 2011*, OECD, Paris. https://www.iea.org/newsroom/news/2011/november/world-energy-outlook-2011.html. Accessed 05/28/2019.
IEA (2015) *World Energy Outlook 2013*, OECD, Paris. https://www.iea.org/newsroom/news/2013/november/world-energy-outlook-2013.html. Accessed 05/28/2019.
IEA (2016a) *World Energy Outlook 2016*, OECD, Paris. https://www.iea.org/newsroom/news/2016/november/world-energy-outlook-2016.html. Accessed 05/28/2019.
IEA (2016b) *Decoupling of global emissions and economic growth confirmed*. https://www.iea.org/newsroom/news/2016/march/decoupling-of-global-emissions-and-economic-growth-confirmed.html. Accessed 05/28/2019.
IPCC (1990) *Emissions scenarios from the response strategies working group of the intergovernmental panel on climate change: Appendix 1*. In Climate Change: The IPCC Scientific Assessment. Prepared for IPCC by Working Group I., Cambridge, UK.
IPCC (2005) *Guidance Notes for Lead Authors of the IPCC Fourth Assessment Report on Addressing Uncertainties*, Geneva. https://wg1.ipcc.ch/publications/.../uncertainty-guidance-note.pdf. Accessed 05/28/2019.
IPCC (2007) *Climate Change 2007: Mitigation of Climate Change: Contribution of Working Group III to the Fourth Assessment Report of the Intergovernmental Panel on Climate Change*. Cambridge University Press, Cambridge, UK.
IPCC (2017) *Activities*. Intergovernmental Panel on Climate Change, Geneva. https://www.ipcc.ch/activities/activities.shtml. Accessed 09/14/2017.
IRENA (2013) *Smart Grids and Renewables*, Abu Dhabi.
Jabareen, Y. (2006) A New Conceptual Framework for Sustainable Development. *Environment, Development and Sustainability* **10**, 179–192.
Jackson, R., Canadell, J. G. & Le Quéré, C. et al. (2015) Reaching Peak Emissions. *Nature Climate Change* **6**, 7–10.
Jackson, T. (2008) The Challenge of Sustainable Lifestyles. In: Worldwatch Institute (ed.) *State of the World 2008: Ideas and Opportunities for Sustainable Economies*. Earthscan, London, pp. 45–60.
Jakob, M., Luderer, G., Steckel, J., Tavoni, M. & Monjon, S. (2012) Time to Act Now? Assessing the Costs of Delaying Climate Measures and Benefits for Early Action. *Climate Change* **114** (1).
Jakob, M., Steckel, J. & Klasen, S. et al. (2014) Feasible Mitigation Actions in Developing Countries. *Nature Climate Change* **2**.
Jakob, M. & Steckel, J. C. (2013) Why mitigation could harm developing countries. *WIREs Climate Change*.
Jellinek, G. (1900) *Allgemeine Staatslehre*. Ö. Haring, Berlin.
Jessoe, K., Mannin, D. & Taylor, J. E. (2016) *Climate Change and Labour Allocation in Rural Mexico: Evidence from Annual Fluctuations in Weather*.

Jonas, A. E. G. & Ward, K. (2016) A World of Regionalisms? Towards a US–UK Urban and Regional Policy Framework Comparison. *Journal of Urban Affairs* **24** (4), 377–401.

Jonas, H. (1984) *The Imperative of Responsibility: In Search of an Ethics for the Technological Age*. University of Chicago Press, Chicago and London.

Kahneman, D., Knetsch, J. L. & Thaler, R. H. (1991) Anomalies: The Endowment Effect, Loss Aversion, and Status Quo Bias. *The Journal of Economic Perspectives. American Economic Association*. **5** (1), 193–206.

Kailitz, S. (2007) Juan J. Linz, Totalitarian and Authoritarian Regimes, In: Kailitz, S. (ed.) *Schlüsselwerke der Politikwissenschaft*, 1. Aufl. VS Verlag für Sozialwissenschaften / GWV Fachverlage, Wiesbaden, Wiesbaden, 241–245.

Kalhauge, A. C., Sjöstedt, G. & Correll, E. (eds.) (2005) *Global Challenges: Furthering the Multilateral Process for Sustainable Development*. Greenleaf Publishing, Sheffield.

Kanitkar, T., Jayaraman, T., D'Souza, M., Sanwal, M., Purkayastha, P. & Talwar, R. (2010) *Meeting Equity in a Finite Carbon World: Global Carbon Budgets and Burden Sharing in Mitigation Actions in Global Carbon Budgets and Equity in Climate Change*, Tata Institute of Social Sciences, Mumbai. https://re.indiaenvironmentportal.org.in/files/TISS-BackgroundPaper31May2010.pdf. Accessed 05/28/2019.

Kapoor, I. (2001) Towards participatory environmental management? *Journal of Environmental Management* **63**, 269–279.

Kappel, R. (2011) Der Abstieg Europas und der Vereinigten Staaten – Verschiebungen in der Weltwirtschaft und Weltpolitik. *GIGA Focus* **1**. https://www.giga-hamburg.de/dl/download.php?d=/content/publikationen/pdf/gf_global_1101.pdf. Accessed 05/13/2017.

Kappel, R. (2014) Global Power Shifts and Germany's New Foreign Policy Agenda. *Strategic Analysis* **38** (3), 341–352.

Karabell, Z. (2014) (Mis)leading Indicators: Why Our Economic Numbers Distort Reality. *Foreign Affairs* **March/April Issue**.

Kemp, R., Schot, J. & Hoogma, R. (1998) Regime Shifts to Sustainability through Processes of Niche Formation: The Approach of Strategic Niche Management. *Technology Analysis and Strategic Management* **10** (2), 175–195.

Kempel, W. (1993) Transboundary Movements of Hazardous Wastes. In: Sjöstedt, G. (ed.) *International Environmental Negotiation*. Sage, Newbury Park, pp. 48–62.

Khan, S. A. (2013) China's new political elite. *The Express Tribune*, March 19. https://tribune.com.pk/story/522700/chinas-new-political-elite/. Accessed 10/5/2017.

Khanna, P. (2017) *Technocracy in America: Rise of the info-state*, First edition. CreateSpace, Kentucky.

Kindleberger, C. (1973) *The World in Depression: 1929–1939*. University of California Press, Berkeley and Los Angeles, CA.

Kjellén, B. (2007) *A New Diplomacy for Sustainable Development*. Routledge, Chapman Hill.

Klintman, M. (2012) Handling issues of scale in global accreditation of sustainable tourism schemes towards harmonised re-embeddedness? *Sustainability: Science, Practice, and Policy* **8**, 59–69.

Knight, P. (2016) Environmental Sustainability and Planning in Jamaica, National Environment and Planning Agency, Kingston, Jamaica.

Knorr-Cetina, K. & Mulkay, M. (eds.) (1983) *Science Observed: Perspectives on the Social Study of Science*. Sage, London.

Kondratieff, N. (1926) Die langen Wellen der Konjunktur. *Archiv für Sozialwissenschaft und Sozialpolitik* **56**, 573–609.

Kornek, U., Steckel, J., Lessmann, K. & Edenhofer, O. (2013) *The Climate Rent Curse: New Challenges for Burden Sharing*. Potsdam Institute for Climate Impact Research, Potsdam, Germany. https://link.springer.com/article/10.1007/s10784-017-9352-2. Accessed 06/12/2018.

Kramer, R. & Messick, D. (eds.) (1995) *Negotiation as a Social Process: New Trends in Theory and Research*. Sage, Thousand Oaks, CA.

Krasner, S. (1983) Third World Vulnerabilities and Global Negotiations. *Review of International Studies* **9**, 235–249.

Krasner, S. (1984) Approaches to the State. *Comparative Politics* **16**, 223–246.

Krasner, S. (1991) Global Communications and National Power: Life on the Pareto Frontier. *World Politics* **43** (April), 336–366.

Kreisky, E. (1979) *Alternative Strategien der Organisation staatlichen Handelns*. Institute for Advanced Studies, Vienna.

Kreisky, E. (2002) In Schlechter Verfassung? Perspektiven einer österreichischen Verfassungsdebatte. In: Graf, D. & Muther, E. (eds.) *Streiten um Demokratie. Beiträge zur Verfassungsdiskussion*. Czernin Verlag, Wien, 59–90.

Kreisky, E. (2008) Geschwächte Staaten, schwächelnde Männlichkeit und neue Kriege. In: Sützl, W. & Wallnöfer, D. (eds.) *Gewalt und Präzision. Krieg und Sicherheit in Zeiten des War on Terror*. Verlag Turia & Kant, Vienna, 137–163.

Kremenyuk, V. (ed.) (2002) *International Negotiation. Analysis, Approaches, Issues*, Second Edition. Jossey-Bass, San Francisco.

Kreuzer, P. & Weiberg, M. (2005) *Framing Violence: Nation- and State-building. An Asian Perspective*. PRIF Reports No. 71, Peace Research Institute Frankfurt. https://www.hsfk.de/fileadmin/HSFK/hsfk.../prif72.pdf.

Kristof, K. (2017) Change Agents in gesellschaftlichen Veränderungsprozesse. In: Reinermann, J.-L. & Behr, F. (eds.) *Die Experimentalstadt*. Springer Fachmedien, Wiesbaden, 165–179.

Kusno, A. (2000) *Behind the Postcolonial. Architecture, Urban Space and Political Cultures in Indonesia*. Routledge, London.

La Viña, A. (1997) *Climate Change and Developing Countries: Negotiating a Global Regime*, Quezon City, Philippines.

Laibson, D. (1997) Golden Eggs and Hyperbolic Discounting. *Quarterly Journal of Economics* **112** (2), 443–477.

Landes, D. (1969) *The Unbound Prometheus*. Press Syndicate of the University of Cambridge, Cambridge.

Larson, M. J. (2003) Low-Power Contributions in Multilateral Negotiations: A Framework Analysis. *Negotiation Journal* **19** (2), 133–149.

Lasco, G. (2018) The tyranny of false dichotomies. *Philippine Daily Inquirer*, January 11. https://opinion.inquirer.net/110182/tyranny-false-dichotomies. Accessed 1/11/2018.

Lax, D. & Sebenius, J. (1986) *The Manager as Negotiator*. The Free Press, New York.

Layer, M. (1980) Political Solutions to the Collective Action Problem. *Political Studies* **28** (June), 115–140.

Leggewie, C. & Messner, D. (2012) The low-carbon transformation—A social science perspective. *Journal of Renewable and Sustainable Energy* (4), 041404 https://aip.scitation.org/doi/10.1063/1.4730138. Accessed 05/28/2019.

Lei X. (2009) *Environmental activism in China*. Routledge, London.

Lewicki, R., Minton, J. & Saunders, D. (1999) *Zone of Potential Agreement in Negotiation*. Irwin McGraw Hill, Burr Ridge, IL.

Li, B. (2013) Welfare state changes in China since 1949. In: Greve, B. (ed.) *The Routledge handbook of the welfare state*, 1. ed. Routledge, New York, pp. 222–231.

Linz, J. J. & Krämer, R. (2009) *Totalitäre und autoritäre Regime*, 3. überarb. und erg. Aufl. WeltTrends, Potsdam.

Litfin, K. (1994) *Ozone Discourses: Science and Politics in Global Environmental Cooperation*. Columbia University Press, New York.

Lloyd, G.E.R. (1992) Methods and Problems in the History of Ancient Science: The Greek Case. *The University of Chicago Press Journals* **83** (4), 564–577.

Löfken, J. O. & Martin, R. (2017) Ökowende: Es wirkt. *Technology Review*, June 19. https://www.heise.de/tr/artikel/Oekowende-Es-wirkt-3746232.html. Accessed 12/19/2017.

Loorbach, D. (2010) Transition Management for Sustainable Development. A Prescriptive, Complexity-Based Governance Framework. *Governance* **23** (1), 161–183.

Lorey, D. (ed.) (1993) *The University System and Economic Development in Mexico Since 1929*. Stanford University Press, Bloomington, IN.

Lotfalipour, M. R., Falahi, M. A. & Ashena, M. (2010) Economic growth, CO2 emissions, and fossil fuels consumption in Iran. *Energy* **35** (12), 5115–5120.

Lucas, Robert, Jr. (2002) *Lectures on Economic Growth*. Harvard University Press, Cambridge.

Luce, R. D. & Raiffa, H. (1957) *Games and Decisions*. Wiley, New York.

Lundvall, B.-A., Joseph, K. J., Chaminade, C. & Vang J. (eds.) (2011) *Handbook of Innovation Systems and Developing Countries: Building Domestic Capabilities in a Global Setting*. Elgar Publishing.

Lynas, M. (2008) A Green New Deal. *New Statesman*, July 17. https://www.newstatesman.com/environment/2008/07/lynas-towards-economy-climate. Accessed 5/23/2018.

Lyytimäki, J., Tapio, P., Varho, V. & Söderman, T. (2013) The use, non-use and misuse of indicators in sustainability assessment and communication. *International Journal of Sustainable Development & World Ecology* **20** (5), 385–393.

Maiden, I. F. A. N. (2004) *Scenarios, Stories, Use Cases: Through the Systems Development Life-cycle*. Wiley.

Makhijani, S., Ochs, A., Weber, M., Konold, M., Lucky, M., Ahmed, A., & Mastny, L. (2013) *Jamaica Sustainable Energy Roadmap: Pathways to* an Affordable, Reliable, Low-Emission Electricity System. Worldwatch Institute. www.worldwatch.org/system/files/Jamaica-Sustainable-Energy-Roadmap-112013.pdf. Accessed 05/28/2019.

Malley, J. & Moutous, T. (1996) Does government employment "crowd-out" private employment? Evidence from Sweden. *Scandinavian Journal of Economics* **98** (2), 289–302.

Malnes, R. (1995) Leader and Entrepreneur in International Negotiations: A Conceptual Analysis. *European Journal of International Relations* **1** (1), 87–112.

Manhit, D. (2017) Dangerous perspectives. *Philippine Daily Inquirer,* March 07. https://opinion.inquirer.net/102224/dangerous-perspectives. Accessed 3/7/2017.

Markard, J. & Truffer, B. (2008a) Technological innovation systems and the multi-level perspective. *Research Policy* **37**, 596–615.

Markard, J. & Truffer, B. (2008b) Technological innovation systems and the multi-level perspective. *Research Policy* **37**, 596–615.

Marsden, G. & Snell, C. (2009) The Role of Indicators, Targets and Monitoring in Decision-Support for Transport. *European Journal of Transport and Infrastructure Research* **9** (3), 219–236.

Martin, L. (2010) Interests, Power and Multilateralism. In: Goldstein, J. & Steinberg, R. H. (eds.) *International Institutions*. Sage, Los Angeles, London, New Delhi, Singapore, Washington DC, 273–300.

Martin, L. & Simmons, B. A. (2010) Theories and Empirical Studies of International Institutions. In: Goldstein, J. & Steinberg, R. H. (eds.) *International Institutions*. Sage, Los Angeles, London, New Delhi, Singapore, Washington DC, 33–64.

Martínez-Cárdenas, R., Ayala-Gaytán, E. A. & Aguayo-Téllez, E. (2015) Confianza y capital social: evidencia para México. *Economía, Sociedad y Territorio* **15** (47).

Maslow, A. (1943) A Theory of Human Motivation. *Psychological Review* **50**, 370–396.

Mathews, J. & Hao, T. (2013) The transformation of the electric power sector in China. *Energy Policy* (52), 170–180.

Mauch, C. & Patel, K. K. (eds.) (2010) *The United States and Germany during the Twentieth Centure. Competition and Convergence*. Cambridge University Press, Cambridge.

Mawhinney, M. (2002) *Sustainable Development: Understanding the Green Debates*. Blackwell Science, Oxford.

Mayer, K. (2009) New Directions in Life Course Research. *Annual Review of Sociology* **35**, 423–424.

Mayntz, R. (2009) *Über Governance, Institutionen und Prozesse politischer Regelung. Schriften aus dem Max-Planck-Institut für Gesellschaftsforschung*. Campus, Frankfurt am Main.

Mazzucato, M. (2013) *The Entrepreneurial State*. Anthem Press, London.

Mazzucato, M. (2015) Toward a Green New Deal. *Project Syndicate,* December 14. https://www.project-syndicate.org/commentary/clean-energy-billionaires-public-investment-by-mariana-mazzucato-2015-12?barrier=accesspaylog. Accessed 5/23/2918.

McCalla, L. (2016) Transportation in Jamaica, Jamaican Urban Transit Corporation, Kingston, Jamaica.

McDonnell, D. & Valbruzzi, M. (2014) Defining and classifying technocrat-led and technocratic governments. *European Journal of Political Research* **53** (4), 654–671.

McGovern, M. (2014) Analysis: Macquarie's Marena Project on the Brink. *Wind Power Monthly,* January 16. https://www.windpowermonthly.com/article/1227498/analysis-macquaries-marena-project-brink. Accessed 12/10/2016.

McKeown, T. (1999) Case Studies and the Statistical World View. *International Organization* **53** (1), 161–190.

McKinsey (2009) *Pathways to a Global Low Carbon Economy*. McKinsey, London.

Meadowcroft, J. (2005) Environmental political economy, technological transitions and the state. *New Political Economy* **10** (4), 479–498.

Meadows, D., Meadows, D., Randers, J. & and Behrens III, W. (1972) *The Limits to Growth*. Universe Books, New York.
Menon, S. (2017) The Unprecedented Promises—and Threats—of the Belt and Road Initiative. *The Wire,* April 24. https://thewire.in/127579/the-unprecedented-promises-and-threats-of-the-belt-and-road-initiative/. Accessed 12/23/2017.
Mensch, G. (1971) Zur Dynamik des technischen Fortschritts. *Zeitschrift für Betriebswirtschaft* **41**, 295–314.
Mensch, G. (1972) Basisinnovationen und Verbesserungsinnovationen. *Zeitschrift für Betriebswirtschaft* **42**, 291–297.
Mensch, G. (1975) *Das technologische Patt: Innovationen überwinden die Depression.* Umschau, Frankfurt am Main.
Merkel, W. (1999) *Systemtransformation. Eine Einführung in die Theorie und Empirie der Transformationsforschung*. VS Verlag für Sozialwissenschaften, Opladen.
Mertha, A. (2009) "Fragmented Authoritarianism 2.0": Political Pluralization in the Chinese Policy Process. *The China Quarterly* **200**, 995.
Messner, D. (2015) A social contract for low carbon and sustainable development: Reflections on non-linear dynamics of social realignments and technological innovations in transformation processes. *Technological Forecasting and Social Change* **98**, 260–270.
Messner, D., Guarín, A. & Haun, D. (2013) *The Behavioural Dimensions of International Cooperation*, Käte Hamburger Kolleg/Centre for Global Cooperation Research, Duisburg. https://www.die-gdi.de/uploads/media/Messner-Guarin-Haun_Behavioural-dimensions_GCRP-1-WEB.pdf. Accessed 05/28/2019.
Miraflor, M. (2017) New DENR chief wants to address misinformation on mining. *Manila Bulletin,* May 13. https://business.mb.com.ph/2017/05/13/new-denr-chief-wants-to-address-misinformation-on-mining/. Accessed 10/17/2017.
Mission Innovation (2015) Joint Launch Statement—Accelerating the Clean Energy Revolution. https://www.mission-innovation.net/joint-statement/. Accessed 5/27/2016.
Mitchell, R. K., Agle, B. R. & Wood, D. J. (1997) Toward a theory of stakeholder identification and salience: defining the principle of who and what really counts. *Academy of Management Review* **22** (4), 853–886.
Montalvan, A., III (2010) The Man with the Sugbu-Anon Accent. *Philippine Daily Inquirer*.
Moomaw, W., Susskind, L. & Kurczak, K. (eds.) (2003) *Negotiating a sustainable future: Innovations in international environmental negotiations*. PON Books, Cambridge, MA.
Moore, C. (1996) *The Mediation Process. Practical Strategies for Resolving Conflict,* Second Edition. Jossey-Bass Publishers, San Francisco.
Morallo, A. (2017) House majority strips anti-death penalty members of key posts. *Philstar,* March 15. https://www.philstar.com/headlines/2017/03/15/1681371/house-majority-strips-anti-death-penalty-members-key-posts. Accessed 3/19/2017.
Morello, C. (2017) U.N. budget cuts highlight new U.S. approach. *The Washington Post,* December 26. https://www.washingtonpost.com/world/national-security/un-budget-cuts-highlight-new-us-approach/2017/12/26/6a313f42-ea69-11e7-9f92-10a2203f6c8d_story.html. Accessed 12/27/2017.
Moss, R. & Schneider, S. (2000) Uncertainties. In: *Guidance Papers on the Cross Cutting Issues of the Third Assessment Report of the IPCC*, Intergovernmental Panel on Climate

Change, Geneva. https://www.ipcc.ch/pdf/supporting-material/guidance-papers-3rd-assessment.pdf. Accessed 05/28/2019.

Moustafa, K. (2015) The disaster of the impact factor. *Science and Engineering Ethics* **21** (1), 139–142.

MSET (2017) *An Overview of Jamaica's Electricity Sector*. Ministry of Science, Energy & Technology, Kingston, Jamaica. https://mset.gov.jm/overview-jamaicas-electricity-sector. Accessed 11/13/2017.

Mufson, S. & Eilperin, J. (2017) Trump seeks to revive Dakota Access, Keystone XL oil pipelines. *The Washington Post,* January 24. https://www.washingtonpost.com/news/energy-environment/wp/2017/01/24/trump-gives-green-light-to-dakota-access-keystone-xl-oil-pipelines/. Accessed 10/18/2017.

Müller, J. A. (1998) *Simulation ökonomischer Prozesse*. MANZ Verlag Schulbuch GmbH, Wien.

Murphy, G. (2010) *Shadowing the White Manas Burden: U.S. Imperialism and the Problem of the Color Line*. New York University Press, New York.

Myint, T. (2007) Environmental governance in the SPDC's Myanmar. In: Skidmore, M. & Wilson, T. (eds.) *Mynmar: the state, community and the environment*. Asia Pacific Press, Canberra, pp. 189–217.

Mytelka, L., Aguayo, F. & Boyle, G. et al. (2012) Chapter 25—Policies for Capacity Development. In: *Global Energy Assessment—Toward a Sustainable Future*, Cambridge University Press, Cambridge, UK and New York, NY, USA and the International Institute for Applied Systems Analysis, Laxenburg, Austria, pp. 1745–1802.

Naess, A. (1989) *Ecology, Community and Lifestyle*. Cambridge University Press, Cambridge.

Najam, A. (2005) Why Environmental Politics Looks Different from the South. In: Dauvergne, P. (ed.) *Handbook of Environmental Politics*. Edward Elgar Publishing Limited, Cheltenham, UK, pp. 111–126.

Najam, A. (2010) The View from the South: Developing Countries in Global Environmental Politics. In: Axelrod, R. S., Downie, D. L. & Vig, N.J. (eds.) *The Global Environment: Institutions, Law, and Policy*. CQ Press, Washington, D.C.

Najam, A., Huq, S. & Sokona, Y. (2003) Climate Negotiations Beyond Kyoto: Developing Countries Concerns and Interests. *Climate Policy* **3** (3), 221–231.

Natal, A., Cadena-Roa, J. & Rappoport, S. G. (2010) Civil Society and Social Capital in Mexico and Central America. In: Anheier, H. K., Toepler, S. & List, R. (eds.) *International encyclopedia of civil society*. Springer, New York, pp. 262–268.

National Science Foundation (2000) *Towards a comprehensive geographical perspective on urban sustainability*. Rutgers—The State University of New Jersey: Center for Urban Policy Research, New-Brunswick, NJ. https://cupr.rutgers.edu/wp-content/uploads/2014/08/sustain.pdf. Accessed 05/28/2019.

Nawrotzki, R. J., Riosmena, F., Hunter, L. M. & Runfola, D. M. (2015) Amplification or suppression: Social networks and the climate change-migration association in rural Mexico. *Global environmental change human and policy dimensions* **35**, 463–474.

NBS (2017) *National Accounts—Gross Domestic Product*. National Bureau of Statistics of China. https://data.stats.gov.cn/english/. Accessed 10/04/2017.

Neale, M. A. & Northcraft, G. B. (1986) Experts, amateurs, and refrigerators: Comparing expert and amateur negotiators in a novel task. *Organizational Behavior and Human Decision Processes* **38** (3), 305–317.

Nery, J. (2017) Duterte's secret. *Philippine Daily Inquirer,* December 05. https://opinion.inquirer.net/109241/dutertes-secret. Accessed 12/5/2017.

Newig, J. & Fritsch, O. (2009) Environmental governance: participatory, multi-level and effective? *Environmental Policy and Governance* **19**, 197–214.

Nietzsche, F. (1883) *Also sprach Zarathustra: Ein Buch für Alle und Keinen*. Verlag von Ernst Schmeitzner, Chemnitz.

Njalsson, G. (2005) From autonomous to socially conceived technology: toward a causal, intentional and systematic analysi sof interests and elites in public technology policy. *Theoria: a journal of political theory* **108**, 56–81.

Nobel Media AB (2014) The Nobel Peace Prize for 2007 to the Intergovernmental Panel on Climate Change (IPCC) and Albert Arnold (Al) Gore Jr., 2014. https://www.nobelprize.org/nobel_prizes/peace/laureates/2007/press.html. Accessed 6/28/2018.

Northcraft, G. B., Brodt, S. E. & Neale, M. A. (1995) Negotiating with Nonlinear Subjective Utilities: Why Some Concessions Are More Equal Than Others. *Organizational Behavior and Human Decision Processes* **63** (3), 298–310.

Northcraft, G. B., Preston, J., Neale, Margaret, A., Kim, P. & Thomas-Hunt, Melissa, C. (1998) Non-linear Preference Functions and Negotiated Outcomes. *Organizational Behavior and Human Decision Processes* **73** (1), 54–75.

Nye, J. (2010a) Smart Power for Global Climate Negotiations. *Climate Science & Policy*. https://www.climatescienceandpolicy.eu/2010/06/smart-power-for-global-climate-negotiations/. Accessed 08/02/2016.

Nye, J. (2010b) The Future of American Power. *Foreign Affairs* **89** (6), 2–12.

Ochs, A., Konold, M., Auth, K., Musolino, E. & Killeen, P. (2015) *Caribbean Sustainability Energy Roadmap and Strategy (C-SERMS)*. Baseline Report and Assessment, Washington, D.C.

O'Connell, B. (1994) *People Power: Service, Advocacy, Empowerment*. Foundation Center, Washington, D.C.

OEC (2017) *Jamaica*. Observatory of Economic Complexity. https://atlas.media.mit.edu/en/profile/country/jam/. Accessed 11/13/2017.

OECD (2011) *Public Servants as Partners for Growth: Toward a Stronger, Leaner and More Equitable Workforce*. Organisation for Economic Cooperation and Development, Paris. https://www.oecd-ilibrary.org/governance/public-servants-as-partners-for-growth_9789264166707-en. Accessed 05/28/2019.

OECD (2017a) *China—Economic Forecast Summary (June 2017)*, Organisation for Economic Cooperation and Development, Paris. https://www.oecd.org/china/china-economic-forecast-summary.htm. Accessed 25 September 2017.

OECD (2017b) *Mexico—Economic Forecast Summary (June 2017)*, Organisation for Economic Cooperation and Development, Paris. https://www.oecd.org/mexico/mexico-economic-forecast-summary.htm Accessed 25 September 2017.

Olchondra, R. (2015) Meralco unit earmarks $1.2B for equity in 3 coal power plants. *Philippine Daily Inquirer,* July 29. https://business.inquirer.net/196109/meralco-unit-earmarks-1-2b-for-equity-in-3-coal-power-plants. Accessed 4/21/2017.

Olson, M. (1965) *The Logic of Collective Action*. Harvard University Press, Cambridge, MA.

Olvera, A. J. (1997) Civil Society and Political Transition in Mexico. *Constellations* **4** (1), 105–123.

OML Center (2014) *2014 Philippine Climate Change Assessment Report*, Manila, Philippines.

Ostrom, E. (1990) *Governing the Commons: The Evolution of Institutions for Collective Action*. Cambridge University Press, Cambridge, UK.

Ostrom, E. (2010) Beyond Markets and States: Polycentric Governance of Complex Economic Systems. *American Economic Review* **100**, 641–672.

O'Sullivan, A. (2003) *Economics: Principles in Action*. Pearson Prentice Hall, Upper Saddle River, NJ.

Ott, H., Winkler, H. & Brouns, B. et al. (2004) *South-North Dialogue on Equity in the Greenhouse: A Proposal for an Adequate and Equitable Global Climate Agreement*, Bonn & Wuppertal.

Oye, K. A. (2011) Explaining Cooperation under Anarchy: Hypotheses and Strategies. *World Politics* **38**, 1–24.

Ozturk, I. & Acaravci, A. (2010) CO2 emissions, energy consumption and economic growth in Turkey. *Renewable and Sustainable Energy Reviews* **14** (9), 3220–3225.

Pan, J. (ed.) (2016a) *China's Environmental Governing and Ecological Civilization*. Springer, Berlin, Heidelberg.

Pan, J. (2016b) Low-Carbon Energy Transformation. In: Pan, J. (ed.) *China's Environmental Governing and Ecological Civilization*. Springer, Berlin, Heidelberg., pp. 129–146.

Parsons, T. (1951) *The Social System*. Routledge, London.

Patwardhan, A., Azevedo, I. & Foran, T. et al. (2012) Chapter 16—Transitions in Energy Systems. In: *Global Energy Assessment—Toward a Sustainable Future*, Cambridge University Press, Cambridge, UK and New York, NY, USA and the International Institute for Applied Systems Analysis, Laxenburg, Austria, pp. 1173–1202.

Paul, R. & Eder, L. (2002) *Critical Thinking: Tools for Taking Charge of Your Professional and Personal Life,* Third Edition. Pearson Education, Inc., Upper Saddle River, NJ.

Pearce, F. (2016) Is it possible to reduce CO2 emissions and grow the global economy? *The Guardian,* April 14. https://www.theguardian.com/environment/2016/apr/14/is-it-possible-to-reduce-co2-emissions-and-grow-the-global-economy. Accessed 10/26/2016.

Peck, S. L. (2004) Simulation as experiment: a philosophical reassessment for biological modeling. *Trends in Ecology & Evolution* **19** (10), 530–534.

Penetrante, A. M. (2010) Politics of Equity and Justice in Climate Change Negotiations in North–South Relations. In: Brauch, H. G., Spring, U. & Mesjasz, C. et al. (eds.) *Coping with Global Environmental Change, Disasters and Security – Threats, Challenges, Vulnerabilities and Risks*. Hexagon Springer-Verlag, Berlin, Heidelberg & New York, pp. 1355–1366.

Penetrante, A. M. (2011) The Entanglement of Climate Change in North–South Relations: Stumbling Blocks and Opportunities for Negotiation. In: Richardson, K., Will, S. & Livermann, D. (eds.) *Climate Change: Global Risks, Challenges and Decisions*. Cambridge Univeristy Press, Cambridge, UK, pp. 356–359.

Penetrante, A. M. (2012) Simulating climate change negotiations: Lessons from modeled experience. *Negotiation Journal* **27** (3), 279–314.

Penetrante, A. M. (2013) Common but Differentiated Responsibilities. The North-South Divide in the Climate Change Negotiations. In: Sjöstedt, G. & Penetrante, A. M. (eds.) *Climate Change Negotiations. A Guide to Resolving Disputes and Facilitating Multilateral Cooperation*. Routledge, London, pp. 249–276.

Penetrante, A. M. (2014) The Case of Arcania: Perspectives in Point-of-Entry Negotiations. In: Melamud, M., Meerts, P. & Zartman, I. W. (eds.) *Banning the Bang or the Bomb? Negotiating the Nuclear Test Ban Regime*. Cambridge University Press, Cambridge, UK, pp. 277–296.

Pentico, D. (2008) The Assortment Problem: A Survey. *European Journal of Operational Research* **190**, 295–309.

Petri, A. (2017) China's 'Great Green Wall' Fights Expanding Desert. *National Geographic*, April 21. https://news.nationalgeographic.com/2017/04/china-great-green-wall-gobi-tengger-desertification/. Accessed 9/27/2017.

Petschel-Held, G., Schellnhuber, H.-J., Bruckner, T., Tóth, F. L. & Hasselmann, K. (1999) The Tolerable Window Approach: Theoretical and Methodological Foundations. *Climatic Change* **41** (3/4), 303–331.

Pfahl-Traughber, A. (2004) Staatsformen im 20. Jahrhundert I: Diktatorische Systeme. In: Gallus, A. & Eckhard, J. (eds.) *Modelle politischer Ordnung. Eine Geschichte der Staatsformen von Altertum bis zur Gegenwart*. Böhlau Verlag, Köln/Weimar, pp. 223–280.

Pfeiffer, S. (2016) 'Rage donations' become an anti-Trump movement. *Boston Globe*, November 21. https://www.bostonglobe.com/business/2016/11/21/rage-donate-becomes-anti-trump-balm/7t4pJvnlbfAW3A3NeltmyL/story.html. Accessed 10/9/2017.

Philipps, T. (2017) The $900bn question: What is the Belt and Road initiative? *The Guardian*, May 17. https://www.theguardian.com/world/2017/may/12/the-900bn-question-what-is-the-belt-and-road-initiative. Accessed 12/23/2017.

Piketty, T. (2014) *Capital in the twenty-first century*. The Belknap Press of Harvard University Press, Cambridge, Massachusetts.

Pilatowsky Gruner, R. (2016) *Mexico Emission Reduction Challenges*, 30 August. https://climatescorecard.org/2016/08/30/mexico-emission-reduction-challenges/. Accessed 30 August 2016.

Pinkse, J. & Kolk, A. (2012) Addressing the climate change-sustainable development nexus: the role of multi-stakeholder partnerships. *Business and Society* **51**, 176–210.

Pissarides, C. (2000) *Equilibrium Unemployment Theory*, 2nd Edition. MIT Press, Cambridge, MA.

Pitkin, H. (1967) *The Concept of Representation*. University of California Press, Berkeley and Los Angeles, CA.

Plous, S. (1993) *The Psychology of Judgment and Decision Making*. McGraw-Hill, New york.

Plummer, J. & Taylor, J. G. (2004) The characteristics of community participation in China. In: Plummer, J. & Taylor, J. G. (eds.) *Community participation in China: issues and processes for capacity building*. Earthscan, London, pp. 36–54.

Polanyi, K. (2015) *The great transformation: Politische und ökonomische Ursprünge von Gesellschaften und Wirtschaftssystemen*, 12. Aufl. Suhrkamp, Frankfurt (Main).

Popper, K. (1959) *The logic of scientific discovery*. Basic Books, New York.

Pora, G. (2017) Of mining and mountains: The audacity of Gina Lopez. *Philippine Daily Inquirer,* March 07. https://opinion.inquirer.net/102202/thinq-audacity-environment-secretary-gina-lopez-mining. Accessed 3/7/2017.

Porritt, J. (1984) *Seeing Green: The Politics of Ecology Explained.* Basil Blackwell, Oxford and New York.

Portney, K. (2013) *Taking sustainable cities seriously.* MIT Press, Cambridge, MA.

Posner, R. A. (2004) *Catastrophe: Risk and Response.* Oxford University Press, Oxford.

Prakash, A. & Gugerty, M. K. (2010) *Advocacy organizations and collective action.* Cambridge University Press, Cambridge, New York.

Pratt, M. L. (2002) Modernity and Periphery: Towards a Global and Relational Analysis. In: Mudimbe-Boyi, E. (ed.) *Beyond Dichotomies.* SUNY Press, Albany, pp. 21–48.

Princen, T. & Finger, M. (1994) *Environmental NGOs in World Politics: Linking the Local and the Global.* Routledge, London.

Pronin, E. & Kugler, M. B. (2007) Valuing thoughts, ignoring behavior: The introspection illusion as a source of the bias blind spot. *Journal of Experimental Social Psychology* **43** (4), 565–578.

Pruitt, D. & Rubin, J. (1986) *Social Conflict: Escalation, Stalemate, and Settlement.* Random House, New York.

Purdy, J. (2010) The politics of nature: climate change, environmental law, and democracy. *Yale Law Journal* **119**, 101–188.

Quirk, R. (1973) *The Mexican Revolution and the Catholic Church, 1910–1929.* Indiana University Press, Bloomington, IN.

Quismundo, T. (2016) Why is PH building 25 more coal-powered plants? *Philippine Daily Inquirer,* March 15. https://newsinfo.inquirer.net/773681/why-is-ph-building-25-more-coal-powered-plants. Accessed 3/18/2017.

Quismundo, T. (2017) Oppositors cite Lopez's 'incompetence' as DENR chief. *Philippine Daily Inquirer,* March 09. https://newsinfo.inquirer.net/879090/oppositors-cite-lopezs-incompetence-as-denr-chief. Accessed 3/17/2017.

Raiffa, H. (1968) *Decision Analysis.* Random House, New York.

Raiffa, H. (1982) *The Art and Science of Negotiation.* Harvard University Press, Cambridge, MA.

Raiffa, H. (2002) *Negotiation Analysis: The Science and Art of Collaborative Decision Making.* Harvard University Press, Cambridge, MA.

Ranada, P. (2015) PH drops in 2016 list of countries vulnerable to climate change. *Rapper Philippines,* November 17. https://www.rappler.com/science-nature/environment/113064-philippines-2016-climate-change-vulnerability-index. Accessed 3/17/2017.

Ravindran, T. (2015) Beyond the Pure and the Authentic: Indigenous modernity in Andean Bolivia. *AlterNative: An International Journal of Indigenous Peoples* **11** (4), 321–333.

Reinelt, C. (1994) Fostering empowerment, building community: The challenge for state-funded feminist organizations. *Human Relations* **47** (6), 685–704.

Reisman, G. (1998) *Capitalism: A Complete Understanding of the Nature and Value of Human Economic Life.* Jameson Books, Ottawa, IL.

Reynolds, O. (2016) Electricity in Jamaica, Jamaica Energy Partners (JEP), Kingston, Jamaica.

Riello, G. & O'Brien, P. (2009) The Future is Another Country: Offshore Views of the British Industrial Revolution. *Journal of Historical Sociology* **22** (1), 1–29.

Rip A. & Kemp, R. (1998) Technological Change. In: Rayner, S. & Malone, E. L. (eds.) *Human Choice and Climate Change*. Battele Press, Columbus, OH, 327–399

Robbins, A. (2006) *Inner Strength: Harnessing the Power of Your Six Primal Needs*, Simon & Schuster Audio.

Robertson, A. (2016) Donald Trump lied about his climate change conspiracy theory, but his tweet is still up. *The Verge,* September 26. https://www.theverge.com/2016/9/26/13067918/donald-trump-presidential-debate-2016-climate-change-hoax. Accessed 11/30/2016.

Rogers, P. (2017) Rebellion against Trump climate change policies. *The Mercury News,* September 27. https://www.mercurynews.com/2017/09/27/states-rebellion-against-trump-climate-change-policies-gaining-momentum/. Accessed 11/1/2017.

Rohde, J. (2017) Richard G. Olson. Scientism and Technocracy in the Twentieth Century: The Legacy of Scientific Management xx + 207 pp., bibl., index. Lanham, Md.: Lexington Books, 2016. $85 (cloth). *Isis* **108** (1), 217–218.

Rong, F. (2010) Understanding Developing Country Stances on Post-2012 Climate Change Negotiations: Comparative Analysis of Brazil, China, India, Mexico and South Africa. *Energy Policy* **38**, 4582–4591.

Rood, S. (2015) *Energy Crisis in the Philippines: An Electricity or Presidential Power Shortage?* The Asia Foundation, Manila. https://asiafoundation.org/2015/03/18/energy-crisis-in-the-philippines-an-electricity-or-presidential-power-shortage/. Accessed 03/18/2017.

Rossi, F. & Bülow, M. von (eds.) (2015) *Social Movement Dynamics*. Ashgate, Farnham.

Roth-Douquet, S. (2016) Post Trump Win: A Silver Lining for Millennials. *17 March 2017,* November 11. https://www.huffingtonpost.com/sophie-rothdouquet/post-trump-win-a-silver-l_b_12890446.html. Accessed 10/9/2017.

Roudometof, V. (2015) The Glocal and Global Studies. *Globalizations* **12** (5), 774–787.

Roy, J., Dowd, A.-M., Muller, A., Pal, S. & Prata, N. (2012) Chapter 21—Lifestyles, Well-Being and Energy. In: *Global Energy Assessment - Toward a Sustainable Future*, Cambridge University Press, Cambridge, UK and New York, NY, USA and the International Institute for Applied Systems Analysis, Laxenburg, Austria, pp. 1527–1548.

Ruiz-Mercado, I., Masera, O., Zamore, H. & Smith, K. (2011) Adoption and sustained use of improved cookstoves. *Energy Policy* **39**, 7557–7566.

Runde, D. (2015) Urbanization Will Change The (Developing) World. *Forbes,* February 24. https://www.forbes.com/sites/danielrunde/2015/02/24/urbanization-development-opportunity/#228f4c226277. Accessed 10/26/2016.

Russell, D. (2017) The real impact of high transportation costs. *Supply Chain Quarterly*, 30–36.

Rutland Bauer, M. (2016) Trump Protests Could Be the Start of a New Civil Rights Era. *Yes Magazine,* November 14. https://www.yesmagazine.org/people-power/trump-protests-could-be-the-start-of-a-new-civil-rights-era-20161114. Accessed 10/12/2017.

Ryan, A., Tilbury, D., Blaze Corcoran, P., Abe, O. & Nomura, K. (2010) Sustainability in higher education in the Asia-Pacific: Developments, challenges, and prospects. *International Journal of Sustainability in Higher Education* **11** (2), 106–119.

Ryan, J. (2017) Green groups see silver lining to Trump win: money and members. *Kuow,* January 19. https://kuow.org/post/green-groups-see-silver-lining-trump-win-money-and-members. Accessed 10/9/2017.

Sadowski, W. (1959) A few remarks on the assortment problem. *Management Science* **6** (1), 13–24.

Sakamoto, Y. (1994) *Global Transformation: Challenges to the State System*. United Nations University Press.

Salaverria, L. (2017) Duterte finally signs Paris Agreement on climate change. *Philippine Daily Inquirer,* March 02. https://globalnation.inquirer.net/153030/duterte-finallly-signs-paris-agrement-climate-change.

Sánchez, M. E. (2010) Globalisation and loss of identity. *International Forum of Psychoanalysis* **19** (2), 71–77.

Sandler, T. (2004) *Global Collective Action*. Cambridge University Press, Cambridge, UK.

Sanna, L. J., Schwarz, N. & Stocker, S. L. (2002) When debiasing backfires: Accessible content and accessibility experiences in debiasing hindsight. *Journal of Experimental Psychology: Learning, Memory, and Cognition* **28** (3), 497–502.

Santos, Soliman, Jr. (1997) The Philippines Tries the Party-List System (A Progressive Perspective). *Kasarinlan Philippine Journal of Third World Studies* **13** (2), 5–18.

Savitz, A. (2006) *The Triple Bottom Line*. Jossey-Bass, San Francisco, CA.

Sawin, J. & Moomaw, W. (2009) *Renewable Revolution: Low-Carbon Energy by 2030*. World Watch Institute, Washington, D.C. https://www.worldwatch.org/bookstore/publication/renewable-revolution-low-carbon-energy-2030. Accessed 01/10/2018.

Scerri, A. & James, P. (2010) Accounting for sustainability: Combining qualitative and quantitative research in developing 'indicators' of sustainability. *International Journal of Social Research Methodology* **13** (1), 41–53.

Schäfer, A. (2008) Krisentheorien der Demokratie: Unregierbarkeit, Spätkapitalismus und Postdemokratie. *MPIfGDiscussion Paper 08/10,* 2008.

Schäpke, N. & Rauschmayer, F. (2011) *Foundations for a common approach. WP 2—Systematic Reflection and Theory Building.: THEME FP7—ENV. 2010.4.2.3-1: Foresight to enhance behavioural and societal changes enabling the transition towards sustainable paths in Europe*.

Schelling, T. (1995) Intergenerational Discounting. *Energy Policy* **23** (4/5), 395–401.

Schofer, E. (1997) Science association in the international sphere 1875.1990: The rationalization of science and the scientization of society. In: Boli, J. & Thomas, G. (eds.) *Constructing World Culture. International Nongovernmental Organizations since 1875*. Stanford University Press, Stanford, CA, pp. 249–266.

Schreurs, M. (2011) Climate Change Politics in an Authoritarian State: The Ambivalent Case of China. In: Dryzek, J., Norgaard, R. & Schlosberg, D. (eds.) *The Oxford Handbook of Climate Change and Society*. Oxford University Press, Oxford, UK.

Schulte von Drach, M. & Schätzl, A. (2010) Vornehm geht die Welt zugrunde. *Süddeutsche Zeitung,* May 19. https://www.sueddeutsche.de/wissen/kein-klimawandel-bei-der-autoindustrie-vornehm-geht-die-welt-zugrunde-1.910994. Accessed 1/19/2017.

Schulte-Uebbing, L., Hansen, G., Hernandez, A. M. & Winter, M. (2015) Chapter scientists in the IPCC AR5—experience and lessons learned. *Current Opinion in Environmental Sustainability* **14**, 250–256.

Schumpeter, J. A. (1934) *Fundamentals of Economic Development*. Harvard University Press, Cambridge, MA.

Schumpeter, Joseph, A. (1935) The analysis of economic change. *The Review of Economics and Statistics. The MIT Press* **17** (2), 2–10.

Schumpeter, Joseph, A. (1954) *History of Economic Analysis*. Allen & Unwin, London.

Schwarz, N., Bless, H., Strack, F., Klumpp, G., Rittenauer-Schatka, H. & Simons, A. (1991) "Ease of Retrieval as Information: Another Look at the Availability Heuristic". *Journal of Personality and Social Psychology* **61** (2), 195–202.

Science News (2017) What's in Trump's 2018 budget request for science? *Science News,* May 23. https://www.sciencemag.org/news/2017/05/what-s-trump-s-2018-budget-request-science. Accessed 11/2/2017.

Scott, J. & Baltzly, A. (1958) *Readings in European History since 1814*. Appleton-Century-Crofts, New York.

SDSN (2018) *SDSN Germany*. https://www.die-gdi.de/sdsngermany/. Accessed 05/28/2019.

Sebenius, J. (1992a) Challenging Conventional Explanations of International Cooperation: Negotiation Analysis and the Case of Epistemic Communities. *International Organization* **46** (1), 323–365.

Sebenius, J. (1992b) Negotiation Analysis: A Characterization and Review. *Management Science* **38** (1), 18–38.

Secretaría de Relaciones Exteriores (2017) *Mexico Reaffirms Its Support for and Commitment to the Paris Agreement to Halt the Effects of Global Climate Change*. 1 June 2017. https://www.gob.mx/sre/prensa/mexico-reaffirms-its-support-for-and-commitment-to-the-paris-agreement-to-halt-the-effects-of-global-climate-change?idiom=en. Accessed 09/22/2019.

Seligman, M. E. P. (2014) *Florecer: La nueva psicología positiva y la búsqueda del bienestar,* 1ª ed. Océano, México, D.F.

Sell, Friedrich, L. & Sauer, B. (2011) Geld-, Kapitalmärkte und Wohlfahrt: Eine Wirkungsanalyse der Target2-Salden. *Die europäische Zahlungsbilanzkrise. Ifo Schnelldienst* **64**, 34–35.

SEMARNAT (2013) *Estrategía Nacional de Cambio Climático. Visión 10-20-40*, México D.F.

Seriño, M. N. V. (2014) Do Philippine Households Lead a Carbon Intensive Lifestyle? *Econstor*. Courant Research Centre: Poverty, Equity and Growth—Discussion Papers 158. https://www.econstor.eu/handle/10419/100100. Accessed 05/28/2019.

Shadi, H. (2003) An Islamic Alternative? Equality, Redistributive Justice, and the Welfare State in the Caliphate of Umar. *Renaissance: Monthly Islamic Journal* **13** (8).

Shambaugh, D. (2013) *China Goes Global: The Partial Power*. Oxford University Press, Oxford.

Shearman, D.J.C. & Smith, J. W. (2007) The climate change challenge and the failure of democracy.

Shelton, T. & Clark, J. (2016) *Technocratic values and uneven development in the "smart city"*.

Shirk, S. (2012) China's next leaders: a guide to what's at stake. *New York Times,* 2012. https://cn.nytimes.com/article/china/2012/11/15/c15shirk/en. Accessed 10/5/2017.

Shiuh-Shen Chien & Fulong Wu (2011) Transformation of China's Urban Entrepreneurialism: The Case Study of the City of Kunshan. *Cross-Currents: East Asian History and Culture Review* **1**.

Siitonen, S., Tuomaala, M. & Ahtila, P. (2010) Variables affecting energy efficiency and CO2 emissions in the steel industry. *Energy Policy* **38**, 2477–2485.

SIJ (2017) *Main Labour Force Indicators*. Statistical Institute of Jamaica, Kingston.https://statinja.gov.jm/LabourForce/NewLFS.aspx. Accessed 11/13/2017.

Simeon, L. M. (2017) Chamber of Mines confident of Lopez rejection as DENR chief. *Philstar,* March 10. https://www.philstar.com/headlines/2017/03/10/1679787/chamber-mines-confident-lopez-rejection-denr-chief. Accessed 3/17/2017.

Simmel, G. (1908) *Exkurs über das Problem: Wie ist Gesellschaft möglich?: in: Ders., Soziologie. Untersuchungen über die Formen der Vergesellschaftung*. pp. 21–30, Berlin.

Simmons, A. (2017) U.S. foreign aid: A waste of money or a boost to world stability? Here are the facts. *Los Angeles Times,* May 10. https://www.latimes.com/world/la-fg-global-aid-true-false-20170501-htmlstory.html. Accessed 12/27/2017.

Simon, H. (1955) A Behavioral Model of Rational Choice. *Quarterly Journal of Economics* **69**, 99–118.

Simpson, Stephen, D. (2011) 5 of the Most Adaptive Companies. *Investopia,* March 22. https://www.investopedia.com/financial-edge/0311/5-of-the-most-adaptive-companies.aspx. Accessed 5/30/2016.

Sinn, H. W. (2007) *Pareto Optimality in the Extraction of Fossil Fuels and the Greenhouse Effect a Note*. NBER Working Paper No. 13453. The National Bureau of Economic Research, Cambridge, MA. https://www.nber.org/papers/w13453. Accessed 05/28/2019.

Sjöstedt, G. (ed.) (1993) *International Environmental Negotiation*. Sage, Newbury Park.

Sjöstedt, G. (ed.) (2003) *Professional Cultures in International Negotiation: Bridge or Rift?* Lexington Books, Lanham, MD.

Sjöstedt, G. (2009) Knowledge Diplomacy: The Things We Need to Know to Understand it Better. *PINPoints* **33**, 4–7.

Sjöstedt, G. & Penetrante, A. M. (eds.) (2013) *Climate Change Negotiations. A Guide to Resolving Disputes and Facilitating Multilateral Cooperation*. Routledge, London.

Skodvin, T. (2000) *Structure and agent in the scientific diplomacy of climate change*. Kluwer Academic Publishers, Dordrecht.

Skorepa, M. (2011) *Decision-making. A Behavioral Economic Approach*. Palgrave Macmillan, Basingstoke, UK.

Slaper, Timothy, F. & Hall, Tanja, J. (2011) The Triple Bottom Line: What is It and How Does It Work? *Indiana Business Review* **86** (1).

Slater, R. O., Schutz, B. M. & Dorr, S. R. (1993) *Global transformation and the Third World*. Lynne Rienner Publishers; Adamantine Press, Boulder, CO, London.

Sliggers, J. & Kakebeeke, W. (eds.) (2004) *Clearing the Air. 25 years of the Convention on Long-range Transboundary Air Pollution*. United Nations Economic Commission for Europe, New York & Geneva.

Smith, A. (2005) The alternative technology movement: An analysis of its framing and negotiation of technology development. Special issue on nature, science and social movements. *Human Ecology Review* **12** (2), 106–119.

Smith, K. R., Balakrishnan, K. & Butler, C. et al. (2012) Chapter 4 - Energy and Health. In: *Global Energy Assessment - Toward a Sustainable Future*, Cambridge University Press, Cambridge, UK and New York, NY, USA and the International Institute for Applied Systems Analysis, Laxenburg, Austria, pp. 255–324.

Smith, S. R. & Lipsky, M. (1993) *Nonprofits for hire: The welfare state in the age of contracting*, Cambridge, MA: Harvard University Press.

Smith, W. K. & Tushman, M. L. (2005) Managing strategic contradictions: A top management model for managing innovation streams. *Organization Science* **16**, 522–536.

Smyrgała, D. (2017) Fukushima and Energiewende: Impact on structure of power generation. *Energy Sources, Part B: Economics, Planning, and Policy* **12** (4), 332–337.

Snidal, D. (2010) Coordination versus Prisoner's Dilemma: Implications for International Cooperation and Regimes. In: Goldstein, J. & Steinberg, R. H. (eds.) *International Institutions*. Sage, Los Angeles, London, New Delhi, Singapore, Washington DC, pp. 1–32.

Solow, R. (1974) The Economics of Resources or the Resources of Economics. *The American Economic Review* **64** (2), 1–14.

Solow, R. (1986) On the Intergenerational Allocation of Natural Resources. *Scandinavian Journal of Economics* **88** (1), 141–149.

Soto, H. de (1986) *El Otro Sendero*. El Barranco, Lima.

Sowers, J. (2007) Nature reserves and authoritarian rule in Egypt: embedded autonomy revisited. *Journal of Environmental Development* **16** (4), 375–397.

Spranca, M., Minsk, E. & Baron, J. (1991) Omission and commission in judgment and choice. *Journal of Experimental Social Psychology* **27**, 76–105.

Staw, B. M. (1976) Knee-Deep in the Big Muddy: A Study of Escalating Commitment to a Chosen Course of Action. *Organizational Behavior & Human Decision Processes* (16(1)), 27–44.

Stearns, P. (1993) *The Industrial Revolution in World History*. Westview Press, Boulder.

Steckel, J., Brecha, R., Jakob, M., Strefler, J. & Luderer, G. (2013) Development Without Energy? Assessing Future Scenarios of Energy Consumption in Developing Countries. *Ecological Economics* **90**, 53–67.

Stedman, S. J. (1997) Spoiler Problems in Peace Processes. *International Security* **22** (2), 5–53.

Stehr, N. (2015) Prima Klima ohne Demokratie. *Frankfurter Allgemeine*, December 01. https://www.faz.net/aktuell/feuilleton/debatten/forscher-glauben-autokratien-koennen-klimawandel-abwenden-13941004.html. Accessed 11/30/2015.

Stein, A. (1983) Coordination and Collaboration: Regimes in an Anarchic World. In: Krasner, S. (ed.) *International Regimes*. Cornell University Press, Ithaca, NY, pp. 115–140.

Steinberger, J. & Roberts, J. T. (2010) From Constraint to Sufficiency: The Decoupling of Energy and Carbon from Human Needs 1975–2005. *Ecological Economics* **70**, 425–433.

Stirling, A. (2008) Science, precaution, and the politics of technological risk. *Annals of the New York Academy of Sciences* **11** (28), 95–110.

Stone, R. W. (2009) Risk in international politics. *Global Environmental Politics* **9** (3), 40–60.

Storck, H. von & Stehr, N. (2010) Knowledge Claims in A Post-Normal Stage: Thoughts on Climate Science and Policy. https://www.climatescienceandpolicy.eu/2010/07/knowledge-claims-in-a-post-normal-stage-thoughts-on-climate-science-and-policy/. Accessed 8/11/2011.

Stringer, L. C., Reed, M. S., Dougill, A. J., Seely, M. K. & Rokitzki, M. (2007) Implementing the UNCCD: participatory challenges. *Natural Resources Forum* **31** (3), 198–211.

Sugiyama, T. & Deshun, L. (2004) Must developing countries commit quantified targets? Time flexibility and equity in climate change mitigation. *Energy Policy* **32** (5), 697–704.

Sutton, P. (2000) *Explaining Environmentalism. In Search of a New Social Movement*. Ashgate, Aldershot, UK and Burlinton, USA.

Sydow, J., Schreyögg, G. & Koch, J. (2009) Organizational Path Dependence: Opening the Black Box. *Academy of Management Review* **34**, 689–709.

Tabuchi, H. & Fountain, H. (2017) Bucking Trump, These Cities, States and Companies Commit to Paris Accord. *New York Times,* June 01. https://www.nytimes.com/2017/06/01/climate/american-cities-climate-standards.html. Accessed 10/9/2017.

Tan, O. F. (2017) Duterte's UP degree and anti-intellectualism. *Philippine Daily Inquirer,* April 24. https://opinion.inquirer.net/103422/dutertes-degree-anti-intellectualism. Accessed 4/24/2017.

Tanaka, K. (2008) Assessment of energy efficiency performance measures in industry and their application for policy. *Energy Policy* **36**, 2887–2902.

Tandon, Y. (2008) *Ending Aid Dependence*. Fahamu, Cape Town, Dakar, Nairobi and Oxford.

Tarrow, S. (1994) *Power in Movement: Social Movements, Collective Action and Politics,* 1st Edition. Cambridge University Press, Cambridge, UK.

Teng, F. & Gu, A. (2007) Climate Change: National and Local Policy Opportunities in China. *Environmental Sciences* **4**, 183–194.

The Economist (2011) Minds like machines. *The Economist,* November 19. https://www.economist.com/node/21538698. Accessed 8/18/2017.

The Gleaner (2016) Dumb 'democracy'—Political system hurting Jamaica. *The Gleaner - Jamaica WI,* February 07. https://jamaica-gleaner.com/article/lead-stories/20160207/dumb-democracy-political-system-hurting-jamaica. Accessed 11/21/2017.

Tilly, C. (1978) *From Mobilization to Revolution*. Addison-Wesley, Reading, MA.

Tilly, C. (1985) War Making and State Making as Organized Crime. In: Evans, P. B., Rueschemeyer, D. & Skocpol, T. (eds.) *Bridging the State Back In*. Cambridge University Press, Cambridge, pp. 169–191.

Tilly, C. (1987) Formalization and quantification in historical analysis. In: Schröder, W. H. & Jarausch, K. (eds.) *Quantitative history of society and economy: some international studies*. Scripta Mercaturae, St. Katharinen, pp. 19–29.

Tisdell, C. (2009) Economic Challenges Faced by Small Island Economies: An Overview. *Economic Theory, Applications and Issues, University of Queensland* **Working Paper No. 58** (ISSN: 1444–8890).

Tocqueville, A. de (1856) *The Old Regime and the Revolution: trans. John Bonner*. Harper & Brothers, New York.

Tokimatsu, K., Ii, R. & Yamaguchi, R. et al. (2013) Measuring future paths of alternative sustainability indicators: An assessment of IPCC SRES scenarios. *International Journal of Sustainable Development & World Ecology* **20** (4), 273–286.

Torero, M., Robles, M., Hernández, M., La Roca, J. de, Webber, M. & Thomas, D. (2006) *The Informal Sector in Jamaica*. Inter-American Development Bank, Washington, D.C. https://publications.iadb.org/handle/11319/4326. Accessed 05/28/2019.

Toth, F., Mwandosya, M. & Carraro, C. et al. (2001) *Decision-making Frameworks: Third Assessment Report (TAR) of the Third Working Group*. Intergovernmental Panel on Climate Change, Geneva. https://www.ipcc.ch/ipccreports/tar/wg3/. Accessed 11/10/2019.

Tria, J. (2017) Coming to terms with mining, Sec. Gina Lopez, dialogue and science. *Manila Bulletin,* February 06. https://news.mb.com.ph/2017/02/06/coming-to-terms-with-mining-sec-gina-lopez-dialogue-and-science/. Accessed 3/19/2017.

Trianni, A., Cagno, E. & Farné, S. (2016) Barriers, drivers and decision-making process for industrial energy efficiency: A broad study among manufacturing small and medium-sized enterprises. *Applied Energy* **162**, 1537–1551.

Trombetta, M. J. (2019) Securitization of Climate Change in China: Implications for Global Climate Governance. *China Quarterly of International Strategic Studies* **5** (1), 97–116.

Tversky, A. & Kahneman, D. (1974) Judgement under Uncertainty: Heuristics and Biases. *Science* **185**, 1124–1131.

Tversky, A. & Kahnemann, D. (1986) Rational Choice and the Framing of Decisions. *The Journal of Business* **59** (4), S251–S278.

Tyfield, D., Ely, A. & Geall, S. (2015) Low carbon innovation in China: from overlooked opportunities and challenges to transitions in power relations and practices. *Sustainable Development* **23**, 206–216.

U.S. Department of State (2017) *FY 2018 Congressional Budget Justification—Department of State, Foreign Operations, and Related Programs*, Washington, D.C.

Ubac, M. L. (2013) Palace: 'Three Furies' will prosecute people in non-Napoles NGO scandal. *Inquirer News*. https://newsinfo.inquirer.net/481885/palace-three-furies-will-prosecute-people-in-non-napoles-ngo-scandal. Accessed 05/28/2019.

UK GOS (2011) *Code of Practice for Scientific Advisory Committees*, London.

Ullbrich, J. & Lipponer, A. (2011) Salden im Zahlungsverkehrssystem Target2 – ein Problem? *Die europäische Zahlungsbilanzkrise. Ifo Schnelldienst* **64**, 34–35.

Underdahl, A. (2002) The Outcomes of Negotiation. In: Kremenyuk, V. (ed.) *International Negotiation. Analysis, Approaches, Issues*, Second Edition. Jossey-Bass, San Francisco, pp. 100–117.

UNDP (2017) *Jamaica Ratifies Paris Agreement*. United Nations Development Program. https://www.jm.undp.org/content/jamaica/en/home/presscenter/pressreleases/2017/04/11/jamaica-ratifies-paris-agreement.html. Accessed 11/21/2017.

UNFCCC (1992) *United Nations Framework Convention on Climate Change*. https://unfccc.int/resource/docs/convkp/conveng.pdf. Accessed 05/28/2019.

UNFCCC (2015) *Intended Nationally Determined Contribution of Jamaica*. https://www4.unfccc.int/sites/submissions/indc/Submission%20Pages/submissions.aspx. Accessed 11/05/2017.

UNFCCC (2016) *Report of the Conference of the Parties on its twenty-first session, Paris, 30 November to 13 December 2016*.

UNFCCC (2017) *Conference of the Parties, Twenty-third session, Bonn, 6–17 November 2017*, Bonn, Germany.

Urpelainen, J. (2011) The enforcement—exploitation trade-off in international cooperation between weak and powerful states. *European Journal of International Relations* **17** (4).

Uy, J. (2016) New groups make it to party-list's Top 10. *Philippine Daily Inquirer*, May 11. https://newsinfo.inquirer.net/784979/new-groups-make-it-to-party-lists-top-10. Accessed 3/14/2017.

van Asselt, H. & Gupta, J. (2009) Stretching Too Far: Developing Countries and the Role of Flexibility Mechanisms of Kyoto. *Stanford Environmental Law Journal* **28**, 311–380.

van der Ploeg, F. (2011) Natural Resources: Curse or Blessing? *Journal of Economic Literature* **49** (2), 366–420.

van Jones (2008) *The Green Collar Economy: How One Solution Can Fix Our two Biggest Problems*. Harper Collins, New York City.

van Mossel, A., van Rijnsoever, F. & Hekkert, M. (2018) Navigators through the Storm: A Review of Organization Theories and the Behavior of Incument Firms during Transitions. *Environmental Innovation and Societal Transitions* **26**, 44–63.

van Vuuren, D., Edmonds, J. & Kainuma, M. et al. (2011) The representative concentration pathways: an overview. *Climatic Change* **109** (5), 5–31.

Varoufakis, Y. (2016) Trump victory comes with a silver lining for the world's progressives. *The Conversation,* November 11. https://theconversation.com/trump-victory-comes-with-a-silver-lining-for-the-worlds-progressives-68523. Accessed 10/9/2017.

Vera, B. de & Domingo, R. (2017) LGUs seen losing P821M from mine closures. *Philippine Daily Inquirer,* February 21. https://business.inquirer.net/224952/lgus-seen-losing-p821m-mine-closures. Accessed 2/22/2017.

Victor, D. (2017) 'Climate Change Is Real': Many U.S. Companies Lament Paris Accord Exit. https://www.nytimes.com/2017/06/01/business/climate-change-tesla-corporations-paris-accord.html, June 01. https://www.nytimes.com/2017/06/01/business/climate-change-tesla-corporations-paris-accord.html. Accessed 10/9/2017.

Volz, U. (ed.) (2015) *Financing the green transformation: How to make green finance work in Indonesia*. Palgrave Macmillan, Houndmills, Basingstoke Hampshire, N.Y., NY.

Walker, H., Rogers, L. & Zelditch, M. (1988) Legitimacy and Collective Action: A Research Note. *Social Forces* **67** (1), 216–228.

Wallsten, S. (2000) The effects of government-industry R&D programs on private R&D: The case of the small business innovation research program. *The RAND Journal of Economics* **31** (1), 82–100.

Walsh, J. P. (1995) Managerial and organizational cognition: Notes from a trip down memory lane. *Organization Science* **6** (3), 280–321.

Wapner, P. (1996) *Environmental Activism and World Civic Politics*. State University of New York Press, Albany.

Warren, M. & Castiglione, D. (2004) The Transformation of Democratic Representation. *Democracy and Society* **2** (1), 20–22.

Watkins, M. & Passow, S. (1996) Analyzing Linked Systems of Negotiations. *Negotiating Journal* **12** (3), 325–339.

WBGU (2009) *Solving the Climate Dilemma - the Budget Approach*, German Advisory Council on Global Change, Berlin.

WBGU (2011) *World in Transition. A Social Contract for Sustainability*, German Advisory Council on Global Change, Berlin.

Weber, m. (1987) Decision making with incomplete information. *European Journal of Operational Research* **28**, 44–57.

Weber, M. (1976) *Wirtschaft und Gesellschaft,* Fünfte, revidierte Auflage. J.C.B. Mohr (Paul Siebeck) Verlag, Tübingen.

Weber, M. (1985) *Die Objektivität sozialwissenschaftlicher und sozialpolitischer Erkenntnis: Gesammelte Aufsätze zur Wissenschaftlehre/ Max Weber*. Mohr Siebeck, Tübingen, 146–214.

Weber, M. (2005) *Wirtschaft und Gesellschaft: Grundriss der verstehenden Soziologie,* 3rd edn. Zweitausendeins, Leipzig.

Weiss, M. L. & Aspinall, E. (2012) *Student activism in Asia: Between protest and powerlessness*. Univ. of Minnesota Press, Minneapolis, Minn.

Weizsäcker, E. U. v., Hargroves, K., Smith, M., Desha Cheryl & Stasinopoulos, P. (2009) *Factor Five: Transforming the Global Economy through 80% Increase in Resource Productivity*. Earthscan, London and Droemer.

Wells, P. (2007) The green junta: or, is democracy sustainable? *International Journal of Environment and Sustainable Development* **6** (2), 208–220.

White, J. & Klein, D. (eds.) (2007) *Family Theories*. Sage, London.

White, M. (2016) Protests won't stop Trump. We need a movement that transforms into a party. *The Guardian,* 2016. https://www.theguardian.com/commentisfree/2016/nov/14/protests-donald-trump-democracy-party. Accessed 10/12/2017.

Wigley, T., Richels, R. & Edmonds, J. (1996) Economic and environmental choices in the stabilization of atmospheric CO2 concentrations. *Nature* **379**, 240–243.

Willard, B. (2002) *The Sustainability Advantage: Seven Business Case Benefits of a Triple Bottom Line*. New Society Publishers, Gabriola Island, B.C.

Wille, J. (2017) „Das Trauma von Fukushima überwinden". *Frankfurter Rundschau,* September 09. https://www.fr.de/wirtschaft/energie/energiewende-das-trauma-von-fukushima-ueberwinden-a-1403395. Accessed 6/8/2018.

William, I. W. & Rubin, J. (eds.) (2002) *Power and Negotiations*. University of Michigan Press, Ann Arbor.

Williams, F. (2016) Transportation Sector in Jamaica, Jamaica Railway Corporation. Interview by Ariel Hernandez, 14 September 2016.

Willie, S. & Morgan, P. (2016) Electricity in Jamaica, JPSCo, Kingston, Jamaica.

Wilson, M. C. & Wu, J. (2016) The problems of weak sustainability and associated indicators. *International Journal of Sustainable Development & World Ecology* **24** (1), 44–51.

Winham, G. & DeBoer-Ashworth, E. (2000) Asymmetry in Negotiating the Canada-US Free Trade Agreement, 1985–1987. In: Zartman, I. W. & Rubin, J. (eds.) *Power and Negotiation*. University of Michigan Press, Ann Arbor, MI, pp. 35–52.

Winham, G. R. (1977) Complexity in International Negotiations. In: Druckman, D. (ed.) *Complexity in International Negotiations*. Sage, Beverly Hills, pp. 347–366.

Winkler, H., Vorster, S. & Marquard, A. (2009a) Who Picks Up the Remainder? Mitigation in Developed and Developing Countries. *Climate Policy* **9**, 634–651.

Winkler, H., Vorster, S. & Marquard, A. (2009b) Who Picks Up the Remainder? Mitigation in Developed and Developing Countries. *Climate Policy* **9**, 634–651.

Winslow, M. (2005) Is democracy food for the environment? *Journal of Environmental Planning and Management* **48** (5), 771–783.

Wiser, R., Z. Yang & M. Hand et al. (2011) *Wind Energy: In IPCC Special Report on Renewable Energy Sources and Climate Change Mitigation*, Cambridge, UK.

Wood, G. (2016) Sustainable buildings in Jamaica, Jamaica Institute of Architects, Kingston, Jamaica.

Woolgar, S. (1988) *Science: The Very Idea*. Tavistock Publications, London.

World Databank (2011) World Development Indicators & Global Development Finance (GDF). https://databank.worldbank.org/ddp/home.do.

WRI (2009) Climate Analysis Indicators Tool (CAIT), Washington, D.C.

WTTC (2017) *Travel & Tourism—Economic Impact 2017 Jamaica*, World Travel & Tourism Council, London. https://www.wttc.org/-/media/files/reports/economic-impact-research/countries-2017/jamaica2017.pdf. Accessed 11/21/2017.

Wu, F. (2016) China's Emergent City-Region Governance: A New Form of State Spatial Selectivity through State-orchestrated Rescaling. *International Journal of Urban and Regional Research* **40** (6), 1134–1151.

Xiaowei, Z. (2004) *Elite Dualism and Leadership Selection in China*. Routledge, New York.

Yao, S. Chan, R. & Zhu, Y. (1992) *Zhongguo de chengshiqun [China's urban clusters]*. Chinese Science and Technology University Press, Hefei.

Young, H. P. (1991) *Negotiation Analysis*. University of Michigan Press, Ann Arbor, MI.

Young, I. M. (1986) Deferring Group Representation. In: Kymlicka, W. & Saphiro, I. (eds.) *Nomos: Group Rights*. New York University Press, New York, pp. 349–376.

Young, O. (2009) Governance for Sustainable Development in a World of Rising Interdependencies. In: Delmas, M. & Young, O. (eds.) *Governance for the Environment*. Cambridge University Press, Cambridge, UK, pp. 12–40.

Zartman, I. W. (1978) *The Negotiation Process: Theories and Applications*. SAGE Publications, Beverly Hills, CA.

Zartman, I. W. (1988) Common Elements in the Analysis of the Negotiation Process. *Negotiation Journal* **4** (1), 31–43.

Zartman, I. W. (ed.) (1994a) *International Multilateral Negotiations*. Jossey-Bass Publishers, San Francisco.

Zartman, I. W. (1994b) Two's company and more's a crowd: The complexities of multilateral negotiation. In: Zartman, I. W. (ed.) *International multilateral negotiation: Approaches to the management of complexity*. Jossey-Bass Publishers, San Francisco, pp. 1–10.

Zartman, I. W. & Rubin, J. (eds.) (2000) *Power and Negotiation*. University of Michigan Press, Ann Arbor, MI.

Zelli, F. (2011) The Fragmentation of the Global Climate Governance Architecture. *Wiley Interdisciplinary Reviews: Climate Change* **2**, 255–270.

Zerriffi, H. & Wilson, E. (2010) Leapfrogging over development? Promoting rural renewables for climate change mitigation. *Energy Policy* **28** (4), 1689–1700.

Zhang, X.-P. & Cheng, X.-M. (2009) Energy consumption, carbon emissions, and economic growth in China. *Ecological Economics* **68** (10), 2706–2712.

Zhang, Y., Lewis, M., Pellon, M. & Coleman, P. (2007) A Preliminary Research on Modeling Cognitive Agents for Social Environments in Multi-Agent Systems, AAAI Fall Symposium: Emergent Agents and Socialities, 116123. https://www.semanticscholar.org/paper/A-Preliminary-Research-on-Modeling-Cognitive-Agents-Zhang-Lewis/ae51a4a099dca38614fc82fcf8a42a02b682a66e. Accessed 05/28/2019.

Zürn, M. (2002) Zu den Merkmalen postnationaler Politik. In: Jachtenfuchs, M. & Knodt, M. (eds.) *Regieren in internationalen Institutions: Festschrift für Beate Kohler-Koch*. Leske und Budrich, Opladen, pp. 215–234.

Zürn, M. (ed.) (2009) *Law and Governance in Post-national Europe*. Cambridge University Press, Cambridge.

The manufacturer's authorised representative in the EU is Springer Nature Customer Service Centre GmbH, Europaplatz 3, 69115 Heidelberg, Germany. If you have any concerns regarding our products, please contact ProductSafety@springernature.com

Printed and bound by CPI Group (UK) Ltd, Croydon, CR0 4YY

30/09/2026

02225697-0001